Praises for
Licensing Best Practices

"A comprehensive digest of national and international advances and developments in licensing! Licensing Best Practices is a veritable anthology and compendium on general and industry-specific licensing practices and licensable intellectual property assets. It is a handbook every licensing executive and intellectual property practitioner will want to peruse and keep on their desk!"

Karl F. Jorda
David Rines Professor of Intellectual
Property Law & Industrial Innovation
Franklin Pierce Law Center
Concord NH

"It was a great privilege to be given the opportunity to preview this outstanding work. The Licensing Executives Society is the world's leading organisation of technology licensing and management professionals. Bob Goldscheider and his team have drawn upon the rich resources of its members to produce a work of immediate impact and lasting influence on a field of economic endeavor which, as the work itself shows, is expanding exponentially. Don't leave home without it."

Des Ryan
Consultant (and former Partner)
Davies Collison Cave, Patent Attorneys and
Barristers and Solicitors
Melbourne, Australia

"This book does serious double duty. It is a helpful primer for business executives and people breaking into the licensing field because it provides broad, often in-depth coverage. It also serves a helpful purpose for seasoned licensing executives and lawyers: first, it endorses many of the things that we do and think and hence serves as a reality check; second, at a deeper level, it proposes techniques and analyses, some of which are necessarily new to each of us because the thing about licensing is that you learn every time out. This book provides learning for even the most seasoned."

Roger M. Milgrim
Partner
Paul, Hastings, Janofsky & Walker LLP

"Licensing Best Practices is a necessary book for any person involved in licensing. The book provides valuable, practical insights that can be readily utilized in licensing matters. The comprehensive contents are set forth in understandable, reader-friendly language. I highly recommend this work."

Michael A. Epstein
Chair, Intellectual Property and Technology
Practice
Weil, Gotshal & Manges LLP

LICENSING
BEST PRACTICES

Intellectual Property—General, Law, Accounting and Finance, Management, Licensing, Special Topics Series

LICENSING BEST PRACTICES

The LESI Guide to Strategic Issues and Contemporary Realities

Robert Goldscheider,
Editor

John Wiley & Sons, Inc.

This book is printed on acid-free paper. ⊗

ISBN: 0-471-21952-5

Printed in the United States of America.

10 9 8 7 6 5 4 3 2

Dedicated to the Licensing Executives Society, a force for good in the world, from a group of its devoted members.

About LESI

The Licensing Executives Society is one of the most dynamic professional organizations in the world. It was born in 1965 when 10 corporate executives and lawyers who were involved in some way with licensing recognized a common need to educate one another about the burgeoning fields of licensing and technology management. They met in Hollywood, Florida, and set up an infant group at that time.

It immediately became obvious to many people that the existence of LES meets real needs. The Society has rapidly and regularly grown in its number of members and geographical presence. As of 2001, there are more than 10,000 members, belonging to 27 national chapters all over the world. About half the membership is in LES (United States and Canada), the current name of the founding group. The backgrounds of the members include scientists in many fields, corporate executives, intellectual property and commercial lawyers, university officers, government officials, and consultants. LES International (LESI) is the coordinating organ of the local societies, and its board of delegates meets twice each year.

LESI is responsible for the Society's respected journal, *les Nouvelles*, as well as other useful publications. Numerous local, national, regional, and global conferences are convened throughout the year, featuring plenary speeches, workshops, and active industry committee meetings. All of these functions provide valuable venues for networking.

For further information, contact the Society's office:

Licensing Executives Society (USA and Canada) Inc.
1800 Diagonal Road, Suite 280
Alexandria, Virginia 22314-2840
USA

LESI Web site: www.lesi.org

Contents

CHAPTER 4 — DREADFUL DRAFTING: THE DO'S AND DON'TS OF LICENSING AGREEMENTS

John T. Ramsay, Q.C.
Gowling Lafleur Henderson LLP

PART TWO: NEW OUTLOOKS ON PATENTS, TRADEMARKS, COPYRIGHTS, AND TRADE SECRETS

CHAPTER 5 — RECENT CHANGES IN PATENTING PROCEDURES AND PROTECTION: DEVELOPMENTS IN THE EUROPEAN AND U.S. PATENT SYSTEMS

Dr. Heinz Goddar
Boehmert & Boehmert
Alan H. Gordon
Alan H. Gordon & Associates, P.C.

CHAPTER 6 — THE CRITICAL ROLE OF TRADE SECRET LAW IN PROTECTING INTELLECTUAL PROPERTY ASSETS

Melvin F. Jager

Brinks, Hofer, Gilson & Lione

CHAPTER 7 — COPYRIGHT, SOFTWARE, AND WEB SITE ISSUES IN THE INTERNET WORLD

Michael A. Lechter

Squire, Sanders & Dempsey, LLP \

CHAPTER 8 — TRADEMARKS, TRADE NAMES, AND TRADE DRESS

Thomas M. Small

Law Office of Thomas M. Small

Kenneth D. McKay

Sim & McBurney

Larry W. Evans
Consultant
With a Contribution from Chi Shaojie
CCPIT Patent & Trademark Office

Dennis Unkovic
Meyer, Unkovic & Scott, LLP

Dr. Natalia Karpova
Government of the Russian Federation

Preface

The genesis of this book was a challenge in late 2000 from Ed Shalloway as he began his term as president of LES International. I had just renewed my term as chairman of the LES Education Committee. Ed's challenge to me and our committee was to do something different and memorable. Thus began an adventure that has resulted in this volume and the analogous audiotapes.

Our original idea was to produce a film of several prominent LES members who would speak about their respective areas of specialty. A two-hour film of four lecturers giving a basic licensing course at an LES USA and Canada annual conference in the early 1980s had been well received. A surprisingly large number of tapes were sold over a period of 10 years. With this in mind, several of our peers were questioned about their interest in participating. Everyone was enthusiastic.

Early on, it occurred to me that a serious film needs a script. It would therefore be useful to have the participants prepare texts that would clearly articulate their ideas. More than 20 different segments were envisaged. Thus, the germination of a book occurred.

Next, we had to locate an appropriate publisher. During the past few years, I have been favorably impressed by several books pertinent to the licensing field that had been published by John Wiley & Sons. A number of LES members are pleased to have their work handled by Wiley. I therefore contacted them and was fortunate to be referred to Susan McDermott, who had just joined the company as acquisitions editor. She was enthusiastic about this LES project, obtained the support of the decision makers, and "the rest is history."

Our goal was to produce an anthology of serious thoughts about many facets of licensing. I contacted a group of LES members whose styles and quality of independent thinking I respect. They have very different backgrounds and experience. Their least common denominator is professionalism, diligence, and intellectual excellence. When discussing the contributions they were invited to provide, I was gratified to note that everyone took this opportunity seriously.

The results have exceeded my optimism. As chapter after chapter was received, I was more than merely impressed. I was genuinely excited that members of the society to which I have devoted considerable effort and emotion for more than 30 years were creating a joint work of exceptional value to the world of licensing.

I consider the chapters to be of a uniformly high standard. Each of them deserves special mention.

Willy Manfroy was asked to write on the somewhat general subject, "Expanding Business of Licensing." He was approached because he has been heading a creative task force that is producing sophisticated sets of new materials intended to instruct licensing executives at the introductory, intermediate, and advanced levels. As such, he is providing important tools to improve the licensing discipline. His eloquent description of the environment in which we work, in the opening chapter of the book, provides a useful keynote for the chapters that follow.

Richard Razgaitis was invited to provide a chapter titled "Technology Valuation" in recognition of his recent, successful book titled *Early-Stage Technologies: Valuation and Pricing.* Rather than merely rest on his laurels, Raz submitted additional, valuable insights about this active subject.

John Ramsay has been stimulating and entertaining LES audiences for years on the subject of "Dreadful Drafting." He has supplemented those materials in an essay bearing the subtitle "The Do's and Don'ts of Licensing Agreements," which contains good-natured wisdom for both veterans and rookies in the field.

Heinz Goddar and **Alan Gordon** have drafted a bifurcated chapter discussing "Recent Changes in Patenting Procedures and Protection: Developments in the European and U.S. Patent Systems." These comments reflect the fact that they are both leading practitioners at the cutting edge.

Mel Jager's chapter on "The Critical Role of Trade Secrets Law in Protecting Intellectual Property Assets" highlights the key thinking in his respected and readable multivolume treatise on the same subject.

Michael Lechter had a particularly difficult assignment in my view, since he was asked to address the rapidly evolving subjects of "Copyright, Software, and Web Site Issues in the Internet World." His chapter is brilliant and taught me a lot. These subjects are very pertinent to all serious practitioners.

The jointly written chapter on "Trademarks, Trade Names, and Trade Dress," by **Tom Small** and **Ken McKay,** covers the pertinent legal situations in the United States and Canada. This is one of the longest chapters in the book, but it has been published in its entirety because of its excellence. Indeed, I consider this to be perhaps the best commentary on these subjects, with which I happen to be quite familiar, that I have ever read.

Cathryn Campbell is senior partner of a thriving IP law firm that focuses on biotechnology inventions. She has written a savvy chapter titled "Licensing in the Biotechnology Industry," describing several actual situations. It is enjoyable to read and highly instructive.

Tom Picone treats the other major area of health care activity in a chapter titled "Pharmaceutical Licensing During the Revolution." This is probably the most active area in all of licensing, and these comments should be useful to the many practitioners in the field.

Two of the most successful operators in the academic area, **Lou Berneman** and **Kathleen Denis,** have written an insightful chapter titled "University Licensing Trends and Intellectual Capital." I thought their original text was just fine, but they insisted on supplementing it, thereby adding even greater value.

Another jointly written article, "What to Do with Technology Rights That Are Financial Assets and Instruments," is a very innovative piece in itself. It was written by the husband and wife team of **Nir Kossovsky** and **Bear Brandegee.** A scenario with a dialog among "players" has been constructed that engagingly explains several novel and somewhat difficult points.

"IC-based Corporate Carve-outs: Strategy, Structure, and Funding," jointly written by **Jim Malackowski** and **Suzanne Harrison,** is a sophisticated discussion of several innovative financial issues. The type of thinking signals the wave of the future to this grizzled licensing executive.

Another duet dealing with "Licensing and Litigation" from the American and European viewpoints has been presented by **Ron Grudziecki** and **Arnaud Michel.** Their interaction and collaboration has been effective and highlights several important issues.

My first and last choice for authorship of a piece on ADR was **Tom Arnold,** who is widely considered to be the dean in this special field. When I contacted Tom's office, I learned that he was recovering from a serious illness and probably would not be strong enough for several months to write a chapter. Tom later sent word that I should look for a substitute. I indicated that, in view of the circumstances, we would omit this subject. In early June, to my complete surprise, I received Tom's brilliant manuscript titled "Alternative Dispute Resolution: Fighting Smarter, Spending Less," which has been included as written. This not only demonstrated that Tom Arnold was as clear thinking as always, but also that he was keenly interested to be a member of this team. It set the tone for the later contributions that steadily streamed in.

A tripartite chapter authored by **Peter Chrocziel, Nigel Jones,** and **Thierry Sueur,** is "Ignore Europe at Your Peril!" This comments on a variety of European developments relating to IP, antitrust, and financial areas that reflect certain respective viewpoints of the British, French, and German contributors. The chapter also tends to reflect the state of flux currently existing in the European Union.

Larry Evans, as expected, delivered a masterful chapter on "Challenges of Licensing to and from China and Hong Kong." He is one of the most experienced and successful LES members in negotiating with Chinese executives. He offers numerous shrewd comments about achieving successful results in this market, which is now prime. A founding member of LES China, **Chi Shaojie** had access to Larry's draft text and has confirmed its accuracy.

Dennis Unkovic provided a candid commentary in his chapter, "Is There a Future for Japan?," which is sobering because of its lack of optimism. At my urging, he added a section on "A Korean Counterpart," which reflects a more positive spirit.

Natalia Karpova forwarded a lengthy and informative essay titled "Licensing in Russia: Opportunities and Pitfalls." One of the most valuable aspects of this work was the comparative treatment of inventions in the former USSR and in modern Russia. We found that the English-language draft received from Professor Karpova could benefit from some linguistic editing by a native speaker. **Marcia Rorke,** who I consider to be the most talented editor in LES (USA and Canada), answered our call. She did her usual splendid work, and the chapter is now both instructive and easily readable.

Rodney DeBoos decided to focus his chapter about Australia on "Australia: Licensing Opportunities in the Medical and Biotechnology Industry." He has thus provided a clear description of important achievements, as well as Australian policies in this area, which compare favorably with certain attitudes in the United States. For instance, there is a description about the freedom to perform stem-cell research Down Under that may attract leading scientists from America and elsewhere to relocate there in order to pursue initiatives in this pioneering field.

Three separate chapters were received from authors describing needs, in their respective jurisdictions, for help from the developed nations of the world and from sister LES societies located at the sources of technology. These chapters are:

- "Challenges to Arab Industries in Acquiring and Selling Appropriate Technologies" by **Talal Abu-Ghazaleh.** An articulate and moving Author's Note about the attitude of enlightened Muslims to the events of September 11, 2001, is appended to this piece. The text is reproduced at the end of Chapter 21.
- "The South African Experience in Economic Development" by **Alan Lewis** and **Don MacRobert**
- "Prospects for Increased Licensing in Latin America" by **Gabriel Leonardos** and **Fernando Noetinger**

All of these pieces describe the strengths and weaknesses in their respective areas, and indicate open-minded attitudes about sensitive assistance. It is hoped that this volume will have a catalytic effect that will inspire some of its readers to answer these calls for input and collaboration.

Finally, I drafted Chapter 3, "The Expanding Role of Technology Management Consultants." It is hoped that this will be the opening move for the formal recognition of consulting activities that should not only be respected, but should also be regulated to the effect that persons intending to utilize the title *Consultant* should qualify to do so by obtaining suitable training and credentials. This activity might be coordinated with the ambitious educational programs that have been developed by LES (USA and Canada), which are currently being expanded from the introductory to the intermediate and advanced levels, and which will eventually be available throughout LESI.

All of the written texts were received prior to the 2001 annual meeting of LES (USA and Canada), and the follow-up meeting of the board of delegates of LES International, which took place in Palm Desert, California, from October 21 to November 3, 2001. We originally planned to produce 10-minute film clips of the authors during this period. This turned out to be too costly. Instead, audio versions of all of the chapters have been substituted for video.

We believe that this electronic analog to the book can be a valuable teaching tool. We produced a set of English-language audiotapes of the authors reading shortened versions of their chapters. This was duly accomplished in Palm Desert, in excellent facilities provided by the organizers of the LES conference. We captured more than 320 minutes of recordings, which are designed to be marketed as a set of CDs. If these prove to be as valuable as hoped, efforts will be made to have translations promptly recorded in several foreign languages, including Chinese, Russian, Arabic, Japanese, Korean, and Spanish.

Several people did "heavy lifting" and/or supplied important moral support to this team effort. **Ed Shalloway** not only issued the initial challenge but also steadily provided encouragement and practical ideas. **Ken Payne** made it clear that financial support for our efforts from the LESI Endowment Fund would be available, if needed. **Clyde Willian,** the LESI general counsel, saw to it that our contractual arrangements, both to LESI, the organization, and the individual authors, were appropriately protected. **Alan Rose** and **Art Nutter,** in their roles as chairpersons at the 2001 LES Annual Conference, provided us with superb recording facilities and administrative support.

Ken Schoppmann, the outstanding director of the LES office in Alexandria, Virginia, has been helpful in the past and will continue to be so in connection with the production, promotion, and distribution of these materials. His attitude and skills made my task much easier.

I have saved the final kudos for **Susan McDermott.** She is bright, creative, and simply wonderful as a person and an editor. Susan is a new member of LES, and will hopefully get as much knowledge and satisfaction from our society as have all of the members of the LES "family" noted in this introduction. I am confident that she and John Wiley & Sons, Inc., will play an increasingly important role in LES.

If this book is as successful as I anticipate, it is tentatively planned to produce succeeding editions in three-year intervals. I am hopeful that *Licensing Best Practices* will come to be known as a leading authority in our chosen field. I already have several ideas for an expanded second edition—but first we must walk; then we will be ready to run.

Robert Goldscheider
November 2001

Part One

The Changing Landscape of Licensing

1

Expanding Business of Licensing

By Willy Manfroy

INTRODUCTION

The profession of licensing has been around for a long time, but its importance in society and in business corporations has evolved dramatically over the years. This chapter presents a brief history of licensing and points out developing trends. It interprets the major factors that influenced these changes and affected the profession as a whole. The chapter concludes with our vision of the future and of the challenges faced by licensing professionals.

HISTORY OF LICENSING

The history of licensing is closely related to the history of patents. A good start is to look at the etymology of both words. *Webster's Dictionary* gives the following definitions:

- *License.* Authority or liberty given to do or forbear any act; especially, a formal permission from the proper authorities to perform certain acts or to carry on a certain business, which without such permission would be illegal; a grant of permission; as a license to preach, to practice medicine, to sell gunpowder or intoxicating liquors. The document granting such permission.
- *Patents.* Open to public perusal—said of a document conferring some right or privilege; as letters patent. Appropriated or protected by letters patent; secured by official authority to the exclusive possession, control, and disposal of some person or party; patented; as a patent right.

The French equivalent, *brevet*, derives from the word *bref*, meaning "short" (time and content), which describes well the content and time life of such instruments. The English patent or letter patent is related to the French *patente* (derived from Latin *patere* or "to open"), which was a privilege delegated by the kings or powers to allow people the privilege to exert certain acts, usually in exchange for something more tangible.

Patents can be traced back thousands of years. They were used by the Phoenicians, for example. Later, they show up in the Republic of Venice, where the first patents were granted in 1474. The interface between patents and licenses dates back to more recent history and the establishment of patent offices in the industrial world. Patents grant exclusion for a specific period of time, whereas licensing is a system developed to allow someone else to remove the exclusion of forbidden knowledge by special permission granted by the patent owner.

After World War II, licensing was extensively and effectively used by Japan to rebuild its industry and develop dominance in fields such as consumer electronics and optics. It was also used as a base to modernize Japan's chemical, petrochemical, and pharmaceutical industries. Japan was and is still running a large deficit in technology-related balance of payment, but its strategy of extensive licensing allowed it to jump start the country rebuilding and, in the case of the consumer electronics, to dominate worldwide markets with its innovations.

Apart from Japan—and, at a later date Taiwan, Korea, and other Asian countries—licensing was not broadly used, particularly in the Western world. The first industry to make use of systematic licensing in Western Europe and the United States was the pharmaceutical industry. In the 1970s, very few companies had a truly global presence. The cost of developing new drugs was considered high at the time ($50 to 150 million/drug), and the probability of finding acceptable new products was low. Merck had not yet pioneered its approach to finding new entities based on fundamental research on the mechanism of action of biological paths. Therefore, most really new drugs were discovered through the tedious process of screening new molecules for interesting pharmacological activities. Pharmaceutical companies were buying the right to screen libraries of chemical compounds, including rights to possible pharmaceutical uses (e.g., Probucol, one of the first cholesterol-lowering drugs, was licensed from a coal-mining company). Microanalysis techniques and combinatorial chemistry had not yet been developed. Thus, the probability of finding the right biologically active molecule was low. It was therefore extremely important to make sure that any discovery reaching commercialization stages be exploited to its maximum potential. This was the golden age of territorial swapping—companies were exchanging rights to specific geographies. Chemical companies believed they could enter the pharmaceutical field based on their extensive libraries of new chemical entities (NCE). The exit of Du Pont from the pharmaceutical business and the sale of BASF's Knoll pharmaceutical mark the end of that period.

During that time, some chemical and petrochemical corporations, under the leadership of Sohio (now BP) and Union Carbide (now Dow Chemical), were initiating programs to sell their process technology—primarily to countries in development and secondarily to their competitors. The engineering companies were the implementers of the technology transfer efforts, combining their project management and construction skills with the know-how generated by the chemical industry. In the rest of the chemical industry, however, licensing was not widely practiced. With a few notable exceptions, licensing was considered an unimportant afterthought and not central to a company's strategy.

RECENT TRENDS

Since the mid- to late 1980s, the situation has changed significantly. Extraction of value from a corporation's intellectual assets (IA) has become big business. The most notable example is IBM, where revenues from IA grew from the low teens to over $1.3 billion annually in a little more than 10 years (see Exhibit 1.1—reference Annual Report and public quotes). IBM is not the only one. It has been widely reported that for a number of years Intel Corporation earned more money from its aggressive licensing deals than from its day-to-day operations.

Also, the size and frequency of publicly available license grants, voluntary or not, has increased over the last 10 years (see Exhibits 1.2 and 1.3).

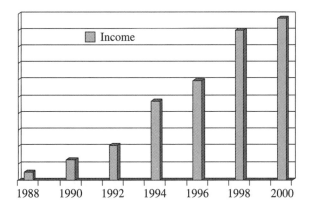

EXHIBIT 1.1   IBM's Reported Licensing Income

Parties	Award (in millions)	Date
Polaroid v. *Eastman Kodak*	$873	Jan. 1991
Hawoorth v. *Steelcase*	$211	Dec. 1996
Smith International v. *Hughes Tool*	$205	Mar. 1986
Exxon v. *Mobil Oil*	$171	Aug. 1998
Viskase v. *American National Can*	$165	Jul. 1999
Hughes Aircraft v. *United States*	$154	Jun. 1994
3M v. *Johnson & Johnson*	$129	Sep. 1992
Fonar v. *General Electric*	$129	Feb. 1997
Honeywell v. *Minolta*	$96	Jan. 1992

EXHIBIT 1.2   Damage Awards for Patent Infringement

Parties	Settlement (in millions)	Date
Digital Equipment v. *Intel*	$1,500.0	Oct. 1997
Texas Instruments v. *Samsung*	$1,100.0	Nov. 1996
Texas Instruments v. *Hyundai*	$1,100.0	May 1999
Medtronic v. *Siemens*	$ 300.0	Sep. 1992
University of California v. *Genetech*	$ 200.0	
Procter & Gamble v. *Paragon Trade*	$163.5	Feb. 1999
Genetech v. *Eli Lily*	$145.0	Jan. 1995
Honeywell v. *Seven Camera Makers*	$124.1	Aug. 1992
Kimberly-Clark v. *Paragon Trade*	$115	Mar. 1999
Rhone-Poulenc Rorer v. *Baxter*	105.0	May 1993

EXHIBIT 1.3   Top Patent Damage Settlements 1990–June 2000

As a result, the subject of technology transfer has moved from the specialized press to center stage. Following are a few examples of the treatment of the subject in the popular press.

- Kevin G. Rivette and David Kline. *Rembrandts in the Attic.* Boston: Harvard Business School Publishing, 1999.
- Pamela Sherrid. "Psst, Wanna Buy A Corporate Secret? Companies are Selling Their Know-how, Too." *U.S. News & World Report*, September 20, 1999.
- "J&J Wins $324M in Patent Suit Against Boston Scientific." *Wall Street Journal*, December 18, 2000.

Simultaneously, world-renowned experts in public accounting (e.g., Baruch Lev from the Stern School of Business, New York University) have been talking about the lack of relevance of current income statements. Steve Wallman, ex-Commissioner of the SEC, has publicly proclaimed the need for corporations to disclose more of their IA strategies in the name of public fairness and corporate health. The result of his efforts led to a thorough report by the Brookings Institute on the subject.[1] Intellectual assets—specifically, technology and service activities—and their relationship to licensing agreements are discussed in detail in Chapter 20.

Merrill Lynch has published data showing that the price-to-book ratio of the S & P 500, which could be considered a fair representation of the U.S. industry at large, went from almost 1-to-1 in 1978 to 6-to-1 in 1998 (see Exhibit 1.4).

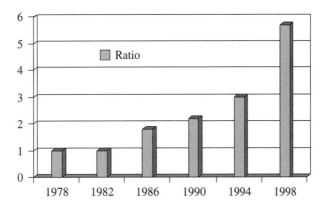

EXHIBIT 1.4   The Average Market-to-Book Ratio of the S & P 500 Companies

In essence, this means that on average, 85 percent of the value of the United States' largest corporations is unexplained in the traditional annual reports. This phenomenon is, of course, not limited to the U.S. and Canadian corporations.

MAJOR FACTORS BEHIND INCREASE IN LICENSING

The reasons for the evolution of the licensing profession stem from four different and equally important factors: legal, business, internationalization, and knowledge management.

Legal

The establishment of the Court of Appeal of the Federal Circuit (CAFC) brought in the most momentous change in the United States. Even though the courts of first instance have not changed, the mere existence of this specialized appeal court has notably altered the practical landscape of patents. In the not-too-distant past, the chief patent counsel of a large chemical company was instructing his attorneys and researchers not to file for end-use applications of existing compositions of matter because they were a waste of time and money and would probably not stand in court. This kind of business philosophy changed in response to the establishment of the CAFC. Studies have shown[2] that since the CAFC was established, the proportion of challenged patents that were invalidated as a result reversed from roughly two-thirds to one-third. The practical consequence has been that for most corporations, patents have shifted from an asset of limited value and high cost to one of strength and potential strategic importance. As a result, the number of patents filed and granted in the United States has grown significantly in the past few years.

Business

The emergence of information technology (IT) as a separate industry segment has also greatly affected the licensing profession. It can be correlated with the growth and wide dissemination of hardware (computers and electronics) and the development of the Internet.

First, as a service to existing corporations and institutions, IT allowed greater access and transparency of information. Second, it created its own set of intellectual assets that were licensed, enforced, or traded. Third, it initiated the dot-com frenzy with its excessive valuation bubble and subsequent correction.

The thirst of industry, government, and institutions for instantaneously available data spurred the growth of software and hardware. New marketing tools (e-markets for technology), data manipulation, and retrieval tools (patent mapping, citation trees, intellectual property (IP) databases) were created for licensing or tech-transfer specialists. This enabled tech-transfer people to increase their productivity and led to more internationalization and globalization of the profession.

Internationalization

The globalization of industry and the leveling effect of the Internet on the availability of information have led to the parallel growth of licensing worldwide. Industries in countries where patents were traditionally filed only in their own domestic markets have increasingly boosted their overseas patent portfolio, particularly in Europe and the United States of America. Korea is typical but not the only representative of this trend. The gross analysis of patent filing by different industry sectors in Korea shows a near simultaneous growth in the number of U.S. patents granted. Samsung Electronics is the most striking example, but companies such as LG Chemicals and others follow the same trend.

Knowledge Management

At the time corporations realized the growing impact of their IP portfolios, major business restructuring was taking place (mostly in North America and later in Europe), leading to a reduction in work force and an important loss of continuity in skill sets. The loss of manpower exacerbated an already existing need to preserve the knowledge of the corporation that resides in its employees and transform it into a more tangible form. Knowledge management became one of the top priorities in companies.

CONSEQUENCES OF INCREASED LICENSING

These four major factors—legal, business, internationalization, and knowledge management—caused a number of significant changes in the licensing field.

They can be grouped in three major areas:

1. Corporate vision and systems development
2. Intensity of technology transfer
3. Impact on tech-transfer professional qualifications

Corporate Vision and Systems Development

Companies, academics, and consultants started building up different models of management to try and capture the new phenomenon and to develop the needed tools and systems. Pioneers in this area include C.K. Prahalad and Gary Hansel of the University of Michigan ("The Core Competence of the Corporation," *Harvard Business Review*, May 6, 1990, 79–90); Nonaka (Nonaka, Ikujiro, and Takachi, *The Knowledge-Creating Company*, New York: Oxford University Press, 1995); Patrick Sullivan (*Profiting from Intellectual Capital*, New York: John Wiley & Sons, Inc., 1998); and Leif Edvinsson (Skandia Corporation, IC Annual Supplements). Leif Edvinsson was the first to apply the new elements and to publish the first Intellectual Capital Supplement for Skandia in the mid-1990s. He was recognized for these pioneering efforts by a Brain of the Year Award.

In many corporations, the practical results of all these efforts have been the development of the *core technology competency concept*, the creation of the chief technology officer (CTO) position, the creation of the *intellectual capital model* of the corporation, and the addition of an *intellectual asset management* function. A final result is that regulatory authorities and corporations have had to better quantify intangible assets.[3] This effort is a work in progress.

Core Technology Competency Concept. Prahalad defines *core competency* as a set of skills and behaviors that consistently provide a competitive advantage. The core competencies have to be defined narrowly enough to differentiate them from similar competencies of competitors. They also need to be defined in such a way as to be able to be managed efficiently (people, technology, impact).

The best-in-class companies have linked core competencies, people, products, and intellectual assets. The process of clearly linking core competencies to intellectual assets has given these companies a powerful tool to decide where to invest their R & D resources and a roadway to extract value from their intellectual asset portfolio.

In order to highlight the importance of the core technology competencies and the systems around them, these corporations have also made them the responsibility of a Board Director or of the newly created position of Chief Technology Officer, with responsibilities beyond R & D.

Intellectual Capital Model. Leif Edvinsson and Patrick Sullivan together with the IC Gathering—and others—have developed models of a company

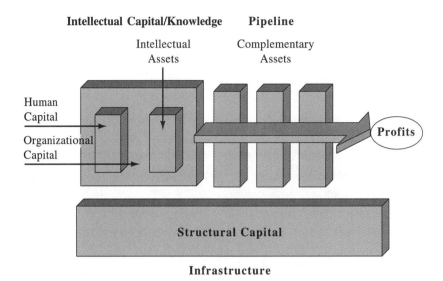

Intellectual Capital/Knowledge   Pipeline

Intellectual   Complementary
Assets   Assets

Human
Capital

Organizational
Capital

Profits

Structural Capital

Infrastructure

EXHIBIT 1.5   Intellectual Assets Business Model

from the intellectual assets perspective. These models are an attempt to explain how the different pieces of a corporation fall together, how they interrelate, and their impact on intellectual assets and profitability (see Exhibit 1.5). Readers interested in a more thorough analysis should consult any of the cited bibliography.

In the model shown, which works well for companies with a manufacturing component, intellectual capital is overlaying the structural capital (physical or hard assets) together with some defined complementary assets (nontechnical competencies) to create earnings. *Intellectual capital* (IC) has two major components: human capital and intellectual assets. *Human capital* is the manpower of a corporation. It includes the manpower's ideas, creativity, and ways of thinking and of resolving problems. *Intellectual assets* (IA) are the systems, processes, designs, operational manuals, show-how and know-how created by the human capital.

The most protected intellectual assets are the traditional elements of intellectual property (patents, provisionals, utility patents, trademarks, copyrights, etc.). It is essential for a company to make sure that whatever is in people's minds (the left side of the intellectual capital box) be transformed into a more tangible form—the intellectual assets. Intellectual assets are an asset of a corporation and belong to it. Human capital is certainly an asset but does not belong to the company because it can freely leave or move. Knowledge management is the critical system developed to ensure that the transfer process from human capital to intellectual capital is taking place in a consistent and effective manner.

Another way to think of this is to express these terms in contrasting equations:

Human Capital = value-creating component

Intellectual Assets = value-extracting component

Intellectual Asset Management.   There are only a finite number of ways in which value can be extracted from intellectual assets (see Exhibit 1.6). Of these, four do or should involve the licensing professional: outright sale, donation, license, and joint venture or alliance. The decision on which avenue to select depends on market and business considerations. Market position, business strategy, and availability of the appropriate complementary assets or the possibility to develop or acquire these will dictate which strategy to pursue (see Exhibit 1.7).

- Outright sale
- Donation
- License
- Joint venture or alliance
- Reduce competitive threat
- Incorporation into existing business
- Create a new business

EXHIBIT 1.6   Value Extraction Mechanisms of Intellectual Assets

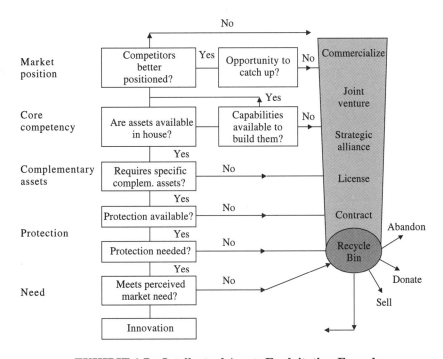

EXHIBIT 1.7   Intellectual Assets Exploitation Funnel

Intensity of Technology Transfer

It is very difficult to obtain accurate statistics on the number and value of licensing deals. The majority of the transactions is of a private nature and is not published. Exceptions include court-related transactions (litigations), which have shown a definite up trend (see Exhibits 1.2 and 1.3).

An estimate of the total value of these deals indicates a considerable increase in the last 10 years (see Exhibit 1.8), from $5 billion to $100 billion/year. These are only rough estimates. The intensity of the growth varies considerably by industry, with the bulk of it concentrated in the IT, computers, telecommunications, pharmaceutical, and biotech sectors. IBM has had consistently growing revenues, well over $1 billion. Lucent, Intel, Honeywell, and Dow Chemical have revenues in the nine digits. Start-up biotech and IT companies regularly announce transactions in the tens of millions. The Association of University Tech Transfer Managers (AUTM) has published data (AUTM Annual Licensing Survey, 1999) showing that the value of licensing transactions between publicly traded corporations and universities has grown to more than $1 billion in the United States and Canada.

The size of each single transaction has also grown. Intel conducted a $1.1 billion transaction with several Korean companies. The size of litigation-based awards reaches well into the hundreds of millions of dollars and crosses industrial sectors. These increases are the direct result of the corporations' movement from a passive to an active mode of exploitation of their intellectual assets.

As a consequence, a number of companies have established licensing as a bona fide business and have created a novel approach toward patenting: *invention on demand.*

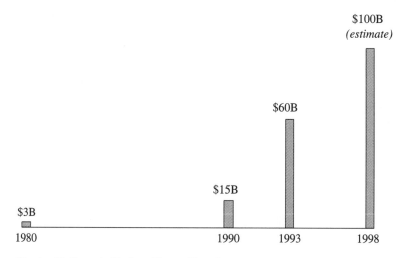

Based on The Economist, The Patent Wars, and SmartPatents.

EXHIBIT 1.8   Patent Licensing Revenues for U.S. Companies*

As a direct result of establishing IP as a strategic tool, companies in fast-moving technological businesses have to make sure that they establish a significant territorial presence in the IP domain. This includes current and future products. It will allow them to secure their freedom of action, to keep their ability to exclude or control their competitors' activities, and to select their most advantageous partnerships.

Impact on Licensing Professionals

The complexity and intensity of current licensing deals have significantly altered the licensing executive profession. In the not-too-distant past, the only things needed were good negotiation skills, an established network, some knowledge or understanding of the field of technology, and a large travel budget.

The situation has changed significantly and the profession has grown more sophisticated and complex. The modern licensing executive has to be fully aware of the tools available to do a better job, to do it faster, and to do it more efficiently. These tools include IP landscape, surveys, patent mapping, and citation analysis, as well as the esoteric use of options analysis, Monte Carlo simulations, and technology for valuation of specific technologies. The field is in constant flux with new systems, tools, and offerings.

It is not the intent of this introduction to elaborate on all of these tools; they will be covered in more detail in subsequent chapters. Here we point to two particular tools as examples. The most used one is *citation analysis,* where proprietary systems are used to graphically show which patents are cited as relevant art during prosecution of a particular patent. Initially restricted to U.S. patents, it has now been expanded to European patents as well. This powerful tool helps business and IP professionals to quickly analyze the IP landscape for a given technology or a given business and to focus on potential infringements, licensing possibilities (in and out), alliance partners, and new business opportunities. They have also been used as a negotiation tool. Exhibits 1.9, 1.10, and 1.11 show such tools as developed by Aurigin Systems. Variations are also available from other vendors such as Chi Research and Manning and Napier. Some systems are now also available as Web interface systems.

Similarly, a number of technology exchange Web sites such as Yet2com, Plx, and Patex have been set up over the last few years to help the licensing professional market its technology or to find a particular jewel. It is still too early to judge the success of such sites, but they very likely fulfill a needed niche in the panoply of industry tools. The number of these competing Web sites will probably shrink to a handful over the next few years. Several of

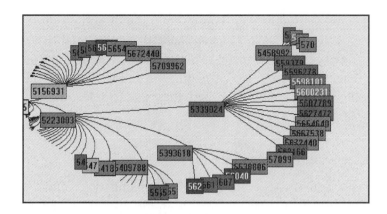

Mining Tool Shows Where to Get "Grandfather"
and "Fence-Hole" Patents Ahead of Competition

EXHIBIT 1.9   Mining for Players in Each Area

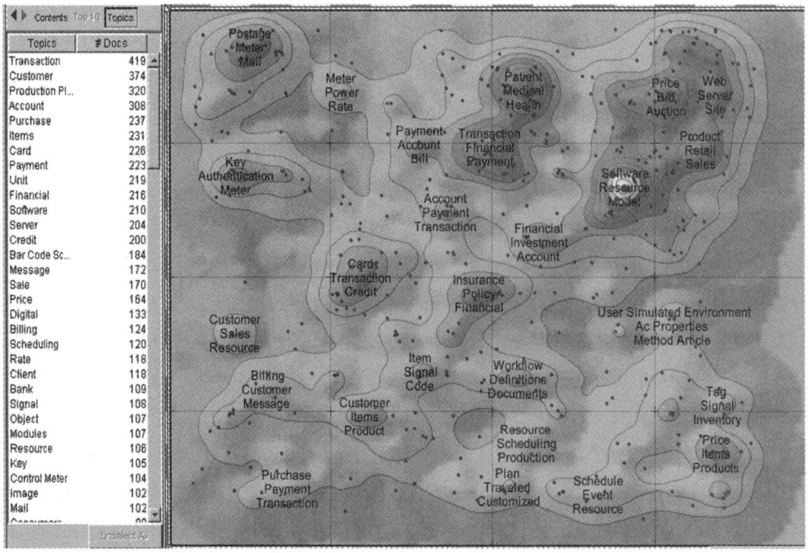

EXHIBIT 1.10   Topographical Landscape of 705 Patent Group

them offer services beyond listing of technologies and have diverse backers
and investors.[4]

The complexity and the expanding role of the licensing business have also
spun a proliferation of specialties, such as valuation, expert witnessing, IAM
databases, IAM consultants, royalty auditing, and so on.

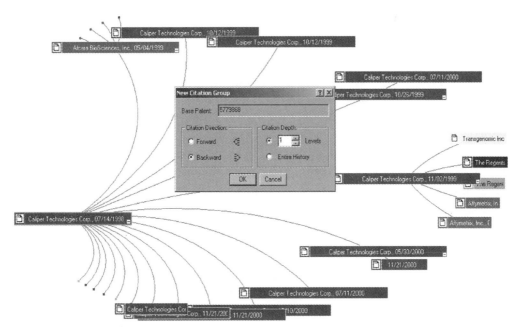

EXHIBIT 1.11   Analysis of Prior Art for Invalidity Studies

EDUCATION AND REMUNERATION

The tech-transfer profession has evolved from a relatively straightforward net-work of IP and negotiation generalists to a complex array of highly specialized and trained individuals segmented by industry and professional skill sets. As a result, to remain on top of its professional expertise, licensing executives have a greater need for education. Recognizing this need, the Licensing Executives Society (LES) has multiplied education initiatives worldwide. These education offerings can be seen on the LESI and associated Web sites. Some are curriculum-based, such as the new Professional Development Series of LES (Canada) and some are topic/instructors based. All have in common broadening subjects encompassing legal, strategy, valuation, and business matters.

The licensing executive of the future will have expanded opportunities but will need a multidisciplinary education or experience. Specialists on issues such as valuation, accounting, IT, IAM consultants, and so on, will help them.

The interconnectivity of all these fields can already be seen by the increasing convergence of professions, with law firms offering valuation and portfolio man-agement expertise, the e-commerce sites offering licensing and negotiation advice, and the big accounting firms including legal, portfolio management, licensing, and valuation advice.

Following the heightened awareness of the value of intellectual assets by industry and governments, the demand for specialists in these areas has grown in parallel. Because of the law of offer and demand, the remunerations offered have also increased significantly, starting to put some financial strain on the traditional *modus operandi* of IP law firms and others.

The biggest challenge—and opportunity—facing the licensing profession will be to train enough qualified individuals. It is not unreasonable to envision the need for a professional certification system to assure industry and government of the licensing executive's qualifications to do the job, not unlike the CPA and other professions. We need to prepare for this eventuality to allow continued growth in the importance of IA and to make sure it is used ethically throughout the world. To reach this goal will require a concerted effort among professional organizations like LESI, governments, and academia.

ENDNOTES

[1] *Unseen Wealth*, Report of the Brookings Task Force on Intangibles, Margaret M. Blair and Steven M. H. Wallman, Task force co-chairs, Brookings Institution Press, 2001.

[2] E. Robert Yoches, *Potent Patents*, Special Report Federal Circuit (March 1999).

[3] Seminar on Valuing Intangibles, Stern School of Business, New York, May 2001.

[4] See Tech Transfer Web sites Table C+EN, July 10, 2000, p.20 and April 2, 2001, p.26 for more details online.

ABOUT THE AUTHOR

Willy Manfroy is principal of Bornival LLC, an international consulting company in intellectual assets. He was director, corporate development, at Eastman Chemical Company, where he was responsible for mergers, acquisitions, divestitures, and licensing. For 25 years he held different positions at The Dow Chemical Company in the United States and in Europe in R & D, business, management, and mergers, acquisitions, and licensing. Mr. Manfroy is a past president of the Licensing Executives Society (LES) Canada, and is an officer of LES International. A Belgian national, Mr. Manfroy obtained a degree in chemical engineering from École Polytechnique of the Université Libre de Bruxelles.

2

Technology Valuation

By Dr. Richard Razgaitis

INTRODUCTION

The subject matter of licensing, insofar as this chapter is concerned, can be characterized by the encompassing word *technology*.[1] Licensed technology may be expressed in patents, patent applications, invention disclosures, software, business procedures, data books, plant manuals and procedures, laboratory apparatus, prototypes of all kinds, factory equipment and even entire production plants, in the minds of people, and many other ways. As discussed elsewhere, technology is protectable by law as *intellectual property*. With the exception of certain niches of licensing, such as brand names and franchising, all licensing—from $99 shrink-wrapped software to a university-owned invention disclosure on a human gene to the design drawings for a $1 billion semiconductor manufacturing plant—can be considered as technology licensing.

Valuation is a more complex concept. Simply put, it is the process of ascribing value, in our context, to technology being licensed. *Value,* or price as an expression of value, is commonly defined as the amount at which an asset would change hands between a willing buyer and a willing seller, each having reasonable knowledge of the relevant facts, neither being under any compulsion to act, with equity to both. Therefore, every license agreement can be considered to be a valuation event. In a sense, even a two-party license, the most common situation, is a type of auction. The licensor (seller) believes that compared to all its other alternatives this particular licensee (buyer) is the most favorable opportunity, given the dimensions of the deal and the risks and uncertainties associated with pursuing an agreement with a third party. Likewise, the buyer, with a world full of alternative investment opportunities, believes that the seller is offering the best incremental return, given the known alternatives and in consideration of the risks and uncertainties in pursuing such alternatives.

Auctions, since antiquity, are known for providing two important, simultaneous business results: the value of price discovery and what is colloquially known as *liquidity*. Until there is the joining of a willing seller and a willing buyer, no price, or value, is certain and, thereby, knowable. In a traditional auction, the seller invites all buyers to bid. In such bidding, the seller and the buyer each discover the value of what is offered. Because the bidders must be *willing-to-execute buyers* for the offers to be meaningful, the process also creates liquidity for the seller, namely the ability to get cash, or any other sought exchange medium, in exchange for the value of the seller's goods, in this case technology.

Technology valuation, then, can be thought of as a business process that *anticipates* the price discovery that will occur between a seller and a buyer after all the marketing and opportunity characterization by the seller and assessment and due diligence by the buyer.

For more in-depth information on valuation and pricing of technology, with a focus on early-stage technology, see *Early Stage Technologies: Valuation and Pricing* (Richard Razgaitis, New York: John Wiley and Sons, 1999), available through online resources such as amazon.com. In this chapter, with a necessarily more limited scope, we will examine *sources*, *expressions of value*, and *methods* (*tools*) of anticipating value (valuation). But, first, we will consider technology valuation in the context of what has become known as the *new economy*.

THE NEW ECONOMY AND TECHNOLOGY LICENSING

At the end of the twentieth century, many began to characterize the business world as the *new economy*. The phrase raises some useful questions: What exactly was the *old economy*? What makes this one *new*? Why might one conclude that something dramatic has happened that warrants such a demarcation? And what might this have to do with *technology licensing*?

First, let us consider what we mean by the old economy.[2] Let me suggest that a useful way of thinking about the old economy is the postulate that there exists a direct, measurable connection between assets and income. The accounting methods that form the foundation of business analysis were invented in Italy about 600 years ago. It was recognized that income from a farm, in the form of crops or animals or animal products like milk or eggs, were directly related, but not solely determined, by deployed assets. In the case of an agrarian economy, such assets were land, water resources, farm machinery and tools, farm buildings, and supplies of seed, animals, fertilizers, and the like. The acquisition costs of such assets were enumerated at the beginning and end of each accounting period, usually a year, in what is known as a *balance sheet*. The income report contained the sales, costs, and net profit that occurred during the reporting period. For our purposes, the key point is this: There is a reason to expect a correlation between the assets given on the balance sheet at the beginning of a year and the revenues, costs, and profit that will be experienced during the upcoming year and later reported on the income statement. Such correlation is not perfect because of the vagaries of drought, pestilence, and other factors such as war, employee and management competence, and diligence. However, the scope and nature of such assets did give an owner, or prospective investor, a reasonable basis by which to anticipate the profit that could be gained in future years. The sum of such anticipated future profits determines the value of the enterprise.

In the dramatic transformation from the agrarian to the industrial economy, starting in about 1850, the nature of the assets on the balance sheet changed to factories, machinery, raw material inventory, and transportation means for many businesses. Yet something important did not change: the asset values could be reliably measured, and there was a direct correlation between such asset values and the anticipated year-to-year profits.

Price-to-Book Ratios

Beginning approximately 20 years ago, the value of business assets, at least insofar as they are traditionally measured and measurable, appeared to have no direct correlation to the actual or anticipated year-to-year profits of many enterprises and, thereby, the market value of the enterprises owning such assets. Three charts support this hypothesis, using *price-to-book ratios* as a measurement tool. The price-to-book ratio is defined in this way:

$$\text{Price-to-book ratio} =$$

$$\frac{\text{Price of 1 share of company stock}}{(\text{Company's asset value / total shares outstanding})}$$

Exhibit 2.1 shows the price-to-book ratio for the Standard and Poor's 500 basket of stocks since 1928.

In Exhibit 2.2, we see the same ratio, but with the scale expanded so that we can better see what has happened since 1989.

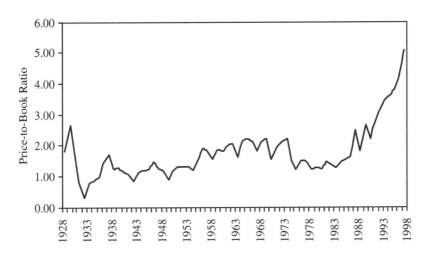

EXHIBIT 2.1   Price-to-Book Ratio for the S & P 500 Since 1928

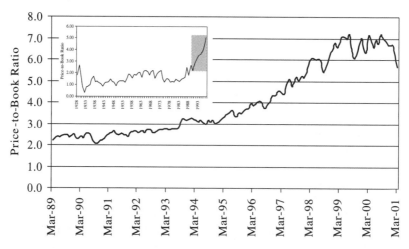

EXHIBIT 2.2   S & P Price-to-Book Ratio Since 1989

These data show, or at least strongly suggest, two phenomena:[3]

1. There is, or at least there was, a more or less steady relationship between what the marketplace said a company was worth (reflected in the share price) and what the accountants said was the value of business assets of the company (reflected in the balance sheet value, or book value per share).

2. This correlation between value and assets has been changing dramatically since about 1990, or perhaps even 1980.

Case Study of the New Economy: Microsoft

Exhibit 2.3 gives us a concrete example, a company some would say is the poster child of the new economy, Microsoft.

Exhibit 2.3 illustrates Microsoft's price-to-book ratio since 1987. These data clearly show that although Microsoft has been gradually accumulating more and more assets, the value of the company is many multiples of the value of such balance sheet assets and, in fact, there is no strong correlation between the two parameters. Further, the volatility of the stock markets—and especially the technology sector—in 1999, 2000, and 2001 affected Microsoft as well. However, its market value remains many multiples of its book value. For interest, Exhibit 2.3 also shows the growth in the annual filing of U.S. patent applications by Microsoft, though no cause and effect with respect to value is suggested here.

So, what is the new economy? One characteristic seems to be that the balance sheet of assets and the income statement of revenues, costs, and earnings no longer appear to be relatable. But is the world's economy itself becoming new?

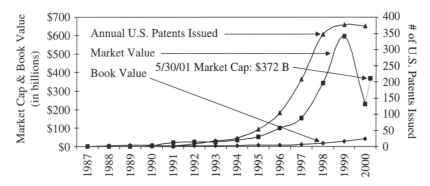

EXHIBIT 2.3   Microsoft's Price-to-Book Ratio Since 1987

The answer is, of course, not completely—there are still farms and factories. However, there does appear to be something genuinely new in the economics of companies that are able to earn returns, and thereby to create company value, far in excess of what would be expected by any accounting analysis of their balance sheets. That leads to the final and most interesting question: How do new economy companies provide such value? The answer appears to be *missing mass on the balance sheet.* What are those missing assets? Primarily, they are technology, which creates value to customers, and thereby to shareholder-owners, in excess of what might be transformed by traditional assets, and which often also provides a barrier to competitors, creating additional shareholder value.

Exhibit 2.4 provides another perspective. This figure shows the steady growth in the U.S. population from 1977 to 1996 in comparison to two other trends: the U.S. gross domestic product (GDP), the economist's standard measure of a country's vitality, which grew dramatically faster than the population, and the GDP of everything that has mass, the kind of assets that easily appear on a balance sheet, which did not grow at all in the period. The difference in the total GDP and the mass-GDP is partially attributable to the services economy, as is widely discussed, but it also includes the effect of real products of the kind that Microsoft sells and ships: such new economy products can have high value and almost no mass (and if delivered as an electronic file of software or content, then it literally has no mass).

It is these unquantified technology assets that have become the principal source of business value for new economy companies. And it is the acquisition, sale, and sharing of such technology assets that have become an enormous source of potential value generation for many industry sectors and for licensing practitioners.

Another signpost of the new economy and its direct role in licensing is the growth in the number and value of merger and acquisition (M & A) activity. Much of the growth in M & A in the late 1990s was driven, in part, by the

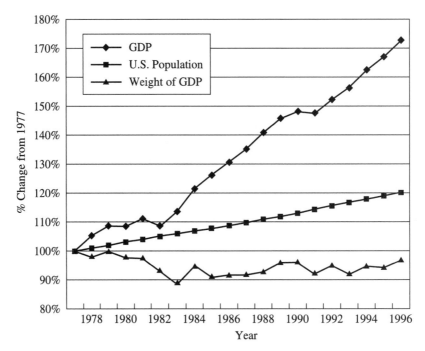

EXHIBIT 2.4   U. S. Population Growth versus GDP

inflated currency of extraordinary share values of acquiring companies. A high-profile example of such a company is Cisco, which averaged two such acquisitions a month. Nonetheless, it appears that companies are increasingly adopting the practice of scouting for potential companies to acquire to supplement, or in some cases replace, internal R & D. In such circumstances, M & A is in a very real sense licensing. It is likely that *game-changing innovation* will continue to flourish in small start-up companies, and this phenomena will affect the course of technology in the twenty-first century. For many of these start-ups, the path to commercial fruition will be through an M & A–originating licensing event.

Do you need more evidence that technology is driving this new economy? Try this: As of March 31, 2001, Microsoft's market value was greater than the sum of the market value of all 25 companies in the S & P index for the four following industry sectors: steel, automotive, chemicals and plastics, and aerospace and defense. That is, *Microsoft alone* is worth more than all the 25 following companies comprising these four sectors *combined*, namely: USX, Allegheny, Nucor, Worthington Industries, Ford, GM, Delphi, Visteon, Goodyear, Cooper, Air Products, Dow, Du Pont, Eastman, Hercules, Praxair, Rohm & Haas, Boeing, Lockheed Martin, Northrop Grumman, Rockwell, General Dynamics, United Technologies, and BF Goodrich.

SOURCES OF VALUE: THE BOX

The critical starting point of any valuation is defining exactly what is being offered for licensing. Yet, it is not uncommon that long into a marketing campaign, or deep into a negotiation, it becomes frustratingly obvious that the parties have not had a common or even similar idea of what is being licensed. Here we wish to consider what a seller may offer and a buyer may seek in a license agreement. In the next section we will reverse the view and consider what a seller may expect and a buyer may offer in consideration for such agreement.

It is useful to develop a shorthand for this discussion: we will use a metaphorical box and its contents to designate the subject matter of a license being valued. What might such a box contain? Clearly, we begin with the right to practice the technology being licensed. But even this simple idea contains two very important terms that must be defined: *technology* and *right*.

1. *Technology.*   What exactly is the *technology* being licensed? How does it relate to the issued patents that might be in the box? For instance, does technology mean that the buyer can use the claims of the licensed patents, however it is able to do so, and only that? Or, is the scope of the technology only incompletely encompassed by the issued patents? What about pending patent applications whose ultimate claims are not known at the time of the negotiation? What about improvement inventions that might arise at the seller's R & D labs or that the seller may acquire rights to in the future? What does improvement really mean in relation to the technology?
2. *Right.*   This is another term capable of a rich range of meanings. What is the uniqueness of licensed right? Is it exclusive? If so, what are the terms? Does it apply to all potential applications (fields of use)? All territories? For all time? Does exclusivity preclude the seller's right to practice? Is the right to sublicense included in such an exclusive right? What about the right to assign?

It is common that sellers are willing to consider alternative boxes with respect to the technology and right issues. There are two things that are important about changing boxes: How does it affect value? How does it affect deal doability?[4]

1. *Valuation.*   Any change in the contents of the box should, in general, cause a change in the value of a license to the box's contents. Accordingly, without locking on a definition of the content of the box, it is not possible for valuation to take place by either the seller or buyer. One is tempted to conceive of creating an à la carte menu by which each element in the box is individually priced, such that any

buyer can self-price the deal by the selections it makes, something like this: nonexclusive royalty is 2%; with exclusivity there is a 3% adder (5% total); the sublicensing right is 1%; two years of improvements cost an additional 2% but five years of improvements are on special today for only 3%; and so forth (or the equivalent in present-value, lump-sum payments).

2. *Doability.*   In licensing situations, the number of possible elements is so large, and their value can so interact with the presence (or absence) of other elements, that to create such a valuation model would require an overwhelming level of analysis. Although such an approach works for restaurants and custom-built homes, the idea of a single box with à la carte pricing incorporating all the possible deal variations is simply impractical for technology licensing. Fortunately there are practical solutions. The obvious solution is for the seller to prescribe only one box and value it accordingly—as Henry Ford said, you could have any color of a Model-T automobile, as long as it was black. Such a one-size-fits-all approach is likely to be rejected by potential buyers as including more than they want to pay for or less than they need. In many cases, a potential buyer will have very particular interests and values, and will seek a licensing box unique to its business situation.

If an à la carte box cannot reasonably be valued, and a one-size-fits-all box has low or no deal doability, what is to be done? As a starting point for marketing and negotiations, the seller creates a baseline box of what it conceives is an appropriate configuration of its interests and its target buyers, but with an analysis of one or two alternatives to establish a range of values and an estimate of value sensitivity. Regardless of these choices and complications, the box must be defined before the valuation process can begin if its result is to have a rational basis.

So far, we have considered technology and rights as two elements of the box. What else is there? Well, the list is long indeed. The following list provides brief descriptions of additional possible elements that could be appropriate to and included in such a licensing box.

- *Patents and other intellectual property.*   This could include pending patent applications, formalized trade secrets, copyrighted content and software, and even trademarks.
- *Proprietary technical information (PTI).*   Although this can be grouped under IP trade secrets, it is useful to consider the wealth of technical information that is typically created by a seller as being broader than the more restrictive, legal term of trade secrets. Included in such PTI could be laboratory notebooks, unpublished white papers, project plans, management presentations, a selected compendium of published articles

whose results are pertinent and valuable to the licensed technology, assessments of competing technologies, market assessments including customer surveys or focus panel results, and the like.

- *People*.   There could be individuals employed by the seller who would be interested in joining the buyer and so continuing to stay involved with the technology. The seller can agree to permit the buyer to recruit selected individuals and even provide inducements to key employees to go with the technology. As part of such transfer, the seller can provide the buyer, and the people transferring employment, the right to use all their "head IP" as it relates to the subject technology. Such seller commitments are subject, always, to the willingness of such people to become transferring employees of the buyer's company, but incentives can be committed to by either the seller or buyer or both.
- *Hardware*.   The technology can be expressed in a wide range of physical forms from special raw materials, to models, R & D prototypes, development breadboards, test samples, and so forth, all the way to saleable inventory.
- *Facilities*.   This can range from the offerings of a complete operable production plant embodying the licensed technology or a factory that manufactures the licensed technology as a product, down to specialized facilities/infrastructure that can be removed, shipped, and reinstalled at the buyer. Alternatively, a lease arrangement could be used whereby the buyer would use the seller's facilities on a short-term or long-term basis.
- *Software*.   The seller could have software programs that model the performance of the technology and are useful in R & D and/or production design and/or production control.
- *Customers*.   Commercial accounts could be transferrable to a buyer. In other cases, there could be trials with potential customers, or expressions of intent to buy that could be available.
- *Suppliers*.   The seller could have identified and even qualified certain vendors who can supply needed materials or services, with the attendant specifications. The seller itself could agree to be a supplier of a needed component (an element that could be a source of high deal value to the seller).
- *External contracts*.   There could be sources of funding, including R & D funding by third parties, such as a government agency, which the buyer would then receive as part of the agreement. Likewise, commercial services that are currently provided by the seller could be transferred to the buyer.
- *External licenses*.   The seller may have operating permits, government approvals, or other licenses to the subject technology collecting revenues that can be transferred. Alternatively, licensed rights to third-party patents could be included here, or under "other IP," and could be an important source of deal value if the seller has the right to sublicense or assign.

- *Patent prosecution and maintenance.*   If the patents are assigned (sold), then their prosecution and maintenance normally becomes the responsibility of the buyer. If the patents are only licensed, then the buyer or the seller could undertake the financial obligation, or it could be shared.
- *Infringement enforcement.*   A common concern is, what happens after the deal is done if a third party infringes or appears to infringe on licensed claims? A seller-licensor could agree to enforce the licensed patents to ensure the buyer's exclusivity. If nonexclusive, the seller may accept the responsibility to take action against unlicensed third parties who compete with the buyer. In either case there may be some threshold of infringement before the seller would be obligated to take action.
- *Infringement defense.*   A different infringement concern by the buyer has to do with the risk associated with its freedom to practice what it licensed from the seller. The seller could indemnify the buyer against claims by the third party against the buyer for a specific product.
- *R & D/consulting services.*   The seller could provide R & D services (commonly termed *tech-transfer assistance*) for a transition period, or an indefinite period. A prescribed level of such services could be included in the license, and/or the commitment to provide such services under specified terms.
- *Regulatory support services.*   There could be circumstances whereby the use of the technology will require some form of regulatory approval and the seller could be of assistance to the buyer in seeking or transferring such approval.
- *General representations and warranties.*   It is, of course, common for the seller to warrant that it has the right to sell or license what it is offering to the buyer, but the seller could offer additional representations and warranties.

Although few agreements have all these elements, it is useful to both the seller and buyer to consider what can, should, and should not be included to maximize the relative value of the opportunity to both parties, particularly for technologies with significant commercial potential. It is especially useful for the seller to create a summary of what is in the box—or boxes, in the case of multiple scenarios. This practice allows all the affected individuals within the seller's organization to possess a common understanding of the dimensions of a potential deal. In any case, such a specification is necessary to create a baseline on which a valuation can take place. Further, it is also useful in communicating with potential buyers so that an early understanding can be reached, or the box appropriately adjusted, to accommodate the deal being envisioned.

These possible elements are not equally important, nor are they unrelated to each other. The IP is, for example, closely tied to both the technology and rights; it would not be uncommon that a license deal would have only these core elements in the box.

EXPRESSIONS OF VALUE: THE WHEELBARROW

In the previous section, the focus was on the value provided by the seller to the buyer, using the metaphor of the box, as the contents for the technology, the rights to use, and the related value-affecting aspects of a license. Here, we wish to consider how the buyer may provide value to the seller. As before, a metaphor will be useful.

One frequent measure of value of a license is the royalty rate, as in "this deal is for a 5 percent license." Actually, a royalty rate by itself is an incomplete description of value. The seller is rightfully concerned about the size of the check that it expects to receive, not the royalty rate used in calculating the amount owed under the license, regardless of the rate, and regardless of whether it is usage-based, time-based, or event-based. To effectively capture the concern of the seller (and buyer), the slang term *wheelbarrow* has been utilized in reference to the buyer hauling cash to the seller in a wheelbarrow. Accordingly, while a royalty rate is a common negotiation point, both parties are ultimately concerned with the size of the wheelbarrow. Here, the wheelbarrow is used to reflect all of the various forms of value provided by the seller to the buyer. The seller provides a box of technology, rights, and other deal elements, whereas the buyer provides, in the form of one or many wheelbarrows, value payments to the seller.

There are two common forms of value contained in such wheelbarrows: a single payment, such as "the buyer paid $10 million for the license," and a royalty rate.

1. *Lump-sum license.* A single-payment license, commonly termed a *lump-sum* or *paid-up* license, is the simplest valuation structure.[5] It represents a check, or more commonly a wire transfer, usually made simultaneously with executing the license. It represents the only payment that the buyer will make. However, even in this simplest of arrangements there may be other important forms of value provided by the buyer, such as granting the seller access to certain patents belonging to the buyer (*cross licensing*), a supply agreement whereby the buyer agrees to provide products made by the licensed technology, or even some other technology, under more favorable terms than are commercially available. Thus, even for such simple, single-payment licenses, the wheelbarrow may contain something notable beyond the closing payment.

2. *Royalty license.* A pure royalty-based license, also known as a *running royalty license*, is the inverse of the single-payment license: the single-payment license is a fixed sum paid upfront for unlimited (or in accordance with the terms of the license), subsequently free use, whereas the pure royalty license has only payments due on use (make, use, or sell) and only on such use. However, a critical factor in determining value is the royalty base against which such royalty rate is applied. A common negotiation involves a determination of the appropriate base. Consider the situation of a quick disconnect that is being licensed for use on the terminals of an automobile battery. The seller may argue that the appropriate royalty base is the selling price of the automobile because such terminals are, say, used only on batteries in automobiles. If the buyer is a battery maker, such an approach will be unacceptable regardless of how low the royalty rate is because the battery maker has no control, or even knowledge, of the selling price of the automobile with the battery in it. Further, the battery maker is likely to argue that the connector royalty should *not* be based on the selling price of the battery itself because the connector is only a small part of the battery and in fact does not contribute to the basic function of the battery. The buyer is likely to propose a royalty base on the selling (or fair market) price of the connector component itself. The negotiated royalty rate will be done in conjunction with the negotiation on the appropriate royalty base: a 1 percent royalty based on the selling price of the battery, for example, could alternatively be a 25 percent royalty based on the connector's cost or fair market value, and yield the same cash amount in the wheelbarrow.

In addition to these two common elements, there are many other possible elements that can be used in any combination in the wheelbarrow to provide value to the seller:

1. *Upfront payment(s).* A common value element is the use of one or multiple *upfront* or *license fee* cash payments. Upfront payments are unconditional and precede the anticipated commercial use by the buyer. One such payment is made on closing or within a specified number of days of closing (e.g., 30 days). Additional "upfront" payments could be made at specified dates, such as on the first and second anniversary of the license. In this case, the term *upfront* is used to specify payments that are committed at deal execution but may be deferred to specific dates after closing. As used here, such form of value is unconditional and additional. It is unconditional in the sense that regardless of the buyer's later decision not to use the licensed technology or even termination of

the license, such payments are still due. It is additional in that other subsequent forms of value payments, such as royalties, are a separate contributor to the wheelbarrow of payment. One important negotiation issue is the ability of the buyer to credit such payments against future royalties owed; not surprisingly, sellers gravitate to no and buyers to yes. The reasonable answer lies in the calculation of the royalty: If the full value of the license has been ascribed to the royalties, and some of the running royalties have been moved to be fixed, upfront payments, then the answer should be yes because they are in fact prepayments; on the other hand, if the royalties were calculated to represent the license value remaining after the upfront payments, then the answer should be no.

2. *Annual payments.*   Another form of fixed cash payments is the use of annual payments payable on each anniversary of the license for as long as the license is in effect. Sometimes this form of payment is referred to as *license maintenance fees* or *minimum royalties* (or simply *minimums*). Normally the use of *minimums* is restricted to those periods when earned royalties can reasonably be expected and the magnitude of the minimums is scaled on some proportion of the magnitude of expected royalty payments, and such payments are commonly credited against earned royalties during that period (and such credits may or may not be applicable, i.e., carried forward, to subsequent periods).

3. *Milestone payments.*   Such payments are specified amounts that become due upon the crossing of some milestone event. In the area of pharmaceuticals, such milestones could be the entry into each phase of clinical testing, or any regulatory approval. Other kinds of milestones could be key R & D achievements, and/or the commitment to building a commercial plant of specified minimum size, and/or the first commercial sale. A special type of milestone payment would be a payment due upon termination of the license.

4. *Option payments.*   One form of option payment is an initial payment made by the buyer to allow it to conduct additional R & D, or market assessment or other feasibility activities, to enable it to make an informed licensing decision. Such a payment has the effect of compensating a seller for withholding the licensing opportunity from the market during the option period. Other types of option payments are possible. One example is the option to maintain exclusivity of the license beyond a certain date. Another example would be to acquire an additional field of use or territorial right. Yet other examples would be to acquire a companion technology, to buy out the license (a one-time payment to end all future royalties), and to make other payments to buy down the royalty rate (a payment that lowers the effective royalty for all subsequent sales).

5. *Royalty adjustments.*   Many creative adjustments have been used with a
baseline royalty rate. A *wedding cake* royalty is one that decreases in rate
with increasing sales, such as 5 percent on the first $5 million, 3 percent
on the next $10 million, and 1 percent for all additional sales. Such sales
could be annual (i.e., with each anniversary the royalty again begins at
5 percent in this example) or cumulative (i.e., total sales since the onset
of the license).

Alternatively, an *escalating* royalty could be used where the royalty
rate actually increases with increasing sales, under the reasoning that
higher sales would correspond to higher licensee profitability. This might
also be used to restrict or control the output of the buyer's licensed goods.
A *multimarket* royalty is another approach, where different, specified
royalties are used for individual products (fields of use) and/or territories.

Yet another strategy calls for certain sales to be *royalty free* (possibly
to aid market introduction or some other purpose). Sellers might seek to
include in the same or an alternative royalty calculation something
called *convoyed* sales, additional products or services that the licensee
might anticipate selling as a result of selling the goods embodying the
licensed technology.

Similar to a milestone payment, a *kicker* is a royalty premium paid
upon the occurrence of some milestone. For example, the baseline royalty rate might be set at 5 percent, but if the performance of the technology exceeds some specified level, there is a 2 percent kicker, making the
royalty paid actually 7 percent. Of course, the opposite could be negotiated by the buyer, such that there is a 3 percent "deflator," making the
royalty paid 2 percent if the technology meets only some lower standard.
Other adjustments in royalty rate could be based on market share, payments made to third parties for the right to practice patents needed to
practice the licensed technology, step-downs in rate if the licensee elects
to convert its license from exclusive to nonexclusive or if certain (but not
all) patents expire, the making public of licensed trade secrets, the passage of a specified period of time, or even the profitability of the relevant product line or company (though such a provision can be perilous
to the seller because of accounting complexities).

Another complex royalty adjustment can exist with respect to the royalty base itself. In some licensing situations, the sales made by a certain
buyer of a technology might be primarily as a result of one or more
patents in the box. Alternatively, such patents could be relatively minor
contributors to a later sale by that same buyer. The parties could deal
with this situation by adjusting the royalty base and possibly the rate
itself to deal with each of these possible future situations.

A final example is that of sublicensing royalties. The royalty amounts paid to the seller under the buyer's sublicenses could be different from that which would have been paid by the buyer for its own making/using/selling. This could be done by apportioning the gross amount of such sublicensing revenues between the buyer and seller.

6. *IP rights.*   A grant-back is one type of IP right in which the buyer can provide rights to its own improvements to the subject technology to the seller, either for the seller's own internal use or to enable the seller to offer additional technology to its other technology licensees. Another example of IP rights provided by the buyer would be rights to patents or other forms of IP owned by the buyer but unrelated to the subject technology; such an arrangement is commonly termed a *cross license.* Another form of this type of value would be an agreement to provide the seller with a product that it, in turn, could sell based on the subject technology, or even some unrelated technology. Publicity by the buyer of the seller's role as a technology provider could create value to the seller in the form of goodwill and market recognition.

7. *Commitment to purchase goods/services.*   The buyer could agree to purchase goods made by the seller at terms that are commercially favorable to the seller in a so-called supply agreement. Another example would be the buyer's commitment to purchase professional services, such as R & D in the area of the licensed technology or some other area; such an arrangement is common when the seller is a university and the buyer is a large company. Depending on the terms of these types of commitments, it could be value neutral to the parties, a value provided by the buyer, or even a value provided by the seller.

8. *Equity.*   The provision of a share of ownership in the buyer can create a source of considerable value, or even the total value in lieu of any cash payments, royalty, or any other form of value in consideration for a license. Another variation is that the seller has an option to purchase a specified number of shares at a prescribed price per share by a prescribed date, and/or similarly the right to convert fixed or royalty payments into equity. Another form of equity value could be provided by the buyer by its infusing capital into the seller in exchange for shares in the seller's company. Such a cash infusion could provide the seller with a strategic advantage with respect to other fund-raising activities. Based on the circumstances, such a transaction could be value neutral, or value favoring the seller, or value favoring the buyer.

Although these eight elements do not exhaust the possibilities, they do reflect the commonly used means of creating a wheelbarrow of value to the seller. As with the box, it is unlikely that there are many agreements that include all possible elements, but the flexibility afforded by the inclusion of an element and its specific implementation can be important in reaching an agreement. Agreements with only unconditional payments, such as paid-up licenses, or licenses with only fixed periodic or event-driven payments, may have higher valuation risks because of their lack of certitude. Generally, though, these agreements result in a simpler document, both in construction and in implementation. Conversely, agreements whose value is primarily dependent upon conditional elements (e.g., royalties) may have less valuation risk but higher complexity in document construction and ultimate implementation.

In general, for less important and less valuable technologies, the parties tend to gravitate to simpler wheelbarrows (and boxes). However, as current trends continue into the twenty-first century, technology owners will increasingly recognize their fiduciary responsibility to maximize their return on assets, and as time to market urgency increases, sellers will be more inclined to license out even their crown jewels for appropriately large wheelbarrows. Likewise, we can expect all buyers to consider quite literally the world of technology in-licensing of boxes based on externally created technologies for the prospect that they can become strategic new businesses and, thereby, warrant highly crafted license-in arrangements. The twenty-first century is expected to become a new economy of licensing by the increasing use of highly tailored boxes and value-optimizing wheelbarrows for opportunities of high importance to both seller and buyer.

PRINCIPLES OF VALUE

Before turning our attention to valuation methods and tools, let us consider certain underlying principles of value and valuation.

Specificity

One valuation method is the use of industry standards, which is based on the concept of identifying a comparable license agreement from public literature. However, for many situations, the contents of the box and the structure of the wheelbarrow will result in a valuation highly specific to the parties and parameters of the deal. This means that it is difficult if not impossible to find an exact or even near-exact comparable agreement on which to base a valuation. Also, this situation should make all of us cautious in characterizing any deal in terms of one or a few simple metrics, or in presuming that whatever the wheelbarrow looked like in our most recent deal is what it should look like in our next deal. There are simple licenses (e.g., the nonexclusive licensing of a single patent in exchange for a single lump-sum payment) where the deal is clearly nonspecific, but this is a less common situation.

Risk

Business planning for future events involves risk. The decision to maintain status quo in a business situation, say by refusing to license, involves risk. *Risk* is business shorthand for saying that the future may turn out more adversely than our most careful planning and forecasting leads us to believe today.

In technology licensing, risk has many potential sources:

- *Technology itself.* Depending on its stage of development, there could be risks associated with R & D activities, product development, and design for manufacture. Unexpected environmental difficulties, rising costs of raw material, or special manufacturing requirements could hamper technological success.
- *The market.* Forecasting market need, acceptance, timing, willingness to pay, and the attendant competitive response can be very challenging, depending on the nature of the technology and the time horizon. Such forecasts naturally tend to underaccount for emerging, unknown technologies that might compete, or might assist, the commercial value of the subject opportunity.
- *IP issues.* The IP protection of the seller's patentable technology might be incomplete at the time of the transaction, leading to risks associated with ultimately allowed claims. IP of third parties may be required, or useful, to the practice of the subject technology, which may add licensing-patent-avoidance costs to commercial estimates. Trade secret protection could be lost by human error or misappropriation.
- *Government and society.* Government policy, or societal values, can make it difficult or impossible to realize commercial value (take the nuclear power industry as a 30-year example).

In fact, any reasonably comprehensive enumeration of risks can be so disheartening as to be disabling, as an ancient (ca. 1000 B.C.) text says:

> Whoever watches the wind will not plant;
>   whoever looks at the clouds will not reap.[6]

Risk is unavoidable, but not all risks are equal. It is possible to characterize the risk of a specific opportunity by specific analysis of the business issues and uncertainties. Such a characterization can be used with various valuation approaches, as will be discussed in the next section, to account for the risk. A particularly useful way to deal with risk is through the framework of the wheelbarrow by using, for example, value heavily weighted by royalties, equity, or conditional fixed payments, where it makes business sense to do so.

Uncertainty

Risk just considered can be thought of as an expression of uncertainty. That is, if we somehow had a time machine that could transport the parties to a time 20 years hence with access to all the business effects, favorable and not, of having entered the license and having not entered the license—a kind of *It's a Wonderful Life* James Stewart movie experience—then the risk would be erased by our privileged future knowledge. Unfortunately for business and valuation purposes (but certainly a blessing in other ways), the future is unknowable to us.

Our purpose here is to consider *uncertainty* apart from its obvious connection to *risk*. When performing most accounting business functions, we expect reasonable exactitude and certitude. If one wonders what the cash balance in liquid accounts is at any moment, one does not accept the answer from the treasurer that such a figure cannot be known, or can only approximately be known. Likewise with raw material inventories: It is either in our control, and therefore on our books, or it is not. If we have it in our control, somebody had better be ready to give a complete and accurate accounting.[7] Selling is perhaps a little more ambiguous, but each business defines (in accordance with generally accepted accounting standards) a criterion for what constitutes a sale, and thus the sales revenue and backlog at any time is similarly knowable. This belief system forms the basis for having an accounting firm audit a company's books and issue a report that represents fairly the financial position of the company and the results of its operations in the past year on a basis consistent with that of the preceding year.

This perspective changes when pro forma (projected) business models are created. The need for internal consistency and mathematical accuracy remains (the columns must sum properly, and the assumptions and related calculations must be self-consistent), but the need for certitude is further relaxed. However, there is a general understanding that pro forma values will be achieved or exceeded or there will be some form of accountability. This causes the responsible parties to be quite conservative, although their managers are known to boost such projections, as has been the source of much of the humor in Dilbert cartoons. In licensing contexts, it is common that the nature of such projections lacks the business history of typical pro forma projections. Further, if only a conservative, can't-miss approach is taken, then it is likely that many worthy licenses will be forgone. Although there are valuation tools that specifically deal with this issue, there is an underlying perspective that licensing technology is a risk-bearing process, and one can rarely afford the luxury of having a high degree of certitude regarding high-value opportunities.

Pricing

Pricing is the specific values that are associated with the wheelbarrow and communicated, frequently by the seller to the buyer. A useful vehicle for such pricing communication is a *term sheet*. A typical term sheet is a two- to three-page document of summary, bullet-like points that characterize the box and the specific values associated with each of the relevant wheelbarrow elements. It can be initiated by either the seller (the most common situation) or the buyer. It provides sufficient summary financial aspirations (or determined expectations) that specify the results of the valuation model and associated trade-offs.

Pricing intertwines with negotiation, much as it would in selling and buying homes. One can price high and expect to wait a long time for just the ideal buyer for whom such price is acceptable, or price low to attract competitive interest to achieve a rapid sale. One can price a little above the expected final value to leave room for counteroffers and the give and take of negotiation, or one can price firm and inform prospective buyers that no offers less than the stated price will be considered (at least at this time). Pricing strategies are outside the scope of this chapter.

VALUATION TOOLS AND METHODS

There are six valuation methods that can be used by both the seller and buyer to value a technology licensing opportunity. These are covered in detail in *Early-Stage Technologies: Valuation and Pricing*. This chapter provides only a brief overview. Refer to Exhibit 2.5 as these methods are discussed.

Before covering the six valuation methods, however, we need to consider the *cost method*. Cost has a long tradition of measuring value. For our licensing valuation purposes, the idea of cost is commonly associated with the buyer's assessment of recreating the subject technology. If it cost the seller $1 million to create the technology, the buyer might be inclined to use this as a starting point for valuation, perhaps even arguing that the value is actually less than the $1 million because of various seller misadventures, or perhaps accepting that the seller is entitled to some return on investment (ROI) consideration but basing such ROI analysis on the $1 million seller cost. This buyer reasoning is buttressed by the implicit notion that the seller's shareholders paid, in this instance, $1 million in forgone dividends to the R & D and possibly other departments. Presumably, the buyer's shareholders could, in the alternative to a license, do the same thing. Likewise, a seller might even resort to an ROI analysis to estimate value, although this is generally a poor basis for determining value: If a seller has somehow, with very little investment, created technology of enormous value, it should license the technology for such value (to a willing buyer), regardless of the ROI calculation. Conversely, if the seller has made significant investments and created technology of nominal value (which could correspond to a negative ROI), the seller is likely to find buyers sympathetic to the investment but willing to pay only such nominal value.

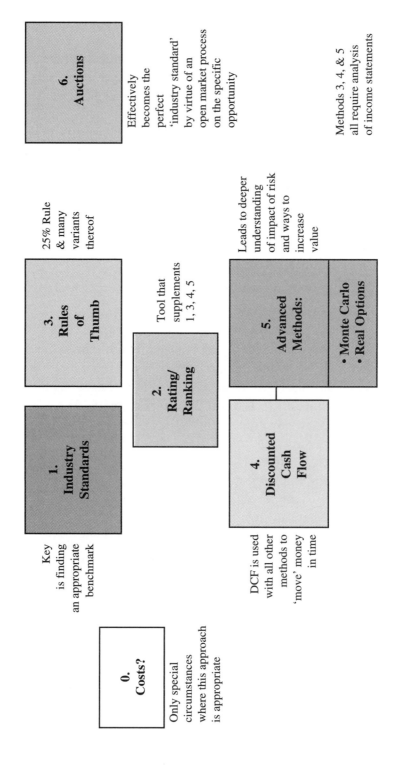

EXHIBIT 2.5   Summary of Six Valuation Methods

However, there are numerous problems with these lines of cost-as-value reasoning.

- Sellers rarely, if ever, know their *true* costs. In many technology development projects, the cost accounting of the work leading to the licensable technology is only part of a continuum of investment.
- When the costs are determined for a seller's technology, the value of the starting or infused IP is almost never assessed.
- The seller's development costs often do not correspond to the costs that the buyer might incur in attempting to recreate the technology, because of the differences in capabilities, insights, and approaches.
- The IP rights of the seller generally make it difficult, and possibly impractical, for the buyer—in terms of investments required, other resources, time delay, and overall project risk—to recreate the seller's technology in a way that the buyer is free to use commercially. So, the replication of the seller's cost is likely to be illusory.
- On the other hand, the seller could have made excessive investments in the development of the technology because of poor choices of approach or other reasons and might thus have a cost basis for the technology in excess of what a reasonable seller should pay, even given the above considerations.
- The risk associated with the commercialization technology is, normally, reduced by the seller's development. Such risk would need to be undertaken by the buyer in an independent development. Even some developments that appear easy turn out to be far more difficult than imagined.
- In some cases there could be an important value of what is sometimes called *negative know-how:* knowledge of processes or approaches that do not work well or at all. It is possible that the seller's technology incorporates an approach that is the only practical way the technology can be made to work, although independent technical experts who have not participated in the development or the technology might believe, wrongly, that another or many other approaches can be made to work commercially.
- There is the seller's value of *now*. In most instances, a reasonable buyer is willing to pay a premium to accelerate its time to market.
- Finally, the cost of creating IP is often simply unrelated to its value. As one far-afield example, Chuck Close is a famous, contemporary artist who paints huge portraitures. Early in his career (1967–1970) he used very highly diluted paints applied by an airbrush technique; he is reported to have painted eight of these amazing paintings with one 60-cent tube of Mars black paint. Technology is not the same as paintings, but the principle is that it is possible to create a valuable technology and not have incurred a commensurate cost.

Yet, if a buyer really believes that its costs to recreate and be free to practice the subject technology are in fact $1 million, including the factors just addressed, which includes the cost to avoid the IP rights of the seller, then this benchmark is likely to be relevant.

Method 1: Industry Standards

Perhaps the most commonly considered valuation method is that of industry standards, also sometimes called the *market* or *comparables method*. It is based on the observation that knowing what other pairs of buyers and sellers agreed to with respect to similar transactions is a useful indication of what a buyer–seller pair should agree on in the subject technology license. It might even be hoped that something like a used-car pricing book or database, such as is commonly available on the Internet, might be available for technology. Unfortunately, such a book does not exist for license valuation. However, it is often possible to discover previously entered agreements that are similar in some important ways to the subject opportunity and thereby provide valuation insight.

Identifying possible comparable agreements, particularly those with the full details of the agreements, is a useful approach. There are many possible sources of such agreements:

- Published results of surveys of licensing practitioners
- Proposed/published licensing norms by various experts
- Published court cases
- Term sheets used by various sellers
- License price lists or rates offered
- Published license agreements
- Previous deal experience
- Lifetime learning and deal experience
- Proprietary databases
- Consultants

For a discussion of the limitations and other issues associated with each of these sources, the reader is referred to *Early-Stage Technologies*. In general, it is rare that one is able to locate agreements that are directly on point with respect to the subject licensable technology with all the related deal terms. (Recall the discussion of the box and wheelbarrow; one would need agreements that had boxes and wheelbarrows similar to the one under consideration.) In practice, one is sometimes able to find a number of agreements that have certain comparable aspects that provide useful insights as to value.

Method 2: Rating/Ranking

Rating/ranking is a general method for comparing two or more things. One popular culture use is in developing *best* lists: best places to live, to retire, to start a business, and so forth. (See, for example, a Web site devoted to such bests: www.bestplaces.com.)

In technology valuation, rating/ranking can be used with agreements found by the use of industry standards to analyze the effect on value for the various distinctions that exist between the near-comparables and the subject opportunity.

The method is based on the following steps:

1. Identify the important distinguishing criteria that affect value, such as the size of the market and profitability margins.
2. Establish a weighting factor for each criterion, so that the more important ones are more heavily weighted.
3. Choose a scoring system on which comparison estimates can be made, such as a 0 to 10 scale or a 1 to 5 Likert scale where a "3" is a neutral score, or some other approach.

Then, using an expert panel, a weighted score is calculated for the subject opportunity with reference to each of the comparable agreements. For example, the use of a 5-point Likert scale provides two levels of *better than* the comparable (a score of 4 or 5) and two levels of *worse than* (1 or 2); a score of 3 is used to designate that with respect to the criterion, the agreements are essentially the same. Then by weighting and adding, one can estimate how the subject opportunity ranks with respect to each of the comparables.

A simple six-criterion system could be based on the following:

1. Market size
2. Product margins
3. IP strength
4. IP breadth
5. Stage of development
6. Market environment

Courts sometimes rely on so-called Georgia-Pacific factors (i.e., nature of the protection, utility over old methods, scope of exclusivity, licensee's anticipated profits, commercial success, territory restrictions, comparable license rates, duration of protection, licensor's anticipated profits, commercial relationship, and tag-along sales) to assist them in developing an estimate of a reasonable royalty in litigation matters. Although litigation valuation is outside the context of this chapter, such factors do address many commonly used measures of value such as market size and profitability. (*Early-Stage Technologies* includes a more detailed discussion of this method.)

Method 3: Rules of Thumb

Certain rules of thumb are commonly used in valuation of technology licenses. The most famous of such rules is the so-called 25 percent rule. It can be applied in either a cost-savings or a new revenues context. For a cost-savings application, this rule calculates, as a starting point, a reasonable royalty corresponding to 25 percent of the savings realized by the buyer in its use of the licensed technology. For a new revenues application, such a starting point for the reasonable royalty calculation would correspond to 25 percent of the net of new revenues achieved by the use of the technology, less the appropriately allocated buyer costs of achieving such revenues. These would include the cost of making the licensed product (commonly termed *cost of goods sold*, or COGS) and appropriate overhead costs associated with sales and marketing and other general administrative costs, which could include R & D. In income statement accounting, such net value is commonly referred to as EBIT, for earnings before interest and taxes.[8]

The *rule of thumb* method is appealing because of its logic, simplicity, and universality. The appeal of its logic is that the benefit to the seller is directly calculated along with the benefit enjoyed by the buyer. The simplicity appeal is that splitting the profit pie by 25:75, or some other ratio, is about as simple as anything can get. Finally, the universal appeal is that it can, in principle, be applied to any industry in any territory for any level of profitability or size of market. Unfortunately, its application is not nearly as simple as it initially appears.

One immediate issue arises with the magnitude of such a split. Some sellers refer to this concept as the *33 percent rule* or the *25 to 33 percent rule*. Other sellers, especially in software or content licensing, adopt the perspective that this method is the *50 percent rule* (or even more). Buyers, not surprisingly, in assessing all the investment and risk associated with transforming the licensed technology into a commercial operation, performing the manufacturing, marketing, and sales, and being responsible for all the cash payments and reporting can conclude that 25 percent to the seller does not leave enough profit to provide an adequate return on assets deployed by the buyer. Accordingly, some buyers refer to this as the *15 to 25 percent rule*. Sometimes, Solomonically, this method is referred to as the *15 to 35 percent rule*, which is a way of saying 25 percent, ± 10 points.

What commonly happens in practice is that 25 percent is treated as a starting point in valuation, in part as recognition that the other side of the negotiation is likely to perform this calculation. Then the specifics of the opportunity are applied to adjust this value up or down. One powerful tool for making such adjustments is the use of the rating/ranking method if one can find near-comparable agreements that were based on various benefit apportionments.

Other challenges in the use of the rule of thumb method include the following:

- *The appropriate costs, direct and indirect, to deduct from the revenues to project the EBIT must be determined.* One way these can be estimated is to determine what such costs are as a percentage of revenues for current operations of the buyer and for comparable companies in comparable industries. Such calculations should account for the distinctions between existing cost structures and those that will be associated with the subject opportunity. It is likely, but not certain or in all cases, that the profitability of a new technology will be higher than that associated with the current mix of products that produce the existing cost structures, because companies in general are seeking new licensing opportunities to raise their profitabilities, not to replicate their averages.
- *A technology license is often specific to a product, or a closely related family of products.* Publicly available financials tend to be for entire operating divisions or for the company as a whole. This obscures potentially significant differences among the individual products (and services).
- *There is discernment required as to what is an appropriate cost deduction.* What about the overhead allocation of corporate headquarters? How lush is too lush for the CEO's office? Are jets and helicopters appropriate deductions? How about the hunting lodge in Kilimanjaro?
- *There appears to be an increasing and alarming lack of reliability in financial reporting.* Sometimes this problem is exacerbated by improper auditing practices and rarely by fraudulent business operations not uncovered by such audits. A common situation is restructuring cost adjustments that can call into question what were the real, historic costs and profits. To the extent that such published financial data are used to determine the starting point for a 25 percent rule, one is advised to consider how to develop independently estimated technology-benefit values based on analysis of the situation.
- *The subject technology license can have important financial repercussions in multiple places in a buyer's operations.* If it has the rights to make, use, and sell Product X, it might now be able to sell more of Product Y, which is not directly related to the licensed technology, or provide more of Service Z, which is related to the technology but can be provided without requiring a license to the IP protecting the technology. How should these benefits be accounted for in a valuation? The seller argues that but for the license, such benefits would not accrue and so it is entitled to some "rule" of profit splits. The buyer tends to argue that

these other benefits are primarily or solely because of other business assets and acumen and the 25 percent (or other value used) for the narrowly construed technology subject matter is the intended full reward.

- *The technology's stage of development at the time of licensing can be an important variable.* Frequently the 25 percent value is associated with characterizations such as a complete or reasonably complete technology package. One interpretation of what this means is that the R & D is finished and a databook that can support design activities is available, so that the next commercial steps involve the design and construction (or adaptation) of a manufacturing facility to make the product.
- *The completeness of the technology package will affect the division of royalties.* If, for instance, there are five related but separate technologies from five sellers, and a buyer must license them all to make one product, then if the buyer uses a 25 percent rule on each license, it will have obligated itself to paying 125 percent of the profits to the combined sellers. This issue is commonly termed *royalty stacking.* In this example, the buyer is likely to say the 25 percent (or other) share of the profits must be apportioned among all the technologies that need to be licensed or acquired to make the product. So if these five were equal contributions, the buyer would suggest a 5 percent profit split to each licensee.

It is also important to observe that this discussion of percentages pertains to the EBIT. Recall that a royalty rate is normally applied against total revenues (sales) (the size of the royalty wheelbarrow is the royalty rate times the royalty base). So if the projected revenues are $100, and all the appropriately allocated costs are $80, leaving an EBIT of $20, and the 25 percent rule is applied, the result is that the seller's share of such profits is 25 percent but its royalty amount is $5 for the revenues of $100, so that, in this example, a 25 percent rule results in a 5 percent royalty rate. What about just using EBIT as the royalty base in a license agreement? This is very seldom done. When establishing a license agreement, there should be as little subject to debate as possible. When auditing a license it is generally possible to come to a relatively unambiguous answer as to the magnitude of royalty-based sales revenues. If EBIT is used as a base, there would likely be an ongoing debate, and even dispute, over how this value is computed.

Method 4: Discounted Cash Flow

A more complex valuation method is to analyze all the projected cash flows to the buyer, net of all costs and investments, and determine what return the buyer is entitled to expect on such investments, given the risks and assets deployed. The excess value is apportioned between the buyer and seller. This approach is sometimes known as the *discounted cash flow method*, or the *net present value method*, or the *income method*, or even the *excess earnings method*.

This method requires the development of a formal spreadsheet model projected sometimes 10 years or more into the future (corresponding to the commercial value of the technology and its IP life), with year-by-year accounting of investments, revenues, costs, royalties, taxes, and so forth, to determine the yearly net cash flow. Such yearly cash flows are then discounted by a risk-adjusted hurdle rate (RAHR) to determine a net, total present value (NPV), where the present value discounted cash flow (DCF) of a given future gross cash flow (GCF) in year n is discounted by such RAHR (expressed as a ratio, not as a percentage), as follows:

$$DCF = GCF / (1 + RAHR)^n$$

The complexities of performing or even illustrating such spreadsheet models are beyond the scope of this chapter. The reader is referred to the following books for more details and examples: *Intellectual Property*, 2nd Edition (Russ Parr and Gordon Smith, New York: John Wiley & Sons, 1998), and *Early-Stage Technologies*.

The valuation tool of cash-flow discounting is also useful with all the other methods to determine the financial effect of various lump-sum payments at various periods.

Method 5: Advanced Methods

Although the DCF method is a powerful valuation tool, there are even more powerful and complex methods. The two principal ones are Monte Carlo and real options.

Monte Carlo methods incorporate probabilistic factors into the development of a DCF spreadsheet. With the availability of PC- (or Mac-) based software tools such as Crystal Ball and @Risk, it is now readily possible to create sophisticated valuation models that account much more explicitly for uncertainties. In a sense, this method extends scenario analysis that is commonly used with the DCF method, where multiple spreadsheet models are created corresponding to baseline, optimistic, and pessimistic projections. The effect of a Monte Carlo method is to create a statistical continuum of possible outcomes.

One of the challenges of the DCF method is the substantial discounting of distant future cash flows in high-risk contexts. For example, using the DCF formula for a net cash flow of $100 million 10 years hence for a RAHR of 30 percent (0.30, as decimal) gives the following result:

$$DCF = 100 / (1.3)^{10} = \$7.25 \text{ million}$$

The DCF method has the effect of discounting each of the future cash flows by the same risk factor (RAHR), even though the risk typically decreases as the project advances and sequential investment commitments are made, or else the project is dropped or redirected. A DCF approach does not directly account for such management interventions and risk adjustments. Real options is a powerful means of taking into account such variables.

To my awareness, there is currently no book that presents real options in a licensing or negotiation context. Part of Chapter 8 in *Early Stage Technologies* addresses Monte Carlo as a license valuation tool. As more significant license deal making occurs, it is expected that such advanced tools will become more commonly used and will lead to more well-considered boxes and wheelbarrows. Although it has taken some time for DCF and NPV methods to achieve their current prominence, it is likely that Monte Carlo and real options will, despite their sophistication, quickly become important for the high-complexity, high-value opportunities.

Method 6: Auctions

With auctions, we return, in a sense, to the first method. *Auctions*, which date to antiquity, are a way of using the market to price the licensing opportunity. However, instead of dealing with comparables, or near-comparables, we are applying the method to the very case at hand.

Well-executed auctions of commodities accomplish two important business objectives: price discovery and liquidity. Determining the price of something, be it wheat or the rights to practice a certain technology for making and selling blue-green lasers, is ultimately tied to what a buyer, dealing at arm's length, is willing to pay for it. An auction provides the seller a forum where price discovery can take place by establishing the standards by which what is being sold can be known and where multiple potential buyers, each acting in their own self-interest or on behalf of the self-interest of others, can compete for the ownership right.

The other principal business value of auctions is liquidity itself. In *open outcry* commodity auctions, such as on the floor of the New York Stock Exchange, or as depicted in the hilarious orange futures scenes in the movie *Trading Places* (Paramount, 1983), price discovery and liquidity take place in the same process: buyers bid openly and competitively and sellers decide whether to sell based on such bids and can select the highest bid and gain an immediate contract to convert the commodity to currency.

For the licensing of technology, unfortunately, the auction method used for commodities requires substantial modification to be workable. For example, an open outcry system is not commonly used with technology licensing; some form of written bidding is normally used either with a closing hour and date or more informally in a back and forth process. To be effective, the seller needs to define the box so that all bids can be in the context of the same deal. Simpler boxes, such as the outright assignment and only that of a single patent or a related group of issued patents, make the auction process easier to use. Also, there must be sufficient time (and interest) for buyers to be able to conduct the appropriate level of due diligence necessary to be willing to make a bid.

Even using an auction, a seller is advised to estimate value using one or some combination of other methods. If there are numerous qualified bidders and rounds of bidding, it is reasonable for a seller to infer that the final price does reflect the value of the technology. However, in a technology auction, there could be few bidders and only a single round of bids. In such case the seller is advised to have an independent opinion as to the range of value of the technology to guide the decision whether to accept even the highest such bid.

For a buyer in a technology auction, relying solely on the prices offered by other bidders to be a measure of the technology value can be a dangerous practice. Even in a commodity auction, buyers do not just top the highest bid, for to do so as a valuation strategy would result in high acquisition costs. For a technology auction, even if a buyer is aware of other bids, the fair value in its hands could be less than the other bids, either because of the unique situation of such buyer or the folly of other bidders or both. Without an independent valuation, how could a buyer know when to stop bidding?

In general, it appears that auctions most commonly take place in two primary and opposite extreme settings: bankruptcy (where the auction is managed by a court disposal of assets process) and the hottest of opportunities (where the auction can evolve almost as a reactive measure by the seller when dealing with multiple, competitive buyers).

CONCLUSION

As noted in Exhibit 2.5, rating/ranking can be used with multiple methods, as can the DCF method, to move back and forth in time. Higher-valued and higher-complexity opportunities will warrant the increased effort and insights afforded by the DCF and advanced methods (Monte Carlo and real options). Special circumstances may enable the use of auctions, as a special case of industry standards. The rule of thumb method is a straightforward cross-check that can be used on profitability estimates that is midway in complexity between industry standards and DCF methods.

Earlier, we considered the matter of uncertainty as an inherent element in future planning. I would like to close with consideration of another aspect of uncertainty dealing with the valuation and pricing methods and outcomes.

Epistemology is one of the core philosophical subjects that in the Western tradition dates back to at least the 400 B.C. Greek classics. Epistemology deals with the question of what can be known and how one can know it, but not with the specifics of what it is that one is trying to know. For us here, the epistemological question is this: What is knowable from the use of these valuation methods, and how do we know that we know?

In our scope of technology valuation, there are two, polar-opposite erroneous answers to the first of these questions: (1) nothing is knowable, or (2) epistemic certitude is possible. The first response has the effect of declaring valuation of technology as an utterly futile effort. This is the equivalent of you thinking of a number between one and a million and inviting me to predict the number. In this situation, nothing is knowable; regardless of my tools and endurance, I am not going to generate a better guess than the first number that enters my head. But is technology valuation really this epistemologically bleak? In general, the answer is no; the future may be dark, but it is not black.

What about the other extreme of contending that epistemic certitude is achievable? There is an old cartoon in which an elementary-school mathematics teacher asks a student: "Quickly, John, how much is 9 times 7?" To which the mathematically unaccomplished, but perhaps future senior management material, student replies, "High 50s, low 60s, somewhere in there." In many, if not most, mathematical settings we demand epistemic certitude. What about technology valuation? One of the virtues of having six methods is the opportunity for comparing results by multiple approaches. Each of the methods reviewed has its strengths and weaknesses. By using more than one approach, one frequently gains insight into a valuation that does not occur by the use of one method. Even though these multiple methods are likely to lead to multiple answers, they are also likely to lead to a deeper understanding of the key factors driving the value and how the process can be refined to develop a wiser answer.

So, in technology valuation, the epistemological aspiration is neither futility nor certitude, but coherence—where multiple methods produce a value or value range that makes sense from such multiple perspectives.

As the twentieth century closed, we experienced what has been artfully termed a *frothy* valuation period, at least with respect to publicly traded stocks and the flurry of merger and acquisition activity. As we enter the twenty-first century, we can expect that at least as a counterreaction, method-based valuations with defendable assumptions and approaches will increase in importance.

ENDNOTES

[1] The scope of this chapter is valuation *outside* of litigation situations. Although many of the observations and tools and methods can be relevant to the analysis of litigation situations, such uses are beyond the scope of this

chapter. Further, the author's comments here are from the perspective of an LES member, not an expert opining on litigation matters, which in every case requires knowledge of the specific circumstances and a much deeper level of analysis than can be presented here.

This chapter reflects the opinions of the author and not those of InteCap, Inc. The concepts and theories covered by this presentation are not intended to be all inclusive on the topic of valuation. The concepts are for illustrative purposes and may not represent approaches that the author or InteCap would recommend in a particular matter. The reader should keep in mind that each case should be evaluated in light of its own facts and circumstances.

[2] Throughout this chapter, our concern is about the business world and not the politicoeconomic issues of society, which have their own unique perspectives on the well-used word *economy*, both new and old.

[3] The S & P data represent a mixture of old and new economy companies, so the averages presented here are necessarily admixtures of business whose values are highly correlated with their balance sheets, and those which are not. Further, the companies comprising the S & P index have changed over time, and these changes by themselves have affected the price-to-book ratio. A careful analysis of this argument is simply outside the scope of this chapter. However, the S & P 500 does reflect a cross section of large U.S. businesses and global industries and as such is a useful indicator of trends and of the argument presented here regarding the increasing importance of unmeasured technology value.

[4] Deal doability is a grammatically incorrect but useful slang expression that expresses the expected ease with which a particular licensing opportunity will be successfully marketed by a seller. One common example of increased deal doability is the seller's ability and willingness to provide post-licensing technical support to decrease the risk of the buyer's successful and speedy adoption of the technology.

[5] Strictly speaking, such form of payment is a royalty—a prepaid, or paid up royalty and, so, should be called a lump-sum royalty. However, as the term *royalty* is normally used as a short hand for "running royalty," that is, a buyer payment that is made in proportion to the buyer's use of the technology, we here will refer to such fixed cash payments without the designation "royalty" affixed.

[6] From the Old Testament book of Ecclesiastes, Chapter 11. The entire paragraph that deals with risk management, and other matters, is as follows: 1 *Cast your bread upon the waters, for after many days you will find it again.* 2 *Give portions to seven, yes to eight, for you do not know what*

disaster may come upon the land. 3 If clouds are full of water, they pour rain upon the earth. Whether a tree falls to the south or to the north, in the place where it falls, there will it lie. 4 Whoever watches the wind will not plant; whoever looks at the clouds will not reap. 5 As you do not know the path of the wind, or how the body is formed in a mother's womb, so you cannot understand the work of God, the Maker of all things. 6 Sow your seed in the morning, and at evening let not your hands be idle, for you do not know which will succeed, whether this or that, or whether both will do equally well (New International Version).

[7] Of course even in such circumstances, there are practical limits to knowledge because of the cost of knowing compared to the value of such knowing. In the raw materials example, one could include the number of pencils in all the company storerooms and desk drawers as a business asset. In principle, such assets could all be counted and known to whatever degree of certainty one was willing to pay to obtain. In practice, a principle of reasonableness is applied that pursues such analysis and measurement only insofar as it is really important to the management of the business or the shareholders. There are other examples, such as the ownership of the right to extract oil, where the magnitude of such reserves are not only subject to the market value of oil and extraction technology, but are also in a real sense unknowable.

[8] The appropriate starting point of the 25 percent rule is the economic benefit of the technology to the buyer. In traditional income statement accounting, this is measured by EBIT (also known as operating profits). However, in licensing, the incremental benefit of the technology may be reflected by a value larger than an accounting-determined EBIT because not all the costs associated with COGS and various overheads are in fact incremental to the practice of the technology.

ABOUT THE AUTHOR

Dr. Richard Razgaitis is a managing director at InteCap, Inc. He has over 30 years of experience working with the development, commercialization, and strategic management of technology, 20 years of which have been spent specializing in the commercialization of intellectual property. He has participated in the licensing-in and licensing-out of numerous technologies, including advanced materials, manufacturing systems, software, and communications products. He has negotiated numerous commercialization agreements with clients in the United States, Europe, and the Far East, ranging from Fortune 500 to small start-up companies.

Dr. Razgaitis holds bachelor, master, and doctorate degrees in engineering, and an MBA. He has been a registered professional engineer in three states and is an inventor of four patents.

A long-time trustee and present treasurer of the Licensing Executives Society USA/Canada (LES), Dr. Razgaitis is also currently a board member and treasurer of the LES Licensing Foundation, and a board member of the National Inventors Hall of Fame Foundation.

He is the author of a published book on valuation, *Early Stage Technologies: Valuation and Pricing* (New York: John Wiley & Sons, Inc., 1999).

3

The Expanding Role of Technology Management Consultants

By Robert Goldscheider

INTRODUCTION

Consulting may be described as an art form whose substance and quality reflect the talents, skills, and diligence of the practitioner. The related fields of licensing and technology management provide an ample arena in which consultants can provide valuable services. Professionals with a broad range of qualifications are meeting the challenges of consulting in those fields in increasing numbers.

A MENU FOR CONSULTANTS

Technology proprietors and corporate decision makers are regularly faced with deciding whether to perform certain tasks in house or to seek and pay for help from outside specialists. To understand the menu for such decisions, one must appreciate the range of knowledge and other assets required to succeed in the licensing process. A realistic spectrum would include the following:

- A sufficient technical background to understand the strengths and weaknesses of a product or process in comparison with the competition
- A knowledge of patents, trademarks, and copyrights, including the different legal protections they provide and the means for their enforcement
- Ability to protect and generate value from trade secrets and know-how
- Experience in dealing with confidentiality during all stages of financing, development, and commercialization of products and processes
- Familiarity with the range of possible transactions within the licensing discipline, such as options, sales agencies, distributorships, assembly agreements, arm's-length licenses, including ancillary sales of goods, joint ventures, strategic partnerships, R & D agreements, and the formation of subsidiaries
- Knowledge about the laws of licensing in every important commercial center of the world, including their interaction with antitrust, tax, and various governmental regulations

- Skills in drafting all types of agreements relating to the licensing process, as well as business plans and memoranda designed to promote technology transfers
- Appreciation of the art of "licensing out" and the organization of effective programs for "licensing in"
- Understanding of the various methodologies for appraising technologies, one analog of which is the ability to propose reasonable royalty rates in a wide variety of situations
- Understanding of the attitudes and techniques for successful negotiations
- Mastering of the tools of the Internet and e-commerce

This list is far from exhaustive because it does not include the personal dimensions of charm, familiarity with different national cultures, history and languages, commitment to meeting deadlines, a sense of humor, and the ability to hold one's liquor when socializing.

THE EQUATION OF MAKE OR BUY

In a learned paper titled "The Nature of the Firm" published in Scotland in 1937, Professor Ronald Coase explained why businesses exist as they do—why, for instance, they choose to produce some goods or perform certain services in house and contract with outsiders for the rest. His thesis, for which he was awarded the Nobel Prize for economics in 1991, was that the level of "transaction costs" determine whether a potential buyer will seek an outside supplier or service provider. Sixty years ago, information was frequently hard to obtain and proprietors therefore tended to integrate, and thereby control, their operations. As communications and distribution systems increased, transaction costs fell, making it more advantageous for businesses to contract out some of their production and service functions. With the advent of the Internet, torrents of information are readily available to all, one result of which is that transaction costs have plummeted. Proprietors are hard pressed to evaluate such information on their own. Moreover, there exists a new element of urgency, because each player is aware that its rivals have equal access to the same information.

The resulting excitement and time pressures promote the increased need for outside help and advice. Companies often do not have the time to master new problems; therefore, they opt to purchase those skills from people who already have them. Consultants also rely on the Internet to access a broad spectrum of information—either as part of a large consulting firm or as a lone wolf operating from an electronic cottage. Considering all of these circumstances, it is not surprising that consulting, itself, has become a growth industry.

The Internet has also leveled the playing field between individual consultants and medium to giant firms. In this connection, individual consultants can also network with other consultants who have complementary skills or are located elsewhere in the world to provide comprehensive and worldwide services. It is therefore relatively easy to enter the field of technology management consulting, although achieving success is not so easy.

SOME ROLES FOR CONSULTANTS

The author recently had a conversation with a fellow consultant who is a senior manager in a 1,000-person consulting firm. This professional had been the top executive handling a major brand for a Fortune 100 company, but he opted to switch firms—in part, because he substantially increased his income and received stock options in the rapidly growing organization. He emphasized, however, that these were not the principal reasons for his career change. It was the challenge of dealing with a much wider variety of problems and the opportunities for creativity that consulting provides. He is certain that he made a career decision that is correct for him.

He thinks consulting services fall into four distinct categories:

1. *Advising a client on a subject in which its knowledge is incomplete.* This type of assignment would include market research in areas to which the client is considering expanding but has limited prior experience. Consultants performing this kind of task can accelerate knowledge acquisition by the client, while also maintaining the secrecy of its new interest from third parties.
2. *Verifying the continuing viability of existing policies and comparing them to the competition.* All consulting should be done with an eye to confidentiality, but it is vital here. The client will not want its strengths and weaknesses to become known in detail by its competitors. This type of work may require the collaboration of the client's regular employees, or the client may not desire to have such employees aware that their actions and policies are being evaluated. This variant highlights another aspect of consulting; namely, that it is important to customize the assignment to the needs of the client. The flexibility inherent in consulting permits this.
3. *Resolving internal conflicts.* Large companies are often the breeding ground of rivalries among individuals and groups whose ambitions clash. Senior management is often reluctant to step in to resolve such conflicts by edict, since this can result in the alienation and even departure of valued personnel. A well-informed, neutral consultant—acting in the role of ombudsman—can sometimes identify compromise solutions and new ideas that can reduce internal tensions of this sort and be beneficial to all parties.

If senior management had already developed a predisposition toward a particular course of action, and the intervention of the consultant can tend to confirm such a policy, the entire matter can frequently be settled more amicably, and hopefully, permanently. One ingredient in such a success would be if the consultant can convince all parties that it is acting objectively, without any personal agenda or ambitions.

4. *Becoming the sounding board to the board of directors, the CEO, or other top executive(s).* This can be a highly desirable, but possibly precarious, role for a consultant. It is usually achieved only after the consultant has attained a positive track record with the people involved. When this occurs, and the senior person or persons thereby desire to take the consultant into their confidence, this can constitute a very satisfying experience.

IN MY EXPERIENCE . . .

The author fondly recalls a relationship that he developed with the chairman and CEO of a Fortune 100 company, starting in the late 1970s. My firm had been commissioned to perform a confidential analysis of an opportunity that the company was considering. The client purposely provided little background about the motivation behind the assignment, in order to prevent my team from forming any preconceived bias. I engaged a highly experienced market economist as my collaborator. We were given three months to perform the task, because the client wanted a thorough job. On the deadline date, we orally presented our findings, together with a 100-page report, to a meeting convened by the CEO and also attended by the president and four vice presidents.

Our recommendation was positive, and we provided several reasons we considered sound to support this conclusion. At the end of our presentation, the CEO thanked us for what he described as a careful and thorough piece of work. He also promptly informed us without having conferred with his colleagues that the company, contrary to our findings, would not proceed with the project.

I was frankly surprised and disappointed. I expressed these feelings in a respectful way and indicated that I was disturbed because my judgment was being questioned by his immediate rejection. The CEO replied that this should be of little consequence, since the work product was respected and, besides, we were being well paid for our efforts. Unsatisfied, I somewhat impulsively replied that I could give the CEO an example of my judgment having been wiser than his.

At that point the others at the meeting became a bit edgy because they were well aware of the short fuse under which the CEO usually operated. Nevertheless (with a twinkle in his eye), he invited me to continue my approach. I reminded him that he had been an active supporter of Richard Nixon's reelection campaign, whereas I had not trusted President Nixon's behavior.

Contrary to the expectation of his colleagues, the CEO chuckled, then smiled broadly and allowed that I was now entitled to learn the reason for his negative decision. I was told that, some years previously, another company that had been acquired at that time by the client had encountered problems and losses in the same market my colleagues and I had studied. We had been engaged to see if some specific conditions considered to be responsible for those losses might have changed. Our findings reflected no such change—even though we were not really aware of that issue. Our analysis made it clear to the CEO that the client should continue to stay away from that business, and he didn't need to ponder the matter.

The CEO then asked me if I was satisfied. I promptly assured him that I was. Whereupon the CEO informed his colleagues that he believed I was the only person in the room who had the courage to question him as I did. He attributed this, at least partially, to the fact that payment of my mortgage did not depend on his continued goodwill. He also indicated that he appreciated my candor and self-assurance, and added that as long as he remained CEO of the client, I was to continue as his personal consultant on licensing-related matters. This was because he was confident that I would always be open, yet careful, in providing advice to him.

I maintained this role for 10 years thereafter. When the CEO retired, my consulting also ended. I accepted this result with good grace. It would have, indeed, been anticlimactic working for the client without the pleasure of my special relationship. My departure was on friendly terms all around.

This anecdote reminds me of an aspect of consulting not yet discussed. This is that a consultant must walk a fine line between indispensable independence of mind and prudence not to be disruptive of the affairs of the client. Put succinctly, a consultant is retained to solve problems, not to create new ones. Moreover, if one finds that advice being provided is frequently negated or ignored, it is appropriate, in my view, to resign from the arrangement and work where one's efforts are appreciated.

ATTITUDES AND MENTALITY

Having said this, a consultant should also be mindful of the fact that this role is something special, beyond the orthodox framework of the client. One should try to be a team player but also someone of whom special abilities are expected to be employed.

When fulfilling this role, care should always be taken to consider the responsibilities and sensitivities of the full-time employees of the client. The client should be made to welcome the arrival of the consultant, not feel threatened. If the consultant can enhance the company's performance and advance the careers of the employees with whom the consultant is collaborating, everyone can realize win-win results.

Several other principles are useful for consultants to bear in mind:

- At the onset of an engagement, identify the executive of the client to whom you are intended to report, and select a backup, should that individual be unavailable at any time. This not only simplifies one's operations, it tends to avoid involvement in the politics of the client. Usually the contact person is sufficiently senior to be above internal tensions; if not, the arrangement should be understood to exist for administrative reasons and not as a display of partisanship.
- Unless there is an overriding reason to preserve confidentiality, the consultant's arrival and mission should be made known to everyone associated with the client who has "a need to know"; moreover, instructions should be given from a senior person that everyone is expected to cooperate and support the consultant's efforts in a reasonable manner.
- Consultants should realize that there is frequently tension with personnel at the client, who might envy the freedom of action that the consultant has achieved.
- Everyone, including the consultant, should realize that the engagement has occurred because the client recognized special talent or experience possessed by the consultant. Otherwise the matter would be routinely handled in house. By displaying an earnest, respectful, and friendly demeanor at all times—but especially at the onset of the relationship—a consultant can help develop the type of mutual regard that is usually an important ingredient for success.
- It is important to develop policies covering remuneration for different types of services. The following specific points should be considered:

  - One basic principle I have followed in almost every instance is to refuse to act on a purely speculative arrangement. My experience is that clients give greater attention to the relationship if they are paying at least part of the consultant's remuneration "up front." These payments are usually in the form of a monthly retainer fee for a minimum of six months, with the possibility of extensions as circumstances warrant.
  - If the focus of the assignment is "licensing out," a success bonus is usually requested and negotiated at the outset of the relationship. This is frequently structured as a percentage of the remuneration received by the client from transactions that have been negotiated within the scope of the consulting arrangement. The bonus continues for the life of these licenses, even if the retainer arrangement may have expired. In order to maintain contact with the deal, and with a view to encouraging the flow of royalties, enlightened consultants perform post-licensing liaison services between the client and the licensee(s), often at no extra charge.

- "Licensing in" consulting is a distinctly different discipline, although consultants frequently perform both *in* and *out* activities under the umbrella of a single consulting assignment. Retainers are also standard here. Success bonuses are often structured as a percentage of sales by the client attributed to the technology licensed in (e.g., 1 percent of such sales for five years from the date of first sale).
- Some assignments are limited to defined advisory tasks in which bonuses are inappropriate. In such cases, it is normal to bill on an agreed hourly basis; the usual procedure is to record professional time daily, in tenths of an hour, and to submit invoices monthly.
- Sometimes, however, a client defines a specific task to be performed by a fixed deadline. In such cases a lump-sum fee can be agreed, usually paid one-third on commission and one-third at some midpoint when progress is reported, with the remaining third paid on completion.
- It is normal practice for consultants to be reimbursed for out-of-pocket expenses relating to telecommunications, postage, express couriers, document reproduction and binding, and preapproved travel. Itemized summaries of expenses, with receipts where feasible, should accompany the reimbursement invoice.

TERMS FOR CONSULTING ARRANGEMENTS

The relationship between a client and a consultant should always be set forth in an agreement that clarifies elements of the relationship. The following provisions are considered appropriate:

- *Defined appointment.* This should formally describe the field of technology pertinent to the client and generally outline the scope of the expected work. Lack of precision about this can lead to counterproductive misunderstandings. The writer also considers it of prime importance that exclusivity be provided within the scope of the defined assignment to avoid an unfortunate rivalry with one or more other consultants; indeed, potentially attractive consulting opportunities have been declined when exclusivity is not available.
- *Confidentiality.* It is indispensable that a client be comfortable in revealing its business particulars and goals to its consultants, in order to provide the necessary ingredients of realism to the relationship. It is my practice to request to sign, in my personal capacity and on behalf of my firm, an undertaking providing the same degree of confidentiality that the client obtains from its own senior executives. In addition, the obligation to maintain secrecy should survive expiration of the consulting relationship. There should also be the usual exceptions, namely, no secrecy obligation if:

- The consultant can demonstrate, in writing, prior knowledge of any divulged information
- Such information enters the public domain without the fault or negligence of the consultant
- The consultant receives such information from a third party who is authorized to reveal it.

- *Duration.*   It has been shown that consultants usually become more effective the better they understand the needs and policies of their clients. This quality is best achieved by experience over a period of time. When handling assignments requiring continual input, the writer therefore requests a minimum initial term of six months, with automatic monthly extensions thereafter if work remains to be done, subject to 60 days' notice of termination.

   For large-scale or long-term assignments calling for a unified body of work and a lump-sum fee, the writer encourages the imposition of milestones to qualify for progress payments, at which times the status of the project is reviewed with the client.
- *Client support.*   Effective consulting cannot be done in a vacuum. Active interface with the client is usually indispensable to suggest courses of action and to comment about initiatives by the consultant. It is also useful for the client to furnish appropriate quantities of company and product literature, and that senior client personnel be prepared to meet with prospective licensees or other contracting parties.
- *Dispute resolution.*   Parties to consulting agreements frequently provide for mediation and/or arbitration to settle disputes that may arise. The delays and expenses in such procedures are usually counterproductive, because they result in an interruption of the work and probable destruction of the relationship. As an alternative, the consultant and client often mutually select a neutral person, in whom they both have confidence, to resolve any differences; this has frequently proven to be the most practicable way to handle matters of this sort. The neutral person is usually paid by both parties and is required to reach a decision in a matter of days.

STRATEGIES FOR A CONSULTING PRACTICE

Consultants have adopted many different strategies within the technology management field. People who leave an established corporate position—either voluntarily or involuntarily—usually begin by offering the same expertise they employed during their corporate careers. Indeed, some former employers frequently soften the blow of separation by becoming the first client of the newly hatched consultant, whose services are retained on a part-time basis for a limited period.

Once established on a familiar work foundation, the consultant can then broaden his or her focus of activities. This can be done individually or else by partnering, on a formal or informal basis, with others having complementary skills or experiences.

In my case, I examined my own strengths and weaknesses and measured those against my understanding of the requirements of licensing and technology management consulting. I divided potential work into four categories, namely:

1. Things I enjoyed doing
2. Areas in which I considered myself to have talent
3. Things I didn't enjoy
4. Areas in which I lacked talent

With the insights thereby revealed, I decided to "accentuate the positive and eliminate the negative." I also decided to collaborate with others, when necessary, in the latter two categories.

In the first two categories, I recognized that I am a people person who enjoys creative dialog and negotiating. I am also an omnivorous reader, and the knowledge thereby gained has enabled me to formulate strategies for clients. Although not an engineer, I am able to grasp the essence of technologies rapidly and articulate their pertinent special features to decision makers, most of whom lack state-of-the-art scientific and technical knowledge because the focus of their work has evolved to overall management issues. I find foreign travel stimulating and have the physical stamina to handle jet lag and long hours. I have developed a real commitment to LES and my many friends in the society. Finally, I enjoy public speaking, teaching, drafting agreements, and writing. These attributes have become the "core competencies" of my professional life.

I had been a practicing attorney, heading the licensing department of a large IP law firm, and have had that position for eight years. During that time I addressed legal problems involving licensing in every important industrial country of the world. I had also worked on problems involving a wide variety of businesses and technologies. My experience at that stage indicated that the spectrum of my exposures qualified me to advise on a broader scope than any individual industry or geographic region. My ambition was thus to be able to advise on several aspects of the "discipline" of licensing, on a worldwide scale.

A skilled musician, sitting at the console of a massive organ with four keyboards, foot pedals, and 100 different "stops" for special effects, can play the works (i.e., inventions) of virtually any composer, be they Bach, Beethoven, Bartok, the Beatles, or the Beach Boys. The organist can adroitly use the large array of enabling tools of the instrument to create wonderful sound. Of course, a musician having lesser skills may produce only unpleasant noise. Likewise, a consultant must master many skills to create a harmonious product.

As I saw it in 1971, at the outset of my life as a consultant, the following specific skills were needed if my existence was to be viable:

- *An understanding of all of the intellectual property rights*, specifically the type of protection and commercial advantages each offered. I am neither a licensed patent attorney nor an academically trained engineer. But, as mentioned, I have the ability to appreciate the "delta" between technologies and reasoned—correctly as it turned out—that this was the key element I needed. It enabled me to serve as a catalyst during licensing negotiations by drawing on others' expertise to point out to the parties the advantages they could realize by the transfer of a given invention or body of technology. To the extent needed, I could obtain input on behalf of the client from its patent lawyers and scientists. At that time, I was already capable of advising about trademarks and trade secrets.
- *Marketing and market research capabilities*. I had some experience in this area, largely by observing the activities of clients of my law firm, but had not personally performed this type of work. To overcome this weakness, I chose a partner who could serve as a mentor in this field.
- *A knowledge of the laws of licensing in the principal countries and regions of the world*, including ancillary issues in the fields of antitrust, taxation, and the export of technology, together with the ability to draft the variety of contracts needed as part of the discipline of licensing. This was my strong point, so I emphasized it from the outset, and continue to do so.
- *Skills in negotiating, including the ability to advise about royalty rates and other forms of remuneration*. Again, this was an area of strength because I had participated in numerous licensing negotiations with clients of my old law firm. I had already employed "the 25 percent rule" for determining reasonable royalties. My partner had complementary skills and was a superb negotiator. We made an excellent team and emphasized this asset from the beginning.

Appreciating the tools of the trade was an indispensable first step in becoming a technology management consultant. The next step was to attract clients. For this, the Licensing Executives Society provided valuable help. By 1971, I had already been a member of LES for four years. We were less than 100 people at that time, and I had gotten to know most of them. Many of these friends expressed concern about my "bold" move in voluntarily embarking on this new adventure and leaving the security of my excellent law firm. However, everyone was supportive, and several of their ideas were very helpful as my consulting practice evolved.

But self-help was recognized to be essential for future success. My partner and I promptly wrote an article titled "The Art of Licensing—From the Consultant's Point of View," published in *Les Nouvelles*. Today, it is considered to be a "classic" in our field. In this text, we "demonstrated our wares" and explained our attitudes about consulting. Reprints of this article, together with biographical notes about ourselves, constituted our mailing pieces when approaching, or responding to inquiries from, potential clients.

Although networking is certainly important, the diversified education provided at LES meetings, and contained in its publications, is even more valuable. I have regularly been stimulated, taught, and kept abreast of developments in licensing from the LES venue.

In the 30 years since I began working in the capacity of a consultant, several events have expanded my professional focus. The most significant has been the explosive growth of litigation in the IP field. This has been largely stimulated by the creation in 1982 of the Court of Appeals for the Federal Circuit, which adopted as its mission greater enforceability of U.S. patents. This has resulted in thousands of patent infringement cases. Section 284 of Title 35 of the Federal Code provides that damages following finding of infringement "in no event will be less than a reasonable royalty." Furthermore, the statute provides that "the court may receive expert testimony as an aid to the determination of damages or of what royalty would be reasonable under the circumstances."

Since the setting of royalties is basic to consulting in the licensing field, I have been regularly contacted as an expert, and to testify in court, on this issue. Indeed, this type of activity has developed into a sort of "cottage industry" in which a cadre of fellow consultants have derived steady revenue. In addition to providing testimony on patent damages, I have similarly testified in cases involving infringements of trademarks and copyrights, and relating to the theft of trade secrets. I have also opined about the acceptability of certain licensing practices and have criticized activities in the field that indicate a "loophole mentality." My view is that this should have no place in licensing, which involves long-term relationships built on mutual trust.

I limit my work in litigation to 25 percent of my professional time, because I enjoy and consider it important to remain "on the playing field" of the real world of commercial licensing. Many practitioners, however, including people in a semiretirement mode, choose to spend virtually all their professional time in expert witnessing.

EXPANDING APPLICATIONS FOR CONSULTING SKILLS

Other areas of consulting, none of which were apparent to me when I embarked on my career, should also be noted:

- *Appraisals of technology.* Most of the people working in this niche have accounting backgrounds, and also provide input to litigating attorneys in calculating infringement damages. I have accurately conducted appraisals, usually for tax or bankruptcy matters, utilizing the tools of licensing. The licensing methodology is usually called the "absence of ownership" or "relief from royalty" approach. It postulates a situation in which a proprietor does not own its property being appraised and is based on the net present value of total royalties, which may reasonably be projected during the economic life of the property. Since this discipline involves objective self-analysis by the proprietor, who may be assumed to know more about its assets than anyone, the conclusions from these appraisals have proven to be difficult to defeat.
- *Internet licensing.* This new phenomenon is having a major impact on licensing, as it has on business in general. It is now possible to expose technologies instantly and on a global scale. Without knowledge of this growing field, a consultant will be missing a huge, dynamic component to his or her consulting business. Chapter 7 covers this topic in detail.
- *Alternative dispute resolution (ADR).* Having considerable firsthand experience with IP litigation as an expert, I am aware of the enormous expense, documentation, and time investments that can be involved with the process of ADR. As an arbitrator under the administrations of both the American Arbitration Association and the International Chamber of Commerce, I have seen serious inefficiencies in both venues. I am therefore currently helping a successful private enterprise company to recruit a worldwide panel of experts focusing on "Licensing and Intellectual Property Disputes." The company possesses efficient e-commerce–based procedures for administering case files and is attracting a group of practicing IP specialists who possess a range of skills not usually found in members of the judiciary. ADR is covered in Chapter 15.

CONCLUSION

The field of technology management consulting has provided a creative environment for a growing number of practitioners. During the past 30 years, this activity has evolved from a staff function in corporations and universities to a respected profession. The technologies being handled are now the "crown jewels" of their proprietors and are the recognized engines for growth and profitability. With the passage of time in which the scientific revolution continues, additional sectors for strategies and advice steadily appear and provide challenges to the practitioners. LES has kept pace with these events and is proving to be both a forum and a clearinghouse for these ideas. The specialty is still young and provides excellent opportunities for ambitious players.

ABOUT THE AUTHOR

Robert Goldscheider is a specialist and recognized authority on the many commercial and legal aspects of the technology transfer process, both in the United States and worldwide. This includes pioneering work in the field of technology management consulting (i.e., providing advice on corporate organization for research, development, marketing, and acquisition of patented and unpatented inventions, as well as strategy for negotiations and maximizing profitability and growth utilizing a technological base as a dynamic asset). This frequently involves the licensing process and strategic partnering.

Mr. Goldscheider is chairman of The International Licensing Network, a firm of technology management consultants established in 1975, with offices in New York City and Delray Beach, Florida. He is a graduate of Columbia (magna cum laude in economics) and Harvard Law School, and he was a Fulbright Scholar.

A regular contributor to the literature in the field, Mr. Goldscheider has written several books, which are regularly updated, that together with more than 30 articles are considered basic texts in the fields of licensing and intellectual property. His writings include: *The Forms and Substance of Licensing*, 5 volumes (West Group, 1978), *Technology Management* (West Group, 1984)—an extensively revised new edition is now in preparation, and *Companion to Licensing Negotiations*, 3rd ed. (West Group, 2001–2002). He has edited several LES publications, including: *The Law and Business of Licensing* (West Group, 1974), *Arbitration and the Licensing Process* (West Group, 1982), and this book, *Licensing Best Practices* (New York: John Wiley & Sons, 2002).

Mr. Goldscheider has regularly served as an expert in intellectual property litigation on issues relating to licensing practices and infringement damages, having been consulted over 100 times. He has acted as an arbitrator in North America and Europe, continually lectured and conducted workshops in LES meetings throughout the world, and speaks regularly at other professional and university venues. In the mid-1980s he was cofounder (with the late Dudley Smith) of the LES Licensing Law Institute.

For over 20 years, Mr. Goldscheider has conducted a four-day course titled "International Licensing and Strategic Partnering for Today's Technology Manager" in Amsterdam and various places in the United States, under the auspices of the Center for Professional Advancement. This course features a mock negotiation in which all students participate. He is recognized as having taught more people about the licensing process than anyone alive.

ABOUT THE AUTHOR (continued)

Mr. Goldscheider has been active in LES since 1967. He is a former vice president–international and a board member of LES U.S.A. and Canada. He has also been active in LESI since its inception and is a continuing member of its Board of Delegates. On several occasions, he has chaired the Publications Committee, the Patent and License Committee, and the Education Committee. In 1982 he was awarded the LESI Certificate of Merit.

4

Dreadful Drafting: The Do's and Don'ts of Licensing Agreements

By John T. Ramsay, Q.C.

INTRODUCTION

We have all experienced the effects of dreadful drafting, either as writer or reader. In this material, we will examine drafting techniques in a licensing context. We will aim to minimize dreadful drafting by the adoption of tactics designed to produce precise but understandable written agreements that set out the parties' intended business and conform to the relevant legal principles.

Drafting is very personal; some of my suggested tactics may appeal to you, while others will be rejected as being unsuitable either to you or your fact situation. In any event, I hope that this material stimulates us to challenge and exterminate dreadful drafting.

DREADFUL DRAFTER: A CASE STUDY

Let us look at a case study that might illustrate the tactics to be discussed. For our case study, let us assume the following three facts:

1. DevCo is a small Alberta software developer[1] that has developed a complex scientific computer program (the "Licensed Software").
2. InterCo is a large international corporation based in Houston, Texas that is a successful international distributor of scientific software.
3. InterCo and DevCo entered into a license agreement in 1999 concerning an earlier version of the Licensed Software; recently, there have been a number of disagreements about the interpretation of the 1999 license agreement.

Using all the negotiating skills known to him,[2] the president of DevCo has spent several weeks convincing InterCo to market the latest version of the Licensed Software, rather than terminating their relationship.

The president of DevCo has written what he considers to be all the pertinent details of the new deal on the back of an envelope and delivers the envelope to our hero, Dreadful Drafter. The details on the envelope are as follows:

- Disputes are settled; it was an unfortunate misunderstanding.
- InterCo gets all of the United States.
- Best efforts in marketing
- InterCo gets source code so it can provide support.
- DevCo gets 5 percent royalty.
- DevCo gets rights to all improvements but InterCo can use the improvements it makes.
- Provide no warranties.
- Five-year term, renewable

Let us look over Dreadful Drafter's shoulder as he wrestles with the items on the president's list.

DREADFUL DRAFTER'S FIRST DRAFT OF RELEASE

The president's first note reads, "Disputes are settled; it was an unfortunate misunderstanding." Dreadful Drafter decides that he should make sure that the issues in dispute are not raised again between the parties. No disputes in the future should relate to anything arising out of the 1999 agreement. He decides that a release will be required.

Dreadful Drafter's First Draft

Like most of us, Dreadful Drafter has a library of precedents that are readily available through a word processor. He calls up a standard form of release, adapts it slightly, and produces the following provision that has a style familiar to all of us; it is a prime example of "lawyer-talk."[3]

FIRST DRAFT

Release. (a) Licensor releases, relinquishes, acquits, and forever discharges Licensee, its officers, directors, shareholders, employees, agents, legal representatives, subsidiaries, affiliates, attorneys, successors, and assigns, of and from any and all debts, obligations, reckonings, promises, covenants, agreements, contracts, endorsements, bonds, specialties, controversies, suits, actions, causes of action, trespasses, variances, judgments, executions, damages, claims, demands, rights, titles, interests, charges, encumbrances, or liens of any kind or sort whatsoever or howsoever arising, in law or in equity, whether known or unknown, whether liquidated or unliquidated, whether in tort or in contract, which they or any of them had, now has, or in the future may have against Licensee, its officers, directors, shareholders, agents, legal representatives, subsidiaries, affiliates, attorneys, successors, and assigns, arising out of, for, under, upon or by reason of or in connection with or relating to, directly or indirectly, the 1999 License

Agreement or any of the following acts or omissions of Licensee, its officers, directors, shareholders, employees, agents, legal representatives, subsidiaries, affiliates, attorneys, successors, and assigns, in connection with or relating to or arising out of or by virtue of any of the following; any loss, cost, or damage relating to or arising out of any breach of fiduciary duty, breach of any duty of good faith or fair dealing, breach of confidence, undue influence, duress, economic coercion, conflict of interest, negligence, bad faith, malpractice, intentional negligent infliction of emotional or mental distress, tortious interference with corporate governance or prospective business advantage, breach of contract, deceptive trade practices, libel, slander, conspiracy, any claim of wrongfully marketing the Licensed Software, or the charging, contracting for, taking, reserving, collecting, or receiving of interest in excess of the highest lawful rate applicable (i.e., usury), or any violations of federal or state law, any violations of federal copyright rules, laws or regulations, or any violation of the federal antitrust acts; Licensor further agrees that neither it nor any of its legal representatives or successors, will institute, prosecute, or in any way aid in the institution or prosecution of any claim, demand, action, or cause of action now existing or hereafter asserted against Licensee, its officers, directors, shareholders, employees, agents, legal representatives, subsidiaries, affiliates, attorneys, successors, and assigns, arising out of or by virtue of or in connection with or relating to any of the foregoing.

Escaping the Trap of Legalistic Style

The long, long sentence in this release contains 420 words. This sentence "not only talks about too many different things . . . [it] says the same thing too many times, and for good measure adds the completely unnecessary. No one, not even the writer, can keep it all straight. . . ."[4]

This peculiar style of legal writing is historic and is perpetuated by habit and standard legal forms. With the development of the word processor, it becomes all too easy to pull together strings of words without bothering to consider whether they make sense to the drafter or the client.[5] By the third line the reader has fallen asleep, lost all hope of ever finishing the sentence, or has let loose with every lawyer joke she knows.

TACTIC:
Do not let the word processor produce verbosity.

Drafter as Negotiator

Frequently, a person will serve as deal negotiator as well as document producer. Dreadful Drafter may have been an integral part of the negotiations during which he facilitated oral communication and interaction between the parties. Unfortunately, all too often when he starts the draft he assumes a wholly different role, the objectives of which sometimes appear to be to obfuscate rather than facilitate. His written communication becomes verbose and stilted: *LBS* as one of my clients puts it (and the L stands for "Legal").

Communicating with the Client

The first draft of a licensing agreement is often designed to communicate with the person instructing the drafter.[6] The drafter usually needs answers to many questions and concerns, for example:

- Have I understood your instructions?
- Have I expressed your instructions as you intended?
- Could you please give me guidance on some business issues I note were not discussed?
- What are the business and legal risks? Please assess the risk/benefits involved.
- Are there some risks that we should perhaps not even consider at this time because they may be too remote or may even be insulting? Please assess and give guidance.

The drafter normally does not have the authority to answer these questions; only the deal negotiators can answer them. It is obvious in our case study that the DevCo president has not fully addressed all the business issues, as we will see in more detail later.

The first draft released to the DevCo president must:

- Be a document that he understands
- Communicate a request for answers to all the drafter's questions
- Clarify the unresolved issues

The DevCo president will want the next draft to be designed to favourably but to fairly communicate DevCo's business position with InterCo as negotiators. The licensing relationship is a long-term affair; the negotiators want to keep the number of surprises to a minimum. Better that they spend their energies developing and marketing the Licensed Software than sorting out misunderstandings.

Unfortunately, with the style of the First Draft, the DevCo president will not easily understand what is being expressed and will have great difficulty explaining and selling to his negotiating counterpart at InterCo the business issues that are expressed in the document.

TACTIC:
Recognise drafting as part of the negotiating process.

DREADFUL DRAFTER'S SECOND DRAFT OF THE RELEASE

It is clear Dreadful Drafter needs help or he will face client rebellion. When the best precedent available is still incomprehensible to persons who must live with it, it is necessary to implement antidreadful drafting tactics. To determine the substance of this release, let us break it down into its individual parts as follows:

SECOND DRAFT

2. Release

2.1 Licensor

(a) releases, relinquishes, acquits, and forever discharges

(b) Licensee, its officers, directors, shareholders, employees, agents, legal representatives, subsidiaries, affiliates, attorneys, successors, and assigns,

(c) of and from any and all debts, obligations, reckonings, promises, covenants, agreements, contracts, endorsements, bonds, specialties, controversies, suits, actions, causes of action, trespasses, variances, judgments, executions, damages, claims, demands, rights, titles, interests, charges, encumbrances, or liens of any kind or sort whatsoever or howsoever arising, in law or in equity, whether known or unknown, whether liquidated or unliquidated, whether in tort or in contract,

(d) which they or any of them had, now has, or in the future may have

(e) against Licensee, its officers, directors, shareholders, agents, legal representatives, subsidiaries, affiliates, attorneys, successors, and assigns,

(f) arising out of, for, under, upon, or by reason of or in connection with or relating to, directly or indirectly,

(i) the 1999 License Agreement, or

(ii) any of the following acts or omissions of Licensee, its officers, directors, shareholders, employees, agents, legal representatives, subsidiaries, affiliates, attorneys, successors, and assigns, in connection with or relating to or arising out of or by virtue of any of the following:

    (1) any loss, cost or damage relating to or arising out of any breach of fiduciary duty,

    (2) breach of any duty of good faith or fair dealing,

    (3) breach of confidence,

    (4) undue influence,

    (5) duress,

    (6) economic coercion,

    (7) conflict of interest,

    (8) negligence,

    (9) bad faith,

    (10) malpractice,

    (11) intentional negligent infliction of emotional or mental distress,

    (12) tortious interference with corporate governance or prospective business advantage,

    (13) breach of contract,

    (14) deceptive trade practices,

    (15) libel, slander, conspiracy,

(16) any claim of wrongfully marketing the Licensed Software, or

(17) the charging, contracting for, taking, reserving, collecting or receiving of interest in excess of the highest lawful rate applicable (i.e., usury), or

(18) any violations of federal or state law,

(19) any violations of federal copyright rules, laws or regulations, or

(20) any violation of the federal antitrust acts.

2.2 Licensor further agrees that neither it nor any of its legal representatives or successors,

(a) will institute, prosecute, or in any way aid in the institution or prosecution

(b) of any claim, demand, action, or cause of action

(c) now existing or hereafter asserted

(d) against Licensee, its officers, directors, shareholders, employees, agents, legal representatives, subsidiaries, affiliates, attorneys, successors, and assigns,

(e) arising out of or by virtue of or in connection with or relating to any of the foregoing.

Now we are able to see what principles the release is addressing. This subdividing or sculpturing of the clause makes it, for the reader, both more visually appealing and easier to analyze.[7]

TACTIC:

Use paragraph sculpturing for ease of reading and analysis.

DREADFUL DRAFTER'S THIRD DRAFT OF THE RELEASE

However, the reader still gets lost in the detail of each segment and will have difficulty finding the clause's essential purpose. Using essentially the same words, let us break the clause down even more, using definitions. Here is the Third Draft.

THIRD DRAFT

2. Release

2.1 Licensor Releases Licensee of all Claims that it now has or in the future might have against the Licensee.

2.2 The Licensor shall not Prosecute any Claim against the Licensee.

2.3 In this Article 2, the following words shall have the following meanings, unless the context otherwise requires:

(a) "Licensor" means the Licensor, its officers, directors, shareholders, employees, agents, legal representatives, subsidiaries, affiliates, attorneys, successors, and assigns.

(b) "Licensee" means the Licensee, its officers, directors, shareholders, agents, legal representatives, subsidiaries, affiliates, attorneys, successors, and assigns.

(c) "Claims" means all debts, obligations, reckonings, promises, covenants, agreements, contracts, endorsements, bonds, specialities, controversies, suits, actions, causes of action, trespasses, variances, judgments, executions, damages, claims, demands, rights, titles, interests, charges, encumbrances, or liens of any kind or sort whatsoever or howsoever arising, in law or in equity, whether known or unknown, whether liquidates or unliquidated, whether in tort or in contract, arising out of, for, under, upon, or by reason of or in connection with or relating to, directly or indirectly, the 1999 License Agreement or any of the following acts or omissions of Licensee Related thereto:

(1) any loss, cost, or damage relating to or arising out of any breach of fiduciary duty,

(2) breach of any duty of good faith or fair dealing,

(3) reach of confidence,

(4) undue influence,

(5) duress,

(6) economic coercion,

(7) conflict of interest,

(8) negligence,

(9) bad faith,

(10) malpractice,

(11) intentional negligent infliction of emotional or mental distress,

(12) tortious interference with corporate governance or prospective business advantage,

(13) breach of contract,

(14) deceptive trade practices,

(15) libel, slander, conspiracy,

(16) any claim of wrongful marketing the Licensed Software, or

(17) the charging, contracting for, taking, reserving, collecting, or receiving of interest in excess of the highest lawful rate applicable (i.e. usury), or

(18) any violations of federal or state law,

(19) any violations of federal copyright rules, laws, or regulations, or

(20) any violation of the federal antitrust act

(d) "Prosecute" means prosecute, institute, or in any way aid in the institution of prosecution.

(e) "Related" includes arising out of, by virtue of, under, by reason of, or in connection with.

(f) "Releases" include relinquishes, acquits, and forever discharges.

Now our business decision makers may understand the materials; it no longer has that peculiar "lawyer look" about it.[8] At last we can see that the substance of this section is: "Licensor Releases Licensee of all Claims which it now has or in the future may have against the Licensee."

The use of definitions in the Third Draft allows the drafter to isolate issues for the reader. We can now more readily see the substance of the release, and see who is doing the releasing, whom is being released, and what is released.[9] Definitions can help the drafter "achieve clarity and consistency without burdensome repetition."[10]

Unless the Context Otherwise Requires

Section 2.3 starts out, "In this Article 2, the following words shall have the following meanings, unless the context otherwise requires." The last five words negatively influence the intent of the definition section. Every time a defined word appears the reader will be required to decide whether the definition applies or whether the context of the agreement here or in any other place otherwise requires another meaning. The goal of the use of definitions was to increase precision and "ease of reading and analysis." Instead, the words "unless the context otherwise requires" reduce precision and make the agreement more difficult to read.

TACTIC:
Drafting laziness should not detract from precision.

Expansive Definitions

Some "definitions" do not define the words[11] (i.e., confine the meaning of the word to certain specifics). Instead, statements often included in the definition section *expand* the meaning of the words used. The Third Draft talks about the word "Releases" including certain things. It does not say that the word "Releases" does not include any other things. Thus, the reader has to decide what the word "Releases" means and whether it adds anything to the list of included items. Sometimes an expansive "definition" is appropriate; more often, it gives rise to confusion.

TACTIC:
Wherever possible, design definitions to limit and not expand the meaning.

Coupled (Tripled) Synonyms

The Third Draft clearly illustrates the longstanding use of strings of synonyms.[12] Here we see well-worn phrases such as "releases, relinquishes, acquits, and forever discharges." For many of us, some strings of synonyms always appear together; we would feel incomplete without all the words being there.[13] Sometimes, strings of synonyms are used by drafters who are insecure about the meaning of the individual word, and as a result of their insecurity, they include them all.[14] Can we safely reduce "releases, relinquishes, acquits, and forever discharges" to "releases"?[15] Similarly, can we use words that have larger scope (such as "affiliates") and eliminate companion words with a narrower but included scope (such as "subsidiaries")?

Dreadful Drafter now should undertake the task of rewriting the release to keep the meat and throw out the filler.

TACTIC:
Eliminate redundant words—less is more.

Boilerplate Produces a Checklist

The Third Draft is now useful as a checklist of the issues to be considered in writing the next draft of the release.

TACTIC:
Precedents (however written) are a valuable source
when developing checklists.

Long, Long Sentences Increase the Risk of Errors.   The First Draft illustrates the significant risk of error due to its length and the resulting stress placed on the typist. In the definition of "Licensee" in the Third Draft, you can see that the word "employee" was omitted. Dreadful Drafter will have difficulty noticing this error because the error is lost in the mass of words.

Will a court find that the licensee's employees are not released due to the omission? It might have to if it follows the rule of law that every insertion and omission is done for a reason.[16]

TACTICS:
Avoid verbose, sloppy writing that may produce surprising results.
Proofread carefully long, long sentences.

Cross-References Must Be Precise.   In Section 2.2 of the Second Draft, Dreadful Drafter provided that the "Licensor . . . will not . . . prosecute . . . any claim . . . against Licensee . . . arising out of . . . or relating to any of the foregoing . . ." In the First Draft this word "foregoing" was the last word of the long, long sentence. Does it refer to the 20 causes of action that are listed in the description of a "claim" or does it refer only to some of them? Does it refer back to anything else? The word "foregoing" does not provide any precise reference back.

Cross-references within an agreement are always a potential source of error, particularly as a document is amended and the references change their position. We do not need to compound the problem by using words that are imprecise and that, many feel, should be dropped from the legal vocabulary.[17]

TACTIC:
Be cross about imprecise cross-references.

Lists.   In Section 2.3(c) of the Third Draft, Dreadful Drafter compiled a list of claims. This compilation must have exhausted Dreadful Drafter's imagination; but is it sufficiently exhaustive? If anything is omitted, he may suffer from the application of the Latin maxim, *Inclusio unius est exclusio alterius* (i.e., if you "specify something but not everything in the same category the reader may infer that the unspecified items have been deliberately omitted").[18] You will notice that Dreadful Drafter did not introduce his list with the saving words "including without limitation." Using those saving words, Dreadful Drafter might now go through his list of 20 causes of action to see if he may safely delete the repetitious or inappropriate ones.

TACTIC:

Phrase lists carefully; avoid application of Latin maxims.

User-Friendly Language. Software developers are making great efforts to produce user-friendly software and related manuals. Borland International, Inc. early on endeavoured to combine user-friendly language with complex legal issues in its standard license agreement. Here is an extract from one of Borland's licenses that set the stage for user-friendly language:

No-Nonsense License Statement

This software is protected by both United States copyright law and international copyright provisions. Therefore, you must treat this software just like a book, except that you may copy it onto a computer to be used and you may make archival copies of the software for the sole purpose of backing-up our software and protecting your investment from loss.

By saying, "just like a book," Borland means, for example, that this software may be used by any number of people, and may be freely moved from one computer location to another, so long as there is no possibility of it being used at one location while it's being used at another or on a computer network by more than one user at one location. Just like a book can't be read by two different people in two different places at the same time, neither can the software be used by two different people in two different places at the same time. (Unless, of course, Borland's copyright has been violated or the use is on a computer network by up to the number of users authorized by additional Borland licenses as explained below.)[19]

My software clients often try to get the technical users to "buy into" the license agreement and push it through the legal department so there will be no delay before they can start using the software. User-friendly language permits the technical users to better assess the risks/benefits and guide the lawyers concerning the level of risk assumption that is acceptable.

TACTIC:

Use user-friendly language if possible.

Concise but Precise. Several years ago, I was involved in the development of a strategic alliance of many parties where the goal of the drafting style had to be articulated to avoid inconsistency as the various drafters proposed changes to clarify the business intent. We decided that our drafting should be "concise, but precise, using business English without ambiguity."

Increasingly our clients are demanding "simple" documents. Too often, this reflects a desire to remove all legal principles and legal language from the document. As Mellinkoff states in "Rule 5" of his superb book on drafting, *Legal Writing: Sense & Nonsense*:

> RULE 5: WRITE LAW SIMPLY. DO NOT PUFF, MANGLE OR HIDE.
> The only thing about legal writing that is both unique and necessary is law. To simplify legal writing, first get the law right. You can't simplify by omitting what the law requires or including what the law forbids. The better you know the law the easier to decide what law ought to go in, and what is overkill or window dressing.[20]

Licensor/Licensee.   In an earlier version of the Third Draft, Dreadful Drafter noticed that Section 2.2 had been typed, "The Licensee shall not Prosecute any Claim against the Licensee." Despite repeated reviews, this error continued; "Licensor" and "Licensee" are not sufficiently visually distinct and errors are almost invited. Occasionally on receiving a long document that uses "Licensee" and "Licensor," I do a find and replace the words with suitable names or acronyms. Virtually every document will have "Licensor" and Licensee" switched at least once. With the current search-and-replace word-processing facilities, there is no continuing reason to use indistinct words like "Licensee," "Licensor," "Lessee," and "Lessor."

TACTIC:
Use distinctive words to describe the parties; avoid both "Licensor"
and "Licensee."

Block Capitals.   Many agreements use block capitals for every defined word, for example LICENSOR and LICENSEE. These blocked words frequently BLOCK the communication flow; a feature that should be retained for emphasis has been squandered on a defined word. Using initial uppercase letters serves the purpose of distinguishing defined words.

TACTIC:
Do not use BLOCK letters for defined words;
it BLOCKS the communication flow.

Visual Appeal.   With improved laser printers and libraries of available fonts, Dreadful Drafter could make his document visually attractive as well as comprehensible. Visual appeal may overcome a reader's initial negative reaction to a complex document.

TACTIC:

Make your documents visually attractive.

To the greatest extent possible, the licensing documents should assist in the marketing of the client's software rather than being a hindrance to the marketing. The marketing process should never stop.

TACTIC:

Market! Market! Market!

DREADFUL DRAFTER WRITES A GRANT CLAUSE

Dreadful Drafter looks at the note: "InterCo gets all of the United States" and recognizes that he needs to grant InterCo certain rights to allow it to use the Licensed Software. He writes, "DevCo hereby grants to InterCo the exclusive right to make, use, and sell the Licensed Software."

Scope of Grant

It would appear that this grant is technology specific and not intellectual property specific—whatever intellectual property DevCo has that relates to the Licensed Software will be included in the grant. Dreadful Drafter has decided that this requires more than what would be required to settle an infringement suit, such as a bare patent license. Since the desire is to have a creative, ongoing relationship, Dreadful Drafter's licensing strategy must have rejected a license based on specific patent claims or copyrighted works and favoured a technology-specific grant that is far more expansive.

TACTIC:

Decide what's in and what's out.

What Rights?

Dreadful Drafter has not made it clear under what rights DevCo grants this license. A license by its nature gives a person the right to do something that is otherwise prohibited. Some intellectual property rights, such as patents and copyright, give the right to exclude others from engaging in specific activities; rather than *monopolistic rights*, these rights are better referred to as *exclusionary rights*. The source code of the Licensed Software could be protected by patents, copyright, and trade secrecy. There may be applications for patents that have not yet issued. Thus, Dreadful Drafter's license must grant permission for something that would otherwise be prohibited, or, in the case of trade secrets, something that would not otherwise be permitted—access to the secrets.

TACTIC:
Specify the exclusionary right that gives the right to license.

What Activities Are Licensed?

The confusion is not helped by Dreadful Drafter's choice of grant words "make, use, and sell," which are words specific to patents. Since there is copyrighted material involved, we would expect to see words such as "copy" or "reproduce, distribute, transmit, and create derivative works." Dreadful Drafter should also keep in mind that trade secrecy is not an exclusionary right as are patents and copyright; it is the right to receive a disclosure of information in exchange for agreement to maintain secrecy and restrict the use of the information to permitted uses. Thus, some would argue that trade secrets are not licensed as patents and copyrights and thus need different language. Goldscheider in Section 7.20 of "Straight Patent Licenses and Integrated Technical Assistance Agreements," writes, "Taking into account the differences in the various intellectual property rights, it is usually advisable to grant licenses to each one in a separate paragraph."[21]

TACTIC:
Co-relate the permitted activity with the exclusionary right
that gives the right to license.

Present and Future Rights?

Dreadful Drafter has not made it clear that the grant covers only the intellectual property that DevCo currently has. Because InterCo's rights are continuing, there could be a suggestion that future intellectual property that DevCo develops could also be included in the grant.

TACTIC:
Plain language still needs to specify the time period: sometimes the present time is not specified by the present tense of the verb.

Whose Rights?

Furthermore, Dreadful Drafter might have indicated by his grant clause that InterCo has the exclusive rights to the Licensed Software or that its reproduction, use, and distribution will not infringe the intellectual property rights of others. He might want to reconsider the clause so that it indicates that DevCo is only granting to InterCo the right to exercise the rights that DevCo has. Warranties as to ownership, validity of patent claims, and noninfringement could then be inserted as stand-alone clauses without contradication of other clauses or implications resulting from ambiguity or lack of clarity.

TACTIC:

Say it once and say it well.

Dreadful Drafter Tries Again

Dreadful Drafter decides that he should draft the grant clause so that it co-relates to DevCo's intellectual property and writes, "DevCo hereby grants to InterCo the right to exploit all intellectual property rights owned by it that cover the Licensed Software."

Cover.   Dreadful Drafter has used a word that is specific to patents, it is unlikely that it applies to copyright, and it does not apply to trade secrecy.

TACTIC:

Properly cover the permitted activities.

Owned.   Some would argue that trade secrets cannot be owned, they can only be possessed; they may have property-like protection but are not property. Also, the choice of this word may have deleted from the grant of intellectual property for which DevCo has a license that permits a sublicense and thus, InterCo may not have been granted all the intellectual property rights that are embodied in the Licensed Software.[22] See the discussion of warranties of ownership later in this chapter, where we discuss the problems of determining what "own" means.

Exploit.   Dreadful Drafter has tried to find one word that covers all the various intellectual property rights that exist under the various exclusionary rights; he is to be commended for his desire for simplicity. However, in some communities, the word "exploit" has a negative connotation of a large entity oppressively taking advantage of a smaller entity. Some might find the word "exercise" more acceptable even if it does not, in the truest grammatical sense, add anything.

TACTIC:

Exercise Sensitivity.

Intellectual Property–Specific Grant

Dreadful Drafter decides that he would like to have a grant that is specific to intellectual property and writes as follows: "DevCo grants to InterCo the license to make, use, and sell software incorporating any inventions disclosed and claimed in US Patent No. 99999."

Scope and Jurisdiction

Note that although the U.S. patent offers exclusionary rights to DevCo only in the United States, this grant may not be restricted to the *benefit* of those rights. It might be technology specific rather than intellectual property specific, because it refers to the technology that is disclosed and claimed, rather than grants a license under the patent itself.[23] Thus, the benefit of the license might not be restricted to the U.S. territory but may be held to apply worldwide.

TACTIC:
Be territorial.

Joint Ownership

Dreadful Drafter decides that he will not be successful in negotiating the grant-back and decides to use joint ownership of improvements as a solution to this problem. The use of jointly owned improvements are particularly perplexing when the nature of the improvement cannot be predicated. So he writes, "InterCo acknowledges that DevCo shall continue to own the intellectual property to the software and improvements thereto contributed by DevCo. DevCo acknowledges that InterCo shall own the intellectual property to the software and improvements thereto contributed by InterCo. The parties shall co-own all improvements made jointly to the Licensed Software. Ownership shall be determined by inventorship under the U.S. Patent Act."

Exercise of Rights by Joint Owners

The law in Canada as to the rights of joint owners is very different from the law that applies in the United States. In Canada, a joint owner may exercise the rights for its own benefit and may assign its entire interest in the innovation without the consent of or requirement to account to the other co-owner.[24] In Canada, unless an agreement provides otherwise, a joint owner may not license or partially assign its interest in the joint invention without the consent of the other party. These default rules are different in the United States. There, according to Gene Dillahunty,

> Each joint owner, or co-owner, not only has the right to commercially practice under the patent without permission of the other co-owner, but also has the right to license whomever they desire under whatever terms they select without permission of the other co-owner and without sharing any profits or royalties with the other co-owner. The end result of this situation is that neither co-owner alone can enforce the patent against a third party to stop infringement, because the accused infringer may be able to obtain a license from the other co-owner. Moreover, a court will not permit a lawsuit toproceed against an infringer unless the entire ownership of patent, i.e., all owners, join in the lawsuit. A co-owner who does not want to be a party to a lawsuit can

license the infringer and keep all of the royalties or license fees, without any requirement to share with the other co-owner.[25]

Dillahunty cautions against joint ownership for the following two reasons: (1) neither party has full rights to exclude others; its marketing plans can be disrupted by an uncooperative joint owner, and (2) if ownership is to be determined by inventorship, each party may try to exclude the other from the inventive process to claim ownership.

TACTIC:
The approach of "what's ours is ours, what's yours is yours,
what's joint is both of ours."

Rather than producing a collaborative environment, Dreadful Drafter might have produced an adversarial or self-serving environment. Dillahunty writes,

> If those involved in a project do not think they can invent anything themselves, and preclude the technical people from the other party from being co-inventors, their natural tendency may be the opposite of the above. They will try to be co-inventor on everything the other party is working on. This is based on a belief that it is better to be a co-inventor and co-owner than it is to have no ownership.

Dillahunty prefers a market-defined, exclusive field-of-use approach, stating that it "will result in a much better planned project with better defined technology and performance goals."[26]

TACTIC:
Consider a market-driven, exclusive field-of-use approach.

Inventorship

Dillahunty points out that *inventorship* is not a good standard to determine ownership.

> The determination of inventorship for a particular invention is not exact; inventorship is subject to differing opinions on the underlying facts, is subject to legal interpretation and may legally change (due to claim amendments) during the prosecution of a patent application. . . . The futility (and frustration) of a technology joint development arrangement which bases future ownership of property rights on inventorship determination is obvious."[27]

TACTIC:
Avoid futility and frustration—do not use inventorship to determine
ownership of jointly developed innovations.

Acknowledgement of Ownership

Dreadful Drafter has asked each party to acknowledge that the other party owns what it contributes. This is unnecessary and, in fact, should be resisted by each party. Each party should only concede that this agreement by itself does not transfer an interest in the software contributed. There is no need to concede ownership to the other party, a fact that might not be within the knowledge of the conceding party.

TACTIC:
Concede retention of rights; do not concede ownership.

DREADFUL DRAFTER WRITES AN INDEMNITY CLAUSE

Dreadful Drafter decides that InterCo will expect an indemnity clause to go along with the warranties against infringement, and writes, "DevCo shall indemnify and hold InterCo harmless from any loss it may suffer on account of any claim that DevCo's intellectual property infringes the intellectual property rights of others."

Claim vs. Actual Infringement

Dreadful Drafter has likely exposed DevCo to liability for infringement claims that are successfully defended since he omitted to write "proven claim"; claims covered by his clause could be vexatious or commenced for competitive reasons that are directed only against InterCo—perhaps to force InterCo to consider settling other claims or to enter into a cross license of other technology. DevCo may decide that it should be responsible for proven infringement; if so, it might want to restrict its liability to successful claims. This is often done in mergers and acquisitions where it is recognized that infringement suits are not always brought because of infringement.

TACTIC:
Consider restricting the scope of the indemnity to successful claims.

Legal Fees

Dreadful Drafter's clause will also make DevCo responsible for the legal fees; Dreadful Drafter may not recognize that in the United States, legal fees are usually 2 to 10 times more expensive than they are in Canada, partially due to the use of the jury system, and also may not recognize that costs are not assessed against the losing party as they are in Canada.

TACTIC:
Assess the economic impact of the scope of the indemnity clause.

Rights by Themselves Do Not Infringe

Dreadful Drafter assumed that intellectual property rights by themselves could infringe the intellectual property rights of others; that is not the case. They are inert; the knowledge that they represent must be implemented before there is an infringement. Thus, holding a patent does not produce an infringement by the holder. The making, using, or selling of a product or process that implements the art disclosed by the patent could result in the infringement of a patent held by another person.

TACTIC:
Activities infringe, not intellectual property.

Trade Secrecy

Since trade secret protection is not an exclusionary right such as patents and copyright, the word *infringement* may be incorrect. Perhaps a better concept is "misappropriate," and a separate provision may be inserted that relates to the misappropriation of any information from a third party.

TACTIC:
Be appropriate.

Withholding Royalty and the Implications for Both Parties

Dreadful Drafter, realizing that InterCo might feel insecure about DevCo's financial solvency if any infringement or misappropriation claim is made, writes, "If, as a result of InterCo exercising its rights under this License, any Claim alleging infringement of any intellectual property right held by another Person is made, or if a Claim is made alleging misappropriation of information from another Person, InterCo may withhold payment of any further Royalty until the Claim has been resolved."

Cash Flow

The withholding of royalty payments could produce just the event that InterCo wished to avoid. Since DevCo is a small company that likely depends on this revenue stream, the *loss of cash flow* might cost it the ability to fund the defense of the claim. Worse yet, DevCo might find, after it successfully defends the claim, that InterCo itself has become insolvent and is unable to pay the earned royalties. This problem will not be resolved by InterCo paying the royalty payments into escrow unless the escrow specifically allows funds to be used for the defense.

TACTIC:
Don't withhold prudence.

DREADFUL DRAFTER WRITES AN EXCLUSIVITY CLAUSE

Dreadful Drafter looks again at his president's second instruction: "InterCo gets all of the United States" and realizes that this refers to the exclusivity of InterCo's distribution rights. Dreadful Drafter writes, "DevCo hereby grants to InterCo the sole and exclusive license to market the licensed Software in the United States."

Use of Specialized Words

What does "sole and exclusive" mean to the reader? Does it mean that DevCo can market the Licensed Software in the United States along with InterCo? Can any of DevCo's other distributors market it in the United States? Can DevCo license the Licensed Software to a company based in Canada for use in its U.S. offices?

The words "sole and exclusive" selected by Dreadful Drafter do not resolve these issues. Indeed, under Canadian law they are a contradiction of terms.[28]

> An exclusive licence gives the licensee the right to exercise the [intellectual property rights] as against all persons, including the licensor. [A] sole licence gives to the licensee the right to exercise the [intellectual property rights] as against all persons except the licensor.[29]

It would be better if words such as "sole" and "exclusive" were not used in the grant clause since their specialized legal meaning is not apparent from their ordinary usage.

TACTIC:
Eat sole; don't write it.

Isolate Separate Business/Legal Issues

Instead of using legal "buzzwords," Dreadful Drafter could write a separate section setting out in detail the extent of the "exclusivity" that is granted to InterCo. When isolated in its own section, the business issues can be more fully communicated to the business decision makers. Examples of issues to be considered are

- Will all licenses to Canadian companies require the user to be situated in Canada?
- How will cross-referrals be dealt with by DevCo and all its authorized distributors? For example, who provides support and installation, and who delivers the Licensed Software and the related manuals?

Consider Footnotes

In the first draft released to the DevCo president, Dreadful Drafter could use footnotes to discuss the risk/benefits of issues raised. This form of communication will let the president more readily understand what issues the drafter is addressing and assess the merits of the various alternatives available.

TACTIC:
Use footnotes in early drafts to improve communication
with the business decision maker.

DREADFUL DRAFTER ADDRESSES BEST EFFORTS

Dreadful Drafter sees that his president had written "Best Efforts" in marketing, so he writes, "InterCo shall devote its best efforts to the promotion and licensing of the Licensed Software."

Best Efforts

"Best Efforts" is often used in agreements, and not always as a result of drafting laziness. It might be used for any of these reasons:

- The parties have developed a trust level between them and do not want to disrupt the relationship by pressing for more precision.
- The parties are unable to predict market acceptance of the product.
- Drafters think it has well-recognized meaning.

Unfortunately, when the trust relationship collapses or the Licensor thinks the product is not being adequately exploited, the parties will find out that, although the term *best efforts* has been the subject of frequent litigation, it is uncertain and ambiguous. In Canada, these words "do not mean second-best endeavours; they do not mean that the limits of reason must be overstepped with regard to the cost of the service, but short of these qualifications the words mean that the [defendant] must, broadly speaking, leave no stone unturned. . . ."[30] A "party that signs a 'best efforts' contract has placed himself in a risky and uncertain situation."[31]

TACTIC:
Avoid the phrase "best efforts"; it may be an invitation to litigation.

Reasonable Efforts

Instead of using "best efforts," Dreadful Drafter decides to use "reasonable efforts." Unfortunately, Dreadful Drafter has made no improvement. There appears to be no Canadian case that defines reasonable efforts. This phrase is as uncertain and ambiguous as "best efforts."

TACTIC:
Use reasonable efforts to avoid the phrase "reasonable efforts."

Performance

The parties might be better served if they addressed what "performance" is expected. The agreement may require, in a software context, any one or more of the following:

- Further research and development to be performed by Licensee

  - Improving existing technology
  - Adding new features

- Funding to be provided by Licensee for research and development to be performed by Licensor
- Obtaining patents or registering copyright in specified jurisdictions
- Modifying the software for a different platform
- Bundling Licensee's technology with Licensor's
- Translation of interface or user manuals into another language
- Establishing production facilities for compact disks, firmware, manuals, floppy disks, and related packaging

  - Quality controls
  - Access to sensitive proprietary source code

- Advertising

  - In what media
  - Minimum budget
  - Prior approval of advertising copy by Licensor

- Other marketing efforts

  - Inclusion in licensee's products list
  - Direct mail catalog
  - Trade show
  - Salesperson

- Training

  - Sales personnel
  - Users

- Support

  - First line of contact with customer

- Second level of support

  - Bug fixing
  - Updates
  - New releases

- Timely response
- Assumption of product liability
- Assumption of risk of infringement
- Assumption of obligation to prosecute third-party infringers
- Establishing a distribution network with specified features

TACTIC:
Specify performance requirements.

DEVCO GETS 5 PERCENT ROYALTY

Dreadful Drafter reads his president's notes concerning royalty: "DevCo gets 5 percent royalty," and decides that instead of a fixed royalty, DevCo is to receive a royalty based on revenues. He writes, "In consideration of InterCo having the right to distribute the Licensed Software, InterCo shall pay to DevCo a royalty equal to 5 percent of net sales."

"Sales" versus "Revenues"

Dreadful Drafter has used the word "sales." Likely DevCo's sophisticated software will be "licensed" rather than "sold." Software developers often refer to grants of fully paid perpetual licenses in the vernacular as "sales," but this word is not an appropriate legal word. DevCo, and perhaps InterCo, will want to retain rights to the Licensed Software; a "sale" could deprive them of these rights. "Sales" might be appropriate in licenses of mass-marketed software, but not elsewhere.

TACTIC:
Beware of vernacular; it may change the legal context.

Source of Revenues

Dreadful Drafter tries again, and this time uses "5 percent of gross revenue from licenses." He has included only fees for licenses of the Licensed Software granted by InterCo to end users. He has not contemplated these possibilities:

- InterCo using the Licensed Software as a consultant or service provider and getting revenue from its own use

- InterCo using the Licensed Software in a joint venture where others gain the benefits of its use
- Consideration for the right to sublicense granted by InterCo to distributors who will market to end users, including:
  - Initial payments for the right to distribute
  - Revenues earned from royalties generated by these distributors
- InterCo providing copies to its staff to be used for marketing purposes
- InterCo providing copies to third parties for the purpose of review and testing

TACTIC:
Define "revenues."

Noncash Consideration

Dreadful Drafter has not considered *noncash consideration* being paid for the grant of license rights—for example, by shares in a closely held corporation or by a grant-back to InterCo of the right to distribute the distributor's software. How will InterCo value noncash consideration that it might receive from a subdistributor at the time of granting the rights to that distributor?

TACTIC:
Consider the effect of noncash consideration being included in the royalty base.

Exceptions from Revenues

Dreadful Drafter did not specify what would be excepted from revenues. Will InterCo be able to deduct amounts resulting from these expenses?

- Sales taxes
- Packaging
- Reproduction of user manuals
- Transportation
- Return allowances
- Commissions

Triggering Event

The event that triggers the royalty right is not stated in Dreadful Drafter's clause. It could accrue when any of the following occurs:

- The Licensed Software is delivered if done before the invoice is released.
- InterCo invoices the licensee.

- A customer no longer has any right to reject the Licensed Software.
- InterCo receives payment.

DevCo will want to have the triggering event as early as possible in the distribution process. InterCo will want to use payment as the triggering event to preserve its cash flow.

With software licenses, "receipt" of the consideration is often chosen as the triggering event. Although DevCo shares the risk of bad receivables with InterCo, this might not be an unreasonable risk because the cost of each copy of software is minimal and this risk might allow wider dissemination of the Licensed Software.

TACTIC:
ROGER! Trigger the ROYalty.

Bundling

InterCo might want to market the Licensed Software as a module within another product it markets (i.e., "bundle" the two products). If there is a single price or license fee, can it be broken down easily to determine DevCo's share?

The Licensed Software could be bundled with InterCo's hardware or with other software marketed by InterCo. The profit margin in the hardware might be very different from the profit margin in the software. The royalty rate might vary, depending on the nature of the products bundled.

TACTIC:
Break the bundle.

License Fee vs. Support Fee

InterCo could decide to make more profit for itself by increasing the amount it receives for support and other services it provides, keeping all such revenues for itself, and correspondingly reduce the license fee for the Licensed Software. Dreadful Drafter might require InterCo to deal with the Licensed Software in good faith and prevent it from obtaining an unfair advantage.

TACTIC:
Avoid predatory pricing.

InterCo's Affiliates

Dreadful Drafter should contemplate InterCo placing a subsidiary between itself and the end user to reduce the royalty payable to DevCo. The license agreement might require InterCo to deal as if at arm's length with its affiliates. If this is not likely to provide adequate comfort, the License Agreement might prohibit dealing with an affiliate. A practical solution will have to be tailored for each situation.

TACTIC:
Prevent affiliates from scooping profits.

Invalidity of Intellectual Property Rights

For the sake of illustration, let us assume that the value of DevCo's software comes from the trade secrets embodied in that software. These trade secrets would be revealed to InterCo on the delivery of the source code to it. Let us assume that after InterCo integrates the software into its product, DevCo's trade secrets become publicly available through a third party's inadvertence. It would seem that a licensee in either Canada or the United States might be obligated to continue to pay the royalties for continued use of the trade secrets even though others can readily gain access to them.

If, however, DevCo had obtained a patent in the United States and the license grant was the right to make copies of the Licensed Software under that patent, under U.S. law InterCo's obligation to pay royalties would cease upon the patent being established as invalid. However, in Canada it is suggested that the licensee would be obligated to continue to pay, even though the patent has been established to be invalid unless there is an express clause to the contrary.

Thus, in any agreement, Dreadful Drafter should do the following:

- Prohibit/permit the Licensee to challenge the Licensor's intellectual property rights. (The ability to prohibit may vary from country to country and may depend on the type of intellectual property.)
- State whether the royalty remains payable after the intellectual property rights cease to be effective.
- State whether the royalty is suspended during the challenge period (consider restraint of trade implications and cash-flow considerations just discussed).
- State whether the royalty remains payable during the challenge period but must be paid into escrow.
- State whether the granted rights are lost if payments are withheld and Licensee loses its challenge of the Licensor's intellectual property rights.

TACTIC:
Crown jewels to costume jewelry: whither the royalty?

DREADFUL DRAFTER WRITES A CONFIDENTIALITY CLAUSE

Dreadful Drafter looks at his president's next note, which says, "InterCo gets source code so it can provide support." Dreadful Drafter recognizes that the source code is the version of the licensed software understandable by computer programmers. It contains all the program's trade secrets, including the algorithms, concepts, and underlying ideas—none of which are likely protected by copyright. The best available protection (apart from patent protection) may be secrecy, but DevCo is about to show all to InterCo. DevCo needs to keep control over these secrets.[32]

Definition of Trade Secret

Dreadful Drafter realizes he has to define what material is subject to the confidentiality and restricted use provisions. He writes, "Trade Secret means the information described on Schedule A."

Dreadful Drafter has taken the easy way out. He has left the definition for another person to draw. Hopefully, he expects someone who understands the technology will develop the proper wording. Unfortunately, one of the following events is likely to occur:

- Schedule A will not be prepared at all and the agreement will be uncertain at best and entirely unenforceable at worst.
- Schedule A will contain "puffery" (i.e., statements as to quality that could be construed as enforceable express representations).
- Schedule A will be so well prepared and so detailed that it will reveal the trade secrets themselves (but no one will be advised to take measures to maintain in confidence the confidentiality agreement that now reveals all).[33]

TACTIC:
Know your technology.

Possible Definition of Trade Secret

As explained earlier, trade secret protection is not an exclusionary right such as patents and copyrights, so trade secrets cannot be *infringed* but can be *misappropriated*. There is no Canadian statutory definition of a trade secret. However, the style of the definition in the Uniform Trade Secrets Act proposed in 1986 by the Alberta Institute of Law Research and Reform may provide some guidance for Dreadful Drafter as he endeavors to draw a definition of Confidential Information. It suggested the following definition:

> "trade secret" means information including but not limited to a formula, pattern, compilation, programme, method, technique, or process, or information contained or embodied in a product device or mechanism which

    (i) is, or may be used in a trade or business,
   (ii) is not generally known in that trade or business,
  (iii) has economic value from not being generally known, and
  (iv) is the subject of efforts that are reasonable under the circumstances to maintain its secrecy."[34]

TACTIC:
Consider adopting a well-known definition.

Categories of Trade Secrets

In deciding on the scope of the definition of "trade secret," Dreadful Drafter might want to decide what kind of secrets (perhaps in addition to the source code) he wants to protect. According to the Alberta Institute of Law Research and Reform:

> There are potentially four categories of trade secrets: specific product secrets (such as a chemical formula); technological secrets (that is, knowledge of some process or know-how that nobody else has yet developed); strategic business information (secret marketing information or customer lists); and specialized compilations of information that, in sum, are not publicly known and have unique value on that account.[35]

TACTIC:
Tailor the definition for the circumstances.

Participation

In the end there is no alternative but for drafters to become familiar, even in a layman's fashion, with the technology that is to be kept secret. Then at a minimum, they can intelligently review Schedule A to make sure it is appropriate.

TACTIC:
Participate in the drafting of the definition.

What Is to Be Kept Confidential

To assist the parties to know what information is subject to the confidentiality obligations and which information can be freely used, Dreadful Drafter writes, "These confidentiality obligations shall apply only to information marked 'confidential.'"

    Dreadful Drafter realizes that one of the standards the courts look for when determining if information constitutes a protectable trade secret is the care the disclosing party takes to prevent unauthorized disclosure. Professor David Vaver reviewed the Canadian jurisprudence and found that the Courts looked to the following eight factors when determining whether information is a trade secret:

1. The extent to which the information is known outside the business
2. The extent to which it is known by employees and others involved in the business
3. The extent of measures taken to guard the secrecy of the information
4. The value of the information to the holder of the secret, and to his competitors
5. The amount of effort or money expended in developing the information
6. The ease or difficulty with which the information can be properly acquired or duplicated by others
7. Whether the holder of the secret and the taker treat the information as secret
8. Custom in the industry concerning this specific type of information.[36]

But is it appropriate to give protection only to information that is marked confidential? Consider the following:

- Disclosures made orally: some agreements require that confidentiality must be claimed within a specified time after a disclosure period. Is this a reasonable expectation in practice?
- Disclosure via electronic transmission, where a confidentiality notice may not be apparent.
- Disclosures where all information is routinely marked confidential—an abusive abundance of caution. Marking information confidential should not make information secret that is otherwise in the public domain.

TACTIC:
Beware of public domain information in a confidential cloak.

Contract versus Trust

Dreadful Drafter decides to establish a standard of care and writes, "InterCo shall hold all the Confidential Information in trust for DevCo."

The use of the word "trust" illustrates the clash between the law of trusts and the law of contracts. Under trust law, the trustee holds the property for the beneficiary and may not use the property for his own benefit except as expressly permitted by the trust. A trustee is expected to act for the benefit of the other party at the expense of his own interest. Generally speaking, such a requirement does not fit the model of North American business reality.[37]

If the trustees breach their fiduciary duty a court will likely order them to restore the beneficiaries to the position in which they would have been had the duty not been breached.[38] There is trust law that indicates that this would require the payment of restorative amounts, no matter how remote or unforeseeable they may be. In contrast, in normal contract law, the awarded damages usually must be foreseeable and closely connected with the breach.

Thus, the use of the word "trust" increases the duties of InterCo so that InterCo is essentially a guarantor against unauthorized disclosure and, on a breach of the trust, exposes InterCo to almost unlimited liability. It is rare that a licensee would be prepared to accept that level of responsibility and exposure to liability.[39]

In *Icam v. Ebco* decided by the British Columbia Court of Appeal on November 19, 1993, the court discussed the remedies that are available for breach of a duty of confidence, summarized as follows:

- A confider may recover damages for breach of contract, or for breach of equitable duty to act in good faith.
- It now appears that the appropriate measure of damages is the sum which puts the confider in the same position "as he would have been if he had not sustained the wrong."
- Depending on the position of the particular plaintiff, that loss may be:
  - The confider's lost profits
  - The value of a consultant's fee
  - The market value of information, as between a willing buyer and willing seller
  - The development costs incurred in acquiring the information
  - The capitalization of an appropriate royalty
  - The depression in the value of the information in consequence of the breach of confidence
- The confider must decide which of the six methods is the most appropriate to satisfy the underlying principles in assessing damages.
- It would be in error to use more than one.[40]

TACTIC:

Consider the appropriate remedies: contract vs. trust.

DevCo knows that, even though it has taken all reasonable measures, there is still the possibility of disclosure of its confidential information occurring at its own offices. Should the obligations for retaining the information as confidential be any higher for InterCo than they are for DevCo? When the goal is to produce a "win-win" agreement, does the drafter of the license have the right to propose a clause that is patently wrong?

TACTIC:
In short-fuse negotiations, design the first
draft to produce a "win-win" result.

The Word "Ensure"

Intending to be fairer to the Licensee in his next draft of the confidentiality clause, Dreadful Drafter writes, "Licensee shall ensure that the confidential information shall not be disclosed." He may not have lessened the duty of care. "Ensure" is defined to mean "to warrant; to guarantee . . . to insure."[41]

Some drafters use the word "ensure" as if it were equivalent to "endeavour" or "take reasonable measures." The dictionary definition seems to result in a very high duty of care, almost to the point that there could be absolute liability. Commonplace usage and the dictionary definition seem to be contradictory. Perhaps the drafter should use a more precise word.

TACTIC:
Use "ensure" only when you mean "guarantee" or "insure";
better yet, don't use it at all.

Precautions to Be Taken

Dreadful Drafter tries again. He writes, "Licensee shall take the same precautions to hold the confidential information in confidence as it takes for its own trade secrets."

Consider DevCo's reaction when it learns that InterCo has lost its trade secrets as a result of its normal (but now proven inadequate) protective measures. To avoid this embarrassment, Dreadful Drafter could select an objective standard combined perhaps with InterCo's standards if they are known to be high. For example, "Licensee shall take all reasonable measures available to it, and in any event not less than those used to protect its own secrets, to keep the confidential information in the strictest confidence."

TACTIC:
Be objective, not subjective.

Steps to Be Taken

In a case of highly sensitive information or in the case of a licensee in a foreign jurisdiction that may not have generally adopted standards of secrecy, Dreadful Drafter might want to set out the reasonable steps DevCo requires of InterCo. For example, Dreadful Drafter could provide that the reasonable steps shall be as follows:

1. Physical security of areas where access may be gained to the Confidential Information
2. Security measures for electronic storage and transmission of data including or derived from any Confidential Information
3. Controls on access to any computer facility and tape or disk library where any Confidential Information may be stored
4. Visitor control
5. Controls over photocopying Confidential Information
6. Document and computer network control systems that limit access to the Confidential Information to employee and agents who have a need to know (the control system should provide for a secured method of protection of sensitive data)
7. Confidentiality agreements with the Licensee's employees, agents, or invitees who are permitted access to Confidential Information[42]

TACTIC:
Consider stating what secrecy measures are required.

Duration of Secrecy Obligations

Dreadful Drafter has not stated how long InterCo must maintain the secrecy. InterCo will be concerned about the costs of maintaining secrecy and the risk of inadvertent disclosure, particularly after an extended period of time. Frequently, drafters pick a figure such as 5 years or 21 years without much justification. It would be preferable to pick a time period more in line with the anticipated economic life of the trade secrets, or at the minimum, the time it would have taken for InterCo to independently develop the technology itself.[43]

Dreadful Drafter has not relieved Licensee's obligations of confidentiality for any portion of the confidential information that enters the public domain. In Canada and the United States, it might be permissible to require continued confidentiality even if the secret has been disclosed.

TACTIC:
Establish and justify the duration of secrecy obligations.

Limited Liability

The Licensee might want to restrict its liability if it has taken all reasonable steps to protect the confidential information but through some inadvertence, there has been a disclosure without some clause limiting the Licensee's obligations. It could be exposed to a claim for significant economic damages.

TACTIC:
Consider limiting Licensee's liability for inadvertent disclosure.

Detailing Permitted Use

As with many confidentiality agreements, Dreadful Drafter has discussed the obligations of secrecy but has not discussed what uses of the confidential information are permitted as well as what uses are restricted. As with any license of technology, the agreement should contemplate what uses are appropriate; for example:

- Evaluation of the technology for inclusion in the recipient's product line
- Permitted modifications of the technology
- Disclosure to employees/contractors who have a need to know
- Disclosures required by a governmental body or court order
- Disclosures to professional advisors

TACTIC:
Specify permitted uses.

DREADFUL DRAFTER ADDRESSES IMPROVEMENTS

Dreadful Drafter looks at his president's notes and sees the sixth instruction: "DevCo gets rights to all improvements but InterCo can use the improvements it makes."

Dreadful Drafter writes the following clause[44] to give effect to these directions of his president: "InterCo shall communicate to DevCo details of all improvements to the Licensed Software during the term of the license granted by this Agreement. Intellectual property rights to such improvements shall belong to DevCo but during the term of its license of the Licensed Software, InterCo shall have the exclusive right to exploit the improvements in the United States."

Does the Word "Improvement" Have a Meaning?

There seems to be little case law on what constitutes an "improvement," and what case law there is provides few clear-cut principles.[45] Here are a few examples of improvements to the Licensed Software:

- An improvement that enhances the Licensed Software's speed of processing and analyzing the user's data
- An improvement that provides processing and analytical features that the Licensed Software does not have
- A program that performs tasks similarly to the Licensed Software but in a different way

These improvements range from something that could be included in the computer program, to something that could be a stand-alone product, to something that is a different but competitive product. How will InterCo know what it is required to disclose and turn over to DevCo? What can it do in related areas without being subject to an infringement claim?

Unfortunately, Dreadful Drafter gives us no guidance as to what improvements InterCo is required to disclose and turn over to DevCo. Dreadful Drafter's improvement clause will be more meaningful if he considers the following factors.

TACTIC:
Use words that have precise meanings or the document invites
"creative misinterpretation."

An Improvement Must Infringe.   Some licensing drafters have chosen to say that an improvement that must be communicated is an improvement that infringes the intellectual property rights of the product involved, in this case the Licensed Software. This solution may be appropriate for a product that is the subject of a patent,[46] but may be of little help if the software is protected by copyright. Does the copyright protect

- Only the literal code of the Licensed Software
- The structure sequence and organization of the Licensed Software
- The Licensed Software's user interface

The case law has established that most of the literal code is protected, but the case law leaves it unclear as to what really is protected by copyright. The method of expressing an idea is normally protected under copyright rules unless it has merged with the idea being expressed (the idea not being protected by a copyright). Recently, Canadian and American courts have been struggling to "weed out or remove from copyright protection those portions [of a computer program] which . . . cannot be protected."[47] Cases relying on *Computer Associates v. Altai* use the abstraction/filtration method.[48] Whether this method is practically sound remains unsettled.

Thus, relying on infringement as a standard for a software improvement provides little certainty to the business decision makers who are involved. It would seem that the word *improvement* will have to be tailored for each agreement. Dreadful Drafter should provide a precise description of the improvements intended by the parties; otherwise a court may be asked to imply what terms were meant by the use of the word *improvement*.

TACTIC:
Define the word "improvement."

Communication of Improvements.   As well, the draft clause does not state when or how details of improvements are to be communicated. Is the communication to be in writing addressed to a stated technical representative or will disclosure in a casual conversation over a beer be sufficient? Does InterCo have to disclose details of the improvement as soon as rudimentary details of the improvement are developed or can it wait until it has developed the improvement sufficiently to establish substantial commercial advantage?

DevCo's ability to patent any improvement may depend on early disclosure. However, InterCo may be reluctant to disclose rudimentary ideas, especially toward the end of the term of the license.

TACTIC:
Make the draft answer "who, what, when, and how."

Term of Use of Improvement.   The improvement clause must address the term during which each party may use the improvement. Dreadful Drafter stated that InterCo had exclusive rights to the improvement in the United States "during the term of its license of the Licensed Software." Let us assume that the term of the license of the Licensed Software is 10 years and the term of protection for the improvement under copyright rules is 50 years. As drafted, InterCo will lose its rights to use the improvement at the end of the 10 years. This could cause significant harm if the improvement was a stand-alone product with an economic life lasting well beyond the 10 years left in the license and still protected by copyright and the right to use the improvement was lost on the termination of the right to use the unimproved technology.

TACTIC:
Co-relate the terms of use of improvements with the term of the
underlying license.

Only in Canada, You Say?

Earlier I mentioned that the improvement clause may be valid in Canada. This is not likely the case in the United States due to its restraint of trade rules. These rules might invalidate any provision that does more than require InterCo to grant to DevCo a worldwide, nonexclusive, royalty-free license with the right to grant sublicenses. In Canada we must always be wary that many of our practices may be in violation of the rules of other jurisdictions that are designed to promote competition.

TACTIC:
Watch applicable antirestraint of trade rules.

WARRANTIES

Dreadful Drafter sees that his president has also written on the envelope "Provide no warranties." Dreadful Drafter decides that a disclaimer of all warranties of quality[49] should be included and writes a clause that was (and still may be) a standard in the U.S. software industry: "DevCo gives no warranties expressed or implied except as specifically provided in this Agreement: WITHOUT LIMITATION, ALL IMPLIED WARRANTIES OF MERCHANT ABILITY AND FITNESS FOR A SPECIFIC PURPOSE ARE SPECIFICALLY DISCLAIMED."

A Warranty by Any Other Name

A disclaimer of "warranties" may be useful in the United States under Section 2 of the Uniform Commercial Code. However, in Alberta, the Sale of Goods Act (Alberta), if it applies, refers to implied "conditions" of merchantability and fitness for a particular purpose.[50] The same words are used in Ontario's[51] sale of goods legislation.

TACTICS:
Design warranties that are "fit for the purpose."
Avoid clauses drafted for the specific rules of other jurisdictions.

You Wanted It to Work?

It is a moot point whether either of the Sale of Goods Act (Alberta) and Section 2 of the Uniform Commercial Code[52] applies to computer programs that are not mass-marketed. None of these pieces of legislation were designed to cover software. The attempts to force software into the unaccommodating legislative schemes produce potentially absurd results. Is the software a *good* if conveyed to the client on a disk but not a *good* if conveyed electronically with no physical copy being delivered?[53] A prudent licensing drafter might want to assume that the sale of goods legislation applies. It is rare that the implied warranties are appropriate for products (particularly computer programs) licensed by a specifically designed licensing agreement. Accordingly, Dreadful Drafter was correct to disclaim the implied warranties of quality but should structure the disclaimer using words appropriate for Alberta and the United States, and at least refer to all "representations, warranties and conditions (expressed or implied, oral or written)."[54]

TACTIC:
Tailor warranties for each technology transfer.

Disclaimer "Fundamentally Breaches Its Essential Purpose"

The DevCo president said there shall be "no warranties." However, the courts in Alberta and the United States are not favorably predisposed to accept complete disclaimers of warranties of quality of goods, particularly if the bargaining powers of the two parties are not equal.[55] Alberta courts look to see if there is a "breach" going to the root of the contract.[56] U.S. courts speak of the agreement "failing of its essential purposes"[57] or of "unconscionability."[58]

DevCo will have to decide whether there are sufficient grounds to justify the exclusions of warranties of quality so it can survive arguments of breach going to the root of the contract, failure of essential purpose, unconscionability, or unreasonableness. If there is any reasonable risk, DevCo should consider providing a few basic warranties designed to prevent opening the door wide to a damage claim.

TACTIC:

Be satisfied that a total disclaimer of warranties of quality is appropriate.

Basic Warranties of Quality

Dreadful Drafter decides that he should provide some basic warranties of quality. He writes, "DevCo warrants that the Licensed Software shall function if used in accordance with the user manual."

Dreadful Drafter might not have specified an objective standard of quality. Did he mean that it would function in accordance with the specifications expressed in the user manual? Or is use in accordance with the user manual a condition precedent to the warranty?

Dreadful Drafter should precisely set out the standards of quality. He might want to consider the following:

- What standards of quality will be used?
  - Are there currently developed functional specifications? Are these specifications clearly and precisely written?
  - If the functional specifications are not yet developed, how will they be approved so they can be used as standards of quality?
- Will there be acceptance tests, and if so, how will they be designed?
- Who will perform the acceptance tests? Where? At whose expense? What periods of rectification are allowed? What are the consequences of acceptance tests not being passed?
- Will there be conditions precedent to a warranty claim? Is it fair for the licensee to lose its remedies if a condition precedent is not satisfied?

- How will the parties resolve disputes over quality?
- What are the remedies of breach of warranty? Are there any limitations on liability?

TACTIC:
Specify standards of quality.

Conditional Warranties

Let us assume that Dreadful Drafter wanted to make the warranty conditional upon the Licensed Software being used in accordance with the user manual. Often the benefits of warranties are available only upon the satisfaction of various conditions precedent. All too frequently, however, the conditions precedent have no correlation with the error that is actually encountered. Did the failure to operate in accordance with the user manual actually cause the quality defect that was encountered? Is it unreasonable to have the warranty voided for the nonsatisfaction of an irrelevant condition precedent?

TACTIC:
Correlate conditions precedent to a warranty to the quality defect.

Back-Up Remedy

Dreadful Drafter might have written as his warranty, "DevCo warrants that the Licensed Software, when installed, shall perform in accordance with the Functional Specifications [defined elsewhere]. All other warranties expressed or implied, including all implied warranties of merchantability and fit for a specific purpose, are specifically disclaimed."

Consider DevCo being unable to install the Licensed Software due to technical errors. A court will be eager to hold that the only warranty is ineffective, and therefore the disclaimer is ineffective.[59] Dreadful Drafter failed to provide any back-up remedy in the event that DevCo's warranties all proved to be ineffective.

Some agreements provide for the possibility that the basic warranties provided are found to be unreasonable or do not cover the breach that actually occurs.[60] This concern is especially significant when the only warranties provided are to repair or replace the defective product. These agreements go on to provide a "back-up remedy," such as payment of an amount pre-agreed to be liquidated damages or payment of the Licensee's direct damages up to a maximum dollar amount.[61]

TACTIC:
Consider providing a back-up remedy.

DREADFUL DRAFTER ADDRESSES THE
WARRANTY OF OWNERSHIP

Dreadful Drafter recognizes that InterCo will want some assurance that it will gain the benefit of the Licensed Software and writes, "DevCo warrants that it owns the Licensed Software."

What Is Ownership?

"Ownership" may connote the following:

- *DevCo has title to the Licensed Software.* Title is a phrase useful in real estate, particularly in those jurisdictions such as Alberta that have a title registry system that is guaranteed by the government. Unfortunately, there is no title registry for intellectual property rights. The issue of a patent does not indicate that the holder of the patent owns it, or even that the claims are valid. The law gives property-like protection to trade secrets, but perhaps not ownership and certainly not a title.
- *An indicia of ownership of property is the right to exclude others from the use and enjoyment of that property.* This might imply warranty that intellectual property rights are valid and subsisting.
- *Another indicia of ownership of property is the right to use and enjoy that property.* This might imply that there is no claim for infringement that might impede that use or enjoyment. Thus, Dreadful Drafter may have difficulty with his client when it discovers the inadvertent scope of the ownership warranty.
- Section 401 of the model *Uniform Computer Information Transactions Act* (UCITA) discusses a warranty of quiet enjoyment, or what is called an *interference warranty*, which also suggests a warranty that there is not, and will not be in the future, any action by the licensor that will diminish the grant by the licensor to the licensee. UCITA suggests in section 401(b)(1), "A licensor warrants (1) for the duration of the license, that no person holds a right to, or interest in, information [a defined phrase] which arose from an act or omission of the licensor, other than a claim by way of infringement, which will interfere with the licensee's enjoyment of its interest."

This clause might become popular if drafters can convince their clients that quiet enjoyment does not mean that there will be quiet, nor that the interest will be actually enjoyed! But for trade secrets, it does seem to be a better phrase than trying to deal with "possession" or such other phrases that may add little to the debate as to what is ownership.

Clarifying Sole Ownership

InterCo might respond that this warranty is fine as far as it goes, but does not go far enough. Dreadful Drafter did not specify that DevCo was the sole owner of the Licensed Software; thus, InterCo could be faced with the surprise that it was sharing the benefits of the Licensed Software with others.

The discussion notes for section 401 of UCITA bring up the issue of exclusivity as to ownership: For a U.S. license to actually grant exclusive rights, the licensor has to have exclusive ownership. One joint owner could defeat another joint owner's exclusive license by granting licenses under its partial ownership interest. Thus Section 401 would require a warranty that there are no other owners; a warranty of ownership by itself is not sufficient. In Canada, unless permitted by contract, the freedom of one joint owner to license without the consent of the joint owner in Canada would not be possible.

TACTIC:
Quietly own the licensed software.

DREADFUL DRAFTER WRITES THE TERM AND TERMINATION CLAUSE

Dreadful Drafter sees the last note from his president: "five-year term, renewable," and writes, "This agreement shall take effect as of February 1, 2001 and shall continue in effect until January 31, 2006 and thereafter for successive periods of five years." He then proceeds to include the usual provisions that the agreement will terminate on insolvency, unremedied breach, or "upon 12 months notice from either party."

Does the agreement terminate January 31, 2006? Note that Dreadful Drafter did not provide that the agreement will renew automatically after every five-year period unless terminated by either party at the end of the fifth year. Thus, the five-year term is irrelevant; the term will not expire after five years but keep running for an indefinite period until either party gives the 12 months' notice. The Courts will not read in different conditions of termination when termination has been provided for in a license.[62]

Frequently, agreements provide for a long term such as five years or life of the patent, but subsequently provide for termination after the expiration of a shorter period following one of the parties giving notice to the other. In these agreements, for all practical purposes, the term that the parties can rely on for business purposes is only the shorter term. The business decision maker could be deceived by the reference to the longer term.

TACTIC:
State clearly the effective term of the agreement.

License Exceeding the Patent Term

Dreadful Drafter should keep in mind that in Canada, parties may contract for the term of a license of technology to exceed the term of its patent protection.[63] In contrast, the U.S. antirestraint of trade rules may limit the obligations under a simple patent license to the term of the patent protection.

TACTIC:
Avoid excesses.

Terminating Events

Dreadful Drafter provided that the agreement itself shall terminate upon the happening of certain events. What happens to all the *rights and remedies* after termination of the agreement? A better approach for Dreadful Drafter might be to determine all the rights and obligations in the agreement that require termination and then draft a termination clause for each group of similar rights and obligations. The converse of this approach is to consider what provisions of the agreement shall "survive" termination of the agreement.[64]

TACTIC:
Define the terminating events for each right and obligation.

Consequences of Termination

Dreadful Drafter could now consider the consequences of the termination, including:

- The Licensee ceasing to use the Licensed Software
- The Licensee ceasing to use the Licensor's trademarks and logos
- The Licensee returning to the Licensor all copies of the License Software in its possession
- If the Licensee does not have the right to return all copies of the Licensed Software which are on hand for the purposes of resale, consider what right the Licensee has to dispose of its inventory.
- If the Licensee has the right to dispose of inventory on hand at termination, the Licensor might want to have the right to perform an audit of this inventory. Otherwise, the Licensed Software might be reproduced surreptitiously following termination, and the Licensor would have no way of separating pre-termination copies from copies made after the termination.

- The Licensee paying all royalties earned pre-termination and, if the Licensee has the right to sell its inventory, after termination
- The Licensor having a right to audit the Licensee's books and premises to satisfy itself that it has been paid in full and that the Licensee has ceased to use and reproduce the Licensed Software

TACTIC:
Forgetting consequences may be damaging.

INCLUSIVE LANGUAGE

Dreadful Drafter included in his boilerplate, at the end of the agreement, a standard provision with an interesting typographical error: "words importing the masculine gender shall include the feminine and *neutered* gender."

This word "neutered" might apply to my Garfield-sized, ex-Tom cat. It would seem to have little other application.

Increasingly, drafters are endeavoring to use inclusive language to avoid a masculine bias.[65] With today's word-processing capabilities, there is no excuse to use the masculine when the feminine could just as easily be used. I am often surprised to see the masculine used when my client is feminine. Unfortunately, writing genderless English is very difficult,[66] and this bias may never be overcome. The use of "you" and "we" in documents may help.

TACTIC:
Strive for inclusive language.

CONCLUSION

Drafters of licensing agreements should facilitate open communication, prevent misinterpretation, and prevent unintended business and legal results. Instead of Dreadful Drafting, licensing drafters can produce precise and comprehensible agreements.

AUTHOR'S NOTE

If you have comments on my material or if you have examples of dreadful drafting you would like to see included in a later version, please contact me, John T. Ramsay, at (403) 298-1996, or fax (403) 263-9193, or email: john.ramsay@gowlings.com.

ENDNOTES

[1] Alberta, fortunately or unfortunately, has very little statutory or case law regulating software licensing and has a significant number of software developers working in a global economy.

[2] His success may be attributed to his adoption of the method of negotiations described in *Getting to Yes, Negotiating Agreements Without Giving In*, by Roger Fisher and William Ury of the Harvard Negotiation Project (New York: Penguin Books, 1991).

[3] Section 2(b) of the draft will be the release of the licensor by the licensee; the release must be bilateral.

[4] David Mellinkoff, *Legal Writing: Sense & Nonsense* (St. Paul, MN: West Publishing Co., 1982), 130.

[5] Mellinkoff, 58.

[6] R.C. Dick, Q.C., *Legal Drafting in Plain Language*, 3rd ed. (Toronto: Carswell, 1995), 12.

[7] Dick, 119, where he lists six conventional rules for paragraph sculpturing.

[8] Mellinkoff, 1.

[9] Now we can recognize that Dreadful Drafter has been too broad in his release; instead of all claims, he should have restricted the release to claims arising out of the 1999 License Agreement.

[10] Dick, 77, quoting from R. Dickerson, *The Fundamentals of Legal Drafting* (Boston and Toronto: Little, Brown and Company, 1965), 98. Dick provides a helpful discussion of the various types of definitions.

[11] Mellinkoff, 26.

[12] Dick, 126.

[13] Mellinkoff says on p. 126: "The explanations for wordiness in legal writing do not justify keeping it that way."

[14] Dick suggests on p. 127 that this insecurity may result from inadequate training. This is true to some extent, but many adequately trained and skilled drafters still suffer from this insecurity.

[15] Dick provides, on pp. 127–129, a list of "couplets" and "triplets" that could be reduced to a single word. The usual drafting jingles that surround the word *releases* is included in that list.

[16] Mellinkoff, 18.

[17] Mellinkoff, 187.

[18] Mellinkoff, 19.

[19] Another company has produced what they call the "Bloodthirsty License Agreement" and the following is an extract from that agreement (I would give credit if I knew where it came from):

Bloodthirsty License Agreement

This is where the bloodthirsty license agreement is supposed to go, explaining that Interactive EasyFlow is a copyrighted package, sternly warning you not to pirate copies of it and explaining, in detail, the gory consequences if you do.

We know that you are an honest person, and are not going to go around pirating copies of Interactive EasyFlow; this is just as well with us, since we worked hard to perfect it and selling copies of it is our only method of making anything out of all the hard work.

If, on the other hand, you are one of those few people who do go around pirating copies of software, you probably aren't going to pay much attention to a license agreement, bloodthirsty or not. Just keep your doors locked and look out for the HavenTree attack shark.

Honest Disclaimer

We don't claim Interactive EasyFlow is good for anything—if you think it is, great, but it's up to you to decide. If Interactive EasyFlow doesn't work: tough. If you lose a million because Interactive EasyFlow messes up, it's you that's out the million, not us. If you don't like this disclaimer: tough. We reserve the right to do the absolute minimum provided by law, up to and including nothing.

This is basically the same disclaimer that comes with all software packages, but ours is in plain English and theirs is in legalese.

We didn't really want to include any disclaimer at all, but our lawyers insisted. We tried to ignore them but they threatened us with the attack shark . . . at which point we relented.

[20] Mellinkoff, 100.

[21] R. Goldscheider, *The New Companion to Licensing Negotiations Licensing Law Handbook 2000–2001* (New York: West Group).

[22] Editor's note: *Embody* is a word that connotes something tangible; the Licensed Software is intangible. Is Dreadful Drafter fictional or really the alter ego of the author?

[23] Thanks to Brian Brunsvold for this example, given in his presentation *Negotiating and Drafting—Transfer of Improvements*, as presented at the Licensing Executives Society (United States and Canada) Summer 2001 Meeting in Kananaskis, Alberta.

[24] *Forget v. Specialty Tools of Canada Inc.* [1995] B.C.J. No. 1653.

[25] T. Gene Dillahunty, *How to (And How Not to) Deal with Inventorship in Joint Development Agreements*, as presented at the Licensing Executives Society (United States and Canada) Summer 2001 Meeting in Kananaskis, Alberta.

[26] Dillahunty, 7.

[27] Dillahunty, 5.

[28] D.G. Henderson, Q.C, *Patent Licensing: Problems from the Imprecision of the English Language* (1970), 4 Ottawa L. Rev, 62, 66.

[29] Ibid.

[30] *CAE Industries Ltd.* v. *R.* (1982), [1983] 2 F.C. 616 at 638, 639 referring to *Sheffleld Dist. Ry. Co.* v. *Great Central Ry. Co.* (1911), 27T.L.R. 451. There seems to be no distinction between best efforts and best endeavors for this purpose. This case law is totally out of line with commercial expectations in technology transfer agreements.

[31] Charles W. Shifley and Bradley J. Hulbert, "'Best Efforts' May Not Be The Best Advice*", les Nouvelles* Vol XXVII, No.1 (March 1992): 37 at 39. This article provides an interesting analysis of best efforts clauses providing a summary of legal decisions, practical examples of difficulties caused by the phrase, and suggested improvements.

[32] For a checklist of what to include in a confidentiality agreement, see the Checklist attached as Appendix A 2.A to the chapter on "Canada, Worldwide Trade Secrets Law," Vol. 1 (Clarke Boardman Callaghan, 1993) at A 2-1 (the Canadian chapter being co-authored by John T. Ramsay and Francois Grenier).

[33] John H. Woodley, "Taking Care of Trade Secrets: Controlling and Exploiting," *Trade Secrets in Law and Practice* (The Law Society of Upper Canada, 1989) C-1 at C-4.

[34] Institute of Law Research and Reform, *Trade Secrets*, Report No.46 (Edmonton: Institute of Law Research and Reform, 1986) 157.

[35] Ibid, 6.

[36] David Vaver, "What is a Trade Secret," *Trade Secrets in Law and Practice* (The Law Society of Upper Canada, 1989) A-1 at A-18.

[37] Quoted from the annotation to *International Corona Resources Ltd.* v. *LAC Minerals Ltd.*, 44 B.L.R. 1 at 9.

[38] *Taylor* v. *Gill* (1991).78 Alta. L.R. (2d) 349 (Q.B.).

[39] Richard A. Brait, an active Licensing Executive Society member with Northern Telecom Canada Limited, Mississauga, Ontario, disagrees with me in his excellent article, "The Unauthorized Use of Confidential Information," 18 C.B.L. 323, at 371. In order to permit full restitution through the constructive trust remedy, he would recommend the use of the word *trust*. Even if a confidant was prepared to accept the exposure to full liability that Brait is advocating, it is my position that the duty of care imposed by the trust relationship is excessive. Additionally, once the confidant has taken

the reasonable measures described in Section 7.10 of this material, he should be free of a liability resulting from an inadvertent disclosure of the confidential information, a position supported by Brait.

[40] [1904] 3 W.W.R. 419 at 425,426.

[41] *The Shorter Oxford English Dictionary*, Vol. I (New York: Oxford University Press, 1973), 663.

[42] J. T. Ramsay, *Drafting Confidentiality Agreements in Canada* (1989) 4 I.P.J. 157 at 175.

[43] Restraint of trade rules may restrict the duration of the requirement to maintain secrecy to this latter period of time.

[44] Adapted from *National Broach & Machine Co.* v. *Churchill Gear Machines Ltd.* [1967] R. Pat. Cas. 99 (H.L.), cited in Henderson, 74.

[45] Henderson, 71. See also *PRC Realty Systems* v. *National Association of Realtors, Inc.* 766 F. Supp 453 (E.D. Va 1991) 459.

[46] Dillahunty would argue that infringement is rarely a good standard; the standard would be better served in a market-defined, exclusive field-of-use approach. Others suggest that patent infringement is not a good standard because it is difficult to be sure when infringement occurs without judicial interpretation.

[47] *Delrina Corp.* v. *TrioJet Systems Inc.* 47 C.P .R. (3d) 1 at p. 37, Ont. Ct. .Gen. Divi., 1993.

[48] 2d Circuit U.S. Court of Appeals. 982 F 2nd at 705.

[49] Let us assume that Dreadful Drafter has handled elsewhere warranties of title and noninfringement and any statutory rights to reject the Licensed Software.

[50] R.S.A. 1980. c. S-2, ss. 17(2) and 17(4).

[51] *Sale of Goods Act*, R.S.O. 1990, c. S-I, s. 15.

[52] For examples of the many articles and cases discussing this issue, see W.P. Andrews, Jr., *Limiting Risks in International Transactions: Current Legal Issues in United States Domestic Transactions for Computer Goods and Services* (Address to the World Computer Congress, April 18–20, 1991).

[53] "UCC Survey: Software Transactions on Uniformity," *The Business Lawyer* 46 (August 1991): 1829.

[54] Working Draft No. 3.0 of the Model Software License Provisions developed by American Bar Association Section on Patent and Trademarket and Copyright Law, Committee on Computer Program of which J. T. Ramsay was one of the committee members (the "Model Software Agreement") provides in Section 6.06 the following:

"LICENSOR DISCLAIMS ANY AND ALL OTHER WARRANTIES, CONDI-
TIONS, OR REPRESENTATIONS (EXPRESS OR IMPLIED, ORAL OR
WRITTEN) WITH RESPECT TO THE LICENSED SOFTWARE OR ANY
PART THEREOF, INCLUDING ANY AND ALL IMPLIED WARRANTIES OR
CONDITIONS OF TITLE, NON-INFRINGEMENT, MERCHANTABILITY,
OR FITNESS OR SUITABILITY FOR ANY PURPOSE (WHETHER OR NOT
LICENSOR KNOWS, HAS REASON TO KNOW, HAS BEEN ADVISED, OR
IS OTHERWISE IN FACT AWARE OF ANY SUCH PURPOSE), WHETHER
ALLEGED TO ARISE BY LAW, BY REASON OF CUSTOM OR USAGE IN
THE TRADE, OR BY COURSE OF DEALING. IN ADDITION, LICENSOR
EXPRESSLY DISCLAIMS ANY WARRANTY OR REPRESENTATION TO
ANY PERSON OTHER THAN LICENSEE WITH RESPECT TO THE
LICENSED SOFTWARE OR ANY PART THEREOF."

[55] In one case, the court had no problem accepting a complete disclaimer
contained in a signed contract where the licensee, Firestone, was a large
sophisticated corporation. See *Bridgestone/Firestone Inc.* v. *Oracle Corp.*,
No. C-91-1420-DL], 2 CCH Computer Cases, para 46,519 (U.S. Dist. Ct.
N.D. C.A. 8/1 1991, as digested by Software Law.

[56] *Bank of British Columbia* v. *Turbo Resources Ltd.* (1983), 148 D.L.R. (3d)
598 (Alta C.A.) Bulletin, Oct/Nov 1991 at 211.

[57] UCC 2-719 (2) as mentioned by "UCC Survey," p. 1851.

[58] See UCC 2-719(3), as mentioned by Andrews, 14. With the U.S. law in
mind the drafter should consider the various tests for unconscionability
articulated under Section 2- 719(3), as referred by Andrews, 14.

[59] See *Hawaiian Telephone Company* v. *Microform Data Systems*, 829 F. 2d
919 (9th Cir. 1987).

[60] For example, see the Model Software Agreement, Section 6.07.

[61] Ibid.

[62] Ronald B. Coolley, "Importance of Termination Clauses," *les Nouvelles*
(December 1990, 1969), referring to *Nicholas Laboratories. Ltd.* v. *Almay.
Inc.* .723 F. Supp 1015 at 1017–1018 (S.D.N.Y. 1989), aff'd 900 F. 2d 19
(2d Cir 1990).

[63] Henderson, 79, citing *British Repetition Ltd.* v. *Formento Ltd.*, [1961] R.
Pat. Cas. 222 (Ch.).

[64] Coolley, 169.

[65] Dick, 165.

[66] Dick, 165.

ABOUT THE AUTHOR

John T. Ramsay, Q.C., has practiced in the areas of corporate and commercial law in Calgary since 1968, first as a partner in a medium-sized firm, and then as a partner with his wife. Before joining Gowling Lafleur Henderson LLP as a partner in January 2001, John was a partner with the firm of Macleod Dixon since 1984. He has acted as counsel to closely held businesses throughout his career and, since 1977, to developers and users of technology, particularly computer software. John has been rated by LEXPERT as one of Canada's leading lawyers in intellectual property and in computer law.

Ramsay is a member of the Licensing Executives Society (United States and Canada) Inc., chairman of the Licensing Executives Society Spring Meeting (June 2001) in Kananaskis, Alberta, and also a member of the Society's Editoral Review Board for that Society's panel, "les Novelles" including doing book reviews. He is also an active participant in Intermediate/Advanced Professional Development Committees, and a contributor of content to their courses.

Part Two

New Outlooks on Patents, Trademarks, Copyrights, and Trade Secrets

5

Recent Changes in Patenting Procedures and Protection: Developments in the European and U.S. Patent Systems

By Dr. Heinz Goddar and Alan H. Gordon

INTRODUCTION

The intellectual property (IP) world in Europe, including licensing regulations, is rapidly changing. Some new laws and regulations have already come into force, and other modifications are to follow shortly. This chapter provides a brief overview with regard to the most important drafts of regulations of this kind, which will affect the world of IP protection and licensing in Europe dramatically.

First, we look at forthcoming changes of the European Patent Convention (EPC), in accordance with a Revision Act approved by a Diplomatic Conference of the EPC member states, which took place at Munich during the period of November 20–29, 2000. The Revision Act and thereby the revised text of the EPC will take effect two years after the fifteenth member state has deposited its instrument of ratification or accession, or on the first day of the third month following the deposit of the instrument of ratification or accession by the last member state taking this step, if this takes place earlier.

The next draft of the Revision Act in this regard is the draft of a European Union (EU) Council Regulation on the Community Patent, which was issued, as Revision Act COM (2000) 412 final, on August 1, 2000, such Community Patent being dealt with in a separate chapter of this book.

Both the Revision Acts, which will probably result in drastic changes of patent protection in Europe over the next few years, will have a heavy influence on licensing in and with Europe. Bear in mind that the general importance of the patent system is to create and protect licensable technology rights.

PLANNED CHANGES OF THE
EUROPEAN PATENT CONVENTION (EPC)

Without attempting to be complete, this section will discuss major changes as intended to take place with regard to the European Patent Convention—first, generally, and then more specifically with regard to certain articles of the EPC that will probably have the greatest importance.

Relation between the Convention and the Implementing Regulations

Many provisions, such as those relating to the manner in which applications filed in languages other than one of the official languages of the EPC (English, French, German), are transferred from the EPC into the Implementing Regulations. This transfer will make it much easier to modify such provisions by a qualified majority vote within the Administration Council of the EPC, and not necessarily by a unanimous vote of the member states of the European Patent Convention; the qualification rules are laid down in the Revision Act.

Patentability

According to the revised Articles 52 and 53 of the Revision Act, European patents in the future will be granted for any inventions in all fields of technology, provided that they are new, involve an inventive step, and are susceptible to industrial application (Article 52(1)).

Article 52(1)(c) will still exclude patents for computer programs and for methods for doing business as such. Practically that will mean, however, that in the future—in view of the rather liberal practice of the EPO—inventions of the aforementioned kind will be patentable under the EPC, provided that in a more-or-less formal manner, technical elements, even in the form of data carrier features, are included into the patent claims.

Novelty

According to the current Revision Act, Article 54(4) is deleted. That provision means that prior applications, not yet published at the priority date, until now have only been considered as prior art, for novelty only, insofar as a contracting state designated in respect of the later application was also designated in respect of the earlier application as published. The new version will mean that contents of European patent applications will be considered for their potential to destroy novelty, even if there is not an overlap of the designated states. This will not, of course, apply to inventiveness, in which case such prior applications also in future will not play any role at all.

Designation of States

In the future, according to the new version of Article 79, all the contracting states party to the European Patent Convention at the time of filing of a European patent application will be deemed to be designated. Designation fees are subject to a "may" clause—that means one possibility is envisaging that no designation fees would become payable some time in future.

Limitation (Restriction) and Revocation

According to a new Article 105(a) suggested by the Revision Act, at the request of the proprietor a European patent may be revoked or limited by an amendment of the claims.

   In the past it was not possible for the proprietor itself to request revocation of the whole European patent. Also, and of greater importance, limitation was not possible. Now that the limitation procedure affecting the whole European patent is possible during the lifetime of the patent (a procedure similar to the restriction procedure already known for German patents, for example), it will be possible to streamline European patents before starting any litigation, thereby minimizing the risk of invalidation requests being successfully filed, at least partially, against European patents in case of litigation.

Petition for Review by the Enlarged Board of Appeal

According to a new Article 112(a), any party to appeal proceedings adversely affected by the decision of a Board of Appeal of the EPO may file a petition for review of the decision by the Enlarged Board of Appeal. The petition may only be filed on one of the grounds exhaustively described in the new Article 112(a), but this exhaustive list contains rather broad formulations, such that in the future the Enlarged Board of Appeal may play a court-like role to supervise the Boards of Appeal of the EPO in a much stronger manner than in the past.

Regional Agreements

According to a new Article 149(a) EPC, all of the contracting states or some of them may conclude special agreements on any matters concerning European patent applications or European patents, which under the EPC are subject to and governed by national law, particularly by establishing a European Patent Court common to the contracting states party to it; the same applying to agreements under which the contracting states party to it dispense fully or in part with translations of European patents into the languages of designated countries, and agreements under which translations of European patents may be filed with and published by the European Patent Office.

The aforementioned provisions will enable the European Union (EU) to establish a Community Patent system as a regional part under the ceiling of the European Patent Convention.

Conference Resolution

The Diplomatic Conference has unanimously agreed on a Conference Resolution by which the Administrative Council and other relevant bodies of the EPC are urged to make preparations for another Diplomatic Conference. Proposals for further revision to be discussed at such a next Diplomatic Conference shall relate to software and any changes that are required to implement the forthcoming Community Patent without delay. This is discussed shortly. The next Diplomatic Conference was expected to take place mid-2002 at Munich.

STATUS OF TRANSLATION PROBLEM IN EPC

On a separate field, different from the revision of the whole EPC as just discussed, a number of member states of the EPC are discussing the possibility of renouncing for their territories the necessity to file full translations of EPC- based patents in situations where the official language of the EPC-based patent is different from the country's language. The status of the respective discussion is that the necessary minimum eight countries—among them France, Germany, and the United Kingdom—have approved the *Language Protocol*, so that now the respective ratification procedures will start in those countries. If everything goes swiftly, within the foreseeable future the language requirements (i.e., necessity of translations to be filed in all designated countries under the EPC) will be considerably smoother.

NEW U.S. PATENT LEGISLATION

The American Inventors Protection Act of 1999 was signed into law on November 29, 1999. This law affects, as of various dates in 1999 and 2000, the operations of the U.S. Patent and Trademark Office (USPTO) and the practitioners soliciting patents on behalf of potential licensors. Some key provisions of the new law are summarized in the following paragraphs.

The Inventors' Rights Act of 1999

The Inventors' Rights Act of 1999, a section of the American Inventors Protection Act of 1999, became effective January 28, 2000, and helps protect inventors from the deceptive practices of certain invention promotion companies. As of the effective date, invention promoters are required to disclose in writing the number of positive and negative evaluations of inventions they have given over a five-year period, as well as the success of their customers in receiving financial profit and license agreements as a direct result of the services provided by the invention promotion company. Customers injured by the failure of the invention promotion company to disclose this required information can recover up to $5,000 or actual damages. Intentional or willful violations may result in a trebling of the amount awarded.

The phrase *invention promotion services* is defined as the procurement or attempted procurement for a customer to develop and market products or ser-vices that include the invention of the customer. There is no general exception for registered patent practitioners. However, persons involved in the offering to license or sell a utility patent or a previously filed provisional patent application are excluded from coverage. Complaints received by the USPTO concerning invention promotion companies, together with the responses to the complaints, are required to be publicized.

The Patent and Trademark Fee Fairness Act of 1999

This section of the American Inventors Protection Act of 1999, effective December 29, 1999, reduces certain patent fees. The original filing fee, the reissue fee, and the international application fees are each reduced from $760 to $690. The initial maintenance fee is reduced from $940 to $830. These reductions are expected to save inventors about $30 million annually.

The First Inventor Defense Act of 1999

This section of the American Inventors Protection Act of 1999 provides a limited defense to certain infringement actions where the asserted claim is directed to a business method. Inasmuch as the USPTO has not been required to change any of its procedures, no rulemaking is likely. Court decisions will guide the evolution of this portion of the AIPA of 1999.

The Patent Term Guarantee Act of 1999

This section of the American Inventors Protection Act of 1999 provides for the adjustment of the term of patents issuing from utility (and plant) applications filed on or after May 29, 2000. An objective of the law is to guarantee a minimum 17-year patent term for diligent applicants so that they are not penalized for certain USPTO processing delays or delays in the prosecution of applications pending more than three years.

The new law provides three bases of adjustment of the patent term. The first basis provides an extension when the USPTO fails to act on an application within specified time periods. The second basis provides an extension when the USPTO fails to issue a patent within three years of the actual filing date, subject to a number of statutory restrictions. The third basis for an extension relates to the time consumed by interferences, secrecy orders, and successful appeals. The other side of this benefit is the reduction of the patent-term adjustment for the time during which an applicant failed to engage in reasonable efforts to conclude the prosecution of an application. Rules promulgated by the USPTO govern the conduct of practitioners who intend to protect the rights offered under this law.

The Domestic Publication of Patent Applications Published Abroad Act of 1999

This section of the American Inventors Protection Act of 1999 provides for the publication of most applications filed on or after November 29, 2000, 18 months after the earliest effective filing date or priority date claimed by the application. The law also provides for the publication of only a portion of an application's disclosure for applicants disclosing more subject matter in the U.S. application than in any corresponding foreign application. The law further provides for publication of applications filed before November 29, 2000, at the request of an applicant, and for publication of applications filed after that date earlier than 18 months after filing.

The law provides for prior art treatment of published applications based on the application's effective filing date. Provisional rights are available from the period of publication of the application to the issue date. An applicant who has not and will not file in a foreign country or under an international treaty that publishes applications after an 18-month period from the effective filing date or priority date may request nonpublication. However, the request for nonpublication must be made at the time the application is filed. Recission of the request for nonpublication may be accomplished at any time and must be done to avoid abandonment of the application if a foreign filing is made after making the request for nonpublication. Regulations govern the particular form for the requests (electronic), the timing of requests for the benefit of foreign priority claims, and procedures for submission to the USPTO by third parties of prior art documents following publication of an application.

The publication of applications under this new section of the law will enable U.S. inventors to see at a much earlier stage an English translation of the applications filed by foreign inventors. This has the dual effect of revealing the state of the art earlier to serve as an input on wise licensing decisions as well as generally making available more prior art for consideration in the prosecution of patent applications.

The Optional Inter Partes Reexamination Procedure Act of 1999

This section of the American Inventors Protection Act of 1999 provides an option to the established *ex parte* reexamination for applications filed after November 29, 1999. The new reexamination option expands the participation of third-party requesters. Under the new option, the requester is permitted to submit a written request each time the patent owner files a response to the USPTO. However, the requester who selects this alternative is not permitted to appeal an adverse decision beyond the level of the Board of Patent Appeals and Interferences or to participate in any appeal taken by the patent owner to the Court of Appeals for the Federal Circuit.

In addition, the requester selecting this option will not be able to challenge in a later civil action any fact determined, or that could have been determined, during the optional reexamination procedure. An objective of this section of the new law is to reduce litigation in district courts and make patent reexamination a more viable and affordable alternative to litigation.

The Miscellaneous Patent Provisions

This section of the American Inventors Protection Act of 1999 makes a number of technical and clarifying changes to the patent law. For example, this section provides for electronic filing, maintenance, and publication of documents. It also provides for the exclusion of commonly owned or assigned patents used in obviousness rejections applied against the later invention if the patent is available as prior art only under 35 U.S.C. §102(e).

NEW U.S. COURT DECISIONS

Decisions by various U.S. courts have affected the way patent law is applied in the United States. This section looks at two key decisions: *State Street Bank & Trust Co.* v. *Signature Financial Group Inc.* and *Festo Corporation* v. *Shoketsu Kinsoku Kogyo Kadushiki Co., Ltd.*

The *State Street Bank* Decision—Business Methods Patents

On July 23, 1998, the decision by the Court of Appeals for the Federal Circuit in *State Street Bank & Trust Co.* v. *Signature Financial Group Inc.* shattered earlier precedent that theretofore had refused patenting business methods as nonstatutory subject matter under U.S. law. The decision announced that it was laying to rest the "ill-conceived exception" to patentability for business methods. The court stated that business methods should be subject to the same legal requirements for patentability as applied to any other process or method. However, the term *business method claim* has not yet been defined when compared with other process claims. As a result, there is some confusion over what constitutes a business method claim.

The *State Street Bank* decision predictably led to a significant increase in applications directed to Class 705 (data processing: financial, business practice, management, or cost/price determination). In 1997 there were 927 applications filed in Class 705. In 2000 this number soared to 7,800 applications. The change in the focus of the applications following the *State Street Bank* decision required a shift in the knowledge base for examiners in Class 705. The USPTO is seeking training for the examiners in more than a dozen new areas for patent applications. For example, there are applications being received for payment schemes, insurance, e-shopping, point of sale, inventory, accounting, coupons and electronic incentive programs, health care management, and reservation systems.

To improve the quality of patents issuing from Class 705 (and perhaps in response to criticism that too many invalid patents are issuing), a second review procedure has been instituted in this area. The USPTO is exploring the use of third-party consultants to create a prior art database.

Class 705 is not the only class into which business methods might be classified. For example, methods of teaching are classified in Class 434; methods of playing games are classified in Class 273; methods of improving crop yields are classified in Class 47. Only computer-implemented processes related to e-commerce, the Internet, and data processing involving finance, business practices, management, or cost/price determination are classified in Class 705. All other applications that may be labeled a *business methods-type application* will be classified, assigned, and examined according to their technology.

The *Festo* Decision—Limitations on the Scope of Claim Coverage

In the year 2000 the U.S. Court of Appeals for the Federal Circuit sitting en banc (all judges sitting) decided an important patent case that changed the law of patent infringement in a major respect. This is likely the most significant opinion from the Federal Circuit in 2000. In *Festo Corporation* v. *Shoketsu Kinsoku Kogyo Kadushiki Co., Ltd.,* the doctrine of equivalents was significantly limited to reduce the scope of coverage of patent claims.

Historically, the U.S. courts recognized the need for some equitable doctrine to prevent infringers from making insubstantial changes to a claimed invention for the sole purpose of avoiding infringement liability. Even though a claim element was not literally found in an accused device or method, if the accused subject matter had an element that performed substantially the same function in substantially the same way to achieve substantially the same result, then infringement was established, nonetheless.

On the other hand, the U.S. courts also have recognized the need for competitors to have a fair notice of the scope of the coverage of patent claims so that legitimate design-around efforts could take place with reasonable certainty that the claims were being avoided. The Court in the *Festo* decision severely limited the availability of the doctrine of equivalents and placed very high priority on the public notice function of patent claims.

In particular, the Federal Circuit decided four significant issues related to the doctrine of equivalents and prosecution history estoppel:

1. *If a narrowing amendment is made to a claim for any statutory reason related to patentability, then prosecution history estoppel (also sometimes called* file wrapper estoppel) *is triggered.* This means that not only will amendments that are made for purposes of novelty and nonobviousness (*inventiveness*) be operative to trigger prosecution history estoppel, but amendments made to comply with requirements such as definiteness, vagueness, completeness, and clarity (for claims already substantially distinct from the prior art) will also.
2. *A voluntary narrowing amendment made by an applicant will have the same force as a narrowing amendment made in response to a rejection by an examiner.*
3. *There is a* zero range *of equivalents for an element that has been narrowed during prosecution.* This departs from the flexible analysis previously adopted by the courts that examined the prior art and determined what vacancies existed in the prior art that could be filled by the claim—even though the claim language did not literally accomplish this coverage. The court replaced this flexible analysis with an absolute bar against use of the doctrine of equivalents, and limited the coverage of the claim element to what is specifically disclosed in the application.
4. *If there is no explanation given by the applicant for a narrowing amendment, there is no range of equivalents for the narrowed element.*

Therefore, in the future (or until the U.S. Supreme Court alters the decision of the Court of Appeals for the Federal Circuit) the closeness of the prior art or the pioneering nature of an invention will no longer affect the scope of elements that were narrowed during prosecution. Competitors now may review the prosecution history, identify an element that was narrowed, design around that element, and avoid infringement. Patent practitioners now may be more inclined to press harder in arguing the allowability of filed claims and may be less willing to negotiate with the examiner moderately narrowing amendments to elements. Now there is greater incentive to appeal the examiner's rejections to avoid patent claims with easily avoided narrow elements.

The value of many U.S. patents may have been reduced by the *Festo* decision. This decision might give licensees a basis for renegotiating their agreements with patent owners. The prosecution history of the particular licensed patent(s) might reveal that the scope of coverage of the patent(s) is more narrow than earlier believed by both parties. This decision also might change whether a particular product or process in the future can be considered a royalty-generating event under the license. The patent community eagerly awaits word from the U.S. Supreme Court on what the situation will be in the future.

ABOUT THE AUTHORS

Dr. Heinz Goddar is a German Patent Attorney and European Patent and Trademark Attorney. He is a partner of Boehmert & Boehmert and of Forrester & Boehmert, with his office at Munich. He has a technical background (as well as Ph.D. degree) in physics and physical chemistry. Before his career as a patent attorney, he was Assistant Professor at the Polymer Department of the University of Mainz, Germany. He is one of the senior partners of his firm and is particularly involved in international patent and licensing matters, including litigation and arbitration, with a special interest in EU (European Union) questions. He is an associate judge at the Senate for Patent Attorneys Matters at the German Federal Supreme Court and lectures Patent and Licensing Law at the University of Bremen, Germany. He is a past president of LES International and of LES Germany.

Alan H. Gordon has more than 30 years of experience in the practice of Intellectual Property Law. In 1998, he established his own firm after having been a shareholder/director of Fish & Richardson, P.C. for 6 years and a shareholder with Arnold, White & Durkee (now Howrey Simon Arnold & White) for 18 years. His practice emphasizes all aspects of litigation in patent, trademark, copyright, unfair competition, employment/noncompetition, and trade secret matters. Mr. Gordon has litigated complex patent, trademark, trade secret, copyright, and noncompetition agreement cases before juries and the bench in both federal and state courts; mediated complex lawsuits and prefiling disputes in intellectual property and other areas; negotiated and prepared extensive licensing agreements in a wide variety of technologies; and prosecuted or supervised prosecution of patent applications in highly technical areas. Mr. Gordon was Adjunct Professor of Patent Law, South Texas College of Law in Houston, Texas; is an author and frequent lecturer in the intellectual property area; and has appeared numerous times as an expert witness in patent, trademark, trade secret, and licensing cases. He is secretary of the Licensing Executives Society (United States and Canada), has served as chairman (Houston Chapter), committee chairman, Central U.S.A. regional vice president, and a United States/Canada delegate to the Licensing Executives Society International Organization. Mr. Gordon also is a member of the American Intellectual Property Law Association, American Bar Association, Houston Intellectual Property Law Association, and the Lawyer-Pilots Bar Association.

6

The Critical Role of Trade Secret Law in Protecting Intellectual Property Assets

By Melvin F. Jager

INTRODUCTION

Trade secret law is the initial form of protection for valuable intellectual property worldwide. Set aside patents, copyright, and trademarks for a moment. In the beginning, a valuable idea is born as a trade secret. Generally, it remains a trade secret until it is voluntarily disclosed or enters the public domain through publications, patents, or disclosure. Trade secrets, often referred to as *know-how*, are therefore a valuable component in an intellectual property asset portfolio. Trade secrets are worth billions of dollars worldwide because most technology is unpatented. They include the information that tells people how things work and how technology can be applied to particular tasks.

In general terms, trade secrets are a component of almost every technology license. The presence of trade secret information or know-how can increase the value of a license for the licensee and the licensor up to 3 to 10 times the value of the deal if no trade secrets are involved.

SCOPE OF TRADE SECRET PROTECTION

Technology licensing today usually involves parties in different jurisdictions and often in different countries. In fact, the global economy demands that licensing be conducted on a worldwide basis. It is therefore important to realize that the protection granted to trade secrets is also generally worldwide. North America and Europe have protected confidential technology in one form or another for hundreds of years. Most recently, compliance with the Tripps agreement has led to increased trade secret protection under the laws in many additional countries.

The Tripps agreement (sometimes written as TRIPS or TRIPPS) stands for the agreement on Trade-Related Aspects of Intellectual Property Rights. Tripps was implemented January 1, 1996, as an agreement that would foster cooperation between the World Intellectual Property Organization (WIPO) and the World Trade Organization (WTO). The WTO succeeded the General Agreement on Tariffs and

Trade (GATT) on January 1, 1995. It is empowered to moderate trade disputes and resolve issues relating to the environment, foreign currency exchange, and labor standards.

In 1991, as an example of compliance with Tripps and GATT, a Trade Secrets Act was enacted in Japan. Trade secret laws were also enacted in Korea in 1992, in China in 1993, and in Taiwan in 1996. Other Far Eastern countries (e.g., the Philippines, Malaysia, Singapore, and Hong Kong) protect trade secret law as well. As a general rule, the unfair competition laws of most major industrial countries now grant protection for confidential technical information, especially when the information is the subject of a well-drafted license or contract.

DETERMINING THE CONTROLLING LAW

The first step in determining whether particular information may qualify for legal protection as a trade secret is to identify the controlling law that defines the trade secret in the first instance. A trade secret must be defined before the scope of legal protection for the information can be ascertained, and before the proper license provisions can be negotiated and drafted to protect the information.

Many factors must be considered to ascertain the proper controlling jurisdiction. The location of the parties to the license should be reviewed, as well as the states or countries that are going to be affected by the transaction. The location of the major license activities is a strong indicator of the best choice for the controlling jurisdiction. As a general rule, courts look favorably on the choice of controlling law elected by the parties in a license agreement. However, such a choice cannot override significant interests in the state or nation in which the license dispute may be litigated or arbitrated.

Once the controlling jurisdiction or country is identified, then a review must be made of the statutes and common law of the country to determine the trade secret definition that applies to the situation. Patent laws and treaties, as well as the provisions of the WTO and Tripps, may be important. The antitrust laws of the particular jurisdiction may also be significant. Several countries and areas, such as the European Economic Community, Japan, and Korea, have block exemption regulations that define the restrictions permitted and prohibited in license agreements. Such regulations should be reviewed if relevant. In the United States, the Department of Justice and the Federal Trade Commission have issued guidelines for the licensing of technology in 1995. However, these guidelines are advisory, not mandatory.

If the United States is selected or determined to be the controlling jurisdiction for the licensing of trade secrets (know-how), care must be taken to determine which state law is used to set the guidelines. There is no federal, civil trade secret law in the United States. Each of the 50 states has its own body of law defining the metes and bounds of a trade secret. Every state has a trade secret common law. In addition, 42 states have enacted the Uniform Trade Secrets Act, which carries statutory definitions and rules. New York and Texas are the two largest U.S. jurisdictions that do not follow the Uniform Act and depend on the common law.

The statutory and common-law definitions of trade secret rights in the United States are fairly representative of the type of definitional approach used in most jurisdictions. Under the Uniform Trade Secrets Act, for example, a trade secret consists of any information that

- Has actual or potential independent economic value
- Is not known to others
- Is not readily ascertainable by proper means by others
- Is subject to reasonable efforts to maintain secrecy

A broader common-law definition is set forth in the 1995 Restatement of Unfair Competition, Section 39, which defines trade secrets as any information that can be used in a business enterprise and is sufficiently valuable and secret to afford an actual or potential advantage over others. Six factors are well accepted in the U.S. as relevant to the determination of the existence of a trade secret:

1. The extent to which the information is known outside the business
2. The extent to which the information is known by the employees
3. The extent of security measures taken to protect the information
4. The value of the information to the owner and others
5. The cost of developing the information
6. The ease or difficulty of acquiring or reproducing the information by legitimate means

COMMON FEATURES OF TRADE SECRETS

Despite the fact that laws vary from country to country, seven common features exist under all trade secret protection regimes:

1. *There is no strict novelty requirement for obtaining protection of information as a trade secret.* Unlike patents, trade secret rights can exist in information and ideas that do not rise to the level of patentable invention and that do not meet the standard requirements of novelty and unobviousness under U.S. law, or inventive acts under other laws. The information only needs to have a modicum of novelty that distinguishes the information from that which is generally known in the particular field. For instance, it is common to have a trade secret that is a combination of

known steps, elements, or components. The fact that each independent component is itself known does not defeat trade secret protection for the combination.

2. *Trade secret laws demand relative, not absolute, secrecy.* A public policy advantage of trade secret protection is the encouragement of technology licensing, while still providing a legal vehicle for protecting the information. It would be counterproductive to demand absolute secrecy. Under those circumstances, no secret could be disclosed to others for licensing without its destruction as a protectable right. Instead, the laws require relative secrecy. The information must be not generally known to people in the field and must be the subject of reasonable precautions to protect its secrecy and confidentiality. Provisions protecting the confidentiality of the exchanged information are common and necessary in employment contracts, vendor contracts, and license agreements.

3. *Technical information is protectable.* If the information is technology based, there is no question that it falls within the definition of a trade secret. Most jurisdictions likewise extend protection to business information such as strategic plans, cost and pricing information, and customer lists. A few jurisdictions, mostly in the Far East, limit the protection of business information under the trade secret laws. Korea protects *managerial* information; China protects *operational* information; and business information is *not* protected under the trade secret laws of Malaysia and Singapore. Thus, care should be taken to review the controlling law if nontechnical business information is a major component of the license agreement being negotiated or drafted.

4. *Protection extends to patentable as well as unpatentable information.* The two forms of protection for intellectual property are not incompatible. They both perform the valuable policy functions of encouraging innovation and commercial morality. They also provide viable vehicles for creating assets that can be protected and transferred by licensing. Both trade secrets and patent laws provide incentives to advance technical arts that would not otherwise exist.

5. *Trade secrets have an unlimited life.* Unlike the patent term, which expires in 20 years or less, a trade secret could last for 100 years or more, as long as it is maintained in secrecy. The unlimited life of a trade secret is important to bear in mind in licensing negotiations and license drafting.

6. *If trade secrets are licensed, the license agreement should specifically provide for the protection of confidential information, should recognize the continuing life of confidential information after the license is terminated, and should provide for the handling of the trade secret information after termination.* Since a license is an agreement not to sue for the use of an intellectual property asset, the expiration of a

license traditionally does not grant any continued rights to use the trade secret information. The licensor who desires to continue to control trade secret technology after a license terminates is well advised to specifically provide for the termination of any rights on the licensee to use the technology after the license has expired. On the other hand, a licensee who expects to continue using the trade secret technology after the licensed patents expire is well advised to specifically provide for that right in the license agreement.

7. *A contract or license to protect trade secret information will be enforced under the laws of the contract.* Whether or not a jurisdiction grants any additional protection for trade secret rights, a contract controlling the rights and allegations of a trade secret right should be enforceable under the normal contract laws and procedures of the controlling jurisdiction. Again, this emphasizes the importance of a well-negotiated and well-drafted license agreement that spells out the rights and obligations with respect to the trade secrets being transferred.

COMMON DIFFERENCES BETWEEN TRADE SECRETS AND PATENTS

Many important differences exist between patents and trade secret rights in most jurisdictions. The three main differences are highlighted here:

1. *The definition of trade secrets is broad and often vague and difficult to apply, whereas patent systems provide for an examination of the novelty and inventiveness of proposed patentable inventions.* Patents also provide for claims that attempt to strictly define the limits of the patent rights. No such technical wording is provided in the law to define the rights of a trade secret. A line between protectable information and nonprotectable information is difficult to draw when trade secrets are involved. Also, the common technique of licensing all rights claimed in a patent does not apply to trade secrets. Instead, the drafter of the license agreement must carefully delineate the subject matter considered to be the trade secrets that are subject to the license.

2. *Unlike trade secrets, patents have a limited life, traditionally 20 years from the date of filing of the application.* Trade secrets can last forever, as long as the information is kept secret. Likewise, they can be instantly terminated by inadvertent or intentional public disclosure, such as through patents, publications, or presentations. A patent right is therefore very stable, but a trade secret right, in contrast, is very volatile. A patent right can be destroyed only through expensive and time-consuming challenges against

the validity of the patent. Trade secret rights can be destroyed easily by inappropriate public disclosure.

3. *As a general principle, patent rights are not subject to independent development or reverse engineering.* For patented products, the subsequent independent development of the same invention does not avoid an infringement charge. Likewise, the subsequent reverse engineering of the invention from products on the marketplace will not excuse patent infringement. In contrast, trade secrets may be discovered and exploited through independent development and reverse engineering. If limitations on independent development or reverse engineering activities with respect to trade secrets are desirable, they should be spelled out in the license contract.

CIVIL TRADE SECRET REMEDIES

A variety of civil remedies are available for protecting against the theft of trade secrets. Most jurisdictions provide for some form of preliminary and final injunctions to prevent further disclosure and use of the trade secret information. Most jurisdictions also provide for recovery of actual damages incurred by the trade secret owner as a result of the misappropriation. These damages could include the loss of profits to the trade secret owner, the gain enjoyed by the trade secret thief, or a reasonable royalty. U.S. and other jurisdictions will permit the award of punitive damages for malicious and willful trade secret misappropriation. In some jurisdictions, the trade secret owner can also be protected by a judgment for attorney fees and for prejudgment interest to recover for the cost of the lost value of money during any ensuing litigation.

These civil remedies for trade secrets are augmented by the contract laws from the various jurisdictions. If the trade secret is a subject of a license, the misuse or inappropriate disclosure would constitute a breach of that agreement, subjecting the licensee to contractual damages and other remedies. If the rights of the parties to injunctive relief and damages are to be curtailed in any way, the license agreement should specifically and clearly provide for the limitations of remedies available to either party.

CRIMINAL SANCTIONS

The United States and most other industrial countries also provide for criminal sanctions against trade secret theft. Virtually all states in the United States have criminal laws protecting trade secrets. Furthermore, the federal 1996 U.S. Economic Espionage Act provides for federal protection against the theft of trade secrets. The sanctions under the Espionage Act can be substantial. A violation of the statute can bring fines of up to $10 million and prison terms up to 15 years for trade secret theft. Keep these criminal statutes in mind when considering the manner in which trade secret rights are defined and controlled in any agreement.

TRADE SECRET LICENSING AGREEMENTS

Three basic types of license agreements are relevant to the licensing of trade secret rights: naked patent licenses, naked trade secret licenses, and hybrid licenses. This section describes these three agreements and discusses the restrictions that can and cannot be imposed upon licenses.

Naked Patent Licenses

A *naked patent license* covers only patents and does not mention trade secrets. These patent licenses, as a general rule, are governed by the contract law of the relevant jurisdiction. However, since patents are involved, the antitrust or unfair competition laws of the controlling jurisdiction must be considered. In the United States, the antitrust and misuse laws come into play in controlling the limitations that can be imposed in patent license agreements. Likewise, the block exemptions or FTC regulations in Europe, Japan, and other countries provide fairly strict regulations on the restrictions that can be included in patent licenses.

The permitted restrictions will vary from jurisdiction to jurisdiction. As already noted, some countries have regulations such as block exemptions, and other countries have case law or common law that control naked patent licenses. They include common restrictions such as these:

- Royalties can be charged before the issuance of a patent.
- Different rates can be charged to different licensees.
- A group of related patents can be bundled into one license.
- Royalties or payments may be continued until the licensed patent or patents expire or are invalidated.

A strong body of law in the United States dictates that all payment obligations in a patent license cease upon such patent expiration or invalidation, whether or not the agreement attempts to extend the payments beyond the patent term.

Naked Trade Secret Licenses

No patent-related issues are raised in a *naked trade secret license*. In the United States, a naked trade secret license is generally controlled by state contract laws. In other countries, block exemption regulations or the like provide for the control of a trade secret license under restrictions that are more liberal than patent licenses.

Trade secret licenses usually require royalties or payment for the use of the trade secret technology for as long as the information remains secret. However, an inappropriately drafted license may create rights and obligations that far exceed the useful life of a trade secret. In the United States, for example, legal decisions have required the payment of royalties for the use of a secret formula (in one case for more than 100 years) after the formula was no longer a secret. The rationale followed was that the contract could have, but did not, provide for the termination of payment after secrecy disappeared. If payment beyond the term of the trade secret rights is not expected, care should be taken in providing for the termination of such obligations in the license agreement.

Hybrid Licenses

A *hybrid license* licenses both patent and trade secret rights. The hybrid license brings into play the laws and regulations dealing with both patent licensing and trade secret or know-how licensing. Some restrictions apply to hybrid licenses that would not apply to pure trade secret licenses. It is important to review these restrictions in the relevant jurisdiction, since the major portion of the licenses negotiated are hybrid-type licenses involving both patents and trade secret technology.

A major error in many hybrid licenses is the intermingling or lumping together of the rights and obligations relating to patents and to trade secrets. It is a common drafting technique to state, for example, that the license is granted for both patents and trade secret technology for a stipulated royalty per unit. In most circumstances, confusion and uncertainty often arise when the licensed patent rights are invalidated or expire. In the United States, if such a hybrid license intertwines the patent and trade secret payment obligation, all obligations to pay cease upon the termination or expiration of the patent rights. This rule applies regardless of efforts in the license to extend payment, such as by providing provisions that require payment to extend for 25 years or the like.

As a general rule, if payment for trade secret technology is expected after the patent rights terminate, the contract should specifically provide for that obligation. If payments are expected beyond the patents, it would be a simple matter to state that royalties or other forms of payments shall continue thereafter, until the trade secrets become in the public domain.

Typical Licensing Restrictions

It is difficult to generalize with respect to the types of restrictions permitted and prohibited in patent and trade secret licenses. Again, the laws and regulations vary substantially from jurisdiction to jurisdiction. However, five general guidelines have been developed that apply to trade secret licensing in most jurisdictions:

1. A license can stipulate payment for the use of trade secret information for as long as it remains secret.
2. The license can be limited to a particular field of use, or a particular limited area.
3. The license can also stipulate minimum production, sale, or use requirements and prohibit the handling of competing goods or using competing technology during the term of the license.
4. The mutual grant-back of nonexclusive licenses for improvements is usually permissible.
5. It is also permissible to continue the obligation of the licensee not to disclose the technology after the license expires, as long as it remains secret.

Restrictions can be used in trade secret licenses that are greater than permitted in patent licensing because a trade secret does not inherently create any monopoly rights in the owner. As already noted, all trade secret rights, whether licensed or not, are subject to independent development and reverse engineering by others that are not a party to the license.

General observations can also be made with respect to restrictions that are prohibited in trade secret licenses. As with patents, a licensor should not attempt to regulate the sale or resale prices of the licensed products. Also, limitations cannot be placed on the use of competing goods by the licensee, or the use of competing technology, after the license is terminated. Exclusive grant-backs of improvements are also subject to question. In the United States, since trade secrets inherently do not convey monopoly power to the owner, such restrictions are reviewed and analyzed under the Rule of Reason of the antitrust laws.

EVALUATION OF TRADE SECRETS

There is no universal method for evaluating trade secrets to be licensed. The value of trade secrets varies substantially from industry to industry. The most effective method of evaluation of a trade secret depends on all of the circumstances relating to the transaction. Several different approaches have been recognized as appropriate under particular circumstances.

One method for evaluating trade secrets is the *auction method*, where the technology is essentially offered for license or sale to the highest bidder. The pros of such an approach are that there are no serious negotiation problems, and it is easy to identify the highest bidder. The cons of such an approach are that the auction process would require widespread disclosure of the information and jeopardize its continued secrecy. Also, the auction method emphasizes only the current price and value afforded to the information.

A second method of evaluation is the *cost method*. Under this method the development costs of the technology are calculated and the requested payments are dictated by the expected return to a licensor for its capital investment. The advantages of this method are that it is relatively easy to calculate the costs and the return expected for the capital investment in developing the technology. The disadvantages of the cost method are that it ignores the risks assumed by the licensee such as unanticipated manufacturing and marketing costs. It also ignores other variables such as unforeseen new applications for the technology.

A further technique for evaluating trade secrets is the so-called *industry standard method*. In this approach, the parties seek to identify and establish a royalty for the particular type of technology. It is easy to identify in some industries and does have the advantage of uniformity in the treatment of related technologies. However, this approach has the disadvantage of basing the evaluation of a trade secret on someone else's prior negotiations. Also, the standard used in the prior deals may be obsolete. Seeking an industry standard also ignores the added value of subsequent developments in the technology, and may cause the parties to focus on a narrow or incorrect market for the technology to be licensed.

The *financial analysis method* of trade secret evaluation is the most frequently recommended technique. This technique employs market-based business economics in an attempt to maximize the value of the technology. It requires a detailed assessment of the risks by both parties and a detailed projection of expected costs and benefits. Under this method of analysis, a successful trade secret license agreement will occur if the expected benefits exceed the expected costs for both parties.

The financial analysis method begins with categorizing the trade secrets for licensing. The information to be licensed should be segregated between information that is of low value and can be easily learned by the licensee, as compared to highly proprietary information that is substantial and valuable, and is difficult to duplicate.

Furthermore, each party must define its expectations. The anticipated gain and anticipated costs to each party should be determined. Potential legislative changes, such as changes in the tax structure, should be reviewed with respect to the potential transaction. Interest rate changes should be considered. From a technology standpoint, the stage of the technology to be licensed should be analyzed, and the need for any special research requirements should be determined. Both parties should remember that the longer the license is to be in effect, the more reality may differ from the expectation of the parties.

The forms of payment should be evaluated. A lump sum would reduce the risk to the licensor in that it receives the payments up front. The failure of the technology, or the advantages of a major success, are borne by the licensee under lump-sum payments. A per-unit fee or running royalty is more common.

In this circumstance, the expected value of the trade secret technology is divided by the expected units or sales revenue for the products. In this circumstance, the licensee avoids the risk of fees without sales, and both parties participate in the future success of the licensed technology.

The ultimate goal of the financial analysis method in trade secret evaluation is to reach an expected range of negotiating criteria. This technique should define the minimum payment that the licensor will accept and the maximum payment acceptable to the licensee. The range of successful negotiation criteria generally lies between these two values.

CONCLUSION

Trade secrets are a valuable part of most licensing agreements. The best licensing practices require that steps be taken by the licensing executives involved in negotiating and drafting the license to identify the scope and value of the trade secrets, determine the controlling law, and clearly specify in the license the rights and liabilities of the parties, both before and after the agreement. A license that is mutually beneficial to the licensor and the licensee is the ultimate goal.

ABOUT THE AUTHOR

Melvin F. Jager has specialized in patent and trade secret law with the Chicago intellectual property firm of Brinks Hofer Gilson & Lione for 34 years. He received a bachelor of science degree from the College of Engineering, and a Juris Doctor from the College of Law at the University of Illinois. He has handled trials and appeals, and testified as an expert witness in patent and trade secret cases throughout the United States and several other countries. He has also had wide experience in drafting and negotiating licenses, counseling, and preparing and prosecuting patent applications throughout the world.

Mr. Jager is the author of a three-volume treatise titled *Trade Secrets Law*, published by Clark Boardman Callahan. This treatise is updated twice a year. He has also written and spoken extensively on patents, trade secrets, and licensing in the United States and other countries. In 1994 he was president of the Licensing Executives Society (USA and Canada), and he currently is president-elect of the Licensing Executive Society International. He is a past president of the Intellectual Property Law Association of Chicago. He was also elected as chairman for the Intellectual Property Litigation Committee of the American Bar Association Litigation Section and chairman of the Patent, Trademark and Copyright Council of the Illinois State Bar Association. Mr. Jager also is on the advisory board for the Practicing Law Institute in New York, and a member of the American Law Institute. He consulted with the American Law Institute on the drafting of the *Restatement of the Law (Third) of Unfair Competition* (Philadelphia, PA: American Law Institue, 1995), which codified the law on trade secrets for the first time in over 50 years. He also was instrumental in the passage of the Illinois Trade Secrets Act. Mr. Jager also holds the position of adjunct professor of patent law at the University of Illinois College of Law.

7

Copyright, Software, and Web Site Issues in the Internet World

By Michael A. Lechter

INTRODUCTION

The Internet has had a profound effect on many aspects of business. It facilitates communications, negotiations, and gathering intelligence. It provides a ready mechanism for worldwide marketing and vehicles for finding co-venturers. It tends to change the mechanics of commercial transactions, and in some instances has caused changes in the very nature of the products offered. New revenue models are being created because of the Internet.

Beyond its effects on business, the new circumstances of the Internet have stretched the existing regime of laws and have given rise to new intellectual property rights and enforcement mechanisms.

COMMUNICATIONS, NEGOTIATIONS, AND INTELLIGENCE— TRANSACTIONS AT THE SPEED OF THOUGHT

The Internet, as a communications media, clearly facilitates doing worldwide business. Through the Internet, communications and documents can be transmitted almost instantaneously, without regard to time zones. At the same time, however, expectations of the time frame in which a transaction will be negotiated have been compressed. The availability of the Internet as a communications medium has created expectations of instantaneous response.

The Internet is also a two-edged sword with respect to the ability to gather intelligence. Although it facilitates research by making volumes of information readily available, the information available to one company on the Internet is also available to its competitors. Through the Internet, essentially everyone has the ability to reach an international audience by making information available on a Web site. However, the cultural norms in some parts of the world tend to discount rights in intellectual property, and material placed on Web sites is also made available, typically in readily reproducible form, to unscrupulous appropriators of intellectual property—pirates—around the world. Early consideration of international protection of intellectual property—particularly that reflected in reproducible media, used, described, or advertised over the Internet—is now much more important.

Historically, pirates located outside of a company's market area were often not aware of a trademark or a new product until the trademark or product found its way into their hands—which often did not occur until the product was shipped or business undertaken on an international basis. This facilitated a planned, gradual approach to international intellectual property. For example, the registration of trademarks in a given geographical area tended to track the expansion of the product or service into that area, and patent protection in those areas tended to be delayed to the maximum extent permitted under the applicable treaties.

Today, with the extensive use of the Internet, the pirates around the world become immediately aware of a product or trademark as soon as the material is placed on a Web site. Moreover, in many cases trademarks, works of authorship (e.g., digitized audio and video), and software are made available to the pirates in ready-to-copy digital form. Accordingly, international protection of intellectual property should be considered sooner than later, and a protection strategy formed, with international access to, and ease of reproduction of, materials on the Internet in mind.

BRINGING DOWN THE BARRIERS TO COMPETITION

In many respects, the Internet has played the role of the great equalizer between large and small business entities. For example, prior to the availability of information on the Internet and inexpensive online reference materials, only relatively large entities could afford extensive research libraries. The Internet, of course, has changed that. The Internet has also tended to pull down a number of historical barriers to competition.

Distribution Channels

In times past, an established distribution channel was a formidable barrier to entry; emerging companies were hard put to compete with larger, better financed competitors with established distribution channels. Before it could bring its goods to the market, the emerging company had to establish its own distribution channels—often a daunting task made more difficult by long-standing relationships and goodwill (and sometimes contracts) between the established company and the entities in the natural distribution channel for the emerging company's product.

The Internet, however, provides an extensive worldwide mechanism for transacting directly with customers. The need for resellers and distributors is minimized. Where downloadable products (such as computer programs, audio and video recordings, and digitized copies of books and other works of authorship) are involved, the Internet also provides a direct-delivery mechanism. In many instances, products have been designed with the conscious intention to eliminate physical media and to facilitate distribution over the Internet. For example, digital versions of audio and video recordings, books, and other works of authorship have been created. In some instances (albeit too few), programmers have attempted to pay attention to coding efficiency to reduce the size of the program. Compression programs have been developed to reduce the size of the digital files, and thus the time required to download the file over the Internet. As wide-bandwidth communication links become more widespread, transmission of audio and video products and multi-megabyte-sized computer programs through the Internet will become more prevalent. Even with respect to hard goods, established distribution channels for delivery of the goods have become less of a barrier to competition. The Internet tends to minimize the infrastructure required for distribution; orders can be taken through the Internet, often on an automated basis, and shipping of the goods to the customer can be outsourced to a commercial fulfillment house.

Identifying Potential Sources, Customers, and Co-venturers

The facility for international networking through the Internet has also tended to minimize yet another historical barrier to competition—the good-old-boy network. In times past, the ability to ferret out deals (often a direct function of an entity's network of contacts) could be a significant competitive advantage. In some instances, brokers and consultants turned their ability to find sources of goods, services, or technology (or someone seeking those goods, services, or technology) into an industry. The Internet is proving to be a great equalizer with respect to the ability to find potential customers and co-venturers. The medium of posting the availability of a product, service, or technology on a Web site (and ensuring that the site is included in the indices of available search engines) provides ready access to a potential "deal" to interested parties all around the world. Identifying and making contact with the potential customers and co-venturers is also facilitated by specialized third-party forums providing matchmaking services and auction sites.

TRANSACTING BUSINESS OVER THE INTERNET—E-COMMERCE

Transacting business through the Internet, often referred to as *e-commerce,* has pushed the bounds of the existing law of contracts. In general, a Web site making a computer program available for sale or license purports to create a contract between the proprietor of the Web site and an end user setting forth the terms and conditions of sale, or the terms of a license. Such a Web site typically includes the following elements:

- *A mechanism for identifying the subject of the transaction.* The Web site includes descriptive material and pricing/fee information regarding the item(s). Generally, when more than one item is available for sale/license, one or more pages of the site are devoted to a catalog of the respective items (descriptive material and associated prices/fees). The purchaser/end user selects (e.g., by clicking representative icons) the particular items of interest from the catalog, causing indicia of the item to be entered in a list (often analogized to a shopping cart). The descriptive material and pricing/fees are directly associated with the transaction process, either through physical proximity on the Web page or through a hyperlink.
- *A mechanism for identifying the end user and billing information.* The Web site typically obtains information regarding the purchaser/end user, typically by prompting, or otherwise soliciting entry of purchaser/end user identification (e.g., name, address, telephone number, and e-mail address) and billing information (e.g., credit card type, number and expiration date).
- *A mechanism for advising of terms and conditions.* In many instances, the Web proprietor intends that specific terms and conditions apply to the transaction conducted through the Web site (such as, in the case of software, a standard end-user agreement). In general, the Web site typically includes either a statement of those terms and conditions (often framed in a scrollable window) or some form of link to those terms. As will be discussed, the manner in which the terms and conditions are presented to the purchaser/end user can determine whether the transaction results in forming a contract according to those terms.
- *A mechanism for signifying intent to place the order.* The Web site typically includes some form of icon or symbol (e.g., a button) to be clicked by the purchaser/end user to signify intent to place the order/participate in the transaction. Often, particularly in the context of a click-through software license, actuating the button is also intended to indicate acceptance of the terms and conditions of the agreement.

E-commerce transactions give rise to a number of questions. Has a contract been formed? If so, what are the terms of the contract? Is the electronic record of the transaction created by the Web site sufficient to meet a requirement for a writing evidencing a contract? Does the transaction process provide a sufficient electronic signature to meet a requirement that the writing be signed by one or both parties? Assuming a contract has been formed, given the relative anonymity of the Internet, can it be attributed to a specific individual? Who actually clicked the order button? In other words, assuming that there is a valid electronic signature, whose signature is it?

These issues are compounded by the use of *electronic agents* to automate commercial transactions. For example, a just-in-time inventory control system at a manufacturer might automatically transmit an order for goods to a Web site, where an e-commerce software package receives the order, automatically acknowledges the order, and initiates shipment of the goods. The inventory control system and e-commerce software package create an electronic record of the transaction. No human is directly involved. The inventory control system and e-commerce software package are electronic agents for the actual parties to the transaction. Is the manufacturer responsible if its electronic agent, the inventory control system, submits an order for 10,000 instead of 10 items?

The applicable law for answering these questions varies from jurisdiction to jurisdiction. For example, in the United States potential sources of law include the common-law contracts; the Uniform Commercial Code (UCC) (adopted in all states); The Electronic Signatures in Global International Commerce Act ("E-Sign"); the Uniform Electronic Transactions Act (UETA); and, in a few isolated states, the Uniform Computer Information Transactions Act (UCITA).

In order for a contract to be formed, the basic requirements of offer, acceptance, and consideration must be met. There must have been an intent to form a contract and agreement as to at least the essential terms. In addition, depending on the value and nature of the transaction, there must be compliance with the statute of frauds—that is, there must be a signed writing. For example, under the UCC (§2-201) a contract for the sale of goods priced at $500 or more must be evidenced by a writing signed by the party against which the contract is to be enforced. Of course, the signature must be authentic—that of (or attributable to) the party against which the contract is to be enforced.

Most jurisdictions have adopted an expansive definition of *writing* and *signature,* and determine attribution based on the logical evidence derived from the circumstances of the transaction. For example, the UCC defines a writing as encompassing any "intentional reduction to tangible form" and a signature as "any symbol executed or adopted by a party with a present intention to authenticate a writing." The UCC, however, does not address the issue of attribution.

E-Sign is a federal statute, signed into law on June 30, 2000, and effective October 1, 2000, applicable to any transaction in or affecting interstate or foreign commerce (§101). In a nutshell, E-Sign validates putting contracts in electronic form and using electronic signatures. E-Sign also validates using electronic agents to automate commercial transactions. However, E-Sign does not deal with the attribution of electronic records or electronic signatures; it specifically leaves the issue of authenticity and attribution to be determined under state law.

UETA was approved by the National Conference of Commissioners on Uniform State Laws (NCCUSL) in 1999, and has been adopted by the majority of states (currently 37). UETA applies to electronic records and electronic signatures relating to commercial transactions. UETA, in effect, equates an electronic record with a writing and an electronic signature with a written signature (§7). An electronic signature is defined by UETA as "an electronic sound, symbol, or process attached to or logically associated with a record and executed or adopted by a person with the intent to sign the record" (§2 (8)). UETA (§9) also specifically addresses the issue of attribution:

> (a) An electronic record or electronic signature is attributable to a person if it was the act of the person. . . .
> . . . The act of the person may be shown in any manner, including a showing of the efficacy of any security procedure applied to determine the person to which the electronic record or electronic signature was attributable.

UCITA was initially conceived as an amendment to the UCC. However, the provisions of UCITA were extremely controversial, and the attempt to amend the UCC was rejected. UCITA was then submitted by its proponents to the National Conference of Commissioners on Uniform State Laws (NCCUSL), where it was approved in 1999. However, UCITA has thus far been adopted in only two states— Maryland and Virginia—and is apparently in the process of being adopted in Iowa. Like UETA, UCITA effectively equates an electronic record with a writing and an electronic signature with a written signature, and determines attribution based on the logical evidence (such as compliance with a security procedure) derived from the circumstances of the transaction. UCITA, however, goes much further, taking an extremely expansive position with respect to the terms accepted by a purchaser/end user by virtue of an electronic signature.

Even when a contract has been formed, the terms of the agreement might still be at issue. For example, in the United States, if there is agreement as to essential terms (e.g., subject, price, quantity), a contract is formed, but terms that had not been agreed upon are not part of the contract. Instead, various terms may be implied under the law (e.g., the UCC). Assuming that the e-commerce transaction created an electronic record and the purchaser/end user manifested assent to the electronic record with a digital signature, the question might still remain as to extent of the assent. Precisely what terms did the purchaser/end user agree to? For example, where the Web page containing the order icon contains only a hyperlink to terms and conditions, and not the terms and conditions themselves, are those terms and conditions part of the contract? Is there a minimum level of clarity required with respect to nature of the hyperlink and the relationship of the hyperlink to the terms?

Consider, for example, Exhibits 7.1, 7.2, and 7.3, which show alternative hypothetical TSI e-commerce Web sites providing for download of its Hi-Bird

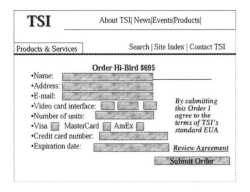

EXHIBIT 7.1   Hypothetical TSI E-commerce Web Site—Example 1

software product. In each instance, TSI intends that its standard EUA will govern the transaction, and the act of placing the order will signify the end user's acceptance of those terms.

In each of the examples, the subject of the transaction is identified as Hi-Bird priced at $695, and identification and billing information (name, address, e-mail, credit card) for the purchaser/end user is acquired. The primary difference between the respective examples is the manner in which the EUA is presented to the end user. In Example 1 (see Exhibit 7.1), a hyperlink, designated by the icon Legal, is provided to a separate Web page containing TSI's standard end-user license agreement (EUA), and the order is submitted by clicking on the "Click here to order" button. In Example 2 (see Exhibit 7.2), the Web page includes a legend ("By submitting this order I agree to the terms of TSI's standard EUA") specifically correlating submitting an order to accepting the terms of the EUA, and a hyperlink to the EUA designated by the icon "Review Agreement," both in proximity to the "Submit order" button. The end user is thus given the opportunity, but not required, to review the terms of the EUA prior to completing the transaction. However, an

EXHIBIT 7.2   Hypothetical TSI E-commerce Web Site—Example 2

EXHIBIT 7.3   Hypothetical TSI E-commerce Web Site—Example 3

affirmative step (using the hyperlink to jump to the EUA) is required in order to review the terms. In Example 3 (see Exhibit 7.3), the EUA is framed and can be reviewed by scrolling without leaving the order Web page. Like Example 2, a legend ("By clicking the accept button, I signify that I have read and accept the terms below") is provided to specifically correlate submitting the order with accepting the terms of the EUA. The correlation is emphasized by the order icon (accept button) itself ("I Agree To Terms Download").

It is likely that, under the law of most jurisdictions, the transactions through each of the exemplary Web sites would result in the creation of a contract (although contract formation under the UCC depends on the intent of the end user). The primary issue is whether the terms of TSI's EUA apply to the transaction. The answer to that question will tend to be different for the respective examples, and tends to vary depending on the applicable law.

For example, under the UCC, the terms of agreement would again be determined by the intent of the purchaser/end user—was there a present intent to accept the terms of the EUA? With respect to Example 1, it is unlikely that such an intent could be inferred from the circumstances. With the increasing correlation between the EUA and placing the order, it becomes progressively more likely (although in no way assured) that such an intent could be established with respect to the transaction using the Web sites of Examples 2 and 3. E-Sign does not address the issue.

UETA requires attachment or logical association between the terms and the electronic signature. The requisite logical association is likely missing from the Web site of Example 1, arguably provided in Example 2, and likely provided in Example 3.

UCITA, on the other hand, deems the electronic signature to be an acceptance of any terms that (a) the purchaser/end user had the opportunity to review prior to completing the transaction, or (b) are made available for review after the transaction is completed, as long as there is a right to return the goods if the terms are not acceptable. Thus, under UCITA, TSI's EUA would apply to the transactions in each of the examples.

WEB-BASED REVENUE MODELS FOR SOFTWARE

Historically, the revenue models for mass-marketed software were relatively straightforward. The primary model was sales of copies (albeit sometimes disguised by shrink-wrap licenses) of the software on magnetic or optical media through either retail channels or direct catalog sales. Direct sale of copies or licensing of software revenue models is still employed on the Internet. In general, an order for the software (or license) is submitted through the seller/licensor Web site, and a copy of the software is either shipped to the purchaser/licensee or downloaded. The mechanics of this type of transaction will be discussed shortly. However, on the Internet other revenue models are also being used: shareware, evaluation copy, application service provider (ASP), and open-source license (general public license).

Direct-License Revenue Models—Click-Through Licenses

In general, the direct-license revenue model on the Web involves an attempt to elicit from the end user a sufficient manifestation of acceptance of a standard end-user license agreement (EUA) to establish the terms of EUA as applying to the transaction. As already described, the Web site includes some form of link to the EUA (preferably together with some form of correlating legend), or more preferably still, a display of the EUA terms and conditions (often framed in a scrollable window). The manner in which the terms and conditions are presented to the end user can determine whether EUA is applicable to the transaction. In general, the most effective direct-license Web site includes a conspicuous display of the terms of the EUA and requires affirmation that the terms were read and agreed to in order to obtain the software.

Shareware Revenue Models

In general, the shareware revenue model involves granting a free limited-use license to the consumer. The shareware copy of the software often has limited functionality, and revenues are generated by requiring a fee-based registration in order to obtain a full-function copy of the software and support. The shareware revenue model is often used with relatively simple (short) programs that are amenable to downloading over the Internet.

Evaluation Copy Revenue Models

Like the shareware revenue model, the evaluation copy revenue model involves granting a free limited-use license to the consumer. However, the evaluation copy is often full function, but limited either in time (typically to one month) or number of uses. At the end of the evaluation period the software is disabled, and a registered copy must be purchased/licensed. The evaluation copy revenue model relies in part upon the *hassle factor*; the evaluation copy can be installed on the user's computer, but when the evaluation license terminates, in order to free computer resources (disk space) the user must go to the trouble of uninstalling the evaluation copy of the software. It is often easier to pay for a registered copy/license than to uninstall the evaluation copy. In addition, in many instances where the evaluation copy is an upgrade to a program already installed on the computer, the earlier version of the software is overwritten by the evaluation copy and must be reinstalled after the evaluation copy is uninstalled. As with shareware, the evaluation copy revenue model is often used with relatively simple (short) programs that are amenable to downloading over the Internet.

Application Service Provider Model

The *application service provider (ASP) revenue model* for software is very much like the service bureau model used during the heyday of mainframe computing. Under the ASP model, the end user is not provided a copy of the software. Rather, the software is maintained on the ASP's server. The end user transmits data to the ASP server (typically over a secure connection on the Internet). The software application is then executed on the ASP server using the end user's data, and the results are transmitted back to the end user. The end user is typically charged either on a subscription, data-flow, or percentage of transaction-value basis. Since the end user is never actually provided with a copy of the software, it is easier for the software proprietor to maintain the software as a trade secret and to control unauthorized use and copying. The ability to prevent unauthorized copying makes the ASP revenue model particularly desirable for use in those parts of the world where cultural norms tend to discount rights in intellectual property. In addition, the necessity of distributing physical media containing the software, or accommodating download, is avoided. Since only copies of the software in the ASP's possession need to be supported and upgraded, the associated costs are minimal when compared to the cost of providing upgrades and support to an extensive customer base.

Open-Source License Model

The *open-source license revenue model* (also sometimes referred to as the *general public license model*) typically relies on follow-on services such as customization and support to generate revenue. In general, a free (or in some instances a fixed fee) license to use the software is granted, and the source code for the software is made available (hence the name *open source*). However, the licensee agrees that the source code for any derivative works will also be made available. In theory, by making the source code generally available, more entities will be examining, debugging, and building on the code. Proponents of the open-source license model contend that this will tend to make developing code faster, with fewer bugs and greater innovation. In practice, the open-source license model has not been widely adopted, and it remains to be seen whether the benefits touted by its proponents will accrue.

UNINTENDED CONSEQUENCES OF DOING BUSINESS OVER THE INTERNET

Doing business over the Internet can have unintended consequences. For example, when a business entity establishes a Web site on the Internet accessible by entities located in various states and countries around the world, conducting business through that Web site may subject the business entity to the jurisdiction of those states and countries. The primary factors determinative of whether a Web site will subject the entity to the jurisdiction of a remote state or country are the nature of the Web site, the location of the server, the domicile of the business entity, and the nature of the transaction.

Web sites can be categorized into three types: (1) *passive* (does not accommodate an exchange of information with the host computer); (2) *semi-interactive* (allows exchange of information with the host computer, but does not actually effect business transactions); or (3) *interactive* (actually used to conduct business over the Web). Generally, at least in the United States, merely providing a passive site that is accessible from a state does not, by itself, subject an entity to personal jurisdiction in that state. However, if the entity actually transacts business over the Net with someone in that state, it will probably be subject to that state's jurisdiction.[1] In other parts of the world, other factors are controlling. For example, the rules governing jurisdiction may be determined by whether a consumer is involved in the transaction. In Europe, under the Brussels I Regulation, where there is a dispute between a consumer in one EU country and an online retailer in another, the retailer is subject to suit in the consumer's home country (with the laws of the consumer's home country applied). In nonconsumer transactions a "country-of-origin"/domicile approach has been applied. Recently, a proposal was made to apply the *country-of-origin approach* to all cross-border Internet transactions.

INTELLECTUAL PROPERTY LAWS AND THE INTERNET

The existing regime of intellectual property laws, of course, applies to the Internet. For example, Internet-based business is the subject of many (if not most) of the business method patents that have become so prevalent; the contents of Web sites are subject to copyright protection; and trademarks are used to identify the source of goods and services related to, or provided over, the Internet, and are sometimes used as domain names. In addition, the availability of the Internet as a communication medium has also made it much easier to create publication bars to patent protection and to disclose (inadvertently or otherwise) confidential information.

Common Internet practices (such as downloading or copying all or portions of files, the use of *metatags, linking,* and *framing*) can violate existing laws (e.g., defamation, trademark, copyright). Reproducing copyrightable material directly from someone else's Web site, or downloading files without permission, would obviously be a copyright infringement, unless it falls into one of the exceptions (e.g., fair use). The Internet is not the Holy Grail; just because material is copied through the Internet does not avoid the copyright law. On top of that, knowingly facilitating the unauthorized copying of copyrighted material (e.g., music files) would be contributory copyright infringement.[2] Converting a file (e.g., music) into a compressed format (MP3), even if provided only to people who already have an uncompressed copy of the file, would probably be a copyright infringement rather than a fair use.[3]

METATAGS

A *metatag* is an invisible code in a Web page that provides information about a Web page without affecting how the page is displayed, and is often used by search engines in locating and ranking pages relative to key words. Using someone else's trademark as a metatag can be a trademark infringement, or it can be fair use depending on the circumstances. If someone else's trademark is used as a metatag in a site in an attempt to divert potential customers from the mark owner's Web site to the site, it can constitute trademark infringement and unfair competition.[4]

LINKING

Linking refers to the use of hyperlinks that permit jumping from one document to another simply by clicking on a *hot spot* (an associated area of a graphics object, or a section of text). As a general proposition, merely providing a link to someone else's home page is not likely to present a problem. However, the context in which hyperlinks are used, or the use of graphics/trademarks in the hyperlink itself, may be problematic. For example, while the use of someone else's trademark as a hyperlink can sometimes be "fair use," if the link tends to cause confusion as to sponsorship or affiliation, it constitutes a trademark infringement.[5] This tends to occur when a graphic or stylized trademark is used as the icon for the hyperlink. Also, depending on the context, linking to someone else's Web site can be defamatory, an invasion of privacy, false advertising, or a contributory copyright infringement. A link is defamatory if its effect is to create an untrue statement that injures the reputation of a person or business (e.g., putting a link to someone's site under the heading "Licensing Scam of the Year"). Similarly, a link constitutes false advertising if it creates an untrue or misleading impression of a product (e.g., putting a link to a competitor's site regarding an FDA-approved product, under a heading "Products Not FDA Approved"). Since linking does not involve copying material, it is typically not a copyright infringement.[6] However, contributory copyright infringement can arise from a link to a site that is known to provide unauthorized copies of copyrighted material, in a context that encourages unauthorized copying.[7]

DEEP LINKING

Deep linking refers to a hyperlink, that bypasses information and advertising on a homepage and goes directly to an internal page of the linked site. Revenues generated by a site are often tied to the number of viewers who pass through their home page. As a result, deep linking into a site can cause the site to lose income. This, of course, tends to make the site owner unhappy. There is, however, no law against deep linking per se. Again, since no copying is involved, deep linking is not typically a direct copyright infringement. However, deep linking might well be a trademark infringement by virtue of creating (1) the impression that the linked sites are associated or endorsed, or (2) a likelihood of confusion as to the source of products shown on the linked site. A form of trademark infringement occurs when one business creates the impression that it is the source of another business's products. (In trademark parlance, this is called *reverse passing off*.) Deep linking tends to cause reverse passing off when, for example, it is not crystal clear that the products are actually being shown on a different, unrelated Web site. As with direct linking, deep linking to someone else's Web site can, depending on the context, also be defamatory, an invasion of privacy, or a contributory copyright infringement.

FRAMING

Frames provide a mechanism for dividing a Web page into scrollable, independently functioning portions, or windows, which are simultaneously viewed in separate parts of the screen. *Framing* issues arise when one entity displays another entity's Web page (or part of the other entity's Web page) within a frame in its Web page. Framing does not actually involve making a new copy of the other entity's Web page—the other party's original Web page (or part thereof) is actually displayed within the frame. This is the basis for an argument that framing is not a copyright infringement. However, since the frame is viewed surrounded by the rest of the Web page, the framing may be considered to modify the appearance of the framed material, thus creating an infringing derivative work.[8] In addition, since framing one entity's site (or a part thereof), by definition, makes it seem a part of another's, it can readily create (1) an impression that the sites are associated or endorsed, or (2) a likelihood of confusion as to the source of products shown on the framed site—and thus become a trademark infringement. Framing someone else's Web site can, depending on the context, also be defamatory, or an invasion of privacy.

DOMAIN NAMES

The Internet has also created what is, in effect, a new form of intellectual property—the *domain name*. In essence, the Internet is a worldwide network of computers, with a common system for uniquely identifying each computer on the network, and certain common sets of rules (protocols). Each location (host) on the Internet is identified by a unique numerical *IP address* (Internet Protocol address). However, humans tend to find it difficult to remember numbers. Accordingly, alphanumeric domain names are used to identify one or more IP addresses, correlated by a database maintained on a set of name servers.

Domain names were initially contemplated to be in the nature of an address or telephone number, and were not intended to be a form of intellectual property. However, the intrinsic value of domain names is now being recognized, and domain names are now considered to be a form of intellectual property with trademark/trade name characteristics.

Domain names can be extremely valuable. The exclusive right to use a particular term as a domain name on the Internet is acquired through registration. In general, the first to register a term as a domain name gets the exclusive right to that domain name. The choice of domain names is, however, subject to the trademark laws—use of someone else's trademark as a domain name can create liability under the longstanding trademark law.[9] In addition, the trademark law has been amended to include provisions specifically relating to domain names. The amendments establish limitations on the liability of domain name registrars for taking actions relating to domain names based on third-party trademarks;[10] create a civil action for cybersquatting;[11] and a parallel action on the part of a domain name registrant for review of actions by domain name registrars that suspend, disable, or transfer a registered domain name based on identity or similarity with someone else's mark.[12] In addition, a new administrative procedure (like arbitration) has been created as an alternative to litigation to deal with the disputes over domain names.

Cybersquatting

As previously noted, the federal trademark statute[13] creates a specific civil cause of action for *cybersquatting*. To establish a claim of cybersquatting, you must show the following:

- The mark was a distinctive (or famous) mark at the time of the registration of the domain name.
- The defendant "registers, traffics in, or uses a domain name" that is identical or confusingly similar to (and/or, if famous, dilutes) that mark.
- The defendant has "a bad faith intent to profit from that mark."

There is no hard and fast rule for determining whether there is bad faith. The basic issue is whether the defendant has a legitimate interest in the domain name, or is merely a cyberpirate. The federal statute[14] provides a (nonexhaustive) list of factors that may be considered:

- *Trademark or IP rights.* The absence of legitimate trademark or other IP rights in the domain name tends to show bad faith. Conversely, the existence of legitimate trademark or other IP rights in the domain name tends to show good faith. The defendant can have legitimate trademark rights where, for example, the mark at issue does not qualify as famous, and the defendant is using the mark with unrelated goods or where the defendant was located outside of the plaintiff's market areas and began actually using the mark with goods before any application for registration was filed, and without knowledge of the plaintiff's use of the mark.
- *Existing relationship to the domain name.* An absence of bad faith tends to be indicated if the domain name registered by the defendant happens to be his or her legal name or a name that is otherwise commonly used to identify the defendant. Likewise, actual use of the domain name in connection with the bona fide offering of any goods or services by the defendant prior to registering the name tends to show that the domain name was not adopted in bad faith. Conversely, if the defendant was NOT actually using the domain name in connection with the bona fide offering of goods or services prior to registering the name, it would tend to show bad faith.
- *Manner in which the defendant uses the mark in the Web site.* Use of the mark in the Web site (other than as the domain name) solely in a manner that qualifies as bona fide noncommercial or fair use (e.g., legitimate commentary, parody, or descriptive sense) tends to show that the domain name was not adopted in bad faith.[15] On the other hand, if the mark is used in metatags in an attempt to divert customers away from the plaintiff's Web

site to the Web site corresponding to the domain name, for the purpose of commercial gain or with the intent to tarnish or disparage the mark, it would tend to show bad faith.[16]

- *Trafficking in domain names.* The ultimate indicator of bad faith is that the defendant is a cyberpirate and traffics in domain names—that is, the defendant registered the domain name with the intent to sell the domain name to someone else rather than use the domain name in the bona fide offering of any goods or services. Indications that the defendant is a cyberpirate include (1) providing misleading or false contact information when applying for the registration of the domain name; (2) intentionally failing to maintain accurate contact information; (3) having prior conduct that shows a pattern of such conduct; and (4) registering or acquiring multiple domain names knowing that they violate someone else's trademark rights.

- *The strength of the mark.* The stronger, more distinctive, and more famous the mark, the more likely that the domain name was registered in bad faith. Conversely, if the mark is weak or descriptive, it tends to show an absence of bad faith.

A cybersquatting action is initiated in the federal district court in the same manner as any other trademark infringement action. As previously noted, the statute also deals with the problem of obtaining jurisdiction over foreign nationals that register domain names by providing for in rem jurisdiction to permit civil actions to obtain forfeiture or cancellation of a domain name that violates a trademark right in instances where you otherwise would not be able to obtain jurisdiction over the registrant.[17] A parallel action on the part of a domain name registrant is provided for review of actions by domain name registrars that suspend, disable, or transfer a registered domain name based on identity or similarity with someone else's mark.[18]

ICANN Uniform Domain Name Dispute Resolution Policy (UDRP)

The Internet Corporation for Assigned Names and Numbers (ICANN) provides an alternative to litigation in the federal courts. Each ICANN-accredited registrar is required to include a provision[19] in the registration contract for a domain name that requires the registrant to submit to a mandatory administrative proceeding before an approved administrative-dispute-resolution service provider.[20] In order to prevail in the proceeding, a *complainant* must prove each of the following elements:

1. The domain name is identical or confusingly similar to your trademark or service mark.

2. The registrant has no rights or legitimate interests in respect of the domain name.
3. The domain name has been registered and is being used in bad faith.

The ICANN UDRP[21] provides a (nonexhaustive) list of things that evidence bad faith:

- Circumstances indicating that the domain name was registered or acquired primarily for the purpose of selling, renting, or otherwise transferring the domain name registration to you or to one of your competitors, for valuable consideration.
- Domain name was registered in order to prevent the owner of the trademark or service mark from reflecting the mark in a corresponding domain name, provided that the registrant has engaged in a pattern of such conduct.
- Domain name was registered primarily for the purpose of disrupting the business of a competitor.
- The domain name is used in an intentional attempt to attract, for commercial gain, Internet users to the registrant's Web site or other online location, by creating a likelihood of confusion with your mark as to the source, sponsorship, affiliation, or endorsement of the registrant's Web site or location of a product or service on the registrant's Web site or location.

It also provides a (nonexhaustive) list of things that evidence good faith and a legitimate interest on the part of the registrant:

- The registrant was using, or had made demonstrable preparations to use, the domain name (or a name corresponding to the domain name) in connection with a bona fide offering of goods or services; or before any notice to the registrant of the dispute.
- The registrant (as an individual, business, or other organization) has been commonly known by the domain name, even if you have acquired no trademark or service mark rights.
- The registrant is making a legitimate noncommercial or fair use of the domain name, without intent for commercial gain to misleadingly divert consumers or to tarnish the trademark or service mark at issue.

The remedies available to you as a complainant pursuant to any proceeding before an administrative panel are limited to requiring the cancellation of the domain name or the transfer of the domain name registration to the complainant.

CONCLUSION

The Internet has probably already affected the way that most companies do business. If it hasn't yet, it probably should have, and sooner or later, it certainly will. With the passage of time, and greater availability of broadband communications, some of the new revenue models, such as the application service provider model, will become more prevalent, and it is likely that more and more software products will be designed specifically with Internet distribution in mind. One thing, however, is clear: The Internet and e-commerce are here to stay—at least until they, too, are supplanted by some new technology.

ENDNOTES

[1] *Mink v. AAAA Development, Inc.*, 190 F.3d 333, 336 [52 USPQ2d 1218] (5th Cir. 1999) (For interactive sites, an exercise of personal jurisdiction is always appropriate, whereas for passive sites, personal jurisdiction is never appropriate. Semi-interactive sites fall somewhere in the middle of the spectrum, and the exercise of personal jurisdiction is determined by the degree of interactivity and commercial nature of the site. Action dismissed for lack of personal jurisdiction because the site merely provided its users with nothing more than product and contact information); *1Cybersell, Inc. v. Cybersell, Inc.*, 130 F.3d 414, 418-419, 44 USPQ2d 1928 (9th Cir. 1997) (When making an interactivity determination, the court must find "something more" than an advertisement or solicitation for sale of goods to indicate that the defendant purposefully (albeit electronically) directed his activity in a substantial way to the forum state.); *Amberson Holdings LLC v. Westside Story Newspaper,* 56 USPQ2d 1847 (DC NJ 2000) (insufficient contacts for personal jurisdiction based on passive site being hosted on Internet server within jurisdiction). See also *Panavision Int'l, L.P. v. Toeppen,* 141 F.3d 1316, 1321, 46 USPQ2d 1511 (9th Cir. 1998); *CompuServe, Inc. v. Patterson,* 89 F.3d 1257, 39 USPQ2d 1502 (6th Cir. 1996).

[2] *A & M Records Inc. v. Napster Inc.* 55 USPQ2d 1780 (N.D. Cal, 2000).

[3] *UMG Recordings, Inc. v. MP3.com, Inc.* , 92 F.Supp.2d 349, 351, 54 USPQ2d 1668 (S.D.N.Y. 2000) (concluding that repackaging copyrighted recordings in MP3 format suitable for downloading "adds no 'new aesthetics, new insights and understandings' to the original" and usurps a further market that directly derives from reproduction of the plaintiffs' copyrighted works.)

[4] *Brookfield Communications, Inc. v. West Coast Entertainment Corp.,* 174 F.3d 1036, 50 USPQ2d 1545 (9th Cir. 1999); *Niton Corp. v. Radiation*

Monitoring Devices, Inc., 27 F.Supp.2d 102, 52 USPQ2d 1380 (D. Mass. 1998); *Oppedahl & Larson v. Advanced Concepts* Civ. No. 97-Z-1592 (D.C. Colo., July 23, 1997); *Insituform Technologies Inc. v. National Envirotech Group,* L.L.C. Civ. No. 97-2064 (E.D. La., final consent judgment entered Aug. 27, 1997); *Playboy Enters., Inc. v. Calvin Designer Label,* 985 F.Supp. 1220, 1221, 44 USPQ2d 1156 (N.D. Cal. 1997) (preliminarily enjoining defendant's Web site, "www.playboyxxx.com" and repeated use of the "Playboy" trademark in defendant's metatags); *Playboy Enters., Inc. v. Asiafocus Int'l, Inc.,* No. Civ. A. 97-734-A, 1998 WL 724000, at *3, *6-*7 (E.D. Va. Apr. 10, 1998), (use of the marks in the domain name and metatags of defendant's Web site enjoined where trademarks used as the metatags such that a search for "Playboy" Web site would produce a list that included defendant's site); *New York State Society of Certified Public Accountants v. Eric Louis Assocs.,* 79 F.Supp.2d 331, 340 (S.D.N.Y. 1999), 79 F.Supp.2d at 341; *OBH, Inc. v. Spotlight Magazine, Inc.,* 86 F.Supp.2d 176, 190, 54 USPQ2d 1383 (W.D.N.Y. 2000); *Bihari v. Gross,* 56 USPQ2d 1489 (DC SNY 2000) (fair use as commentary); *Terri Welles v. Playboy* 47 USPQ2d 1186 (S,D Cal, 1999) (found to be fair use of mark in descriptive sense); *Bally Total Fitness Holding Corp. v. Faber,* 29 F.Supp.2d 1161, 1165, 50 USPQ2d 1840 (C.D. Cal. 1998) (fair use as commentary)

[5] *Playboy Enterprises Inc. v. Universal Tel-A-Talk Inc.* 48 USPQ2d 1779 (E.D. Pa, 1998); *Ticketmaster Corp. v. Tickets.Com Inc.* 54 USPQ2d 1344, 1346 (C.D.Cal, 2000).

[6] *Ticketmaster Corp. v. Tickets.Com Inc.* 54 USPQ2d 1344, 1346 (C.D.Cal, 2000).

[7] *Intellectual Reserve, Inc. v. Utah Lighthouse Ministry, Inc.* 75 F. Supp. 2d 1290, 53 USPQ2d 1425 (D. Utah 1999).

[8] *Futuredontics Inc. v. Applied Anagramics Inc.* 45 USPQ2d 2005 (C.D. Cal, 1997).

[9] 15 U.S.C. §§ 1114, 1125

[10] 15 U.S.C. § 1114 (2)(D) (i)–(iv)

[11] 15 U.S.C. § 1125(d)(1)

[12] 15 U.S.C. § 1114 (v)

[13] A person shall be liable in a civil action by the owner of a mark, including a personal name that is protected as a mark under this section, if, without regard to the goods or services of the parties, that person:

(i) has a bad faith intent to profit from that mark, including a personal name which is protected as a mark under this section; and

(ii) registers, traffics in, or uses a domain name that:
(I) in the case of a mark that is distinctive at the time of registration of the domain name, is identical or confusingly similar to that mark;
(II) in the case of a famous mark that is famous at the time of registration of the domain name, is identical or confusingly similar to or dilutive of that mark; (15 U.S.C. § 1125(d)(1))

[14] 15 U.S.C. § 1125 (d) (1)(B)

[15] See *Bihari v. Gross,* 56 USPQ2d 1489, 1499 (S.D.N.Y. 2000).

[16] *Eli Lilly & Co. v. Natural Answers Inc.,* 56 USPQ2d 1942 (7th Cir 2000).

[17] 15 U.S.C. § 1125(d)(2)

[18] 15 U.S.C. § 1114 (v)

[19] ICANN UDRP ¶4(a)

[20] Approved ADR service providers currently include CPR Institute for Dispute Resolution [CPR]; eResolution [eRes]; The National Arbitration Forum [NAF]; and the World Intellectual Property Organization [WIPO]. A complete list of approved ADR service providers can be found at http://www.icann.org/udrp/approved-providers.htm.

[21] ICANN UDRP ¶4(b)

ABOUT THE AUTHORS

Michael A. Lechter of Squire Sanders and Dempsey LLP, adjunct professor at Arizona State University and longstanding LES member, holds a B.S.E.E. from the University of Maryland and a Juris Doctor from Seton Hall University. He is the author of *Protecting Your #1 Asset: Creating Fortunes from Your Ideas* (New York: Warner Books, 2001), *The Intellectual Property Handbook* (Techpress, 1994), is coordinating editor of *Successful Patents and Patenting for Engineers and Scientists* (Piscataway, NJ: IEEE Press, 1995), and is contributing author to *Encyclopedia of Electrical and Electronics Engineering* (New York: John Wiley & Sons, Inc., 1999). He has lectured extensively throughout the world; submitted, upon request of the House Judiciary Committee, testimony to the U.S. Congress; and participated in various U.N. and governmental proceedings on intellectual property law and technology transfer.

8

Trademarks, Trade Names, and Trade Dress

By Thomas M. Small and Kenneth D. McKay

INTRODUCTION

A century ago, trademark licensing was considered to be improper, even illegal. Today, it is a widely used business tool that accounts for many billions of dollars in business revenue annually throughout the world. Licensing begins with a protectable right owned by one party and the desire of another party to have permission to use that right. Thus, the licensing process is two-pronged: establishing a protectable right and then contracting with others to establish the terms under which permission for use of that right will be granted.

The governing contract between the parties, or *license agreement,* must define the nature and extent of the rights that are being licensed to the prospective user, the compensation or consideration that will be required for the permitted use, and the conditions that will be attached to that use, including controls by the owner of the right with respect to the use and display of the trademark. The same license agreement will contain the assurances that are to be given by the owner regarding the licensee's ability to use the trademark in the intended manner, including the degree of protection, if any, that the owner will provide against unlicensed competition from others.

For these reasons, it is essential in any licensing negotiation for both parties to understand the nature of the rights that are involved and the incidents of ownership, protection, and enforcement of those rights. The would-be licensor needs to know how strong are his or her rights, the extent or scope of the business to which they apply, and any vulnerability that might exist, so as to have a realistic view of the negotiations. The licensee, on the other hand, has need of the same type of knowledge so as to be able to evaluate the grant that will be made, and to project a realistic profit picture that will be a fundamental factor in determining what the licensee should pay, and can afford to pay, for the grant. In addition, the licensee needs knowledge of the protection that the licensor's rights will provide for the licensee's business under the license. These factors all depend on the intellectual property laws and procedures of the jurisdiction or jurisdictions in which the licensee will be doing business under the licensed rights. Accordingly, an understanding of applicable basic principles should be the starting point from which to approach trademark licensing.

The fundamental principles of trademark protection and transfer, including licensing, are similar in most jurisdictions, but important differences exist in some countries. Although the primary focus of this chapter will be on the laws and practices of the United States and Canada relating to trademark rights, handled primarily in separate sections, general mention will be made of some of the more significant aspects of protection and licensing in other jurisdictions.

HISTORICAL DEVELOPMENTS REGARDING TRADEMARK TRANSFERS

A brief history of trademarks will be helpful in understanding the technical requirements of trademark ownership, protection, and transfer. The origins of trade symbols can be traced back thousands of years, one of the earliest known examples being the branding of cattle. In fact, the word *brand,* now sometimes used interchangeably with *trademark,* is derived from a word meaning *to burn,* and continues today as the symbol of ownership on cattle, and also is used in a totally unrelated field to refer to the brand names for consumer products.

In addition to signifying ownership of animals, early trade symbols were used on crafted products such as swords and cloth. One early function was to identify the maker in case the product was defective, a function that evolved into the identification of high-quality products made by a skilled craftsman. Later, special symbols were used to mark the products of the early guilds. Thus, the functions of source identification and quality assurance grew as the principal functions of trade symbols.

As the use, recognition, and value of marks developed, a new legal claim developed as well. This was in the broad field of unfair competition, and in English law was a part of the law regarding fraud and deceit. *Passing off,* or *palming off,* applied to the selling of one's goods as the goods of a competitor. The primary focus of the law was the protection of the consumer from fraudulent acts, with a secondary purpose of preventing unjust enrichment of the seller through unfair competition. The property right of the owner of the mark was only incidentally protected.

These limited views of trademarks prevailed well into the twentieth century in both the United States and Canada, with the result that protection of trademarks continued to be focused on source identification and consumer protection. Indeed, the transfer of a trademark from one owner to another was foreign to the underlying principle—that a trademark identified a single source. Only when there was a transfer of the entire business could ownership of a particular mark be transferred. This view prevailed in England, Canada, and the United States in the early 1900s.[1] This principle remains in effect today, in modified form—ownership of a trademark cannot be validly transferred except with the goodwill of the business with which the mark is associated. In England, this modification was codified in 1938; the United States and Canada followed suit later.

In the United States, accordingly, trademark transfers have been subject to close examination to determine whether the goodwill associated with a trademark actually has been transferred with the mark. If not, a serious question will exist as to the validity of the trademark rights of the transferee. It is important, therefore, to include in any assignment of U.S. trademark rights a recitation of the transfer or goodwill. Further, it is advisable to transfer enough of the incidents of the business to establish that the activity of the transferee is a continuation of that business. These incidents may include, in a given situation, customer lists, labels, inventory, packaging, and the like. If this is not done, the validity of the transfer may be questioned.

Historical Developments in U.S. Trademark Licensing

Given the early view that a trade symbol indicated only one particular source, permitting use of the trademark by another was philosophically impossible. A licensee technically would have been a different source, and, therefore, use of the licensor's trademark by a licensee would have been a false or deceptive representation as to the source of the licensee's goods. This view existed during most of the first half of the twentieth century, although limited exceptions began to appear. During the 1930s, trademark licensing was approved in some instances where the licensor remained in control of the nature and quality of the licensee's goods. In this manner, consumers were assured that the goods delivered by licensees would not be materially different from the goods of the licensors, and the consumers thus would be protected against fraud or deception.[2] The U.S. Congress recognized this concept in the Lanham Trademark Act enacted in 1946, which established that legitimate and controlled use by a "related company" does not affect the validity of a trademark and, indeed, "shall inure to the benefit of the registrant or applicant for registration."[3] Since the enactment of the Lanham Act, U.S. licensing of trademarks has been fully recognized and has become widely practiced.

Historical Developments in Canadian Trade-mark Licensing

Prior to 1868, provincial laws in Canada governed trade-marks and trade-name rights in at least two provinces, the Province of Canada and the Province of New Brunswick. In 1868, these acts were repealed and the Trade-mark and Design Act of 1868 became the law in Canada governing trade-marks.

The Trade-mark and Design Act essentially provided for registration and cancellation of trade-marks, assignability, and penalties for unlawful use as well as civil actions for damages relating to infringement of registered marks. Dissatisfaction grew with regard to the limited rights under this act, as there were no provisions relating to common-law trade-mark rights or unfair competition. The Unfair Competition Act of 1932 remedied some of those problems. Ultimately, because of the awkward language of this act and some questionable judicial interpretation of its provisions, the dissatisfaction with this act became even more widespread and vocal than with its predecessor.

The Trade-marks Act of 1953 (the Canadian Act) was structured to resolve these problems and to consolidate other existing statutes relating to trade-marks and trade-mark issues and to include appropriate provisions to reflect Canada's International Treaty obligations at the time.

As it relates to licensing and the ability of trade-mark owners to freely assign their rights, this act was the first statute to recognize, at least to some extent, the commercial reality of the day. Trade-marks could be assigned without the entire goodwill of the business, which radically changed the law of assignment for the future and ratified any historical assignments that would have been contrary to prior trade-mark laws. Under the new act, a trade-mark could be assigned, and was deemed always to have been assignable, whether registered or unregistered, either in connection with or separate from the goodwill of the business. This distinction as to assignment of trade-marks differed from U.S. law at the time and continues to do so. Section 48(1) of the Canadian Trade-marks Act reads as follows:

> (1) A trade-mark, whether registered or unregistered, is transferable, and deemed always to have been transferable, either in connection with or separately from the goodwill of the business and in respect of either all or some of the wares or services in association with which it has been used.

Although this gives trade-mark owners the commercial freedom to assign with or without goodwill, the courts have made it clear that where there is an assignment, particularly without the goodwill of the business associated therewith, there is a positive obligation on the new owner, the assignee, to make the consumer of its products or services aware of the change of ownership or source of the trade-marked products or services. If this is not done, the courts have held in certain circumstances that the goodwill or distinctiveness continues to attribute to the former owner. The new owner in these circumstances runs the risk of having the mark found nondistinctive and therefore unenforceable against would-be infringers. Distinctiveness does not attach to the new owner until the consuming public has been informed of the transfer or the new ownership. Mere recordal of a transfer of ownership at the Trade-marks Office is not enough. This means that in Canada, an assignee cannot hide behind or ride on the reputation of the former owner without disclosure of the new ownership or source.

ACQUISITION AND MAINTENANCE OF TRADEMARK RIGHTS

Trademarks are creatures of national laws, and important differences exist in the legal bases of trademark rights in different jurisdictions around the world. In the United States and Canada, the trademark systems grew out of the early English common-law system in which the courts recognized acquisition of trademark rights based on adoption and first use. Later, governments in common-law countries began registering trademarks as a way to recognize and formalize existing common-law rights acquired through use, thus providing statutory benefits such as notice and presumptions of ownership, nationwide effect, and statutory damages.

In contrast, trademark rights in European and other non-Anglo jurisdictions operating under civil-law systems typically are granted by the government to the first party to apply for a registration of the mark. A prior user who has not obtained a registration has little, if any, right to protection. Accordingly, priority of application for a registration is critical in civil-law countries, while *use rights* exist, without registration, in common-law countries.

Both the United States and Canada now have statutory systems that permit applications for trademark registrations based on *intent to use,* but both require the applicant to establish actual use of the mark before the registration will be granted. This enables an applicant to establish a priority filing date (a *constructive use date* in the United States accorded by Section 7(c) of the Lanham Act). Eventual actual use is required to convert the constructive use date into actual trademark priority. An important change in U.S. federal law that accompanied the *intent to use* legislation was the elimination of *token use* as a legitimate way to acquire trademark rights. Since 1989, *use,* as defined in Section 45 of the Lanham Act, has required "the bona fide use of a mark in the ordinary course of trade, and *not made merely to reserve a right in a mark.*" (Italics added.) Similarly, Canada requires use in the "normal course of trade."

The use requirement prior to the registration in Canada and the United States is unique, as most countries do not require use prior to registration. Canada does not require proof of use for renewal purposes. This is covered in Section 4 of the Canadian Act.

In the United States, trademarks and service marks are registered on the Principal Register, which is for distinctive trademarks only, whether inherently distinctive or having acquired distinctiveness. *Collective* and *certification* marks are special categories of marks that also are registrable on the Principal Register.

Registrations on the Principal Register are entitled to presumptions of validity and of the registrant's ownership and exclusive right to use the registered mark in U.S. commerce in connection with the goods or services specified in the certificate (Sections 3, 4, and 7, Lanham Act). In addition, there is a U.S. Supplemental Register for all terms that are capable of distinguishing an applicant's goods or services but are not registrable on the Principal Register, usually because of limitations on registration of "merely descriptive" terms and surnames (Section 23, Lanham Act). These prospective marks must be capable of acquiring distinctiveness through use, and if such distinctiveness can be shown, a mark that has been registered on the Supplemental Register then can be registered on the Principal Register.

Section 44 of the Lanham Act, relating to International Conventions, authorizes applications for U.S. registration of marks of nationals of countries who are parties to conventions or treaties with the United States. Subsection 44(d) provides for Convention priority for corresponding applications filed within six months of the first filed foreign application, and subsection 44(e) provides for U.S. registration of marks that are duly registered in the applicant's country of origin, on the Principal Register if eligible, otherwise on the Supplemental Register. No registration will be granted under this provision until the mark has been registered in the country of origin, unless that applicant alleges use in U.S. commerce. Applications for registration of marks that have been registered in the country of origin must state the applicant's bona fide intention to use the mark in U.S. commerce, but are not subject to proof of use before registration.

In most, if not all, countries around the world, use by the registrant is required in order to maintain a registration after it is granted. Proof of use is required either as a part of the renewal process or as a defense to or avoidance of a cancellation proceeding, typically within three to five years after registration. In the United States, proof of continuing use is required in the sixth year of the term of a registration and every 10 years when registrations are renewed.

Typically, proof of continuing use in a particular jurisdiction may be satisfied by actual sales of the goods or services under the mark in the jurisdiction, either by the registrant or a distributor of the registrant or by a licensee who manufactures or sells in the jurisdiction with authority of the registrant. In most jurisdictions, registration or recording of a license agreement between the registrant and a licensee is either required or strongly recommended, so that there is a public record of the licensing relationship between the owner of the mark and the user. Such records protect the public by giving notice of the actual source of trademarked goods, and they protect the owner by preserving the source-indicating function of the trademark.

In some jurisdictions, such as Benelux, Italy, many Latin American countries, and Russia, recordal of trademark licenses is required. In Russia, for example, the absence of recordal renders the license agreement void and unenforceable in the courts. This leaves the licensor unable to control the actions of the licensee in accordance with the terms of the unregistered agreement, and also prevents the licensor from relying on the use of the mark by the licensee to maintain the licensor's registration. In such a case, if there is no other use of the mark in that jurisdiction, the trademark rights of the licensee may lapse or be subject to cancellation.

Recording of licenses is permitted in the United States, but is not required for validity or for inurement of the benefits of the licensee's use to the licensor. License recordal is not regularly done, but is an effective way to create a public record of the rights of the licensee.

Abandonment of a mark is a basis in the United States for loss of rights in a mark. The federal law defines abandonment as cessation of use with intent not to resume, and makes nonuse for a period of three consecutive years the basis of a presumption of abandonment (Section 45, Lanham Act). The presumption of abandonment can be overcome by proof that the requisite intent did not exist.

TRADEMARK PROTECTION AND LICENSING: THE U.S. PERSPECTIVE

In principle, the concept of what is a trademark and what are the characteristics of a trademark are not decidedly different as between Canada and the United States. Both countries consider the one-source theory a primary characteristic in determining trademark. However, there are important differences between the laws of both countries that go far beyond the fact that Canada's statute includes a hyphen in "trade-mark" and "trade-name" and the United States does not. Therefore, the remainder of this chapter will look at trademark issues in the United States and Canada separately. Interesting similarities or differences between the two will be noted.

In the United States, a generally recognized definition of *trademark* is "a word, name, symbol or device, or a combination thereof, that is adopted and used by a person or other entity to identify his or her goods and distinguish them from the goods manufactured or sold by others, and to indicate the source of the goods."[4] Thus, a trademark (frequently referred to simply as a *mark*) is used on or in connection with goods, on tags or labels, containers, or, in some circumstances, other documents associated with the goods. It identifies goods that are from one particular source. The identity of the actual source need not be known to the purchaser.

Trademarks used in connection with services are sometimes called *service marks,* now recognized in most jurisdictions as a protectable category of trademarks. Service mark use typically is in the advertising or promotion of the services, such as on brochures, in advertisements, or on signs or other displays associated with the service business.

Technically, *trade name* is a term that is properly used as the name of a business entity, such as the name of a corporation or partnership. An example is General Electric Co. A trade name, or its dominant terms, may be incorporated in or used as a trademark or service mark, such as GENERAL ELECTRIC, and may be applied to the goods of the company as a source indicator, perhaps along with the well-known GE logo mark. The technical distinction is maintained between trade names and marks, and trade names are not registrable as such. Incidentally, approval of a corporate name by a state's corporations department is not a guarantee that the name is free of infringement problems. Such departments do not conduct trademark searches, and their approvals are not clearances for use.

Finally, *trade dress* is a term that probably is of U.S. origin, referring to the "dress of goods" in their packaging or labeling. Trade dress that has become distinctive as identifying the source of the goods is protectable in the United States. In some instances, the configurations of goods themselves have been recognized and protected as trade dress, which in the United States has come to be regarded as a separate category of protectable trademarks and service marks. A landmark decision regarding the trade dress of a restaurant as a service mark is *Two Pesos Inc. v. Taco Cabana International Inc.,* 505 U.S. 763 (S. Ct. 1992).

There is virtually no limit in the United States as to what a trademark can be. Scents, sounds, and colors can qualify. See *Qualitex Co. v. Jacobson Products Co.,* 514 U.S. 159 (S. Ct. 1995), the landmark case regarding protection of a nonfunctional color (for ironing-board covers) that had become distinctive and recognized as an indication of the source of the covers. In this respect, the distinctive color is trade dress of the goods.

Scope of U.S. Trademark Rights

Throughout the world, the scope of trademark rights is determined in relation to the goods or services with which the mark is associated, whether as identified in a registration or through actual use, or both. The general rule in the United States is that rights do not exist in a trademark in the abstract, or *in gross,* but rather, are limited to the goods or services for which the mark is registered or has been used. These rights will extend beyond those goods or services only to such other goods and services as to which the use of the same or a similar mark would be likely to cause confusion of purchasers or prospective purchasers.

Likelihood of confusion, considering the similarities in the marks and the relationship of the goods or services, is the almost universal test of infringement. In a few jurisdictions that follow rules of stricter limitation, trademark rights under a registration are restricted to the scope of the goods or services expressly identified in the registration, but the modern trend has been to broaden this coverage.

Famous marks and highly distinctive or arbitrary marks generally are recognized as being *strong* marks that are entitled to enforcement against a broader range of goods and services, the rationale being that the strength of the well-known mark will cause prospective purchasers of even noncompetitive goods or services to assume that the owner of the mark has expanded into a new field, either by direct entry or by licensing. In contrast, marks that are composed of words that are descriptive or suggestive of properties of the owner's goods or services typically will be regarded as *weak,* and will be protected against infringement, if at all, only in the narrow field of the owner's actual use or registration. Descriptive terms will remain available for use by others in that field in identifying their products, and suggestive terms—those that have at least a limited degree of distinctiveness with respect to the owner's goods or services—will be protected against use on competitive products and services, but usually not outside the owner's field of business. More detailed attention will be given later in this chapter to recent developments in U.S. law regarding special protection of famous marks against dilution of the distinctiveness of the marks, even through noncompetitive use and in the absence of likelihood of confusion.

Both registrability and infringement of trademarks are determined by the *likelihood of confusion test* or an equivalent in most countries of the world. A trademark or service mark is registrable if it meets all of the technical requirements to be a mark and is not confusingly similar to a mark or name previously registered or used (in the United States) by another, and not abandoned.[5] Similarly, infringement of a trademark occurs when a person uses, without the owner's consent, a copy or colorable imitation of a mark:

> In connection with the sale, offering for sale, distribution, or advertising of any goods or services on or in connection with which such use is likely to cause confusion, or to cause mistake, or to deceive . . . .[6]

The detailed aspects of the law and practice regarding trademark infringement are beyond the scope of this chapter, but awareness of the general rule represented by the U.S. trademark act is important in the licensing process.

Limitations on Trademark Protection for Trade Dress

The United States is at the forefront of new developments and viewpoints in intellectual property law, and has been active in recent years in both new legislation and judicial interpretations of U.S. trademark law. The *Taco Cabana* and *Qualitex* landmark decisions of the U.S. Supreme Court dealing, respectively, with trade dress and color as protectable trademarks, have been mentioned and are recommended reading for the principles that apply in these matters.

In 1992, the *Taco Cabana* decision resolved a split between various circuit courts of appeal. The U.S. Supreme Court held that inherently distinctive trade dress was protectable without proof of acquired secondary meaning. Following the *Taco Cabana* decision, the protection of trade dress on the same basis as other trade symbols received increased attention, both in the federal registration of trade dress as trademarks and service marks and in litigation of claims of infringement of allegedly protectable trade dress, whether registered or unregistered. Before this decision, Section 43(a) of the Lanham Act had been the primary basis of federal jurisdiction for claims of infringement of unregistered trademarks (including trade dress) and other causes of action generally constituting unfair competition. These were presented under the broad headings of *false designations of origin and false or misleading descriptions or representations of fact.* In 1986, Congress substantially rewrote Section 43(a) to incorporate the expanded court interpretations that had been made and to clarify and strengthen the federal law regarding disputes over a variety of matters, including trade names and trade dress.

Then, in 1999, Congress added Section 43(a)(3), which placed upon the party asserting infringement of any trade dress that had not been registered as a trademark on the Principal Register the burden of proving that the matter sought to be protected is not functional. More recently, however, the Supreme Court has held that product configurations cannot qualify as inherently distinctive trade dress, so that proof of acquired secondary meaning is an essential element of protection of such configurations. In *Wal-Mart Stores, Inc.* v. *Samara Brothers, Inc.*, the Supreme Court ruled that Wal-Mart, a mass retailer, did not infringe the unregistered trade dress in the sale of knock-off clothing copies.[7] The key holding was that a product's design, like a color, "is distinctive, and therefore protectable, only upon a showing of secondary meaning."

Another Supreme Court decision, in *TrafFix Devices, Inc.* v. *Marketing Displays, Inc.*, brought the U.S. trade dress developments to their current status.[8] It focused on the issue of functionality of the allegedly distinctive aspects of a design claimed to be protectable trade dress. In this case, the product design at issue, a traffic sign supported on dual springs to withstand windy conditions, had been the subject of a utility patent, which raised an evidentiary inference of functionality. After acknowledging that trade dress can be protected under federal law if it has acquired distinctiveness that serves to identify the product as to source, the Court cited the Lanham Act Section 43(a)(1)(A) as confirming this statutory protection and Section 43(a)(3) as placing the burden of proving nonfunctionality on the proponent of the protection. In this context, the Court considered the effect of the expired patent and concluded that it was "strong evidence that the features therein claimed are functional" and found that the patentee "did not, and cannot, carry the burden of overcoming the

strong evidentiary inference of functionality based upon . . . the expired patents."
The Court noted in passing that an attempt to protect, as trade dress, "arbitrary, inci-
dental or ornamental aspects" of a patented device could lead to a different result.

Accordingly, the law of trade dress protection in the United States has been clarified in the very recent past, in a manner that should assist a prospective licensor in
identifying what will be licensable subject matter. On the other hand, these clarifica-
tions also may enable a prospective licensee to determine what should not be owned
by a licensor as trade dress, and, therefore, should not be subject to royalty payments.

U.S. Antidilution Protection of Famous Marks

Antidilution protection of trademarks and names has been present in the laws of the
U.S. for many years, but until recently was only a matter of state law. It should be
understood that, although trademark dilution is part of the law of trademark protection, it is not an aspect of trademark infringement. Instead, dilution is a different
wrong. Whereas trademark infringement has been tested through the years by considering similarities in the marks and the relationship of the goods or services
with which they are used to evaluate the likelihood of confusion of purchasers,
the concept of dilution is based on the recognition that a distinctive mark has
inherent value that can be diminished, or even destroyed, by other marks or names
that do not create a likelihood of confusion. This harm is the lessening of the
capacity of the mark to identify and distinguish goods or services, through blur-
ring or whittling away of the distinctiveness of the mark, or by tarnishment of
business reputation by association of the mark with unsavory goods or services.

State dilution laws in the United States have been enacted since 1956 and
exist in approximately one-half of the states. Typically, only injunctive relief is
available, and a high degree of distinctiveness is required to qualify for dilution
protection. There has been a lack of consistency in the application of these laws,
and the results in any given conflict have been unpredictable.

Effective in January 1996, the Federal Trademark Dilution Act was added to
the Lanham Act as Section 43(c), to provide uniform and consistent federal dilution protection, limited to famous marks, to replace the patchwork quilt produced by state laws. This act accomplished several objectives:

- It set forth eight factors to be considered in determining whether a mark is
  "distinctive and famous."
- It limits relief to an injunction unless the defendant's actions were willful,
  in which case the full damages provisions of the Lanham Act are available.
- Federal registration became a complete defense to state dilution actions
  (but the act did not eliminate such actions).
- It set up three exclusions, or defenses—for fair use in advertising, noncommercial use, and news reporting and commentary.

The goal of uniform and consistent protection against dilution has not been achieved. Instead, the several federal courts of appeal have developed differing tests for dilution, and a serious split has developed between the circuits as to whether actual, present injury has to be proved under the Dilution Act before relief against dilution can be granted.

The source of this split is the wording of the act:

> The owner of a famous mark shall be entitled, subject to the principles of equity and upon such terms as the court deems reasonable, to an injunction against another person's commercial use in commerce of a mark or trade name, if such use begins after the mark has become famous and causes dilution of the distinctive quality of the famous mark.[9]

The words *causes dilution* have been held by the Fourth Circuit to mean that the owner must prove, at trial, "actual economic harm to the famous mark's economic value by lessening its former selling power . . ."[10] Proof of prospective harm, alone, is not sufficient to entitle the claimant to injunctive relief. This view also has been adopted by the Fifth Circuit and followed by several district courts, including the Central District of California.[11]

In contrast, the influential Second Circuit has expressly disagreed with the Fourth Circuit, and interprets the Dilution Act "to permit adjudication granting or denying an injunction . . . before the dilution has actually occurred."[12] The Second Circuit and other courts following this interpretation of the Dilution Act find that it is within the intent of Congress to provide for an injunction to prevent harm before it occurs.

The practical effect of the Fourth Circuit's more stringent interpretation is to make it very difficult for any claimant to obtain relief under the Dilution Act because of the problems of proof regarding actual economic injury. In addition, this more stringent interpretation often will subject claimants to uncompensable injury, since damages are recoverable only for willful dilution. Thus, this question is ripe for another Supreme Court decision to resolve a split between the circuits.

This issue also will be faced by the Trademark Trial and Appeal Board, which handles oppositions and cancellation proceedings as well as deciding appeals from the decisions of trademark examiners in the U.S. Patent and Trademark Office. The Board held in 1996 that the Dilution Act did not provide that dilution would be a new ground for opposing or cancelling a registration, but Congress amended the Lanham Act in 1999 to override this decision.[13] Thus, the Board is facing the same dilemma as that faced by the district courts.

In this regard, the Board has an additional circumstance—many oppositions pertain to intent-to-use applications in which the mark in issue has never been used.

Despite this fact, Congress now has directed that "dilution under 43(c)" is a ground for opposition to a registration, so the Board must resolve the "causes dilution" question in a way that permits the determination of oppositions against marks that have not been used.[14]

The outcome seems to be predictable: "causes dilution" will have to be interpreted as meaning "likely to cause dilution" so that the Board can decide these cases. Further, this test logically would apply in cancellation actions as well—the statutory language is the same—so that proof of actual economic harm to a mark's value, as required by the Fourth Circuit's stringent test, is not likely to be required in Board proceedings, and the Second Circuit's approach is likely to be followed by the Board.

Interestingly, a more recent decision by the Second Circuit injected another obstacle into the paths of claimants seeking federal dilution protection. In this case, *TCPIP Holding Co.* v. *Haar Communication, Inc.*, the court held that trademarks that are not inherently distinctive but have acquired secondary meaning do not qualify for federal dilution protection.[15] The decision seems to equate *fame* with *acquired distinctiveness* and makes *inherent distinctiveness* a prerequisite to dilution protection. In doing so, the court misinterprets basic trademark principles in relation to the dilution law.

A clear conclusion from the recent dilution cases is that the goal of uniform and consistent protection against dilution has not been achieved. Both before and after the federal Dilution Act, the courts frequently exhibited an unwillingness to give antidilution statutes their literal effect, and have granted or denied dilution protection inconsistently. Nevertheless, dilution remains one remedy that can be sought to protect a distinctive trademark against noncompetitive and noninfringing use, under appropriate circumstances but without predictable results.

The Internet, Cyberpiracy, and Domain Name Conflicts

With the growth of the Internet, an entirely new arena of trademark and trade name conflicts has arisen, resulting from the use of the same or similar terms in domain names. Companies have registered domain names, including the trademarks of their competitors, and some Internet entrepreneurs have registered hundreds, or even thousands, of combinations of words, some trademarks and some not, to serve as stock-in-trade for future sales and licensing. Others have registered well-known trademarks in domain names for Web sites that are critical of the trademark owner, raising constitutional issues of free speech. The registration of large numbers of domain names containing well-known trademarks to which the registrant has no claim of right, other than being the first domain name registrant, has led to the coining of new terms: *cyberpiracy* and *cybersquatting*.

Other chapters in this book deal in more detail with the Internet and the registration and use of domain names. This chapter will be limited to a review and general summary of the developments regarding the use and protection of trademarks and trade names in this field.

Although the Internet was conceived more than 30 years ago, domain names exploded into the public's awareness and emerged as trademark issues during the mid-1990s. There were no specific laws regulating the adoption and use of domain names, which were registered on a first-come, first-served basis by Network Solutions, Inc. (NSI). This agency administered domain names in several top-level domains that now are well known: *.com, .org, .edu, .gov, .mil, .net* and *.int.* NSI's policies attempted to limit abuses and resolve conflicts between competing claims of ownership, but were of limited effectiveness in dealing with allegations of trademark infringement. A difference in a single digit from a registered trademark was sufficient to take a dispute outside NSI's limited ability and willingness to resolve a dispute as to ownership.

Early court cases dealing with allegations of infringement of intellectual property rights on the Internet relied on traditional legal principles in dealing with activities in this new medium. Examples include *Playboy Enterprises* v. *Frena,* 839 F. Supp. 1552 (M.D. Fla. 1993), (trademark and copyright infringement) and *Religious Technology Center* v. *Netcom On-line Communications Services, Inc.,* 907 F. Supp. 1361 (N.D. Cal. 1995) (copyright and trade secrets infringement). These and other early cases established that the courts would consider allegations of infringement in Internet activities on the same grounds that were applied in other media.

In early domain name litigation, trademark owners had little difficulty in preventing use of confusingly similar domain names in connection with Internet business activities related to the goods or services with which the trademarks were used. Traditional *likelihood of confusion* analyses resulted in court decisions, or, more often, settlements, in favor of the trademark owners.

Where the businesses of the parties were unrelated or the domain name registrant had not used the domain name in connection with any activity, likelihood of confusion often was difficult to establish, so traditional infringement approaches did not provide a clear remedy. Resorting to state antidilution statutes was uncertain, at best, and sometimes was defeated by lack of actual use of the domain name.

In 1999, the U.S. Congress added the Anti-cybersquatting Consumer Protection Act to the Lanham Act as new Section 43(d), creating a new federal right for owners of marks and names against a person who:

> with bad faith intent to profit registers, traffics in or uses a domain name that—
>
> > (I) is identical or confusingly similar to a distinctive mark, or
> > (II) is dilutive of a famous mark.

The act, headed "Cyberpiracy Prevention," sets out nine factors that may be considered in determining whether bad faith is present, including the accused pirate's intellectual property rights and activities regarding the domain name and the extent of distinctiveness or fame of the mark, and provides for *in rem* civil actions under some circumstances.

Some of the states also have enacted similar statutes. California, for example, passed a "Cyber Piracy" statute in 1988 (Business and Professions Code Sections 17525–17528) also directed to the bad-faith registration, use, or trafficking in domain names that are identical or confusingly similar to the personal names of other living persons or deceased personalities.

In view of the expense and complexity of litigation, these statutory remedies do not provide prompt and economical disposition of domain name disputes and, therefore, have not been widely used. In recognition of the need for a different solution, the World Intellectual Property Organization (WIPO) has cooperated with the relatively recently formed Internet Corporation for Assigned Names and Numbers (ICANN) to establish an expedited alternative process, known as the Uniform Domain Name Dispute Resolution Policy (UDRP). This process initially applied to the original seven top-level domain names, including *.com, .org,* and *.net,* and subsequently has been expanded to include numerous two-letter country code domain names. It is, essentially, a limited arbitration procedure that is mandatory for the domain name registrant after it has been invoked by a complainant, who must show the following:

- The domain name is identical or confusingly similar to a mark owned by the complainant.
- The domain name registrant has no legitimate interest in the domain name.
- The domain name has been registered and used in bad faith, specifying the following four types of circumstances constituting evidence of bad faith:
  1. Indications that the domain name was acquired primarily for the purpose of sale or other transfer to the complainant;
  2. A pattern of conduct of registration for the purpose of preventing the owner of a mark from registering;
  3. Registering for the purpose of disrupting a competitor's business; or
  4. Use of the domain name to attract Internet users, for commercial gain, by creating a likelihood of confusion with the complainant.

The relief granted by the UDRP proceeding is limited to the cancellation of the registration, or transfer to the successful claimant, and does not bar the complainant (or the registrant) from taking judicial action, either before or after the administrative proceeding. In fact, ICANN's policy is to delay for 10 days before notifying the domain name registrar of the outcome, so that the registrant can take legal action to protect the registration.

The UDRP process has served its intended purpose for relatively simple disputes, many of which are not contested. Its limitations lie primarily in the inability of the process to consider complex or unusual issues, which are more effectively addressed in court proceedings.

Although the United States has been the leader in the Internet/domain name field, and the initial registry, NSI, is based in this country, foreign courts have been active in deciding disputes over domain names that infringe local trademark rights. For example, a Canadian company that owned the YELLOW PAGES mark obtained an injunction in Canadian court against a Web site in the United States identified as *cdnyellowpages.com* that was controlled by Canadians and targeted the Canadian market.[16]

Additional Internet issues similar to domain name issues exist regarding the use of metatags on Web sites. These are index words that are inserted on Web pages in a manner that is invisible to an observer but is detectable in electronic searches as key words for identifying the subject matter on the site. Trademark owners generally have been successful against competitors who are attempting to divert business away from the trademark owner with infringing metatags, unless the allegedly infringing use is justified as a truthful statement or is protected, nonconfusing free speech as criticism of the trademark owner.[17]

Merchandising and Franchising as Specialized Fields of Trademark Licensing

Trademark licenses are the foundations of both merchandising and franchising, each of which has special characteristics that set it apart from other trademark licensing fields. Although general licensing principles apply, additional considerations receive special attention in agreements in these fields.

Merchandising, sometimes called *character licensing,* often is combined with the licensing of copyrighted subject matter from motion pictures or other literary or entertainment properties and personalities, and is based on the use of publicly recognizable characters or other properties that are used on or in association with products or services to foster the sales of those products and services. Examples of merchandising are STAR WARS toys, clothing, and videogames, HARLEY DAVIDSON jackets, belts, and T-shirts, and MICHAEL JORDAN as a sponsor of shoes, underwear, and hot dogs. Special attention is given in merchandising agreements to the field of use, form of display, and graphics, advertising, and protection of the licensor from possible adverse effects, and, in the case of *personality* merchandising, the personality's rights in his or her name, likeness, or other aspects of persona.

These rights are protected in the United States under the rights of privacy or publicity and thus are licensable for use by others.

Franchising, in turn, is the granting of a trademark/trade name license by a franchisor to one or more franchisees, together with a comprehensive business plan or system for the operation of the franchised business, in return for payment of a franchise fee for the right to operate the franchise, under the franchisor's supervision and control.

Franchises can be categorized in at least three different recognizable types:

1. *Business format franchises,* in which the franchisees operate retail sales outlets in accordance with the franchisor's business plan, licensed trademark/trade name, and usually overall image (such as a fast-food or restaurant chain of licensed, franchisee-owned outlets).
2. *Distribution franchises,* under which the franchisees/distributors market trademarked products of the manufacturer/franchisor, as the official or authorized outlet for those products (such as automobile and gasoline dealerships).
3. *Manufacturing franchises,* in which the franchisees receive a basic product or protected right from the franchisor, enabling the franchisees to manufacture and sell the completed product (such as soft ice cream, a bottled beverage, or mattress and bedding products).

In the United States, both state and federal laws apply to the regulation of franchise activities. The Federal Trade Commission (FTC) has promulgated the FTC Franchise Disclosure Rules, and states have enacted laws regulating both the offering and the termination of franchises. Before entering into the granting of franchises in any state, the franchisor typically will be required to register the franchise offer, and the registration procedure will include the filing of an application with the state's regulatory agency, with copies of the offering prospectus, the proposed franchise agreement, and any advertisements offering the proposed franchises.[18]

Care must be taken in drawing nonfranchise license agreements to avoid imposing on the franchisee the requirements of a business plan or system that might bring the license under the various franchise laws and regulations. This is a particular risk in cases where several nonexclusive licenses are to be granted, perhaps with exclusive licenses in their respective territories, and all using the same licensed trademark. All that distinguishes such a licensing program from a franchising business is the nature and extent of the quality control in the trademark license agreement. If it rises to the level of "a marketing plan or system prescribed in substantial part by [the licensor]," it may well subject the licensor to the franchise laws applicable to the jurisdictions in which the licensees will be operating.[19]

TRADE-MARK PROTECTION AND LICENSING:
THE CANADIAN PERSPECTIVE

As with the U.S. Lanham Act, the Canadian Act defines the concepts of trade-name and trade-mark as well as the use, enforcement, and protection of trade-marks in Canada. A trade-name is defined in the Trade-marks Act as "the name under which any business is carried on, whether or not it is the name of a corporation, a partnership or an individual." This is quite straightforward. A *trade-mark,* however, is defined as:

> (a) a mark that is used by a person for the purpose of distinguishing or so as to distinguish wares or services manufactured, sold, leased, hired or performed by him from those manufactured, sold, leased, hired or performed by others,
>
> (b) a certification mark,
> (c) a distinguishing guise, or
> (d) a proposed trade-mark.

Certification mark and *distinguishing guise* are further defined as follows:

> Certification mark means a mark that is used for the purpose of distinguishing or so as to distinguish wares or services that are of a defined standard with respect to
>
> (a) the character or quality of the wares or services,
> (b) the working conditions under which the wares have been produced or the services performed,
> (c) the class of persons by whom the wares have been produced or the services performed, or
> (d) the area within which the wares have been produced or the services performed,
>
> from wares or services that are not of that defined standard.

Although a definition of certification mark exists in the Canadian Act, it is little used in Canada because the distinction between a certification mark and an ordinary mark is essentially a distinction without a difference. Historically (prior to June 1993), there were some advantages to certification marks; these have essentially disappeared.

Distinguishing guise means

> (a) a shaping of wares or their containers, or
> (b) a mode of wrapping or packaging wares
>
> the appearance of which is used by a person for the purpose of distinguishing or so as to distinguish wares or services manufactured, sold, leased, hired or performed by him from those manufactured, sold, leased, hired or performed by others.

Not unlike *trade dress* in the United States, essentially everything from the trademark or the name of the product down to the way a product is shaped, wrapped, contained, or packaged through a distinguishing guise can be the subject of trademark protection and therefore the proper subject matter of a license. The most recent application of the Canadian Act can be found in the case of the *Canadian Olympic Association* v. *Konica Canada Inc.,* et al. (1991) 39 C.P.R. (3d) 400. In that case the Federal Court of Appeal determined that the definition of distinguishing guise was broad enough to include a book entitled *The Guiness Book of Olympic Records* shrink-wrapped with the Defendant's photographic film. The Court held that the Defendant's use of the Olympics on the book shrink-wrapped with its film was an attempt to use the Canadian Olympic Association's Olympic mark to sell its "film." The offending use was enjoined as a distinguishing guise, "a mode of wrapping or packaging wares," which offended the Canadian Olympic Association's rights in its Olympic mark. As to services, the trade-marks used for the services, together with the manner or method by which they are delivered—and even the sound, smell, and color associated therewith—are all fair game for trademark protection and therefore licensing. Add to that patented processes, domain names, software, know-how, trade secrets, and confidential or proprietary business techniques, and we have a whole array of rights that can enter into a licensing situation. Most licensing agreements contain not one but a series of grants of rights relating to various different technologies and intellectual property categories.

In addition to traditional trade-mark and trade-name licensing, Canada, by statute, also provides a *trade-mark-like* licensing vehicle directed to government institutions, and, more importantly from a licensing point of view, to universities and other not-for-profit entities called *public authorities* that provide services and goods to the public. Interestingly, this protection is *not* limited to Canadian public authorities or Canadian universities. This protection is available to public authorities and universities throughout the world, provided the organization meets the criteria set by Section 9 of the Trade-marks Act and the applicable case law.

In Canada, there is only one register for trade-marks; it is not divided as to Principal or Supplemental Registers. However, marks that are initially considered by a trade-mark Examiner during the application process to be "clearly descriptive" might be found to be registerable on the Canadian Trade-mark Register if the owner can establish to the satisfaction of the Registrar of Trade-marks that the mark has, by use in Canada by the owner or its predecessor, become distinctive as of the date of filing of the trade-mark application for registration.[20] This concept is often referred to as establishing *secondary meaning.*

In order to establish secondary meaning, an affidavit or affidavits proving such notoriety as of the date of filing must be filed with the Trade-marks Office during the examination process. As well, Canada, unlike the United States, also permits the registration of *clearly descriptive marks* by foreign entities under Section 14 of the Canadian Act. A foreign applicant can, if the "clearly descriptive" objection is raised, claim the benefit of Section 14 if it has a registered trade-mark in its country of origin for substantially the same mark and the mark is "not without distinctive character in Canada" with regard to all circumstances including its use in *any* country.[21] As with secondary meaning, the requirements of Section 14 are proven by way of affidavit evidence filed during the examination process.

Sections 30 and 34 of the Canadian Act provide for the same six-month priority filing benefit as in U.S. law, as well as filing based on use and registration in a foreign country. However, unlike the United States, Canada allows for filing of a Canadian application based solely on use and application abroad, even if filing the application in Canada is beyond the priority period. Registration in the foreign country and use must be achieved prior to registration being allowed in Canada on this basis.

Registration is for a renewable 15-year period, and no proof of use is required upon renewal, nor is there any interim statutory proof-of-use requirement. As in the United States, cessation of use without the intent to resume is abandonment. Under Section 18 of the Canadian Act, a registration of a trade-mark can thus be expunged on this basis. The statute does not, however, state that three years of nonuse is deemed to be abandonment, nor does it provide any presumption in that regard. An expungement proceeding on the grounds of abandonment must be brought in the courts, and while the provincial courts can give a declaration of abandonment, only the Federal Court can expunge a registered trade-mark from the Trade-mark Register under Section 57 of the Canadian Act.

Unlike the United States and unique to Canada, a summary cancellation procedure is available to cancel or expunge trade-mark registrations that are not in use in Canada. Section 45 of the Canadian Act provides for cancellation of registered trade-marks that, essentially, have been registered for more than three years but are not currently in use in Canada. This procedure is an administrative procedure carried out in the Trade-marks Office by the filing of a request with the Registrar of Trade-marks. Any person can bring such a proceeding upon payment of the prescribed fee. The test is whether the mark has been in use in Canada in association with each and every one of the wares and services set out in the registration within the three-year period immediately prior to the date of issuance of the notice by the Trade-marks Office pursuant to Section 45. The registrant must file an affidavit proving use, failing which the mark will be expunged or at the very least the wares and services for which evidence of use was not provided will be deleted. The only exception to the requirement of proof of use is provision for an affidavit attesting to exceptional circumstances (i.e., circumstances beyond the control of the registered owner) that prevented the registrant from using the mark at issue within the relevant period for some or all of the wares and services. Failure of the owner to file an affidavit in response results in expungement of the mark. This procedure is actively used in Canada because it is inexpensive, summary in nature, and effective.

In Canada, confusion can be found between trade-marks, whether or not the wares or services are of the same general class. This principle is stated in Section 6 of the Canadian Act. There is no special statutory protection or case law protection, however, for *famous marks*. The traditional causes of action such as infringement, passing off, and unfair competition are, of course, available to owners of famous trade-marks. The only additional cause of action that is somewhat similar to dilution is the *damage to goodwill* basis set out in Section 22 of the Canadian Act. It reads

(1) No person shall use a trade-mark registered by another person in a manner that is likely to have the effect of depreciating that value of the goodwill attaching thereto.

(2) *Action in respect thereof.* In any respect of a use of a trade-mark contrary to subsection (1), the court may decline to order the recovery of damages or profits and may permit the defendant to continue to sell wares marked with the trade-mark that were in his possession or under his control at the time notice was given to him that the owner of the registered trade-mark complained of the use of the trade-mark.

Unfortunately, the Canadian courts have severely restricted the effectiveness of this cause of action to date by limiting its application not only just to *registered* marks as proscribed by subsection (1) but also just to situations where the unauthorized user is using the identical mark to the mark registered. This section, although often raised by plaintiffs in their pleadings, has never resulted in any significant deterrent to unauthorized users, either from the damage or injunction point of view.

Although not all trade-marks are created nor treated equally in Canada, a trade-mark is a trade-mark is a trade-mark. The confusion test in Canada is the method by which the relative strength of trade-marks or trade-names is measured, whether they are registered, common law, famous, or otherwise. Section 6(5) of the Canadian Act reads:

In determining whether trade-marks or trade-names are confusing, the court or the Registrar, as the case may be, shall have regard to all the surrounding circumstances including

(a) the inherent distinctiveness of the trade-marks or trade-names and the extent to which they have become known;
(b) the length of time the trade-marks or trade-names have been in use;
(c) the nature of the wares, services or business;
(d) the nature of the trade; and
(e) the degree of resemblance between the trade-marks or trade-names in appearance or sound or in the ideas suggested by them.

As can be seen, there are at least five elements to the test—namely, the criteria of Section 6(5)(a) to (e) and any additional circumstances. Certainly, strong and convincing evidence as to any element listed above could lead to a conclusion that a mark is very strong, unique, distinctive—dare we say famous—or so weak and virtually unenforceable except against an essentially identical mark for identical wares or services.

The test for confusion in Canada is the imperfect recollection of the ordinary consumer. The question that must be determined is whether a person, on a first impression, knowing of one mark only and having an imperfect recollection of it, would be likely to be deceived or confused as to source or believe that the source of the second mark is somehow authorized by the owner of the first mark.

The most recent case and decision in Canada as to the *famous mark* is *United Artists Corp.* v. *Pink Panther Beauty Corp.,* (1998) 80 C.P.R. (3d)247, a decision of the Federal Court of Appeal. Leave to appeal the decision was sought and granted to the Supreme Court of Canada. Unfortunately, the parties settled the matter before it could be heard and decided by the highest court. This decision essentially removes any special status or protection for famous marks. The case originated as an opposition proceeding before the Opposition Board in the Canadian Trade-marks Office. The principle issue was whether PINK PANTHER, in association with "beauty supplies," was registrable over the United Artists' famous THE PINK PANTHER for feature films and related services. At the Trade-marks Office level, the opposition was dismissed because the Registrar held that there was no likelihood of confusion and that while the mark THE PINK PANTHER was well known, it was not famous. Contrary to the finding of the Registrar, the Trial division of the Federal Court found THE PINK PANTHER trade-mark of United Artists to be very famous and allowed the appeal and refused the application by Pink Panther Beauty Corp. for registration of Pink Panther.

At the Court of Appeal level, the bench was divided two to one in its decision. The majority believed that while THE PINK PANTHER mark was famous and inherently distinctive, that did not automatically result in a finding of confusion. Rather, the Court decided it still had to consider the various criteria of confusion under Section 6(5), as above. The majority stated:

> "In a case with a famous mark, it's necessary to adjust the weight given to the individual criteria or to the surrounding circumstances." The Court went on to find that "the fact that [United Artists'] mark was world renowned could not be a factor so important as to make the differences in wares and services irrelevant." The Court decided it had to divorce THE PINK PANTHER (pink cat) character from the words PINK PANTHER and, as a result, found that the use of the words alone would not give rise to "confusion" in view of the divergent wares and the nature of the trade of the respective parties.[22]

The dissent essentially held that because of the famous nature of the trade-mark THE PINK PANTHER, a consumer of ordinary intelligence would believe the wares of PINK PANTHER BEAUTY CORP. originated from or were authorized by United Artists. This case is an excellent review of the law as to famous marks in Canada.

Special Protection in Canada for Marks Used in Foreign Jurisdiction

Although Canada and its courts do not give special protection to famous marks, they do allow for legal action under passing off and unfair competition for trade-marks that are essentially used only in the United States. The theory is that Canadians are exposed to United States trade-marks while residing and traveling in the United States. This minimal goodwill or notoriety among Canadians traveling and temporarily residing in the United States, even where the U.S. company had done no business in Canada, was sufficient to maintain a successful action for passing off and unfair competition in Canada. This principle was recently confirmed in the case of *Enterprise Car & Truck Rentals Ltd. et al.* v. *Enterprise Rent-a-Car et al.* (1996) 66 C.P.R. (3d) 453 and affirmed on appeal at (1998) 79 C.P.R. (3d) 45. Goodwill in a trade-mark sufficient to sustain a legal action in Canada can be created by use in another country where the trade-mark came to the attention of Canadians either through use or advertising in that other country. Interestingly, while the preceding situation is sufficient to maintain a legal action and obtain injunctive relief in Canada, that same use is not of a sufficient level to obtain registration of a trade-mark in Canada.

Cyberpiracy in the Land of .ca

In Canada, the land of .ca, the law as to cybersquatting or cyberpiracy is not well developed. Canada has no equivalent or, for that matter, any statute in the nature of an Anti-cybersquatting Consumer Protection Act. Again, Canadian trade-mark and trade-name owners, as well as trade-mark owners from around the world, must look to the courts in Canada. Traditional intellectual property causes of action must be used to enforce their respective trade-mark or trade-name rights as against .ca cybersquatters and cyberpirates throughout the world, except where they can qualify for, or are entitled to, protection or enforcement rights in foreign jurisdictions. Canada has not recognized ICANN or any organization for .ca dispute resolution. Clearly a Canadian can take action as against .com or other Internet breaches through ICANN or other dispute resolution agencies that exist in other jurisdictions. However, with regard to .ca, the courts or negotiated settlement are presently the only alternatives, although the final policy and rules for a Canadian Domain Name Dispute Resolution Policy are being put in place.

Presently, the aggrieved parties must seek redress in the provincial courts or the Federal Court under trade-mark infringement, passing off, unfair competition, or depreciation of goodwill under the Trade-marks Act or at common law. Numerous actions against offending domain name users have been commenced in various courts throughout Canada. To date, there have been no final decisions by the Courts after a full trial on merits. There are several interlocutory decisions, most of which have sided with the trade-mark owner. The difficulty with many offending .ca domain names is that while they are owned by a third party and may be offending, they may not be in use or may never have been in active use. The issue, then, is whether traditional trade-mark causes of action are appropriate where only the mere ownership of an offending domain name is at issue. Is ownership alone without use enough to trigger rights under infringement, passing off, unfair competition, or damage to goodwill causes of action? Probably not.

In this vein, there is a recent decision of the British Columbia Supreme Court trial division that largely adopted the U.S. approach to conspiracy. In the *British Columbia Automobile Association* v. *Office and Professional Employees' Union Local* 378 (2001) B.C.J. No.151, the Union, which was on legal strike, had created a Web site that was accessible through the domain name bcaabacktowork.com, bcaaonstrike.com, and picketline.com. After several changes to the Web site relating to objections as to trade-mark use and copying of various aspects of the look and feel of the plaintiff's Web site, the matter went to hearing.

Although the Court did find at least to some extent that the defendant had passed off and depreciated the goodwill of the plaintiff in some of its trademarks through its use, the criteria the Court applied is of interest:

- Were the trade-marks identical?
- Are the entities commercial competitors?
- Is there evidence of actual confusion?

The Court ended up balancing the plaintiff's trade-mark rights against the rights of the union to present its message to customers of the plaintiff or its right to freedom of speech. Of significance to the Court was the disclaimer on the union Web site as to any affiliation with the plaintiff and the lack of evidence of any actual confusion. In other words, even though customers of the plaintiff might have been misdirected to the union Web site for various reasons, once they were on it they knew it was not the plaintiff's.

While cybersquatting is an active area of the law in Canada, it would appear that the traditional forms of action under trade-mark law are meeting the needs of owners or that the matters are settling through negotiation. Cybersquatting is clearly alive and well in Canada and may be lucrative. However, the

Canadian Internet Registration Authority (CIRA), the entity involved in the recordal registration and transfer of .ca names, has recently released a final policy and rules for public comment. The revised policy shares some similarities with ICANN UDRP but differs in the responsibilities of the complainant and respondent. For example, the complainant is only required to prove bad faith registration and confusion (along with some evidence that the respondent has no legitimate interest in the name). However, the respondent retains the domain name if he or she is able to demonstrate any legitimate interest in the name, including a good faith noncommercial use. As well, the policy requires a three-member panel for all cases. The criteria under the new Canadian system are:

1. Is the .ca registrant's mark similar to trade-mark in which the complainant had rights prior to the registration of the .ca domain name?
2. Does the registrant have a legitimate interest in the name?
3. Has the registrant registered the domain name in bad faith?

Once the system is operational, it will be interesting to see the effect in Canada on cybersquatting.

Statutory Trade-mark License Provisions for Trade-marks and Trade-names

In Canada, under the Trade-marks Act of 1953 and until June 1993, the Canadian Act created a central registry of licensees for *registered* trade-marks and therefore recognized only registered trade-mark licensing. The licensees were referred to as registered or permitted users, and the recorded agreements were Registered or Permitted User Agreements. In June 1993, the so-called simplification of trade-mark licensing resulted in Section 50 of the Trade-marks Act, which reflected commercial licensing reality by recognizing both registered and unregistered trade-marks as well as trade-names. However, as licensing was no longer subject to government approval, an even greater onus was placed on the licensing professional and the owner of trade-marks and trade-names to make sure that proper licensing is completed both quickly and correctly and that obligations under license agreements are complied with. Section 50 requires self-discipline on the part of the owner to ensure that license arrangements are timely put in place, monitored, and maintained, even in related corporate or related party or controlled situations. Although in certain controlled or wholly owned corporate situations, quality control might be implied by the courts, I suggest it is a risk that should not be taken and that a proper written license agreement should be created and the obligations complied with and monitored.

Licensees under Section 50 of the Canadian Act include any persons other than the Canadian owner who are using a trade-mark or a trade-name. This applies to independent third parties, related or associated companies, and wholly owned subsidiaries. Anyone who uses a trade-mark or trade-name other than the owner of that trade-mark or trade-name is required to comply with Section 50 or risk the validity of its mark.

Under the statutory regime of Section 50, the use, advertisement, or display of a trade-mark or a trade-name by a licensee will be considered to be used by the owner if the conditions of Section 50(1) are met. These are:

- That the entity using the mark or name is licensed by or with the authority of the owner; *and*
- The license gives the owner direct or indirect control of the character or quality of the wares or services sold or provided in association with the trade-mark or trade-name and the owner actually exercises that control.

Specifically, Section 50 reads as follows:

(1) For the purposes of this Act, if an entity is licensed by or with the authority of the owner of a trade-mark to use the trade-mark in a country and the owner has, under the licence, direct or indirect control of the character or quality of the wares or services, then the use, advertisement or display of the trade-mark in that country as or in a trade-mark, trade-name or otherwise by that entity has, and is deemed always to have had, the same effect as such a use, advertisement or display of the trade-mark in that country by the owner.

(2) *Idem.* For the purposes of this Act, to the extent that public notice is given of the fact that the use of a trade-mark is a licensed use and of the identity of the owner, it shall be presumed, unless the contrary is proven, that the use is licensed by the owner of the trade-mark and the character or quality of the wares or services is under the control of the owner.

(3) *Owner may be required to take proceedings.* Subject to any agreement subsisting between an owner of a trade-mark and a licensee of the trade-mark, the licensee may call on the owner to take proceedings for infringement thereof, and, if the owner refuses or neglects to do so within two months after being so called on, the licensee may institute proceedings for infringement in the licensee's own name as if the licensee were the owner, making the owner a defendant.

It is *not* mandatory that a license be in writing, although a written license is always recommended and preferred even in situations where related, associated, or wholly owned licensed users are involved.

At a minimum, in order to maintain and sustain a protectable right, any such license should cover the basic elements of licensed trade-mark or trade-name use such as attribution of all use to the owner, termination provisions, quality control, inspection, and proper marking as to ownership, preferably in compliance with Section 50(2). This should be the case whether the parties are in related, associated, or controlled relationship or arm's-length, since Section 50(1) is directed to the control of the trade-mark or trade-name use by the owner rather than the concept of corporate control as between parties.

Section 50(2) provides that if the public is notified of the identity of the owner of a trade-mark or trade-name and the fact of its use under license, then there will be a rebuttable presumption in favor of the owner that the use is properly licensed and that there is the necessary control. Therefore, requiring a licensee to mark packaging and other materials as to ownership of the marks and the fact that marks are used under license can be quite beneficial, particularly where no written license agreement exists. It should prove far more difficult for a would-be infringer to disprove deemed proper licensing obtained by way of the presumption of Section 50(2) (and therefore deemed in compliance with Section 50(1)) than it would be for an owner of a mark, particularly where only an oral license is in place to prove compliance with that section. Each and every trade-mark license should require the licensee to include such a notice on its packaging and promotional material to reverse the onus of proof onto the infringer.

These sections deal with statutory minimum requirements as to license wording to be included in a trade-mark/trade-name license agreement. Perhaps more critical, if not at least equally important, is the need for the actual monitoring of that licensed use to ensure compliance. It cannot be emphasized enough to a trade-mark owner that the drafting of a good license agreement is only the first baby step in the effectiveness of a license. It is incumbent upon a trade-mark owner during the currency of a license agreement to police not only infringing use by third parties but also to monitor the use by its licensee or licensees. Section 50 and trade-mark licensing law traditionally have required the owners to ensure that quality control standards are being maintained and to monitor to ensure compliance by the licensee.

Mere paper obligations are not enough. Trade-mark owners should set up a regular, recorded, quality control program that can be produced and provided, should the issue of proper and monitored licensing be raised in any enforcement or cancellation proceedings. This issue is, almost without exception, raised as an issue in any adversarial proceeding, whether it be expungement, cancellation, opposition or infringement, or passing off litigation. No matter how thorough and detailed the written trade-mark/trade-name license drafting may be, it is the actual and consistent monitoring and enforcement of those provisions in terms of quality control and monitoring that completes the proper quality control licensing requirements and will most likely make the difference between being able to enforce trade-mark rights or defend against third-party action with respect to a protectable trade-mark or trade-name.

Right of Licensee to Take Legal Action for Infringement

Section 50(3) also provides trade-mark licensees with the right to take separate legal action for infringement, should the owner refuse to do so. As an owner, you should include a clause within any license agreement dealing with the licensee's right to sue, if any, and the circumstances governing that right. Failure to deal with this issue might result in an embarrassing and perhaps damaging situation where the licensee may bring an action that ultimately negatively affects the trade-mark rights of the owner. Strangely, Section 50(3) only speaks to infringement (which, of course, relates only to registered trade-marks). It does not address *passing off* or unfair competition as it relates to common-law trade-marks and trade-names, nor does it address unauthorized use of Section 9 or official marks, the latter of which will be dealt with later in this chapter.

Licensing and Pharmaceutical Marks

Please note, as well, that there are particular *attribution-of-use* guidelines provided under Section 51 of the Trade-marks Act for trade-marks relating to "Pharmaceutical Preparations." If your licensing situation involves pharmaceutical preparations, careful attention should be given to these guidelines as to use, labeling, and attribution rights.

Licensing of Trade-marks for Trade-name Use

As already mentioned, Section 50(1) also contemplates that a trade-mark owner may permit licensees to use a trade-mark in or as a trade-name. This use should also be monitored and controlled by a license agreement in the same manner as licensed trade-mark use. As well, provisions that provide for deregistration of the business trade or corporate names that consist of or include a trade-mark, upon termination of a license, are a must. In particular, clauses that allow for the unilateral deregistration of a trade or corporate name by the owner of the trade-mark, upon termination, are recommended as the licensee may no longer exist or may not be particularly co-operative upon termination.

Existing Registered User Agreements Recorded Prior to June 1993

As noted above, prior to June 1993, a registered or permitted user system for licensing of registered trade-marks existed in Canada that required submission of licensing documents or a summary thereof in the form of a registered user or permitted use application to the Trade-marks Office for approval and recordal prior to the implementation of the license.

As to registered or permitted use agreements relating to registered trade-marks, many such agreements included either no definite termination date or an *indefinite term*. Many historical registered or permitted user agreements may at least technically still be in force in Canada and, for all intents and purposes, may still govern relationships between parties to those agreements, unless they have been subsequently terminated. These prior registered user agreements recorded under the pre-1993 system are maintained by the Trade-marks Office, which must maintain a Register of former permitted users. Following enactment of the Intellectual Property Law Improvement Act of June 1993 and Section 61 thereof, the Trade-mark Office published in the *Canadian Trade-marks Journal* the following "Practice and Procedures," concerning the repeal of the old Section 50 of the Trade-marks Act on September 8, 1993, and again on September 22, 1993, as follows:

> All the requests received before June 9, 1993, for the registration, cancellation or the variation of a user of a registered Trade-mark should have been processed by now.
>
> All the requests, received before June 9, 1993, for the registration, cancellation or the variation of a user of a pending Trade-mark that was not registered as of June 9, 1993, will not be processed. The fees received to effect such registrations should have been refunded by now, and the requests should have also been returned by now.
>
> All the requests, received on or after June 9, 1993, for the registration, cancellation, or the variation of a user of either a pending or registered Trade-mark were not to be processed. The fees received to effect such registrations should have been refunded by now, as well as all such requests. In that connection, with former registered user matters, there is always the possibility that files have been missed and processing left in an incomplete state.
>
> All former registered user files are to be stored at various locations of the National Archives of Canada in Ottawa, since there is no longer a registered user department within the Trade-marks Office. The files are available upon request via the Trade-marks Office within one to three working days.[23]

Recordal of Trade-mark Licenses in Canada

As a result of the amendments to the Canadian Act in June 1993, Section 26(1)(b) prescribed the obligations on the Registrar of Trade-marks to maintain the Register of registered users in view of the ongoing rights contained in some of the documents. Under the pre-1993 system, approval and recordal of licenses was a requirement, if not prerequisite, to proper licensing under the Canadian Act. No specific recordal provisions now exist; however, the Canadian Act and Trade-mark Office practice appear to provide for the recordal of a trade-mark license under subsection 26(2)(c) of the Canadian Act as against *registered* trade-marks only. This section reads as follows:

Section 26

   (1) There shall be kept under the supervision of the Registrar
        (a) a register of trade-marks and of transfers, disclaimers, amendments, judgments and orders relating to each registered trade-mark; and
        (b) the register of registered users that was required to be kept under this subsection as it read immediately before Section 61 of the Intellectual Property Law Improvement Act came into force.
   (2) Information to be shown—The register referred to in paragraph (a) shall show, with reference to each registered trade-mark, the following:
        (c) a summary of all documents deposited with the application or subsequently thereto and affecting the rights to the trade-mark;

This section, and particularly subsections 26(1)(a) and 26(2)(c), requires the Registrar to keep a register showing various information pertaining to each registered trade-mark including, among other information, a summary of all documents deposited with the application or subsequently thereto and affecting the rights to the registered trade-mark. Again, like Section 50(3), this provision does not appear to apply to common-law trade-mark or trade-name licenses or licenses under Section 9 (this provision will be dealt with later) of the Canadian Act. The Canadian Trade-marks Office initially indicated that trade-mark license agreements would be included within the definition of documents "affecting the rights to the trade-mark" under this section. Although this procedure is not likely to be of significance to or of great attraction to trade-mark owners, a trade-mark licensee, particularly an exclusive trade-mark licensee, may wish to have his or her trade-mark license agreement recorded to ensure that any assignee of the owner (licensor) of the registered trade-mark will have notice or will be deemed to have notice of the existence of the licensee's trade-mark license agreement rights by virtue of this recordal.

Trade-mark owners, on the other hand, might not want licenses recorded against their registered trade-marks, as it might hinder or delay the assignment of rights because the existence of any recorded license would be revealed in any due diligence to a potential purchaser. As well, since Section 26 is not clear as to what will be recorded and therefore reflected on the Trade-mark Register or by whom, several questions arise:

- Who will be able to record a trade-mark license? The licensor or licensee or both?
- How and where will it be recorded?
- Who can cancel or remove such a recordal once made?
- What is the procedure involved in each step?
- What is the legal effect, if any, of such a recordal?

The Trade-marks Office had indicated initially (at least informally) that *only* the owner of a registered mark would be able to file and record a trade-mark license document and that the actual agreement might not necessarily need to be filed. For instance, all that may be required is a letter stating the fact of the existence of a trade-mark license. Query whether this truly reflects what is intended by Section 26 and whether the Trade-marks Office has the authority to make such a limitation on recordal without a change to the Canadian Act or, perhaps, the Regulations. In any event, it appears that the Trade-marks Office has changed its position somewhat, as it has allowed the filing and recordal of a complete trade-mark license agreement by the licensee alone without the notice or consent of the owner. It is doubtful that the owner of a registered mark would want all of the terms of his or her license agreement, including financial, to become part of the public record.

It should be borne in mind that any filing of documents with the Canadian Trade-marks Office *cannot be done on a confidential basis.* In other words, all documents filed are fully and publicly available for review or copying. The filing of the complete license agreement allows any third party to obtain a complete copy without restriction. It may, therefore, be more appropriate to file an expurgated version of the agreement, a summary thereof, or simply notice of its existence. Interestingly, under the pre-June 1993 registered user system, the act provided for confidentiality of the actual license agreement or any document, information, or evidence furnished under then Section 49(6) of the Canadian Act.

Trade-mark Licensing and Franchising in Canada

No discussion of trade-mark and trade-name licensing in Canada would be complete without at least mention of the important subcategory of franchising. As a result of the dramatic growth in the area of franchising, the law relating to trade-mark licensing has been greatly affected by decisions relating to clauses contained in franchise agreements (i.e., the fairness concept of licensing, particularly where the parties are not equal in licensing sophistication). Currently, only the provinces of Alberta and Ontario have in place statutory legislation governing franchise relationships. However, many provinces have draft legislation in the works, much of which mirrors the Ontario and Alberta process. Any person engaged in trade-mark licensing in Canada should be careful to consider both of these franchise statutes prior to finalizing any licensing arrangement, as the statutory definition of what is a *franchise,* particularly in Alberta, is quite broad. The breach of these franchise statutes can result in severe consequences, particularly for the owner of the trade-mark rights. In Alberta, The Franchise Act (the Alberta Act) defines *franchise* as:

> a contract, agreement or arrangement, either expressed or implied, whether oral or written, between 2 or more persons by which a franchisee is required to pay directly or indirectly a franchise fee in consideration for any of the following:

(i)   the right to engage in the business of offering, selling, or distributing the goods manufactured, processed or distributed or the services organized and directed by the franchisor,

(ii) the right to engage in the business of offering, selling or distributing any goods or services under a marketing plan or system prescribed or controlled by the franchisor,

(iii) the right to engage in a business which is associated with the franchisor's trade-mark, service mark, trade-name, logo type, advertising or any business symbol designating the franchisor or its associate,

(iv) the right to engage in a business in which the franchisee is reliant on the franchisor for the continued supply of goods or services, or

(v)   the right to recruit additional franchisees or sub-franchisors, but excluding contract, agreements or arrangements between manufacturers or if the franchisor is the Crown, a Crown agency or a municipal corporation.

The Ontario Act, called The Arthur Wishart Act (Franchise Disclosure) 2000, was, for the most part, enacted in 2000 and included various regulations to complement, explain, and particularize several of its provisions. The Ontario Act defines *franchise* more narrowly than the Alberta Act:

a right to engage in a business where the franchisee is required by contract or otherwise to make a payment or continuing payments, whether direct or indirect, or a commitment to make such payment or payments to the franchisor, or the franchisor's associate, in the course of operating the business or as a condition of acquiring the franchise or commencing operations and,

(a) in which,

(i)   the franchisor grants the franchisee the right to sell, offer for sale or distribute goods or services that are substantially associated with the franchisor's, or the franchisor's associate's, trade-mark, service mark, trade-name, logo or advertising or other commercial symbol, and

(ii) the franchisor or the franchisor's associate exercises significant control over, or offers significant assistance in, the franchisee's method of operation, including building design and furnishings, locations, business organization, marketing techniques or training, or

(b) in which,

(i)   the franchisor, or the franchisor's associate, grants the franchisee the representational or distribution rights, whether or not a trademark, service mark, trade-name, logo or advertising or other commercial symbol is involved, to sell, offer for sale or distribute goods or services supplied by the franchisor or a supplier designated by the franchisor, and

(ii) the franchisor, or the franchisor's associate, or a third person designated by the franchisor, provides location assistance, including securing retail outlets or accounts for the goods or services to be sold, offered for sale or distributed or securing locations or sites for vending machines, display racks or other product sales displays used by the franchisee.

The Alberta Act, at the outset, was a proactive act (similar to the registered user system under the pre-1993 Trade-marks Act) requiring would-be franchisors to file documentation including copies of the proposed franchise agreements, which were to be used in the province for approval by a government agency *prior to* any franchise activity or execution of a franchise agreement in or affecting the province. This procedure became unmanageable because the extreme delays caused by the government approval process did not meet with commercial reality. The Alberta Act and its regulations were subsequently amended to move to a *fairness* system. The act now requires a certain and defined prior disclosure by the franchisor to the franchisee in a disclosure document. Certain specific information must be included in that document, and certain provisions must be included in all franchise agreements. The failure to comply by the franchisor, even with the consent or knowledge of the franchisee, may result in unilateral termination of rights under the franchise agreement, together with the right of the franchisee to sue for damages even where the franchisee knowingly agreed to the terms of the agreement and had prior legal advice with regard to the franchise agreement.

The Ontario Act has followed this latter pattern of requiring certain disclosure of information and the form and content of that disclosure, all being about fairness in the franchisor/franchisee relationship. In addition, although the Ontario Act did not come into force until 2000, it has, to a certain extent, had retroactive effect on all prior franchise relationships. In particular, Section 3 of the Ontario Act, titled "Fair Dealing," retroactively affects franchise agreements entered into both prior to and after the coming into force of the Ontario Act.

Section 3 and its three subsections state:

3. (1) Every franchise agreement imposes on each party a duty of fair dealing in its performance and enforcement.

    (2) A party to a franchise agreement has a right of action for damages against another party to a franchise agreement who breaches the duty of fair dealing in the performance or enforcement of the franchise agreement.

    (3) For the purpose of this section, the duty of fair dealing includes the duty to act in good faith and in accordance with reasonable commercial standards.

The concept of *fairness* that is embodied in these two statutes will likely become the basic tenet of both technology and trade-mark licensing, for practical as well as legal reasons. The first decision under the fairness doctrine has now been rendered in the province of Ontario. In the case of *Shelanu Inc.* v. *Print Three Franchising Corp,*[24] Shelanu, the franchisee, had purchased two printing franchises from Print Three, the franchisor. The franchisor subsequently created a new business that competed with the franchisee's business, called Le Print Three. Subsequently, a dispute arose between the parties as the franchisee sought to close one of its operations due to economic conditions.

The franchisee sued for a declaration that the franchise agreement be terminated. The court held that the franchisor's establishment of a competing business was an act of bad faith and a breach of the underlying reasonable commercial standards that governed the business relationship of the parties. This was a fundamental breach that relieved the franchisee of compliance concerning the restrictive terms of the franchise agreement. This decision is presently under appeal.

If a license agreement is not fair to both parties, it will not likely be workable and will not last through time. The concept of win-win in terms of licensing is a longstanding motto of all good license drafters and negotiators. This does not mean that negotiations are not tactical, tough, or hard fought—only that in the end there is a fairness as to the ultimate terms and conditions of the agreement entered into by the parties. An agreement that is totally one-sided or unfairly drafted will only result in ongoing disagreement and animosity between the parties, which in the end will likely result in a breach or a series of breaches of the agreement by the aggrieved party, ending in termination, litigation, and/or arbitration.

In these one-sided situations, the cost of legal advice, litigation, arbitration, and enforcement will, in the end, likely far outstrip the advantages gained as a result of the one-sided terms of the license agreement. In many cases—particularly where it is made to appear to the court or the arbitration panel that one party was at a disadvantage in the negotiations and was taken advantage of in the license drafting process—the egregious clause or clauses in issue will be struck down or declared unenforceable.

For example, in recent decisions of Ontario Courts, *noncompetition clauses* (particularly in employment contract situations) that *generally* restrict an employee from competing within a specific territory for a specific period of time after the termination of an agreement have been held to be unenforceable. The court, on the other hand, has indicated that *nonsolicitation clauses* restricting a former employee from soliciting actual customers or likely potential customers of the employer are not similarly offensive. This principle will likely apply equally to all licensing and franchising situations. The concept of *fairness* (in this case the right to earn a living) is creeping into all aspects of licensing and contract law in general. As in the Shelanu case, the court incorporated some of the principles of employment law into the franchise case law and applied the statute. With the fairness principle now included as a statutory concept in the Ontario Act, this crossover concept has and will be applied generally to licensing relationships involving any and all aspects of technology.

Another development in licensing in Canada is the apparent willingness and ability of the government to impose or terminate license agreements as a part of regulating competition. Government intervention through a vehicle such as Section 32 of the Competition Act R.S.C. 1985, c. C-34, which provides, among other things, that where trade-mark rights are used so as to unduly restrain competition, the Federal Court may make an order, including a declaration that a license is void or directing that there be a grant of a license. An order may only be made under this section at the request of the attorney general of Canada. As such, it may not normally be invoked in a civil action between private litigants. This section of the Competition Act has received little judicial interpretation. The Canadian Competition Tribunal in *Canada (Director of Investigation & Research) v. Tele-Direct*[25] considered whether selective refusal to license a trade-mark is an anticompetitive act for the purposes of the Competition Act. The Tribunal ruled that selective refusal to license a trade-mark is *not* anticompetitive.

The Tribunal did not consider the further question as to whether the Tribunal has the jurisdiction to order that a license be granted if the circumstances warrant, pursuant to Section 32 of the Competition Act.

It will be interesting to see what future positions the federal court and Competition Tribunal will take with regard to technology licensing, trade-mark licensing, and anticompetitive practices, since the granting of a trade-mark monopoly, particularly where it involves an exclusive licensee, is perceived by some to be inherently anticompetitive. The question of whether, and the extent to which, the government is prepared to or should intervene in what are essentially private rights still remains to be answered.

Section 9 Prohibited or Official Marks: A Licensing Opportunity

In Canada, the Trade-marks Act and Section 9 thereof create a special class of organizations that are entitled to protect marks, badges, crests, or emblems—normally the subject of trade-mark protection—in a very particular manner. These marks, badges, crests, or emblems held by these organizations are usually referred to as *prohibited marks* or *official marks*. Generally speaking, they are marks that have been adopted and used by Royalty, Crown corporations, state authorities, governmental institutions, and certain international organizations such as the Red Cross and the United Nations, universities, and public authorities. Interdiction against the use of prohibited or official marks under the Trade-marks Act is widesweeping in scope. According to the Trade-marks Act, except for the owner of a prohibited mark and those to whom consent to use and/or register has been granted by the owner, no person shall use a prohibited mark *as a trade-mark or otherwise in connection with business.* Therefore, the existence of a valid prohibited or official mark prohibits all third parties from adopting and using the same or similar mark on wares and services, after the said mark has been published in the *Canadian Trade-marks Journal.*

Two of the more controversial subsections of Section 9 are subsections 9(1)(n)(ii) and (iii), which provide that a prohibited mark includes any badge, crest, emblem, or mark adopted and used by any university or public authority as an official mark *in Canada.* Subsection 9(1)(n) further provides that any university or public authority wishing to adopt such a mark shall notify or request the Registrar of Trade-marks, which shall then issue a public notice in respect of such adoption in the *Canadian Trade-marks Journal.* Subsections 9(1)(n)(ii) and (iii) read as follows:

> *Section 9 Prohibited Marks*
>
> (1) No person shall adopt in connection with a business, as a trade-mark or otherwise, any mark consisting of, or so nearly resembling as to be likely to be mistaken for,
>> (n) any badge, crest, emblem or mark
>>> (i) . . . ,
>>> (ii) of any university, or
>>> (iii) adopted and used by an public authority, in Canada as an official mark for wares or services,
>
> in respect of which the Registrar has, at the request of Her Majesty or of the university or public authority, as the case may be, given public notice of its adoption and use....

There is, as indicated above, no indication as to whether the reference to *university* and *public authority* in subsections 9(1)(n)(ii) and (iii) of the Canadian Act respectively includes only Canadian universities and public authorities exclusively or foreign universities and public authorities as well. A review of the Canadian Trade-mark Office records as to universities and public authorities that have acquired Section 9 marks reveals that at least at the *Trade-marks Office level,* both Canadian universities and public authorities and foreign universities and public authorities have been allowed protection under Section 9 by the Canadian Trade-mark Office. The three-part test created as to whether an organization is a public authority for the purposes of the act are that the organization must satisfy the following conditions:

1. It has duty to the public.
2. There is a significant degree of governmental control.
3. Any profit must be for the benefit of the public and not for private benefit.

In addition to the extensive protection afforded by Section 9(1), Section 9(2) of the Canadian Trade-marks Act allows Section 9 mark holders to license third parties; even entities that are not public authorities or universities may use Section 9 marks and/or register them in their own name for their own purposes. This licensing would not appear to be governed by the trade-mark/trade-name licensing provisions of the act. The preamble to Section 9(2) reads:

> Nothing in this section prevents the adoption, use or registration as a trade-mark or otherwise, in connection with a business, of any mark
>
> > (a) described in subsection (1) with the consent of Her Majesty or such other person, society, authority or organization as may be considered to have been intended to be protected by this section; or
> >
> > , . . .

Query whether a university or a public authority could adopt as an official or prohibited mark such well-known marks as Xerox or Coca-Cola and then license third parties to use such marks without recourse from the owners of these marks.

In the past, some Section 9 mark owners have used their rights and entitlement under this section to be used for the benefit of third-party organizations. By analogy, during the last papal visit to Canada the Toronto Transit Commission (which operates the public transit system) adopted, applied for, and obtained Section 9 protection for a series of prohibited or official marks on behalf of the Catholic Church and licensed them back exclusively to the Catholic Church for sublicensing, policing, and protecting the marks and design emblems signifying the papal visit. This adoption and use by the public authority was done at the request of the owner of the rights to enable it to obtain better protection more quickly. The outstanding issue is what would prevent a public authority from adopting existing third-party marks and using them or licensing them to third parties or both.

CONCLUSION

The ever-changing landscape for trademarks and related intellectual property rights has experienced numerous significant changes in the past few years; it continues to develop in a steady fashion, both in North America and elsewhere in the world. The commercial world, and LES, have been giving increasing attention and importance to these rights, as significant and valuable components of intellectual capital. They require careful handling and nurturing to realize their optimum value.

ENDNOTES

[1] See, for example, *MacMahan Pharmcal Co.* v. *Denver Chemical Mfg. Co.,* 113 Fed. 468 (8th Cir. 1901).

[2] See *K Mart* v. *Cartier, Inc.,* 486 U.S. 617 (S. Ct. 1988).

[3] Section 5, Lanham Trademark Act (15 U.S. Code §1051 *et seq.*), which will be referred to simply as the Lanham Act.

[4] Section 45, Lanham Act.

[5] See Sections 1 and 2, Lanham Act.

[6] See Section 32, Lanham Act.

[7] 120 S. Ct. 1339 (2000).

[8] 121 S. Ct. 1255 (2001).

[9] See Section 43(c)(1), Lanham Act.

[10] *Ringling Bros.-Barnum & Bailey Comb. Shows, Inc.* v. *Utah Div. of Travel Dev.,* 170 F. 3d 449 (4th Cir. 1999).

[11] See *Playboy Enterprises* v. *Netscape Communications Corp.,* 55 F. Supp. 2d 1070 (C.D. Cal. 1999).

[12] *Nabisco, Inc.* v. *PF Brands, Inc.,* 191 F. 3d 208, 224–225 (2d Cir. 1999).

[13] See Lanham Act Sections 13 and 24.

[14] Lanham Act Section 13(a).

[15] 2d Cir. No. 99-7744, 2/28/01.

[16] See *Tele-Direct Publications Inc.* v. *Canadian Business Online, Inc.,* 83 C.P.R. 3d 34 (1998). An example from France is *Saint-Tropez* v. *Eurovitel,* PIBD 1997 III 558 (T.G.I. de Draguinan) in which the city of Saint-Tropez was successful against the domain name *saint-tropez.com* that was accessible in France.

[17] See, for example, *Brookfield Communications, Inc.* v. *West Coast Entertainment Corp.,* 174 F. 3d 1036 (9th Cir. 1999), *Playboy Enterprises* v. *Welles,* 7 F. Supp. 2d 1098 (S.D. Cal.) *aff'd* 162 F. 3d 1169 (9th Cir. 1998), and *Bally Total Fitness Holdings Corp.* v. *Faber,* 29 F. Supp. 2d 1161 (C.D. Cal. 1998), respectively, for examples of these three situations.

[18] See, for example, the California Franchise Investment Law, California Corporations Code Sections 31000 *et seq.*

[19] See California Corporations Code Section 31005, definition of *franchise.*

[20] Section 12(2) of the Canadian Trade-marks Act.

[21] Section 14(1)(b) of the Canadian Trade-marks Act.

[22] *United Artists Corp.* v. *Pink Panther Beauty Corp.* (1998) 80 C.P.R. 247 at p. 265.

[23] *Canadian Trade-marks Journal,* September 8, 1993 and September 23, 1993.

[24] 2000 *Carswellont 4040.*

[25] 73 C.P.R. (3d) 1.

ABOUT THE AUTHORS

Thomas M. Small has been practicing as an intellectual property lawyer for more than 40 years, first in the Chicago, Illinois area and since 1968 in Los Angeles, California. He has an engineering degree from Purdue University and a law degree from Indiana University School of Law. Mr. Small is active in a variety of intellectual property areas, both domestic and international, with emphasis on trademark matters, licensing, and merchandising, and, to a lesser extent, on patent counseling, prosecution, and litigation. While maintaining an active law practice, he has found time to serve as president of Licensing Executives Society (United States and Canada), president of the Los Angeles Patent Law Association, and chair of the California State Bar Patent and Trademark Section, and is active in ADR in the intellectual property field.

Kenneth D. McKay is an active litigator in the Intellectual Property Bar in Canada. He is the co-author of several books and papers relating to intellectual property, marketing, and the licensing of technology, including the *Canadian Marketing Law Handbook* (DeBoo, Canada) and *Trade-marks—Canadian Forms and Precedents* (Butterworth, Canada). Mr. McKay has appeared as lead counsel and co-counsel on several leading intellectual property cases at the trial and appeal level. As well, Mr. McKay appears on a regular basis before administrative boards such as the Trademark Opposition Board and has an active trademark agency practice. In addition to these publishing endeavors, Mr. McKay is active as a speaker and workshop leader in the trademark and technology transfer/licensing area. As a very active member of the Licensing Executives Society (United States and Canada), and the Licensing Executives Society International (LESI), Mr. McKay is well versed in negotiating and license drafting as it relates to intellectual property, technology transfer, commercial contracts, and licensing in general. Mr. McKay is also a member of the Canadian Bar Association (CBA), a member of the International Trademark Association (INTA), a member of the Law Society of Upper Canada, and a Fellow of the Patent and Trademark Institute of Canada.

Part Three

Advances in Industry-Specific Licensing

9

Licensing in the Biotechnology Industry

By Dr. Cathryn Campbell

INTRODUCTION

The last 25 years have witnessed a revolution in the biological sciences. From the development of recombinant DNA technology in the mid-1970s to produce biological factories churning out proteins, through sequencing of the human genome at the turn of the twenty-first century, the pace and scope of innovation has been dizzying. The methodology of both biological research and medicine has been radically changed.

Such rapid technological progress presents enormous challenges to the patent systems of the world. According to the U.S. Patent and Trademark Office, at the beginning of the twentieth century a full one-third of all U.S. patent applications related to bicycles. Such mechanical inventions are a far cry from the complex technologies of microelectronics, computers, and aeronautics with which the patent system must wrestle today. Perhaps in no field, however, have the challenges to existing patent law been as great as in biotechnology. The advances in technology and patent law necessitate new strategies and practices in licensing.

In order to structure biotechnology licenses, it is imperative to understand both the technology and the proprietary protection issues. Further, developing strategies to license early-stage inventions presents a unique challenge to the licensing professional.

This chapter will focus on several points that, if not specific to biotechnology licensing, are at least of unique importance in this field. Many of the defining inventions in biotechnology—and the proprietary protection available for them—are qualitatively different from those in other technical fields. These differences reflect the fact that much of the technology emerging from the biotechnology industry relates to methods of designing or identifying useful compositions, rather than to the novel compositions themselves. In addition, many of the discoveries were developed in academia, where publication is considered essential. Therefore, patent applications must be filed very early in the development of the technology to avoid the inventor's own work being a bar to patentability.

Two case studies will be presented to illustrate and explore these themes, each of which will exemplify commercially valuable inventions and well-reasoned licensing strategies. As previously noted, I am of the firm belief that an understanding of license strategies must begin with an understanding of the technology and proprietary protection. The principles of biotechnology often seem daunting not only to the layperson but to the professional as well. Despite the fact that the results of these technological advances are so extraordinary and the terminology so complex, the inventions are actually quite straightforward and comprehensible, at least on a conceptual level.

In addition, biotechnology companies are often faced with the necessity of licensing out early-stage technology to raise the funds required to sustain their often large burn rates. Crafting licenses with other biotech companies or pharmaceutical companies to provide needed capital without giving away the technological crown jewels can be a challenge.

THE COHEN–BOYER RECOMBINANT DNA TECHNOLOGY

Higher organisms, such as mammals, contain in the neighborhood of 100,000 proteins, each encoded by a different sequence of DNA. In a cell, a sequence of DNA is called a *gene*. The gene is *translated* into its corresponding protein, whose function is determined by its sequence of amino-acid building blocks. As the workhorses of the body, proteins perform a variety of physiological roles whose manipulation can often be therapeutically useful. However, while their effects may be critically important to the organism, many proteins are present in vanishingly small amounts in the body.

A longstanding problem prior to the 1970s was the difficulty of obtaining sufficient quantities of a particular protein for either further research or therapeutic administration. The recombinant DNA techniques developed by Stanley Cohen of Stanford University and Herbert Boyer of the University of California (UC) at San Francisco provided the single most important means of overcoming this deficiency.

Let's look at how recombinant DNA works with reference to Exhibit 9.1. Remember that the goal here is to efficiently produce large amounts of protein— large at least in biological terms. As shown at the top of the exhibit, a single gene is inserted into a host cell, which is usually a bacterium, to create what is called a *transfected cell*. The transfected bacterial cells can then be grown in quantity and manipulated so as to produce the protein encoded by the introduced gene. These bacteria become, in effect, biological factories churning out the desired protein, which can be isolated in useful amounts.

What aspects of this elegant technology were claimed in the three patents issued to Drs. Cohen and Boyer in the early 1980s? The major claims can be broken down into three groups, each indicated by the circles in Exhibit 9.2.

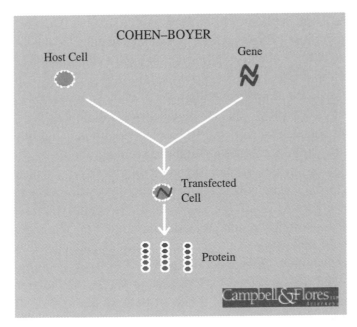

EXHIBIT 9.1   How Recombinant DNA Works

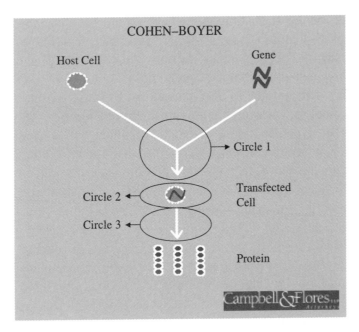

EXHIBIT 9.2   Cohen–Boyer Patents

First are claims to the method of inserting a particular gene into a host cell (shown schematically as Circle 1). Second are claims to the transfected cells, containing the inserted gene (Circle 2). Finally, claims are directed to the method of culturing the transfected cells to produce the desired protein (Circle 3).

At least as important as understanding what is claimed is recognizing what is not claimed. The final product—the expressed protein produced by practicing the invention—was not claimed, nor could it have been. Although it is beyond the scope of this chapter to go into the issues relating to the unpatentability of the recombinant product, suffice it to say that the recombinantly produced proteins generally are not novel over the same proteins purified from nature. As we patent attorneys would say: A protein does not know where it came from. There are also issues of enablement and written description that would preclude claiming of the recombinant protein in the Cohen–Boyer application.

The licensing strategy developed at Stanford University to commercialize the pioneering Cohen–Boyer technology is attributable largely to Neils Reimers, a long-term and active member of LES. Although the Cohen–Boyer patents expired in 1999, the Cohen–Boyer license still provides a classic example of thoughtful and effective licensing strategy.

Stanford was charged with handling the licensing of the Cohen–Boyer technology and took a very aggressive approach to signing up licensees. The guiding principles of the strategy were several: encourage use and dissemination of the technology; provide income to the universities; and avoid legal challenges to the patent.

The terms of the license were deliberately generous, thus encouraging the execution of licenses and decreasing any incentive to engage in litigation. The basic license terms required an upfront and annual licensing fee of $10,000. For licenses executed within five months of the issuance of the first patent, five times the license and annual fees was credited against earned royalties. The royalty rates were set between 1 percent and 3 percent, depending on the methods used and products sold. Royalty-free licenses were given to all nonprofit organizations. All licenses were nonexclusive. In excess of 350 companies took licenses during the patent term. No legal challenge to the patents was ever mounted.

More interesting, however, was the royalty base, the sales upon which the royalty percentage is calculated. For example, where batches of transfected cells—those made by claimed methods and falling within the scope of the composition claims—were sold, a 2 percent royalty was due on the net sales. The most commercially important products, however, were the recombinant proteins made by these transfected bacteria. Although these proteins were made using the patented methods and the patented transfected cells, the recombinant proteins themselves did not fall within the scope of any patent claims. Nevertheless, where the recombinant protein was sold, the royalty rate was set at 3 percent of net sales.

During the term of the patent, it is estimated that the sales value of products covered by the license was in excess of $30 billion. These products included such therapeutically important drugs as human insulin (to treat diabetes), TPA (to treat heart attacks and stroke), EPO (to increase white blood cell production), and human growth factor (to treat a number of deficiencies). The total royalties received by Stanford and UC from license fees and royalties was in excess of $255 million, the largest single source of royalty income in UC's history.

The key aspect of this analysis is that although the final product—the recombinant protein produced by the bacterial factories—was not itself covered by the patent, the patented methods and transfected cells were, by definition, repeatedly used in the production of recombinant protein. Sales of the nonpatented final product served as the royalty base to compensate the patent holders for the repeated use of the patented methods and materials necessary to generate the nonpatented product.

Royalties based on a nonpatented product have been described as *reach-through* or *flow-through* royalties. Both legal and ethical objections have been raised against the use of such royalties. However, as the final product is often the best measure of the use and value of claimed methods and intermediate materials, the use of the commercial product as the royalty base seems wholly reasonable and justified for technology such as Cohen–Boyer, where patented methods and materials are repeatedly used to produce the commercial product. I will refer to the Cohen–Boyer royalties as *flow-through* where they are based on a nonpatented product manufactured by means of patented technology. As discussed next, royalties based on the repeated use of patented methods and materials to generate product need to be carefully distinguished from royalties based on products that result from a single, or limited, use of patented methods or products.

THE LADNER PHAGE-DISPLAY TECHNOLOGY

An important development of the early 1990s was a method of producing vast numbers of short proteins, or *peptides*, each having a unique amino acid sequence. Rather than using bacteria to produce a single protein at a time from a known gene, the methodology—here termed *phage-display*—permits the production of millions of short peptides that may or may not occur in nature.

Exhibit 9.3 is a schematic illustration of the phage-display methodology. An array of short pieces of DNA are synthesized. Each piece is inserted into a single cell, which translates it to produce an array of short proteins, or peptides. The array of different peptides, called a *peptide library*, can then be screened to find those that have desired biological properties. The screening step can take a variety of forms and is depicted by the *black box*. The selected peptide or peptides can then be made by various well-known methods.

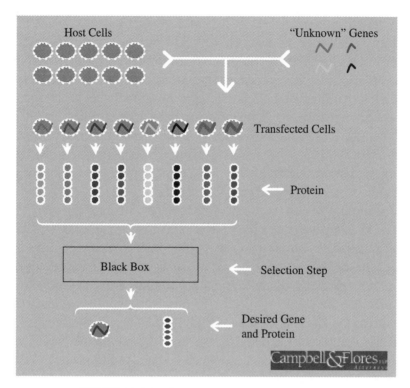

EXHIBIT 9.3   Phage-Display Methodology

Patents on this phage-display technology were filed in 1988 by Robert Ladner and others, and rights were ultimately controlled by Dyax Corporation. Again recognizing that this technology was of wide interest to both academia and industry, Dyax developed and pursued an aggressive and successful licensing strategy, which provides an interesting comparison to that of Cohen–Boyer.

Let's look at what aspects of the technology are claimed (see Exhibit 9.4). Again, the claims can be broken down into groups. Because the description of the technology has been simplified, the claims must be also. The composition claims can be categorized as relating to the library of peptides (Circle 1) and the library of cells each transfected with a different short DNA sequence (Circle 2). In addition, there are claims relating to methods of producing both of these types of libraries (Circle 3).

Again, at least as important as what is claimed is what is not claimed. While here the library of peptides is claimed, such a gamish of peptides has little use except as a source from which to identify desired individual peptides. The individual peptides identified or selected through the black-box screening procedures are not, and cannot be, claimed. It is these selected peptides that will ultimately be the commercial product.

A critical difference between the Cohen–Boyer technology and the phage-display technology is that while the claimed methods and compositions are repeatedly used

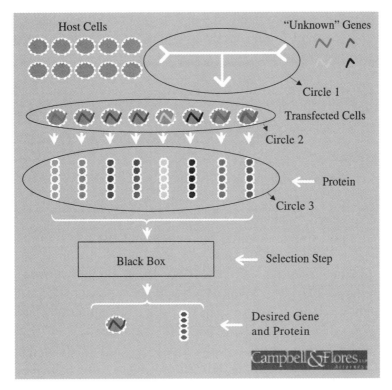

EXHIBIT 9.4   Patent Claims on Phage-Display Methodology

to manufacture the final products in the Cohen–Boyer methodology, with phage-display the claimed methods and compositions are used only to identify but not manufacture the final product. In other words, the claimed methods of phage-display can be thought of as being used only once, often in the privacy of one's own laboratory. Once a desired peptide is identified, the technology is not used again; the identified peptides are then manufactured by other methods appropriate to produce quantities of the single peptide, rather than producing a library of varied peptides. The Dyax licensing strategy thus needed to realize the value of the patented technology as an *early-stage invention*, used only at the outset of the product-development pipeline.

Dyax began contacting potential licensees in earnest shortly after the first patent issued. Its license agreement also shows considerable strategic forethought. Both its similarities to and differences from the Cohen–Boyer license are instructive.

As with the Cohen–Boyer license, Dyax offered nonexclusive licenses that carried signing fees, maintenance fees, and earned royalties. Two accommodations reflect trends in biotechnology licensing that became common as the industry grew and diversified:

1. Milestone payments were due to the licensor as products proceeded toward FDA approval.

2. The licensee was provided the option of choosing relatively higher licensing fees and lower earned royalties, or lower licensing fees and higher earned royalties.

The former option is generally seen as favorable to the larger pharmaceutical companies that do not wish to share their ultimate profits, while the latter is preferred by the often cash-strapped smaller biotech companies.

An even more interesting aspect of the license is the royalty and royalty base. Earned royalties are again set low, ranging from 1 percent to 2 percent, depending on the trade-off against licensing fees. The royalty base is net sales of *licensed products*, which are themselves defined as any product which is "discovered, made, or developed using a method covered by a claim . . . or which is otherwise covered by a claim" of the licensed patents. Note the reference to the terms *discovered* and *developed*. Patent law does not define as infringement the discovery or development of products using patented methods. Thus, the royalty base reflects a product that may be identified through a patented method but that itself is neither claimed nor commercially made using patented methods. It is important to distinguish these royalties, which I term *reach-through* from the previously discussed flow-throughs. Reach-throughs can be defined as having as a royalty base a product that was discovered by patented technology, but neither claimed itself, nor manufactured by a patented method.

While Stanford made the decision to allow royalty-free use of the Cohen–Boyer patents by nonprofits, Dyax has sought licenses from nonprofit institutions and universities. For nonprofits, the signing and maintenance fees are waived. However, if any product is transferred to another party or if the nonprofit provides services relating to the claimed technology, transfer fees are owed. In addition, the nonprofit must assure that any party receiving product or services must sign a provided *third-party agreement* committing that party to the general terms and conditions of the Dyax license.

According to its press releases, Dyax has successfully licensed both commercial companies and nonprofits under these terms. As the term of the license depends on the term of continuing patents that may not yet have been issued (and may receive the benefit of the pre-GATT patent term of 17 years from the date of issuance), a potentially large number of products may fall within the terms of the Dyax license.

THE LICENSE FOR FUNDING DILEMMA

The previous examples relate to the licensing of widely applicable and mature platform technology. The licensing revenues in these cases benefit the nonprofit or for-profit owners without jeopardizing their core business. Perhaps an even more pervasive—and characteristic—type of licensing in the biotechnology field is that of early-stage technology where the driving force is the need for capital.

An almost universal issue for the start-up biotechnology company is the continuing need for capital to sustain the enormous costs of drug development. Although estimates vary widely, it is not uncommon to see quotes of more than $100 million as the cost of taking a therapeutic drug to market. For many biotechnology companies, such financial pressure necessitates licensing of their intellectual property rights.

Traditionally, biotechnology companies have been started to develop inventions made by either academics or other independent inventors. Early funding is often provided by the founders, "angels," or even family members. Even after several rounds of venture funding, however, a product may still only be in preclinical trials. Joint ventures or alliances with other biotechnology companies, or more likely, licensing arrangements with large pharmaceutical companies, may be the only feasible sources of the funds necessary to support the studies required for regulatory approval.

Particularly for companies with a limited array of proprietary technology, entering into early-stage licensing arrangements presents difficult issues. How can a small company with obvious cash requirements obtain fair value for its technology from a large and sophisticated phamaceutical company while retaining sufficient rights to remain a viable entity? The playing field may be far from flat. Two strategies are common to such situations: *license rights to future technology* and *partitioning the rights to current technology.*

When licensing future rights, the biotech company is likely to prefer upfront payments over future royalties in order to satisfy its capital needs. Big pharma, on the other hand, may prefer to divide the risk of untested technology by paying earned royalties rather than high upfront payments. Depending on the biotech's needs, it may have to settle for an undervaluation in order to consummate the deal.

Several additional issues arise in this scenario. Accurately valuing early-stage technology might be quite difficult, and mortgaging its future technology might leave the company with no long-term technology assets. Moreover, out-licensing of the technology can have a negative effect on the company's innovators, who may view inventing for big pharma as undesirable, causing the best and the brightest of these innovators to leave. Perhaps most importantly, granting of future rights to the biotech company's strategic plans runs the risk of leaving it money rich but vision poor and directionless.

If the existing technology is widely applicable—in terms of field of use or geography—the biotech company may be able to structure licenses that grant partial rights to another company while retaining the crown jewels for itself. Often these deals are structured as joint ventures rather than merely licenses, so that both companies can benefit from the technical developments of the other. Not infrequently, biotech companies in the United States will seek foreign partners to develop and distribute technology in their home countries while retaining the lucrative U.S. rights for themselves. Alternatively, companies might try to license diagnostic uses, for example, while retaining the therapeutic applications. Or a company might try to license technology for some medical indications while retaining those that best fit its internal expertise.

Several important issues arise from such partitioning of the rights. First, the company must accurately predict which indications and areas will be the most valuable so as to retain them for itself—or at least obtain fair value for them. It is fundamental that the parties must be able to work together effectively as partners. Even so, developments of one partner can either help or hinder the progress of the other. For example, if one party approaches the FDA with data relating to a compound's usefulness in treating one indication, this data might affect the regulator's view of the compound's utility for another indication. Further, if the FDA turns down an application for the licensee's application, this decision may negatively affect the licensor's chances of obtaining approval for another indication.

On the other hand, partnerships between small biotechs and large pharma may provide important benefits. The licensed technology may complement the portfolio of the licensee. In addition, it might be important to the licensee to maintain market share by providing a technological edge over a competitor. In addition, big pharma's cash position and manpower can permit it to develop and market the products with an efficiency and a speed unavailable to the biotech.

In drafting such licenses, certain provisions should be given particular attention. First, of course, is the amount and structure of compensation to the licensor. In addition to upfront payments, milestone payments should be negotiated to provide a continuing source of funds. And, ideally, achievement of the milestones should not be left entirely in the hands of the licensee, unless stringent due-diligence provisions are included. Big pharma's interest in the technology may reflect more on its desire to keep the technology out of the hands of its competitors than its actual intent to develop a product.

Termination provisions are also critical. Partnerships, like marriages, may run into irreconcilable differences that could not have been predicted at the outset. In particular, the licensor should be sensitive to the inclusion of provisions that allow it to exit gracefully and without undue financial burden, if necessary. If the licensee has had rights to a product for some time without product approval or development approval, the technology may have greatly reduced value as other companies have developed competing technology. The licensor should ensure that there are incentives to remain in the partnership. Or in the case of termination, the responsibility for the decreased value should be borne by the licensee.

Confidentiality provisions are also important in the biotech/big pharma deal. The licensor should negotiate rights to both positive and negative data developed by the licensee. Finally, control of patent prosecution and litigation, though ideally not their costs, should always remain with the licensee to avoid its patent rights being jeopardized or biased toward the licensor's field.

CONCLUSION

So what lessons are there for the biotechnology licensing professional? Several. As Willy Manfroy has pointed out in Chapter 1, the licensing profession in general has evolved over the years to have more appreciation for and skill in the technologies; no field requires this more than biotechnology. In addition, however, biotechnology licensing practices require familiarity with both general principles of patent law and the details of the proprietary protection of the licensed technology. Although it is by no means necessary for licensing professionals to be lawyers, they and their institutions will benefit enormously from an understanding of the metes and bounds of the existing and available protection. Close communication between those responsible for patent protection and those responsible for commercializing the inventions can only benefit the dissemination of the enormous value that biotechnology promises.

ABOUT THE AUTHOR

Dr. Cathryn Campbell is a founding partner of Campbell & Flores LLP, a law firm specializing in biotechnology intellectual property. She holds degrees from Wellesley College (B.A. Biological Sciences), the University of California Davis (M.S., Ph.D. Population Genetics), and UCLA (J.D.). Over the past 20 years her practice has focused on issues unique to the biotechnology industry, particularly those pertinent to patent prosecution, portfolio strategy, and licensing. She represents biotechnology companies, from the earliest stage through initial public offering and numerous non-profit universities and institutions. Ms. Campbell has published and lectured extensively on both science and law and was named one of the top patent attorneys in California by *California Lawyer*.

10

Pharmaceutical Licensing During the Revolution

By Dr. Thomas A. Picone

INTRODUCTION

Today, about 11 percent of the population consists of people over the age of 65. Over the next 30 years, this figure is expected to double. Since these people are heavy users of pharmaceutical products, sales are expected to double from approximately $325 billion in 2000 to more than $750 billion. Although this truly is a large figure, we need to keep pharmaceutical spending in context. In the United States, the projected per capita spending on alcohol, tobacco, and entertainment in 1999 was $413, whereas the pharmaceutical product purchases were only $358 per capita.[1] Furthermore, we see the percentage of health care spending on pharmaceuticals to be a small percentage (less than 7 percent) of total health care spending.

In the year 2000 there were more than 7,000 pharmaceutical products in development in the United States.[2] Of these compounds, 70 percent were in the preclinical stage—they had never been tested in humans (for safety and efficacy); 11 percent were in Phase I (determination of safety); 13 percent in Phase II (determination of safety and efficacy); 3 percent in Phase III (large-scale testing for safety and efficacy); and 1 percent were in Registration (under review by the FDA). The cost of bringing a single product to market varies from $25 million to $50 million (for small products targeted toward niche indications) to $600 million to $1 billion (for large products developed to treat conditions such as heart disease).[3] If we use an average price of $250 million for development, the cost of R & D for all products currently in development would exceed $1.75 trillion. Many products do not make it through full development, but it is clear the investment required to bring us the medicines of tomorrow is substantial. Last year the top 15 large pharmaceutical companies spent almost $40 billion on R & D (see Exhibit 10.1).[4]

The investment of research dollars to develop medications has shifted somewhat from the large companies to the smaller biotech companies over the past decade. The risk involved in developing early-stage compounds is great. Some of this risk has shifted from the big companies to the public sector, as much of the capital raised by the biotech community is from venture capital funding and initial public

COMPANY	2000 R & D EXPENDITURE ($/BILLIONS)	% CHANGE FROM 1999
Pfizer	$4.44	9.9%
GlaxoSmithKline	3.84	10.5
Aventis	3.20	10.4
Johnson & Johnson	2.93	12.5
AstraZeneca	2.89	(1.0)
Novartis	2.76	9.7
Pharmacia	2.75	(2.2)
Merck & Company	2.34	13.3
Hoffmann–La Roche	2.34	4.4
Bayer	2.19	11.3
Eli Lilly	2.02	13.2
Bristol-Myers Squibb	1.94	10.2
American Home Products	1.69	6.3
Abbott	1.35	13.2
Schering-Plough	1.33	11.9

**EXHIBIT 10.1   Research and Development Expenditure of
Fifteen Pharmaceutical Companies**

offerings. This year, about 50 percent of the worldwide R & D expenditure will come from biotech firms. In 1980, only 10 percent came from this segment.[5] Large companies complement their internal development projects with investments in biotech products to ensure an adequate pipeline of products within therapeutic areas of interest to the large company. Companies such as Pharmacia Corporation are also now investing in products targeted to specific customers (physician specialists and consumers), in addition to more traditional investing in specific therapeutic areas such as cardiology and psychiatry. This new structure has increased the focus on primary-care products in late-stage development, and products in Phase III development are in high demand. Evidence of this can be seen by examining the payments that larger companies make to smaller companies to get products. Over the past 10 years, pharmaceutical companies have paid three times as much in precommercial payments to smaller biotech companies for pharmaceutical products that are in late-stage development.[6] In 1990, large pharmaceutical companies were paying about $24 million in precommercial payments, whereas in 2000, they paid an average of $76 million to the smaller company for a late-stage compound.

With the new genomic techniques, it is possible to generate 7 million new drug candidates per year. Of these 7 million, 1,000 will be validated to actually be viable products for clinical development, 12 may actually make it into preclinical evaluations, 6 will make it through clinical development, and 1 will actually reach the market. With the amount of spending required to bring this one product to market, it is no surprise that buying these compounds later on in the stage of development lowers the risk. We can easily see why there is increased value for late-stage products.

Products that are within two to three years of marketing only make up 4 percent of the compounds in development. These products are sought out by many large companies, thereby increasing their value. In addition to the value placed by competition, there are issues with FDA approval that further increase the value of an approved product. In 1996 the FDA granted 131 new drug applications (NDAs). As of August 2001, there had been only 25 NDA approvals.[7] Once a company gets an approved product, it must invest heavily in commercial advertising and sales representative calls on physicians. In addition, large launch costs must be figured into the equation. Seminars for doctors, sample kits, advertising, and numerous documents must be prepared for review with the FDA.

The dramatic increase in the value of late-stage compounds to meet the needs of the large numbers of people that will require pharmaceutical intervention as they exceed age 65 is clearly the driver of the revolution we are seeing. These people will be more demanding. They will be more active, will have more disposable income, and will require products that enhance their lifestyle—not just prevent or treat disease.

PHARMACEUTICALS ON DEMAND

In 1999, the U.S. pharmaceutical industry spent $1.8 billion on direct-to-consumer advertising.[8] In 2000 this figure had climbed to $4.5 billion.[9] Future consumers are going to know more about treatment options and will demand very good products. They will expect pharmaceuticals to work well and provide great benefit—and they will be able to pay for performance. Future consumers of pharmaceutical products will be very well educated. Information on various medical conditions is widely available on the Internet. Also, direct-to-consumer advertising on television, radio, and in print will increase consumer awareness and demand.

The use of lifestyle drugs will increase dramatically. Common conditions such as increased visits to the bathroom are now being addressed. It is no longer necessary to plan your day or your car trip around where bathroom stops will fit. Products like Detrol have decreased the problems of urinary incontinence. Consumers are now aware of alternatives and no longer accept lifestyle inconveniences. In addition, it is not uncommon to hear that consumers with an allergy to cats would take a product such as Zyrtec or Claritin daily to suppress their allergy because of their love of cats or because of their love of someone else who loves cats. Products like Viagra are the quintessential lifestyle drugs in many cases. As seen recently, advertising targeted toward consumers has shown a much younger target population than was first popular in the days of the Bob Dole advertising. Products for sexual performance, hair loss, energy enhancement, immune modulation, and general well-being will increase dramatically.

Primary-care physicians (doctors like OB/GYNs, internists, and doctors who see patients for routine care) will play a critical role in the diagnosis and treatment of the ailments of the general population. They have become the focus of advertising campaigns and sales calls that pharmaceutical company representatives make on doctors. This is because this group of physicians prescribes approximately 75 percent of the total pharmaceutical products sold. Primary-care physicians (PCPs) are the frontline for many consumers. They can best interpret the data for patients. They must have the best information. If a patient has a serious illness, the PCP will often refer the patient to a specialist. For instance, if a patient has a cardiac problem he may see a PCP because of a symptom. If the PCP believes he can treat the patient (i.e., for hypercholesterolemia) the physician might prescribe a cholesterol-reducing product and/or diet and exercise. If a PCP thinks the patient requires a specialist, she might refer the patient to a cardiologist. PCPs often refer to specialists for specific product recommendations, and the promotion of specialized products to medical specialties will always be critical to drive product sales both in a particular category (i.e., cardiology) as well as in the PCP's office. For instance, Detrol, a product for overactive bladder, is promoted heavily to urologists so that urologists are comfortable with the various aspects of overactive bladder and can distinguish between this condition versus more serious prostate abnormalities. However, the large market for overactive bladder products is driven by PCPs, who will often see a patient who would complain of overactive bladder during a routine annual physical. Many times, patients will not recognize this as a specific medical condition. The PCP is critical to diagnosing and treating many illnesses of the general population.

Another phenomenon dramatically influencing the importance of the PCP is the managed-care organizations. Most managed-care organizations require individuals to see their primary-care physicians before authorizing further expenses on a specialist or before specific pharmaceutical prescriptions can be written. This dramatically increases the value of the PCP, as most patients in America are covered by some managed-care organization. Through the promotion of products to the specialist and the proper education of the PCP, a drug company can maximize its return on the investment it put into developing the product, and the general population will be healthier.

There are several good examples of new pharmaceutical products that have been promoted to physicians and consumers. The new COX-2 inhibitor drugs are an improvement over ibuprofen or nonsteroidal anti-inflammatory drugs (NSAIDs) because they dramatically reduce the incidence of stomach ulcer when compared with NSAIDs. The sales of billions of dollars of Vioxx and Celebrex indicate the importance of safety advantages in product profile. Products like the stomach-acid-blocking drugs Tagament and Zantac surely illustrate how products are saving dollars by keeping the patient out of the hospital. In 1977, before such drugs were available, surgeons performed approximately 100,000 operations for peptic ulcers. In 1993, despite dramatic population growth, the number of operations had decreased to 19,000 and in 2001 was expected to be less than 5,000, partially due to the impact of the COX-2 products replacing NSAIDs.[10] The COX-2 products may be expensive, but they are much cheaper than abdominal surgery. We must pay for performance.

Today's megabrands are safe, more convenient, and better tolerated. The current statin (class of products that reduce cholesterol) market, of which Lipitor is the current market leader, is approximately $13 billion. There are approximately 80,000 sales representatives detailing products in the United States alone. Sales force size has roughly doubled from 1996 to 2001.[11] The future will be very intriguing.

Two opposing forces could change the landscape of the pharmaceutical industry. The description that we have been portraying of the market with very large emphasis on global brands targeted primarily to primary care physicians and focused on large-scale, one-size-fits-all type pharmaceuticals will run smack into the face of the future of personalized medicine through the practice of pharmacogenomics. It is possible that by the end of this decade we will see an era where a blood sample is given before any diagnosis is made and then a specific type of diagnosis for your particular type of disease is made. Multiple etiologies of depression or hypertension will be sorted out. Each will require pharmaceutical intervention, from targeted products specifically intended to meet the needs of an individual. This specialized medicine will require point-of-care diagnostic equipment that can be used rapidly in a physician's office but will also require the segmentation of markets into many subsets. For instance, antidepressives are currently prescribed to anyone with the proper diagnosis of depression. In the future, a blood test might determine the type of depression that each individual has, and a specific pharmaceutical intervention for that particular mechanism of action that is causing the depression will be given. It remains to be seen if this type of specialized medicine can be practiced in a primary-care physician's office—which will drive the prescribing of medicines away from mass-marketing tactics and into the individual physician's office with specific expertise for different mechanisms of actions. The focus of precise tools will change drug discovery, which will rely less on serendipity and more on specific validated targets. As a result, companies will make difficult decisions as to which therapeutic franchises to invest in and will become more focused. Depth of knowledge versus broad-based approaches to drug development may develop.

With few exceptions, today's large franchises were built from opportunities amid serendipity. When the patent expires, that usually signals the decline of that franchise. The serendipitous nature of drug discovery has allowed for companies to dominate a therapeutic class overnight. The commitment of a company to a particular franchise may be required in the future. More expense will be required to dominate a franchise. A sustained business presence will be necessary. Companies will become much more focused on customers and specific mechanisms of action within specific diseases that will result in the most profitable and efficacious product. The top five therapeutic areas—cardiovascular, central nervous system, metabolism, anti-infectives, and respiratory problems—generate more than 60 percent of total pharmaceutical sales. The necessity to focus within those broad categories on specific mechanisms of action to develop products with specific efficacy without dose-limiting side effects will be what the consumers of the future demand. Time will tell if this technology-driven approach to product development will lead to commercial success. Other important factors such as massive consolidation within the industry may lead to other business models. Perhaps one giant company will have divisions that specialize in particular disease states and specific mechanisms of action. We will explore the consolidation of the industry in the next section.

ALLIANCES

There has been a remarkable increase in the value of alliances in recent years. Biotechnology companies raised $28 billion in 2000 in public and private equity—seven times the amount raised in the previous IPO window in 1996 and nearly triple the amount raised in 1999.[12] The upfront fees paid for late-stage compounds now often exceed $30 million. In comparison, in 1996 Pfizer paid Warner-Lambert $25 million upfront for the co-promotion rights to Lipitor, which is likely to become the biggest selling drug of all time. Bristol-Myers Squibb just paid $2 billion for access to Imclone's monoclonal antibody, C225 (cetuximab) for head and neck cancer. This deal has been widely described within the industry as a very rich deal for Imclone. They got a $500 million premium to the most optimistic, peak, annual sales potential for the drug. The agreement calls for Bristol to make a $1 billion upfront equity investment at a 40 percent premium to the market and a $200 million cash licensing fee. Bristol would pay another $300 million when the BLA is formally accepted by the FDA, and another $500 million on approval.[13]

The large impact of the increase in alliances between companies can be felt in a variety of areas. First, alliances are critical to the success of a company that does not have a global presence in all major markets. The United States, Europe, Japan, Latin America, Asia, the Middle East, Africa, and Canada all have significant pharmaceutical businesses (see Exhibit 10.2).[14] If a company wants to maximize its return on each drug, it must find a way—through organic growth from within or use

COUNTRY	VALUE IN $ BILLION 2000	% OF TOTAL	% CHANGE FROM 1999
United States	$138	2%	16%
Europe	83	25	8
Germany	17	5	4
France	17	5	4
United Kingdom	11	3	9
Italy	11	3	12
Japan	48	15	5
Latin America	21	7	7
Asia Pacific	18	6	11
Middle East, Africa	11	3	10
Canada	6	2	15
Total	**325**	**100**	**11**

EXHIBIT 10.2   The Global Pharmaceutical Market

of partnerships—to maximize the sales of each and every approved drug. Traditionally, Japanese companies have licensed products to U.S. companies to maximize sales outside the United States. Today more and more joint ventures are being formed giving the Japanese partner more control. Also, Japanese companies such as Takeda have established their own U.S. presence.

Second, because of the consolidation in the industry, some alliances require renegotiation of preexisting contracts. If one company co-promotes another company's product in a particular class, say cardiovascular products, noncompete arrangements that the former company had prior to the new alliance might need to be renegotiated. If two companies co-promote an oral therapeutic for cardiovascular disease, they might need to renegotiate aspects of the former deal to co-promote a topical or combination drug. Also, major intellectual property and patent issues surface when cross-licensing intellectual property. This will be covered in more detail in Chapter 14.

Alliances are often completed with a company that is recognized for its specific therapeutic strengths. Of 75 licensing deals completed in 1998, 53 percent of the compounds went to a licensee that was a recognized leader in the therapeutic area.[15] Thirty-six percent went to licensees with a strong presence in that particular therapeutic area, whereas only 11 percent went to companies with no previous experience. A product licensed to the correct partner can triple its value. Stronger partners bring distinctive clinical and development abilities, world-class sales force staff with multiple countries covered, a well-defined plan for launch and support, and strong clinical support during and after the commercial launch to be sure physicians are comfortable with the product. Also, any widescale use of product must be carefully monitored for any side effects that might occur in small populations. As companies continue to collaborate in specific therapeutic areas, it will be inevitable that major companies occasionally compete head-to-head with a sales force in one therapeutic area while they collaborate as partners with that sales force in another therapeutic area.

MEGAMERGERS

The number of large industry deals has increased dramatically in the last decade. Exhibit 10.3 indicates some of the data in this category. Even in 2001, a relatively slow year, the number of merger and acquisitions deals worldwide involving pharmaceuticals rose by 9 percent in the first six months of the year. This is in contrast to a 25 percent reduction across all other industries.[16] Before we examine in depth some of the rationale for these mergers, it is important to point out some of the characteristics of companies that stay independent. Even in these days of large numbers of megamergers, there are good rationales and good examples of companies that have succeeded with an independent philosophy. Merck, Lilly, and Johnson & Johnson claim to be diversified enough and have strong enough pipelines to not require a megamerger for successful growth into the future. Time will tell.

Going alone is better in certain indications. For instance, when a company is in a small franchise area that is well defined, it is possible to cover it alone without a megamerger. Within these areas, small companies can avoid large marketing costs without compromising profit growth. However, when large numbers of customer relationships are required and sales forces that will reach 8,000 to 10,000 in the United States alone will be required to promote products to a large number of primary care physicians, large megamergers will be necessary to

BUYER	TARGET	DATE ANNOUNCED OR COMPLETED	VALUE OF DEAL
1. Pfizer	Warner–Lambert	Feb. 2, 2000	$91.5 billion
2. Glaxo–Wellcome	SmithKline Beecham	Jan. 17. 2000	78.4 billion
3. Zeneca Group	Astra	Dec. 9, 1998	31.8 billion
4. Sandoz	Ciba–Geigy	Dec. 17, 1996	28.0 billion
5. Pharmacia & Upjohn	Monsanto	Dec. 20, 1999	26.8 billion
6. Glaxo Holdings	Wellcome	May 1, 1995	13.4 billion
7. Bristol-Meyers	Squibb	Oct. 4, 1989	11.9 billion
8. Sanofi	Synthelabo	May 24, 1999	11.2 billion
9. Roche Holding	Corange	March 5, 1998	10.2 billion
10. American Home Products	American Cyanamid	Dec. 21, 1994	9.3 billion

SOURCE: Press release announcements of each deal.

EXHIBIT 10.3   Pharmaceutical Industry Deals

meet the needs. It is important to realize that today the 15 largest companies only control 50 percent of the pharmaceutical product sales. This industry is still very fractionated and will continue to see further consolidation. The strategy of going alone versus a megamerger will be heavily influenced by external factors such as clinical trial design, profitability of various drug classes, the impact of HMOs, and pharmacogenomics.

Demand for all drugs will continue and will drive up the price of R & D. Investment in pharmaceutical product development for products targeted at 100,000 patients or less actually requires smaller clinical trials in more targeted populations. These trials are cheaper to conduct than large-scale clinical trials aimed at the masses. NSAIDs are consumed by hundreds of millions of people worldwide, as is the case for cholesterol-lowering drugs or other cardiovascular medications. Large-scale studies in tens of thousands of patients over several years are essential to bring one of those products to the market. One of the fundamental driving forces of the industry is the fact that approximately 50 percent of all pharmaceutical products consumed today are generic and do not result in any significant profit to the manufacturing company. This means that the entire research and development effort to bring these medications to the market rides on the back of the 50 percent of products that are covered by patents.

The effect of HMOs and pharmacogenomics will also be a factor. Both variables will drive development of targeted pharmaceutical products to smaller segments of the population. Their goal will be maximum efficacy with minimum side effects. Drug development will parallel clothes design. One size does not fit all. These goals will impact company strategy, drug development, and the need for megamergers.

ENDNOTES

[1] Uwe Reinhardt Presentation, May 13, 2001. Extracted from *Health Affairs* (March/April 2000).

[2] IMS Health Statistics (February 2001).

[3] Roger Longman, *Big Deal: The Search for Certainty.* Presentation for Windhover's Pharmaceutical Strategic Alliances Conference, October 1, 2001.

[4] "A Reference of Prescription Drugs in Development," *Med Ad News* (July 2001), p. 4.

[5] Mark Edwards, *Recombinant Capital.* Signal Mag. NSF, Council Research.

[6] Mark Edwards, *Recombinant Capital.* Personal Communication (April 24, 2001).

[7] "Research Moving to USA," *Affarsvarlden* (September 19, 2001).

[8] S. Woloski, L. Schwartz, J. Tremmel, and H. Welch, "Direct-to-Consumer Advertisements for Prescription Drugs: What Are Americans Being Sold?" *Lancet* 2001 6(358): 1141–1146.

[9] "The Global Pharmaceutical Market," *Med Ad News* (September 2001), p. 5.

[10] Ronald Bailey, "Goddamn the Pusher Man. Why Does Everybody Seem to Hate the Pharmaceutical Industry?" Reason Online (April 2001).

[11] "The Global Pharmaceutical Market," p. 5.

[12] Roger Longman, "Dealmaking for the Revolution." *In Vivo: The Business and Medicine Report* (March 2001).

[13] F–D–C Reports, Inc., *The Pink Sheet* (September 24, 2001): p. 20–21.

[14] "The Global Pharmaceutical Market," p. 5.

[15] Longman.

[16] Carlos Grande, "Companies and Finance International: Drugs M & A deals on the rise," *Financial Times* (October 1, 2001).

ABOUT THE AUTHOR

Dr. Thomas A. Picone received his Ph.D. in biochemistry from the University of Connecticut in 1980. He worked for two years at American Hospital Supply Company in R & D on pediatric pharmaceuticals. In 1982, Dr. Picone joined Abbott Laboratories and spent the next eight years in R & D. He focused on preclinical development for four years and clinical development for four years. In 1990, he started a licensing group at the Ross Division. He led the team to two acquisitions, including the acquisition of Puleva, and 33 licensing deals, which included the co-promotion of MedImmune's Synagis. In 1999, Dr. Picone joined Pharmacia Corporation as executive director of global licensing, and in 2000, he was promoted to vice president of global licensing. He has been involved in the merger of Pharmacia Corporation with Monsanto and has led the team to an agreement with Searle to co-promote Detrol in the United States. In addition to his corporate responsibilities, he has been the chairman of LES Healthcare Group since 1999 and was just elected to the board of LES.

11

University Licensing Trends and Intellectual Capital

By Dr. Louis P. Berneman and Dr. Kathleen A. Denis

INTRODUCTION

Academic–industry technology transfer is the process of moving research results from the laboratory to the marketplace. In FY2000, according to the Association of University Technology Managers (AUTM) annual licensing survey, more than 347 new products resulting from academic research were introduced into the market by licensees. The previous year AUTM survey indicated that in FY1999 this activity contributed $41 billion to the U.S. economy, supported 270,000 jobs, and produced $5 billion in new tax revenues.

Research universities engage in the transfer of technology to do the following:

- Facilitate the commercialization of university discoveries for the public good.
- Reward, retain, and recruit faculty and students.
- Forge closer ties to industry.
- Promote economic growth.
- Generate income.

University technology managers seek to achieve these goals by resolving the conflicting cultures and values of academe and industry. To do so, university technology managers focus on the common interests of universities and companies in commercializing new and useful technologies. Inventions resulting from university research are protected through patents, trademarks, and copyrights. As not-for-profit entities, universities do not engage in product development, marketing, and sales. Therefore, promising technologies with commercial potential are licensed to a for-profit partner for further development.

Challenges in academic-industry technology transfer have their basis in the multifaceted, complex, and occasionally competing goals of technology transfer and in the embryonic and fundamental nature of many university scientific discoveries. University discoveries and the associated intellectual property are often the basis for future product development and market protection, rather than the definition of an exact product or the basis for patent prosecution itself.

Licensing when the eventual product is not precisely known presents challenges in setting and extracting fair value, as well as in numerous other contractual issues.

Universities are currently struggling with the appropriate role that academic technology transfer should play in the innovation chain of scientific discovery, technology development, and product commercialization. However, creative partnerships between universities and companies will continue to reward both corporate shareholders and the public with new products and services based on university research. Of late, universities are increasingly involved in creating start-up ventures to further develop and commercialize embryonic discoveries. Public scrutiny of the conflicts created in such ventures has become a major issue of which both universities and industry must be mindful for continued success.

America's investment in science and technology has been the principal source of our nation's unrivaled national security, increasingly good health, and unprecedented economic growth. Federal funding of research at academic institutions has yielded discoveries that have attracted the risk capital necessary for subsequent product development. The public has benefited not only from products and services based on these discoveries, but also from the trained work force and tax revenues those discoveries have enabled.

> Scientific researchers have a strong responsibility to work for the public good. Regardless of where those researchers reside—in universities, corporations, or government laboratories—this obligation remains undiminished. From each source, ideas must be transferred inexorably to evermore real application, and to evermore public benefit. Probably, some money will be gained along the way, but so will much more of a greater currency: improvements in human lives and economic prosperity. —*Gertrude Elion, D. SC., Nobel Laureate*[1]

FOUNDATIONS OF TECHNOLOGY TRANSFER IN THE UNITED STATES

University technology transfer in the United States has its roots in the technological advances made by university researchers during and after World War II. Recognition of the contribution of university research led to broader support for basic science by the federal government at research universities. This funding was intended to yield national economic benefits by increasing the flow of knowledge and creating a skilled work force to benefit U.S. industry.

Public law 96–517, the Bayh–Dole Act, was signed into law on December 12, 1980, and became effective in July 1981. For our purposes, the Bayh–Dole Act can be summarized as follows:[2]

- The act established a uniform federal patent policy governing inventions made at universities using federal research funding.
- Universities are encouraged to collaborate with industry to promote the development and commercialization of these inventions.
- Universities have the right to elect title to inventions made with federal research funding, and this right cannot be assigned to a for-profit entity.
- Universities have the obligation to file for patents on inventions they elect to own.
- The government retains nonexclusive license to practice the invention throughout the world and retains a march-in right.
- Preference in licensing by universities is to be given to small businesses (less than 500 employees).
- The licensee needs to substantially manufacture licensed products in the United States that are sold in the United States.

Timing of the Bayh–Dole Act was fortuitous, given the concentration of bio-medical inventions and expansion of the biotechnology industry throughout the 1980s. In addition, the Circuit Court of Appeals for the Federal Circuit (CAFC) has steadfastly upheld the rights of intellectual property owners and the value of intellectual assets. These factors have contributed to the impressive expansion of university–industry collaborations over the past two decades.

GROWTH OF UNIVERSITY TECHNOLOGY TRANSFER ACTIVITY

AUTM began tracking university patent and licensing activity in 1991 (see Exhibit 11.1). Consistent with the growing federal funding for basic research, legislation enabling universities to assert title to inventions (Bayh–Dole), and other factors noted previously, university technology transfer has grown steadily throughout the decade as measured by invention disclosures, patents filed and issued, licenses executed, and gross licensing income.

In FY2000 alone, according to the AUTM Annual Licensing Survey, the 190 U.S. and Canadian universities, nonprofit research institutions, teaching hospitals, and patent commercialization companies participating in the AUTM survey reported

- $29.5 billion in sponsored research expenditures, including $18.1 billion from federal government sources and $2.7 billion from industry
- 13,032 new technology disclosures
- 6,375 new U.S. patent application filings
- 3,764 U.S. patents issued

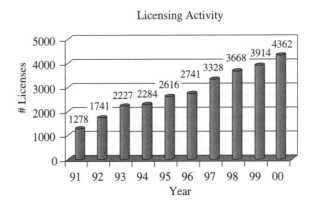

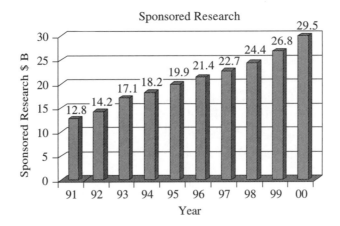

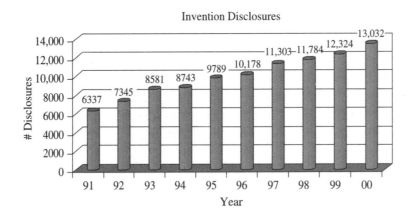

EXHIBIT 11.1   University Patent and Licensing Activity, 1991–2000

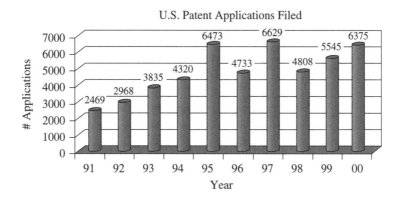

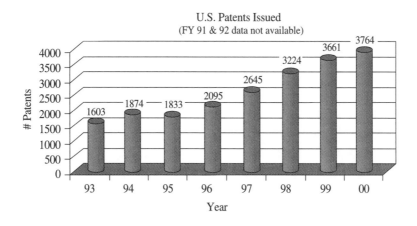

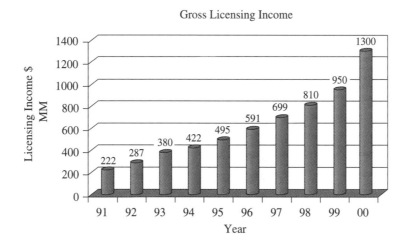

EXHIBIT 11.1   Continued

- 4,362 new options and licenses, 454 granted to new start-up ventures (80 percent of which established operations in the state of the discovery institution); 90 percent of the start-up venture licenses were exclusive in nature; 50 percent of the 4,362 licenses were granted exclusively and 50 percent were granted nonexclusively
- $1.3 billion in adjusted gross income

Analysis of previous AUTM licensing surveys indicates that based on substantial research funding from the National Institutes of Health and the emergence of the biotechnology industry and new biomedical products, approximately 67 percent of university inventions and 86 percent of licensing income were in the life sciences (see Exhibit 11.2).

Consistent with the Bayh–Dole preference for small business, 66 percent of university licenses in FY2000 were granted to small companies, including start-up ventures (see Exhibit 11.3).

AUTM annual licensing surveys and other information suggest that since 1980 more than 3,376 new companies have been created based on an intellectual property licensed from universities, including the 454 formed in FY2000. Of these 3,376 new companies, 2,309 were still operating as of the end of 2000. Universities report receiving equity interests in 372 transactions in FY2000, including 252 (56 percent) of the new companies formed.

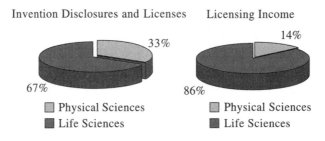

EXHIBIT 11.2   University Inventions and Licensing

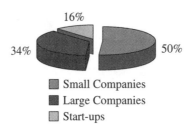

EXHIBIT 11.3   University License Grants in 2000

TECHNOLOGY TRANSFER PROCESS

The technology transfer process is frequently envisioned as the linear model depicted in Exhibit 11.4. Research at universities, funded in large part by federal government dollars, leads to technology disclosures from faculty and staff inventors. These disclosures are reviewed for a number of criteria in a process called opportunity assessment. Those disclosures found meritorious during opportunity assessment are submitted for intellectual property protection, generally performed by outside counsel. A customized commercialization strategy is determined and, if executed successfully, results in the licensing of the technology to an existing company or a new entity formed to exploit the technology.

Opportunity Assessment

Inquiry-driven, federally funded research generates approximately one invention disclosure per $2 million of funding. According to AUTM, during the period 1991–2000, $204 billion in research expenditures at the universities and research institutes surveyed yielded 97,182 technology disclosures.

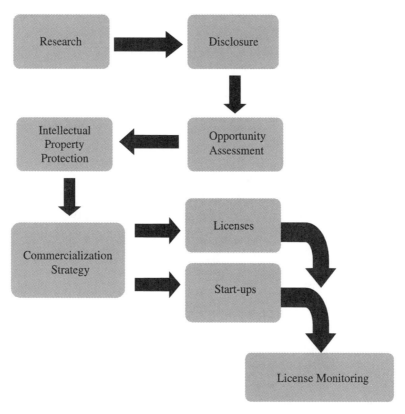

EXHIBIT 11.4   The Technology Transfer Process

Although systematically implemented to varying degrees across institutions, universities generally use four criteria to assess invention disclosures:

1. Commercial potential
2. Technical merit
3. Protectability
4. Inventor profile

Opportunity assessment is among the thorniest of all technology transfer tasks, even for experienced university technology managers. Most experienced technology transfer managers recognize that it is difficult (if not impossible) to select *winners* among disclosures, as there are numerous uncertainties in the product development and commercialization pathways. However, with the right process, it should be possible to avoid *losers*. The objective is to invest resources—time and money—on discoveries that are likely to be attractive to potential licensees and are likely to be successful in the marketplace.

Confounding the already challenging task of opportunity assessment are the multifaceted objectives of technology transfer. Each university must keep in mind its own hierarchy of technology transfer objectives, as discussed in the Introduction, when performing opportunity assessment on its own disclosures. Before moving on, let's look at those objectives in more detail:

- *Facilitate the commercialization of university discoveries for the public good.* Discoveries likely to yield large public benefit with minimal commercial benefit will often be pursued if there is any chance of finding a licensee. Importantly, though, no public good can be served by having a huge inventory of technology disclosures and/or patents that are not marketed and are unlicensed.
- *Reward, retain, and recruit faculty (and increasingly students).* Although initially faculty may be pleased that a submitted technology disclosure is being filed as a patent application that might eventually issue as a patent, these same faculty become disenchanted with the technology transfer process and the technology licensing office if, after having invested considerable time and effort in patent prosecution, no marketing effort is conducted and/or no commercial partner is found to license their technology.
- *Forge closer ties to industry.* Universities are increasingly desirous of improving relationships with industry. However, it is counterproductive to market technologies that have not been carefully assessed in the triage process to companies that do not have a strategic interest in that specific technology. Companies have little time or patience for unsolicited offers to license technologies outside their strategic interests.

- *Promote economic growth.* Increasingly, universities recognize the value of technology commercialization to promote economic development. As previously cited, the AUTM data indicate that 80 percent of new start-up ventures based on university-licensed technologies locate in proximity to the discovery institution. Universities are ever more cognizant of keeping their intellectual assets (technology, faculty, and graduates) close to home. With this goal in mind, universities are licensing their technology to new ventures that will employ their faculty as consultants and their graduates as employees, and will create new jobs and wealth in the region.

- *Generate income.* All universities want to generate income from technology transfer activities, although its importance as an objective varies greatly from university to university. Although this income may represent a small percentage of the university budget (on average, less than 4 percent of the total research budget), these dollars are unrestricted in their use, unlike virtually all other dollars in an academic budget. Bayh–Dole requires that universities use licensing income for educational and research purposes and that faculty be awarded a share of income personally. During periods of fiscal constraint, income generated from technology transfer is increasingly valued.

Systematic opportunity assessment of invention disclosures provides technology managers with credible, defensible, and objective data essential for communicating decisions with faculty inventors. Scientists are accustomed to receiving critiques of their research grants, projects, and publications. Generally, faculty can appreciate and accept valid criticism of their technology disclosures. However, faculty are unwilling to accept either a lack of responsiveness from the technology transfer office and/or subjective evaluations of their technology disclosures that are not effectively communicated. Valid opportunity assessment critiques also help faculty to understand and improve subsequent invention disclosures. We propose that technology managers focus on the following four criteria for opportunity assessment: protectability, technical merit, commercial potential, and inventor profile.

Protectability (Patentability). Protectability (patentability) is often used as the baseline for opportunity assessment. Unfortunately, a number of institutions use patentability as the sole criterion. Many institutions use internal or outside patent counsel to help determine patentability. Patent searches may be used to help determine the breadth and depth of possible patent claims, freedom to practice, and difficulty for nonlicensees to reverse engineer. Patentability assessments may also assist in determining the ability of the patent assignee or licensee to detect infringement and/or withstand litigation. Patent searches and other patentability reviews determine the extent of patent activity in a given field. These reviews help determine the depth and breadth of prior art and encumbrances. Patentability reviews, especially of the inventor's own prior art, help determine whether any damage might be caused to the faculty inventor from automatic publication of the patent application and the need or urgency to make a patent filing decision. Although protectability (patentability) is a necessary component of comprehensive opportunity assessment, by itself, it is insufficient.

Technical Merit. The determination of technical merit as part of opportunity assessment is another essential aspect. However, many university technology managers are loathe to question their faculty inventors' technology disclosures in terms of technical merit. Clearly, attention must be paid to the sensitivity of an administrative staff person "evaluating" the quality of a faculty member's science. A review of technical merit requires the faculty member to provide an adequate description of the technology and to support the invention's novelty, utility, and unobviousness. An adequate description of a technology in the form of a detailed disclosure will help the technology manager, whether the invention represents a composition of matter (or new chemical entity) or a method of use invention. The description should be supported by the availability of data demonstrating utility or by evidence of a prototype. The description also helps determine whether the invention falls within a hot commercial market scientific discipline or an emerging field of research. A review of technical merit helps to identify both an individual technology manager's experience with similar technology and a particular technology transfer office's experience and success in patenting and licensing similar technology.

The technical merit review helps identify features (and benefits) of the innovation that are thought to outweigh its limitations, the probability of gaining industry support to further develop the invention, and whether the invention is a core discovery (disruptive technology) and as such might stand alone as the platform or foundation for a new company. Technical merit review assists in determining the development status of the invention in relation to the time to market, taking into account the milestones, hurdles, and obstacles to commercialization. This review also helps to determine the extent to which established industry channels to commercialization exist for the technology, including manufacturing and distribution channels.

Commercial Potential. Determining commercial potential is often a function of the ability to use the description of the technology to define a product or service that would be based on the invention. Defining the product assists in identifying customers and end users, as well as the perceived need, commercial value, and market size for the product coming from the technology based on the scientific discovery.

During this definition of product, prospective licensees can be identified and used to determine the availability and nature of competing technologies and the predisposition of potential industry licensees to licensing. A review of commercial potential also reveals both an individual technology manager's and the technology transfer office's experience in licensing into that particular industry.

Inventor Profile.   Although it is possible to license embryonic discoveries without the willing and able assistance of a faculty inventor, it is far more difficult to do so. Therefore, the ability and willingness of a faculty inventor to participate in the technology transfer process, including patenting and licensing, is highly desirable. This participation in the process also tends to reveal the faculty member's expectations of rewards from the technology transfer process and presents the opportunity to establish realistic expectations.

A faculty member's knowledge of the industry in which an invention is being licensed and that faculty member's standing in terms of research funding and recognition by both academic and industry peers are also essential. The extent to which faculty inventors' publications are frequently referenced, their involvement with and/or knowledge of potential licensees and company contacts, their tenure status, and the support of their academic superiors are all determinations of inventor profile. Faculty are often the best source of leads for potential licenses. Inventions by faculty who have little knowledge or contacts within the industry into which their technology would be licensed are a major red flag.

Determinations around these four opportunity assessment criteria provide the basis for communicating results of the technology assessment to inventors. The goal of this process is to be firm, fair, and flexible. Technology managers must be willing to revise their assessments of a particular technology upon receipt of new information. In addition, results of this evaluation can and should be used not only to improve future technology disclosures, but also to refine the process for the next invention.

AUTM productivity metrics for the period from FY1991–FY2000 indicate that participating universities filed patent applications on 35 percent of technology disclosures (see Exhibit 11.5). A breakout of select top-tier research universities shows that up to 50 percent of their disclosures are filed as patent applications.

Intellectual Property Protection

Even for technologies that appear promising using each of the criteria in opportunity assessment, obtaining appropriate intellectual property protection for embryonic technology remains a large challenge in university technology transfer. As compared to industry patent applications, university applications generally are filed much earlier in the research discovery process than patents from industry. Faculty are in the *recognition business* and strive to publish early and

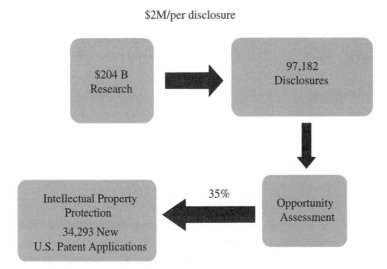

EXHIBIT 11.5   AUTM Productivity Metrics

often. University technology managers must make decisions based on discoveries that define scientific research results rather than technologies, markets, or products. Generally, universities must file patent applications with relatively little notice prior to publication or with limited data to support the application. University faculty are under intense pressure to publish, which forces technology managers to make decisions to file patent applications far earlier than their industry counterparts and often prior to the availability of any prototype or utility data. University patents are also generally filed before any commercialization strategy or commercially sound claims can be structured. These realities are often the basis for industry criticisms of university inventions, patents, and licensing ventures.

Limited patent budgets generally do not permit universities to file national foreign patent applications without licensee sponsorship. In an ever-more global marketplace, the lack of foreign intellectual property protection is often problematic in licensing. However, while university inventions can be the basis of a new product, subsequently developed research results are often even more critical for patent and market protection to industry. Thus, a U.S. patent alone may be a limitation in the licensing opportunity, but still represents a worthwhile asset (and the basis for 50 percent of product revenues in pharmaceuticals).

In addition, universities are increasingly being challenged in their quest for patent protection of life-science research tools and materials. The National Institutes of Health and other private foundation research sponsors have published guidelines urging universities to either not file patents for such tools and materials or, if filed, to license them on a nonexclusive basis.

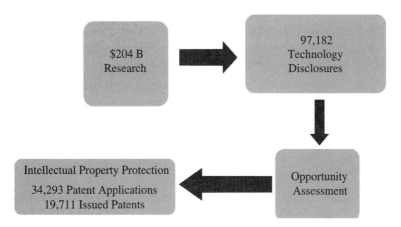

EXHIBIT 11.6   University Patent Applications

Finally, given these constraints, managing outside counsel is another intellectual property protection challenge. Not only are patent budgets limited, but also because of the embryonic nature of discoveries and the lack of commercial focus, outside patent counsel are often left on their own to formulate the patent strategy and claims. Patent applications are thus often prosecuted without appropriate commercial (market, product) focus, which is usually provided by company strategy. Although many university patent budgets are still very limited in terms of filing patent applications for technologies for which no industrial sponsor/licensee exists, most universities now recognize the need to assess invention disclosures on their merits and file patents to protect embryonic discoveries. Despite these challenges, more than half (57 percent) of university patent applications are issued as U.S. patents (see Exhibit 11.6).

Licensing to Established Companies

As discussed earlier in "Opportunity Assessment," university inventions are often embryonic in nature. The markets and products made possible by such early discoveries might not be known or defined for many years. Often, academic discoveries represent a window into the future. Licensing such technologies requires that the university technology manager and faculty inventor have either a sense or a vision for how the discovery will be utilized in the marketplace. The commercialization (licensing) strategy emanates from this vision. Most discoveries from universities eventually become the basis of or an addition to a single product or a narrow group of products. These discoveries represent an evolutionary change in science. Such inventions are generally the basis of a license to an established company with channels for manufacturing, distribution, and sales of products based on the invention. Virtually all university technologies (97 percent) are licensed to established companies (see Exhibit 11.7).

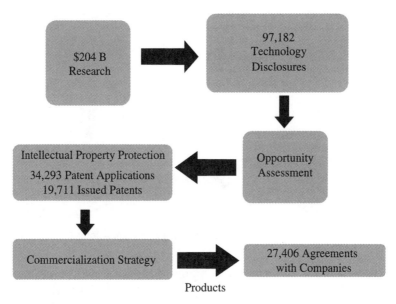

EXHIBIT 11.7   University Licenses to Established Companies

In their licenses to established companies, universities seek a variety of financial considerations:

- Initiation/upfront and maintenance fees
- Milestone and diligence payments
- Running and minimum royalties
- Sharing of sublicensee revenues
- Patent and licensing expense reimbursement
- Sponsored research

Although rarely a stumbling block in terms of consummating a license, valuation and pricing discrepancies in negotiations are frequent in university–industry licensing. It is beyond the scope of this paper to address various approaches and methodologies for valuation and pricing. Suffice it to say that win-win negotiations generally occur in these transactions when neither party seeks to take unfair advantage of the other.

One increasingly difficult issue in early-stage licensing is in defining the basis for future royalty payments, or deciding if there will be royalty payments at all. Often the university technology is many steps removed from product identification and may be one of many aids to future product definition. In such cases it might be unfair to reach through to an eventual royalty, and the university might need to be satisfied with yearly payments while the technology is in use. In other instances where the technology is critical to future product definition, both sides may agree that a royalty on future sales is warranted.

Although financial terms may be the most frequently discussed and hotly debated issues between university technology managers and industry licensing executives, the *nonfinancial terms* should be far more important to the university, and thus may be far more problematic and difficult to negotiate. These nonfinancial terms include

- Scope of the license (including field of use and territory and rights to improvements)
- Definition of product or other royalty basis
- Confidentiality
- Diligence requirements and termination consequences
- Milestones and timing to commercialization
- Control of patent prosecution
- Warranties, indemnification, and insurance

Given universities' statutory obligation to facilitate the commercialization of federally funded discoveries for the public good, diligent commercialization by licensees is essential. University technology managers often seek written, contractually obligated commitments for the timely development of the licensed technology to first commercial sale. Payment penalties, reversion of rights or scope of the license, and possible termination of the license are all considerations to assure diligence. The prospective licensee often regards these measures as harsh and unnecessary. The strategic objectives of a company may change over the years of a license agreement, and the university should be able to recover neglected technologies that would fit another company's strategy.

Reputation risk and institutional endowment are among the greatest concerns for high-level university administrators. As such, restricted use of name and appropriate indemnification and insurance coverage are essential safeguards for risks associated with institutional reputation and endowment and will be components of all university licenses. In addition, universities are generally unwilling to provide any warranty as to utility of the licensed technology, potential freedom to use, or patentability.

University technology managers recognize that companies seek a competitive advantage and benefit from their collaborations with universities. However, universities are not able to grant broad rights to future discoveries, including those from the faculty member developing the technology being licensed, even in the same field of use. Companies seeking to own future inventions by a faculty member or in a given field of use from that laboratory are wise to sponsor research for several years in that laboratory, which will enable them to have an option to license future discoveries.

Licensing to New Companies/Creating Start-ups

Discoveries that are revolutionary in nature (also referred to as *disruptive technologies*) represent a paradigm shift in scientific thinking and may serve as the foundation for a platform of new products serving multiple markets. These types of discoveries can be the basis for the creation of a new venture to develop and commercialize university inventions. Such platform technologies often require substantial additional research and proof-of-concept validation prior to focused product development initiatives.

Universities have adopted a wide variety of philosophies and approaches in licensing to new companies and creating start-up ventures. These approaches range from mere facilitation of the new venture all the way to managing and venture funding new companies. They are summarized in Exhibit 11.8.

The most basic approach in licensing a start-up company involves facilitating creation of the new company by perhaps developing the business concept, recruiting experienced entrepreneurial management, and attracting seed investment. Acknowledging and understanding the differences in licensing to an established company and a newly formed company are very important here. Some universities go one step further by creating a new company (NewCo) and issuing stock to investors and management. Some universities take the next step of providing interim management to guide further development of the technology through proof-of-concept testing to making the discovery more investable (and valuable) to future venture investors. Some universities provide a small amount of seed capital to perform proof-of-concept development. Finally, a few universities invest their own operating or endowment funds (directly or through

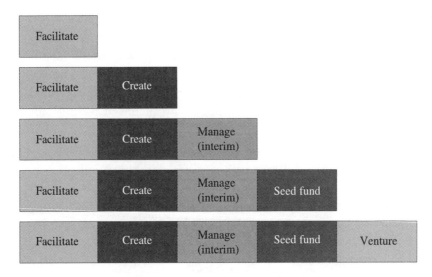

EXHIBIT 11.8   Philosophies and Approaches in Licensing to New Companies

affiliated venture funds) to make seed investments and in later round venture investments in their own start-ups.

Many faculty and university administrators mistakenly believe or wishfully think that a large proportion of inventions are the basis for a new entrepreneurial venture. However, AUTM data indicate that only 3 percent of disclosures rise to the level of an invention that is adequate for start-up creation (see Exhibit 11.9).

Equity is an important consideration in start-up licenses. In effect, equity represents a prepaid royalty or consideration in lieu of license initiation fee. Financial considerations in these start-up licenses often include similar considerations seen in licenses to established companies. The amount or percentage of equity taken by the university is a determining factor in other financial considerations. That is, the greater the university's share in equity, the lesser requirement for other financial considerations.

Conceptually, at the pre-seed stage of investment, there are three value components in a start-up—intellectual property/technology, management, and money. As a university provides the intellectual property and technology, the university is entitled at this preseed investment stage to approximately one-third of the equity. Universities providing interim management and a portion of seed investment may wish to take a greater portion of equity. In these situations, it might not be appropriate for the university to also take a license initiation fee, which, in effect, penalizes the company and uses cash that might be

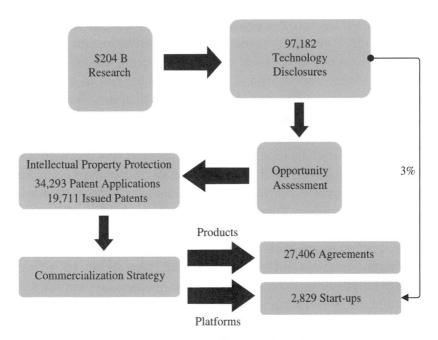

EXHIBIT 11.9   Start-up Creation

more appropriately used for technology development. However, in start-up ventures in which the university takes a single-digit percentage of equity, financial considerations common in licenses to established companies, including license initiation fees, are generally appropriate.

Universities that receive a large proportion of their funding from state or local sources often take a much more aggressive approach to start-up licensing. This approach is based on the recognition that 80 percent of start-up ventures locate in proximity to the discovery institution. Thus, new-company formation is seen as an effective tool to promote economic development by creating local investment and jobs. In addition, many of these universities are relatively new to technology transfer and view equity and its multiplier effect as an opportunity for short-term financial success. These institutions often value their technology and associated intellectual property rights as equal to other value contributions in new ventures—management and money—and seek double-digit equity positions in lieu of license fees and milestones.

License Monitoring

License monitoring is an essential part of any licensing transaction, including university–industry licenses. Many universities now recognize the need to monitor licensee performance and payments. In addition, for inventions funded in whole or in part by the federal government, universities are obligated to report annually on invention usage. Setting up appropriate systems and procedures before things go off track is a necessary component of technology transfer.

The first step in license monitoring is the creation of a sound recordkeeping system. This system could be either a written ledger or computerized database that records licensees' reporting and financial obligations to the licensor. For reports or payments due upon performance, rather than time-based events, projected dates of completion can be docketed to prompt an inquiry.

An individual or office must be designated to monitor licensees' obligations. This monitoring should include gathering data from the licensee and other sources, receiving payments or acknowledgements of payments, and identifying and reconciling differences between the obligations noted from the recordkeeping system to those made in compliance by the licensee.

Information gathered from a variety of sources can be used to monitor this compliance. Formal sources include progress reports, development plans, and other information required in the license. Public information, including annual and quarterly reports, investor relations information, and news articles, can provide important insights into licensees' activities related to development and commercialization of licensed technology. Finally, researchers often become aware of information that is not generally available to the public through their professional meetings and personal grapevines.

Information gleaned from these sources provides a picture of licensees' activities. In those instances where a university's interpretations of licensees' obligations are consistent with licensees' progress reports, sales reports, and payments, no additional action is necessary. However, when information differs or seems inconsistent, it is helpful to use increasing levels of inquiry to reconcile differences. These levels of inquiry can include telephone calls, personal visits, formal written requests for additional data or interpretation, royalty audits, demands for payment, and ultimately, legal action.

Increasingly, it is recognized that periodic telephone calls and/or personal visits to licensees, especially those licensees considered to be important from a financial or technology standpoint, are very appropriate. Such activities can often preclude future differences in interpretation of license terms. University technology transfer offices should also consider conducting royalty audits within a year of first sales for licenses predicted to generate significant royalties. Such audits can confirm the appropriate basis for the royalty payments. In addition, some universities require licensees to conduct an independent audit of sales and royalties on a periodic basis (e.g., every two years) once annual sales of licensed products achieve a certain level (e.g., $5 million annually). However, such audits may be unlikely to identify differences in interpretation of terms leading to royalty basis.

Monitoring licenses and maintaining good communication with a licensee should not be viewed as contentious activities. As partners in the commercialization of a technology, both the company and the university must share appropriate information. Regular communication and diligent monitoring should assure that both partners are treated fairly and should thus short-circuit many causes of future litigation.

TECHNOLOGY TRANSFER: BRIDGING THE GAP BETWEEN ACADEMIA AND INDUSTRY

Universities manage intellectual assets to promote and support their core teaching and research missions. Technology transfer is *not* universities' primary interest or activity, and universities need to approach the risks and rewards inherent in technology transfer accordingly. Universities cannot play the role of the profit-driven corporation, nor the public-driven charity, in technology development. Being neither fish nor fowl results in a turmoil that is difficult to explain to the outside world. This ambiguity of role results in numerous misunderstandings with the public and press but also increasingly among technology transfer professionals and academic administrators.

Universities in the twenty-first century must address and resolve the compelling and competing imperatives represented in Exhibit 11.10.

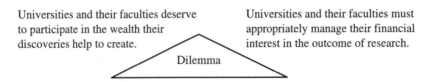

Universities and their faculties deserve to participate in the wealth their discoveries help to create.

Universities and their faculties must appropriately manage their financial interest in the outcome of research.

Dilemma

EXHIBIT 11.10   Intellectual Assets Versus Teaching and Research Missions

In effect, university technology transfer must bridge two worlds—academia and industry—and resolve the conflicting cultural values that define each. University technology transfer managers must do their part to help:

- Preserve traditional academic values
- Encourage appropriate institutional and faculty entrepreneurship
- Manage risks
- Manage conflicts of interest and commitment

One of our greatest challenges in the twenty-first century will be determining for ourselves how we define and measure success. Some observers of university technology transfer view the growth of these activities over the past two decades as an indication of great success. These observers point to the over $1 billion of gross licensing income reported by the most recent AUTM Annual Licensing Survey as an indication of success. Those of us in the field have struggled mightily during this period to achieve this growth, and we look forward to sales of products now in development as the basis for even more spectacular success. However, this $1 billion in collective income is less than what some *individual* companies earn from licensing and related intellectual asset management activities.

Clearly, licensing income is a measure of success. However, is financial success the defining metric for university technology transfer? University technology managers struggle with the mixed agendas and mixed messages inherent in the complex and multifaceted goals of academic technology transfer. Despite these challenges, products and services based on university technologies have made and will continue to make vast improvements in the quality of life for people throughout the world. U.S. investment in research creates new knowledge and discoveries. University technology transfer facilitates the exploitation of these discoveries by the private sector that contributes tens of billions of dollars to the U.S. economy, supports hundreds of thousands of jobs, and produces billions of dollars in new tax revenues. This repayment on investment will continue to grow impressively in the twenty-first century and reward all participants handsomely.

ENDNOTES

[1] Scott McPartland. *Gertrude Elion: Master Chemist* (Vero Beach, CA: Rourke Enterprises, Inc., 1993).

[2] For a comprehensive discussion of the legislative history and regulations affecting university-industry technology transfer, see Howard W. Bremmer, "History of Laws and Regulations Affecting the Transfer of Intellectual Property," *AUTM Technology Transfer Practice Manual III* (1994).

ABOUT THE AUTHORS

Louis P. Berneman, Ed.D., is an experienced intellectual asset management and business development executive. Dr. Berneman is managing director, Center for Technology Transfer (CTT), at the University of Pennsylvania. CTT obtains and manages patents, copyrights, and trademarks derived from the university's academic enterprise. CTT creates relationships with industry to develop, protect, transfer, and commercialize intellectual property resulting from the university's research program.

Dr. Berneman is a past president of the Association of University Technology Managers (AUTM). He is also a trustee and vice president of the Licensing Executives Society (LES) and board member of the Pennsylvania Biotechnology Association. Prior to joining Penn in 1995, Dr. Berneman was director for Licensing and Business Development at Virginia's Center for Innovative Technology. Previously, he co-founded and was a director of Innotech, Inc., co-founded and was president and CEO of Response Technologies, Inc., was vice president of marketing and sales of Immuno Modulators Laboratories, Inc., and was assistant professor of education at the University of Houston. Dr. Berneman received his undergraduate degree in history from the Pennsylvania State University, a teaching credential from the University of California at Santa Barbara, and masters and doctoral degrees in education from Columbia University.

Kathleen A. Denis, Ph.D., is the senior director of technology transfer at The Rockefeller University, a premier biomedical research institution located in New York City. Managing the intellectual assets of the university, she works with their elite group of researchers to establish partnerships with industry in order to develop and commercialize technologies for the public good. Formerly a consultant specializing in the management of intellectual assets in the life sciences, she worked with academic and industry clients to manage intellectual property portfolios, evaluate new technologies, market and license technologies, and start new technology-based businesses.

Dr. Denis is active in numerous professional organizations and speaks frequently about early-stage technology evaluation, formation of start-up companies, conflict of interest, and other issues of academic technology transfer. She is a trustee and vice president of the Licensing Executives Society (LES), and has served on the board of directors of the AUTM and the Pennsylvania Biotechnology Association.

ABOUT THE AUTHORS (continued)

From 1995 through 1998, Dr. Denis was vice president of technology development at Allegheny Health, Education, and Research Foundation. She managed the intellectual property and research assets of Allegheny University of the Health Sciences (formerly and currently the Medical College of Pennsylvania and Hahnemann University), as well as Allegheny General Hospital and Allegheny Singer Research Institute. Responsibilities of this position included the evaluation and marketing of technologies, building collaborative relationships with the biomedical and biopharmaceutical communities, and promoting economic development in Pennsylvania.

Dr. Denis was a director at the University of Pennsylvania Center for Technology Transfer from 1991 to 1995, where she managed a large portfolio of biotechnology and pharmaceutical-related technologies. Previously, she was an investigator at the Molecular Biology Institute at UCLA for eight years and was a senior scientist at Specialty Laboratories, Inc. She has more than 30 scientific publications.

Dr. Denis holds a Ph.D. in immunology from the University of Pennsylvania, a masters in Human Genetics from the University of Texas Medical Branch at Galveston, and an undergraduate degree in genetics from Cornell University.

Part Four

Financial Issues, Legal Protection, and Litigation Developments

12

What To Do with Technology Rights That Are Financial Assets and Instruments

By Dr. Nir Kossovsky and Bear Brandegee

INTRODUCTION

Technologies and the intellectual property (IP) rights that control their economic exploitation are the foundation of the *knowledge economy*. Recent changes in financial market behavior, accounting practices, business strategy, and the global information infrastructure are transforming intellectual property rights into financial instruments. Going forward, IP management strategies will be fully integrated into corporate financial strategies.

A GUIDE FOR INTELLECTUAL CAPITALISTS

Technology licenses are valuable assets. To the owner of technology rights, licenses and their attendant real or potential cash flows are a source of economic value. The licenses may generate cash directly through royalty and milestone payments or indirectly through debt instruments secured by cash flows, equity instruments, and derivative securities created from single or aggregated debt instruments.

In the late twentieth century, licensing executives devoted most of their energy to matters of law, technology, and market analysis. The range of monetization opportunities just described were not yet part of their licensing toolkit. But with the dawn of the knowledge economy, finance became a potent driver of IP management decisions. Now in the twenty-first century, licensing executives need to be expert in both law and finance. They need to be *intellectual capitalists*.

In the sections that follow, we offer four case studies that illustrate intellectual capitalist strategies for managing intellectual property, as a financial asset.

IP AND VOLATILE FINANCIAL MARKETS

It was 6:30 A.M. on August 10, 2000. Martha Koontz, CEO of Diasyn Drugs, Inc., pressed the snooze button of her obnoxious alarm clock for a third time. It was a bad morning after a bad night that capped a bad day, and she wasn't yet prepared to face the new day.

Tuesday, August 8, had been a banner day. After several years of laboratory research, Diasyn Drugs announced the successful formulation of a new anxiolytic drug and the filing of patent applications for the new product in several key jurisdictions. The marketing department had developed a special investor relations campaign to roll out NoProblem and NoProblemPlus, a formulation combining the anxiolytic activity of the basic drug with a short-term amnestic agent. The analysts were ecstatic, the stock market was buoyant, and Diasyn Drugs stock rose 15 percent to a new high of $22.50 per share. Life was good.

Wednesday, August 9, the party ended abruptly. A U.S. appeals court ruled against Eli Lilly & Co., one of the leading producers of anxiolytic and other neuroactive drugs, stating that its Prozac patent extension was invalid. Financial markets panicked. Within minutes, Eli Lilly & Co. lost almost a third of its market capitalization. Its shares fell $33.56 to $75.00. Furthermore, in the setting of intellectual property uncertainty, investors expressed doubts about the value of drug patents belonging to Pfizer Inc., Merck & Co., Johnson & Johnson, and others. That day, drug stocks collectively accounted for almost three-quarters of the S & P's decline.

Diasyn Drugs and its CEO, Martha Koontz, were caught in this maelstrom. By nightfall, its stock had fallen to $4.25. The company's telephone circuits were overwhelmed. Investors, brokers, dealers, and analysts each wanted a meeting. The board of directors demanded that Martha present a corrective plan at an emergency meeting. Company employees, most of whose stock options were suddenly under water, were demanding a town hall meeting.

It was now the morning after, and the laptop computer surrounded by her breakfast bowl of coffee and a salad plate decorated with one chocolate donut, meticulously sliced in eighths, showed that the stock opened at $4.10. Martha weighed her options and made her first executive decision of the day—she reached for and meticulously sliced a second donut. She then made her second decision: Diaysn Drugs was going to hedge its IP risk.

Discussion: The Effect of Market Volatility on Intangible Assets

Market volatility is a healthy phenomenon. It helps differentiate various grades of debt and quality of equities, and it provides investment opportunities for individuals with different risk appetites and investment horizons. Excessive volatility, however, is disconcerting to primary issuers, investors, and the many market intermediaries. It can create capital shortages and it can drive you to eat too many chocolate donuts. A contributor of present-day volatility is uncertainty over the value of the primary driver of market cap in most companies—intangible assets.

Intellectual property is the most valuable of the many intangible assets (other assets include earnings momentum, management reputation, and human know-how). Until the mid-1980s, the value of intangible assets in the S & P 500 companies tended to equal the value of the tangible assets (book value), and the average market capitalization of these companies was twice book value. Prior to the millennium meltdown of financial markets in the 2000 to 2001 period, the market capitalization of new economy companies was many times their book value and accounted for five of every six dollars of market capitalization. One year after this ratio peaked, at least four of every five market capitalization dollars are still based on the value of intangibles.

Baruch Lev, professor of Accounting and Finance at New York University, notes in a study recently published by the Brookings Institution that the rise in the value of intangibles is due to the confluence of two major forces: changes in the structure of business enterprises and technological innovation. Insofar as it appears these forces will continue to bear down on us for quite some time, financial risk-mitigation strategies associated with IP value volatility might be useful.

Secrets of the Intellectual Capitalist

The intellectual capitalist of the twenty-first century has several alternative financial hedging instruments to reduce the company's stock price volatility insofar as it relates to uncertainties in IP valuation. The first strategy is to lock in the value of IP through a securitization. An alternative strategy is to protect against value loss through insurance (see Exhibit 12.1).

Securitization. In an IP securitization, an underwriter assesses the present value of a company's IP asset, pays a lump sum for the rights to the future cash flows, and then sells a bond to investors whose interest payment and final principal payment are financed from the purchased cash flows. Through this mechanism, the risks associated with volatility are transferred from the company to the bondholders. The underwriter plays an intermediary role in creating the investment instrument and providing certain assurances that promote investment.

Insurance. In an IP value insurance strategy, an insurance underwriter assesses the present value of a company's IP asset and, for a premium, the underwriter agrees to pay a lump sum in the event that the value falls to some agreed level as the result of some unforeseen event. Through this mechanism, the risks associated with volatility are transferred from the company to the insurer.

Today several global companies offer commercial intellectual property securitization and insurance products. They tend to favor well-capitalized entities with a large IP portfolio—a profile that helps mitigate the attendant risks. However, as

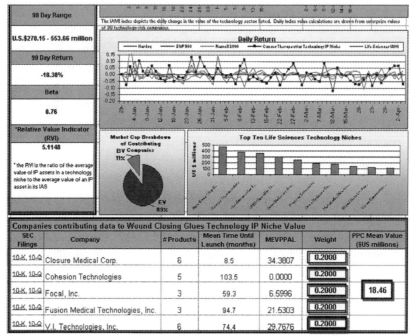

Image courtesy of the Patent and License Exchange, www.pl-x.com.

EXHIBIT 12.1   Advanced IP Value Metrics and Other Management Tools

these relatively exotic financial strategies become more commonplace, these services will be available to a larger range of potential customers. As soon as they do, Martha Koontz will be on the phone contracting these services.

IP AND FASB STATEMENTS 141 AND 142

Mark Aiken, the CFO of Diversified Global Technologies, was so happy he felt like a kid. He was going to spend the Thanksgiving holiday with his family. As he drove home, singing to himself, Mark recalled that only five months ago, the chances of his enjoying Thanksgiving, or even Christmas, with his family, were slim to none.

On Friday, June 29, 2001, the Financial Accounting Standards Board of the United States (FASB) unanimously approved the final standards resulting from its deliberations on the business combinations project. Shortly thereafter, the FASB issued Financial Accounting Standards (FAS) No. 141, "Business Combinations," and No. 142, "Goodwill and Other Intangible Assets." The new rules required significant changes in how his company recorded the value of its intellectual property.

In the past, Mark would have simply delegated the task to his firm's auditors. With budgets being tight after two consecutive poor quarters, a down market, and a looming recession, Mark didn't think he would be able to find the resources to support this massive additional project. "No," Mark said to himself, "this is something we are going to have to manage in-house." It was August, the weather was oppressive, most of the senior executives were on vacation, and he was faced with a daunting task.

Shortly after Labor Day, Mark called Janice Kimura, senior IP counsel.

"Janice, I'm starting to implement our FAS 141/142 compliance initiative, and I'd like to review with you the IP of our various acquisitions and see how their values may map against what we have on our books as goodwill."

"Will you need a legal opinion from me on the validity and strength of every patent?" she asked.

"Perhaps," Mark said. "How many patents are there?"

"From the merger this past spring we brought in about 12,000, so overall we have about 17,000."

"Janice, what if we bundled them into asset units and treated them as a portfolio with assumed averages?"

"I'm not sure I could define an average patent, Mark. That sounds more like a financial concept than a legal concept. But informally, I would say that if you are bundling them into commercial assets, you'll need Robertson from Marketing or Choi from Strategy to give you a market assessment so that you can run your financial models."

"How many asset units, then?"

"Well, Mark, it would take me some time to determine which patents will bundle into reasonable packages that represent future product."

The going was slow. Janice, also working under severe budget constraints, had recruited volunteers from R & D to help organize the patents into asset bundles. The conference room was commandeered and was piled high with stacks of patent documents that were being organized by potential product based on a consensus opinion reached by an ad-hoc committee. Mark was glum. Surely, he reasoned, there must be some software package that was designed to organize technology in such a way that one could visualize what products they yielded, or at least what intellectual property space they dominated. "More importantly," he thought, "what I really need is a practical tool that can help me estimate the market value of an IP asset bundle in real time."

Discussion: Goodwill

In July 2001, FASB developed a standard for how intangible assets, namely *goodwill,* should be treated and reported to investors. This standard was designed to improve the accuracy of the reported fair market value of goodwill and any related amortization. FASB and its counterparts in the United Kingdom, together with the joint Steering Committee on Financial Instruments of the International Accounting Standards Committee and the Canadian Institute of Chartered Accountants, all concluded that measuring financial instruments at fair values is an idea whose time has come. The FASB recently extended this line of reasoning to include intangible assets.

The FASB describes fair value as "an estimate of the price an entity would have realized if it had sold an asset or paid if it had been relieved of a liability on the reporting date in an arm's-length exchange motivated by normal business considerations."[1] The European Commission describes fair value as

> (a) a market value, for those items for which a reliable market can readily be iden-
> tified. Where a market value is not readily identifiable for an item but can be
> identified for its components, the market value of that item may be derived from
> that of its components; or
> (b) the value resulting from establishing valuation models and techniques, for those
> items for which a reliable market cannot be readily identified. Such valuation
> models and techniques should ensure a reasonable approximation of the market
> value.[2]

The practical consequences of periodically determining the fair market value of intangible assets, for example goodwill, per the FASB pronouncement are significant. Fair market value of goodwill determinations could be required annually or on an interim basis whenever certain *triggering events* occur at the reporting-unit level. Such events include, for example, ongoing operating cash-flow losses, significant decline in market share or revenues, or significant cost increases.

The art of determining the fair market value of IP using traditional valuation methods such as income, market, and cost approaches can be a time-consuming and expensive task. Financially oriented metrics, such as market-to-book ratios, Tobin's Q, and the calculated intangible value, provide enterprisewide measures of intangible value but are too coarse for meaningful financial reporting.[3] Given the operational requirements set by the FASB, the business world may soon seek to rely on valuation tools to streamline an art form into a reliable and reproducible financially oriented business process.

Secrets of the Intellectual Capitalist

The intellectual capitalist uses two basic valuation methods: discounted cash flows and options pricing. These two approaches tend to yield different value estimations (see Exhibit 12.2).

Discounted Cash-Flow Method. In using the discounted cash-flows method, present value is related to the sum of all future cash flows (read, *profit*), C that, due to the inherent uncertainty and therefore riskiness of actual payment, are

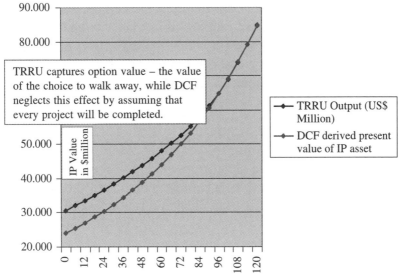

Image courtesy of the Patent and License Exchange, www.pl-x.com.

EXHIBIT 12.2   Discounted Cash-Flow Models

discounted by r, the discount rate. The implicit assumption is that the profits are generated by a going concern, and in the setting of early-stage technologies with little or no history of revenue generation, both the estimates of cash flow and the estimates of risk are subject to guesstimation. The discounting, or reduction in value, of the present value of an asset whose value today depends on events in the future reflects the skepticism that the future will in fact materialize as predicted by the cash-flow models.

$$PV = -Outlays + \sum_{n=t}^{L} \frac{C_n}{(1+r)^n}$$

Advanced desktop computer–based applications have attempted to address the challenges of arbitrariness by expressing the value of C as a distribution with a mean (μ), a standard deviation (σ), and a distinctive shape to the distribution curve. Iterations can be run repeatedly, and the resulting distribution of present values better helps the user estimate this expected value and the degree of risk.

$$PV = -Outlays + \sum_{n=t}^{L} \frac{f(C_n, \mu, \sigma)}{(1+r)^n}$$

PV = present value
L = limit of the period for which cash flows are being projected into the future

n = a subscript and exponent representing the compounding of uncertainty into the "nth" future year, ranging from time t to the limit

t = the first year of the period for which the cash flows are being modeled. For example, if the first cash flows are expected 3 years into the future and occur for an additional 3 years, then $t = 3$ and $L = 6$.

Real Options Method. In using the real options method, the present value is a function of five variables: estimated cost to develop the IP to the next stage of value K, estimated time to reach that stage τ, the present value of comparable technologies S, the variance in the log of the return on a hypothetical investment in those comparable technologies (in contrast to the estimated risk r of discounted cash flows, this is an observed risk σ^2), and the risk-free cost of capital.

Real options are the most transparent and market sensitive of the methods for calculating net present value. Thus, the real options method is the most useful method for determining the value of raw, undeveloped technology assets where there is little evidence of cash flows, and the technology in effect represents a future *call option*. The disadvantage of this financially sophisticated model, based on the 1997 Nobel Prize–winning Black–Scholes options pricing model, is that significant effort is needed to maintain the databases required for tracking the present value and the return on hypothetical investments. But for professional IP valuation companies and for power users such as Mark Aiken and Janice Kimura, there are Internet-based software services that provide both the necessary background data and real-time computational algorithms.

$$PV = S_t N(h) - Ke^{-r\tau} N(h - \sigma\sqrt{\tau})$$

where

$$h = \{\ln(S_t / K) + r\tau + \sigma^2\tau / 2\} / \sigma\sqrt{\tau}$$

$$\sigma^2 = \frac{Var\left[\sum_{}^{t} \ln\left(\frac{S_{t+\Delta t}}{S_t}\right)\right]}{\Delta t}$$

IP AND BUSINESS STRATEGY

Sara Garwell, the chief technology officer for ElectroProducts, Pty, a leading international provider of signal processing devices, was proofreading her field report, "The Global ElectroProducts R & D Initiative: Leadership for the 21st Century and Beyond," when her assistant, John, announced that the CFO was on line two.

"Sara, it's Vic. The boss had a rough meeting with the board this morning. The share price problem is not going away, and he thinks that as a financial engineer, I can build him a better market cap. He wants a plan before the end of the week. Can I come up and chat?"

"Sure, Vic," replied Sara, taking care that her voice masked the fatigue from her recent month-long, four-continent tour of the company's global R & D operations. "Let's start at three. Anything specific you would like me to have ready in advance?"

"Yes. It's the usual. We're looking for cost savings and revenue opportunities. I can run numbers to tell the boss what the impact will be on our key metrics, but my numbers are no better than the inputs from your department. You're fresh from an inspection, so I expect that you have a sense of what projects from our recent acquisitions are duplicative and provide cost-savings opportunities, which have short-term revenue prospects, and which ones are promising but should be delayed."

"In a flash, Vic. See you at three." Sara turned to her intercom. "John, quickly, please. In my field report, I observed that the labs in San Jose, Osaka, and Upsalla are working on what seem to be related projects. Search our database for all projects in the 250 to 700 nanometer range, all switching rates of less than 50 nanoseconds, and all superconductor projects in the 253 to 273°K range. Sort them by time to market at 6, 12, and 18 months, and then sort each group by projected development cost. Also, give me a summary of the present value of each. And I'll need that by two, so you've got about one hour. Thanks."

The meeting in CFO Victor Chang's office started promptly. With the data that John had drawn from the IP enterprise software Sara had installed the previous year, the tasks were easily managed.

"So, Sara, let me summarize what we have," Victor began. He pointed to a list on the flat-panel display that dominated the eastern wall of his office (despite the pleadings of his wife's Feng Shui consultant) (see Exhibit 12.3).

"It looks about right, Victor," Sara said. "But the boss's background is in marketing. Can you do this up as a visual?"

"No problem," Victor replied. A few keystrokes later, Sara and Vic were looking at the screen reproduced as Exhibit 12.4.

Discussion: Lifecycle Model

Companies noting the rise in the value of intellectual property are developing new intangible asset monetization strategies and increasing their production of intellectual property. Kevin Rivette, author of *Rembrandts in the Attic,* reports that revenues from intellectual property licensing rose more than 700 percent between 1990 and 1999.[4] Over the same period, the USPTO reports that the number of applications filed for U.S. patents by non-U.S. entities rose by 45 percent and by U.S. entities rose by 49 percent, for a total of 243,000.

Abort ten patent filings – low value	$200,000
IP tax donations (net 35%)	$8,750,000
Consolidate 16 redundant R & D	$13,500,000
License ten sleeping patents (est.)	$10,000,000
Enforce one non-core patent	$5,000,000
Transaction and marketing costs	($2,000,000)
Consulting/Legal support services	($2,000,000)
Net Value	$33,450,000

©2002 Heisenberg Principals, Inc.

EXHIBIT 12.3   IP Monetization Proposal

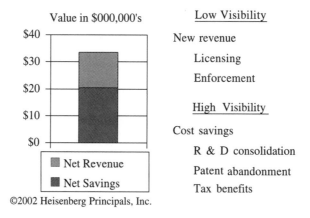

Value in $000,000's	Low Visibility
	New revenue
	Licensing
	Enforcement
	High Visibility
	Cost savings
	R & D consolidation
	Patent abandonment
	Tax benefits

■ Net Revenue
■ Net Savings

©2002 Heisenberg Principals, Inc.

EXHIBIT 12.4   Simplified IP Monetization Proposal

Furthermore, companies are beginning to view IP production and IP management as part of a business process to be measured using the financial metrics of cost, revenue, return on assets, and return on investment.

Today, senior corporate executives recognize that there is a supply chain along which IP is transformed from its origins as an idea into cash flow (see Exhibit 12.5).

IP begins with an idea, and that expertise resides with R & D. But the moment that idea requires resources to test it or otherwise transform it into a monetizable asset, other experts are called on. Legal transforms the idea into perfected rights. Finance assesses whether the expected capital investment will yield an acceptable return. And a C-level executive determines the strategic fit if the research is going to be commercialized. If the return is to be realized through an alternative monetization strategy, such as licensing or assignment, then the licensing and marketing offices get involved. However, if the return will be realized through a securitization, collateralization, or a tax-credit strategy, finance weighs in.

IP Lifecycle Solutions

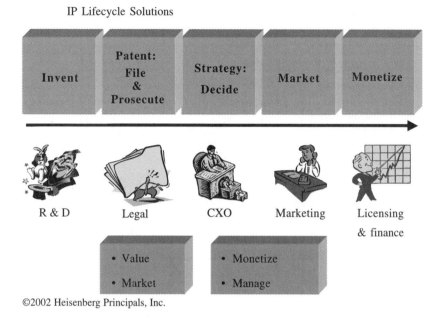

©2002 Heisenberg Principals, Inc.

EXHIBIT 12.5   IP Lifecycle Model

Secrets of the Intellectual Capitalist

The intellectual capitalist of the twenty-first century understands that enterprise-level software solutions are an integral component of supply-chain management. Although such solutions have been commercially available for manufacturing, human resource management, and customer relations, most IP management solutions have been proprietary. In 2000, however, several IP software and solutions providers began releasing client-server and hosted applications that begin to address this growing enterprisewide IP management need. Intellectual capitalists such as Sara Garwell and Victor Chang are passionate users.

IP, MARKETING, AND THE GLOBAL INFORMATION INFRASTRUCTURE

Wallace Felder, the newly appointed head of licensing for General Technologies, one of the world's fastest-growing companies, sat down at the head of the long, dark conference table in the COO's work area.

"Hello again. I'm Wally, and as you know, Chairman Rigby brought me on board to breathe life into our IP licensing program. Let's start by looking at the vision." He then projected the slide shown as Exhibit 12.6.

"IBM generated 26 percent of its total net income from licensing last year—an impressive $1.65 billion at a 98 percent margin, if one assumes that the R & D

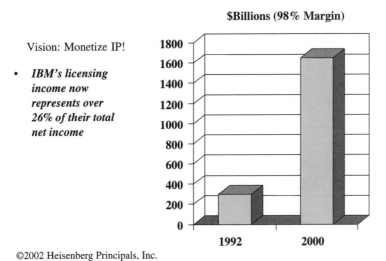

Vision: Monetize IP!

- *IBM's licensing income now represents over 26% of their total net income*

$Billions (98% Margin)

©2002 Heisenberg Principals, Inc.

EXHIBIT 12.6   The GT IP Marketing Mission

behind all this work is sunk cost. Our patent portfolio is in the same league with IBM. Our businesses span the globe, we have been in business longer, and we are more nimble. Our licensing revenue, however, is not where it should be. This chart shows you where we should be."

"We tend to use our IP internally rather than license it," said Earl Black, VP of R & D. "Our competitors are large and few in number. I can understand the theory of licensing to many small companies, but they can't compete in this space. And I don't see why we would license our technology to our large competitors. We do much better building and selling. That is our strength."

"We've built our patent portfolios to defend our product lines," said Jonas Liteman, the chief IP counsel. "I am not sure we are prepared to offer blanket warranties and indemnifications for technology you may want to out-license."

Charlene O'Brien, VP of marketing, spoke up. "Our marketing activity is targeted to markets we know well. From what I've read on licensing, the real opportunities are outside of our traditional network."

"Excuse me," interrupted Anna Marie Harrison, VP of Human Resources. "My understanding is that a substantial portion of this licensing revenue is generated through the so-called stick approach. Are we planning a corporate cultural change?"

Wallace Felder was prepared for this. The resistance was the result of fear. Everyone knew that GT managed by objectives, and success or failure was clear-cut. No one had enough experience with licensing to know what it would require, and to have IP managed to a revenue target was frightening.

"To help direct our energies toward generating revenue on a new, aggressive licensing program, I've invited Cornelius Welks from Man's Best Consulting. Cornelius has been a partner with MBC for more than 20 years and currently heads its IP marketing and monetization practice. Mr. Welks and I have been developing this roadmap for GT. It is a leading practice, and it is a plan that will make us the number-one IP monetizer in the world. Everyone, meet Mr. Welks."

And so the morning was spent. Later that evening, Earl Black from R & D and Charlene O'Brien from Marketing found themselves side by side on the treadmill at Bodies in Perpetual Motion, the preferred health club of senior GT employees.

"Your take?" asked Earl.

"Licensing is more than the transaction. Transactions are the easy part."

"Only if you can effectively mitigate risks," Earl corrected.

"Agreed. But we saw some interesting concepts that work effectively in both financial and real property markets."

"You mean escrow, insurance, and standard contract terms."

"Yes," said Charlene. "But the hard part is creating awareness. We can blanket the world with outbound messages. E-mail and the Web-based tools are terrific. But it seems to me that the really important information is highly technical, and I don't know how to send highly technical information around in such a way that I don't turn off the market segment that is not interested in a particular technology but might be interested in my next mailing."

Earl took a sip of red Gatorade from his GT—The Power Is On water bottle. "You can make your mailings entertaining. I've seen the great materials you guys produce."

"Thanks." After a brief pause, Charlene asked, "How do you find technologies today, Earl?"

"We create RFPs in technical language and distribute them through channels that target the people we know who do the kind of work we want. We thought of posting materials on the Web, but no one wants to read through all that text online. And the natural language search engines are no good. What we really need is an effective tool that can search both the patent and nonpatent literature for the detailed quantitative information unique to each technology."

Charlene suddenly turned up the pace on her treadmill. "Yes," said Charlene excitedly, "that's exactly what I want, too. But in reverse. I need a software tool that will let me describe technology in the quantitative language that technology people understand."

"Do you think engineering could build something like that for us?" yelled Earl over the rhythmic pounding of their running shoes as both treadmills increased the pace.

"Sure. And then maybe we can license it to others!" Charlene laughed.

Discussion: Management Tools

IP information management tools are in demand today as companies with large IP portfolios ask these questions:

- What IP do we have that we can exploit internally?
- What IP do we have that we can license, assign, or otherwise monetize?
- How do we inform the world or let the world find our offering?

For many years, IP managers have struggled with the limitations of natural, language-based disclosures. Both the IP licensor and potential licensee tend to communicate internally in the language of engineering and science. This language is quantitative and is often documented in the form of charts and graphs. It is a rich and precise language. In transforming a technology into a patent, much of the richness of the original language is lost in the translation to the prose used in law and business. This loss is the foundation of the communication challenge that confronts a buyer seeking a specific technology (see Exhibit 12.7).

Nevertheless, today technology buyers and sellers typically communicate their interests in prose through personal networks, cold calls and letters, trade show visits, and Web postings. Although both Internet and intranet-based bulletin boards have increased the efficiency of prose-based disclosures and searches, these sites are still hampered by the limitations of prose-based searches.

Fortunately, today IP licensors and licensees can benefit from the newest Web-based products that allow users, such as Earl and Charlene, to search internal repositories, private exchanges, and the global markets; and to broadcast to these same channels, with standardized units of measure and to locate

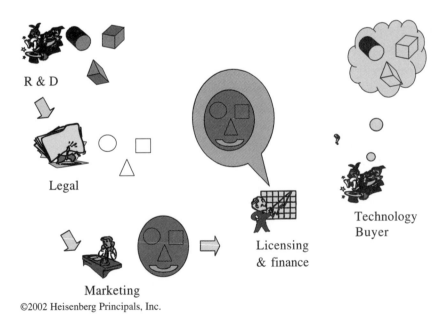

R & D

Legal

Marketing

Licensing & finance

Technology Buyer

©2002 Heisenberg Principals, Inc.

EXHIBIT 12.7   Communication Difficulties

technology based on disclosures and ranges of values (see Exhibit 12.8). Such tools overcome the limitation of prose and searches. Licensing officers and CTOs can market and search for technologies using a search engine that finds IP assets on the basis of performance criteria, commercial application, value, and transactional considerations. These multiple-search categories make it possible to find business and technology solutions starting with technology needs, patent claims, budget limitations, and other business constraints.

Secrets of the Intellectual Capitalist

The intellectual capitalist of the twenty-first century uses the same information technology tools that transformed financial markets to transform IP markets:

- Technology tools are used to find needed technologies.
- Technology tools are used to broadcast technologies the intellectual capitalist wishes to license and monetize.
- Risk-mitigation tools of disciplined financial markets are used to assure that when the intellectual capitalist finds a technology, the transaction can be completed quickly and safely.

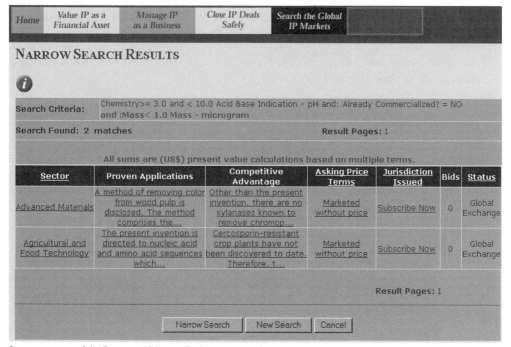

Image courtesy of the Patent and License Exchange, www.pl-x.com.

EXHIBIT 12.8 Technology Search Engine Using Quantitative Attributes

CONCLUSION

As law and finance converge, patent management strategies will fully integrate into corporate financial strategies. This convergence is being accelerated by recent changes in financial market behavior, accounting practices, business strategy, and the global information infrastructure. By using the tools of disciplined financial markets, intellectual capitalists will be at the forefront of IP monetization and the creation of corporate value and growth.

ENDNOTES

[1] FASB: Preliminary views on major issues related to reporting financial instruments and certain related assets and liabilities at fair value, Financial Accounting Series No. 204-B, Dec. 14, 1999.

[2] Proposal for a Directive of the European Parliament and the council amending Directives 78/660/EEC and 83/349/EEC as regards the valuation rules for the annual and consolidated accounts of certain types of companies, February 24, 2000.

[3] Market-to-book ratio is the market value of a firm divided by the firm's book value; Tobin's Q (Q ratio) is the market value of a firm's assets divided by their replacement value; and the calculated intangible value is the market value of a firm less the market value of all of the firm's tangible assets.

[4] Kevin Rivette and David Kline, *Rembrandts in the Attic* (Boston: Harvard Business School Press, 1999).

ABOUT THE AUTHORS

Dr. Nir Kossovsky is a principal with Heisenberg Principals, Inc., an intellectual capital venture advisory group. He is the founder and former CEO of The Patent & License Exchange, Inc. (www.pl-x.com), the leading provider of Web-based intellectual property valuation and management services. At pl-x, he led the development of several novel financial tools to establish the value and reduce the risk of IP asset-based transactions. Nir holds more than 20 patents in life sciences, electronics, and business, and is a former UCLA faculty member. He holds degrees in philosophy, business, and medicine; is an alumnus of the Universities of Pittsburgh, Chicago, and Southern California; and is a Captain (select) in the U.S. Navy Reserve.

Bear Brandegee is co-founder and former president and COO of The Patent & License Exchange, Inc. ("pl-x"). Bear raised more than $30 million in venture capital; negotiated key strategic and product development alliances with Ernst & Young LLP, Swiss Re, and Chicago Title/Fidelity Financial (NYSE-FNF); and oversaw the build-out of U.S. operations. Bear also developed and deployed pl-x's educational and awareness marketing program, which captured three Belding Awards, the *Fortune* Small Business Advertising Award, and the *Forbes* Best of the Web Award. Prior to founding pl-x, Bear held various marketing leadership positions for consulting, marketing, and corporate entities, including Mitsubishi Electric America and Fleishman-Hillard.

13

IC-Based Corporate Carve-outs: Strategy, Structure, and Funding

By James E. Malackowski and Suzanne Harrison

INTRODUCTION

The latter half of the 1990s have been an extraordinary time for technology-driven new business start-ups and new capital and value formation. We have watched as companies from the new and old economies alike—Amazon.com, and IBM, to name just two—have made billions of dollars from their ideas without ever manufacturing a single product! Today ideas are licensed, sold, carved out, or bartered in their raw state for immense sums. But how do companies determine which technologies should be licensed or carved out? What should be done with technology that is no longer strategic or related to the current or future business of the firm? More and more, companies are turning to *corporate carve-outs* as the best way to capitalize on such intellectual capital (IC). As will be seen, Fortune 500 companies now rely on and actively promote their IC to create shareholder value.

What is the best way to assess the risk/reward for companies interested in exploring this value-extraction mechanism? This chapter will address a series of questions that companies must answer before they can determine if this is the best value-conversion mechanism available to them.

Specifically, this chapter will discuss these questions:

- What is a carve-out, and why are companies interested?
- When should you consider a carve-out?
- What is the role of IC in creating value through a carve-out?
- What criteria should be used to judge potential opportunities?
- What criteria should you use to select potential partners?
- How should a carve-out be structured?
- How should due diligence be applied to selecting venture investments?

For ease of discussion, the authors will use the following terms throughout this chapter: *The company* will refer to the existing corporate entity that holds and likely developed the relevant IC to be commercialized. *The subsidiary,* or *NewCo,* refers to the newly created entity formed as a joint venture between the company, management, and a financing partner.

WHAT IS A CARVE-OUT, AND WHY ARE COMPANIES INTERESTED?

A corporate *carve-out* occurs when a company itself desires to hold the assets of its business in two or more sister corporations. There are three major differences between a spin-out and a carve-out:

1. Shares in a spin-out are distributed to existing shareholders; a carve-out establishes a new set of shareholders.
2. Stocks issued through a carve-out generate positive cash-flow to the firm; a spin-out does not have immediate cash-flow consequences.
3. Firms that divest through a carve-out are subject to more stringent disclosure requirements by the SEC.[1] In contrast, a spin-out is usually encouraged where there is a strong business reason to hold the assets in separate entities.

Typically, a company will drop select related assets into a new wholly owned subsidiary and then distribute the stock of the new subsidiary to the company's shareholders. If the transaction meets the detailed requirements of Section 355 of the U.S. Tax Code, then the transaction will be tax-free to the company and its shareholders. The subsidiary may then issue additional shares in exchange for cash or other assets and may direct its business as it deems appropriate.

For the purpose of this chapter, we will deal primarily with carve-out transactions. The success of a carve-out varies based on the strategy for the transaction and the partners selected in the process. The leading motivators for a carve-out transaction are as follows:

- *Financing.* The creation of a new subsidiary allows a third party to easily invest in the assets or business of the subsidiary without interest in the core operations of the company. A carve-out can often attract investment or venture capitalists who would be unwilling to invest in the company generally.
- *Strategic partnerships.* Every business does not possess all of the skills necessary to maximize the success of every business line. Such a realization often leads to a search for strategic partners that provide the miss-

ing expertise. A carve-out can facilitate such an alliance and more clearly align incentives for business development.

- *IC value realization.* Large companies may often develop proprietary systems that improve operations and profitability but are not core to the strategic mission of the company. A carve-out may provide an opportunity to capture value from such IC by offering such systems to others within or outside the company's industry.

The concept of IC value realization is often the core strategy behind what might be perceived to be a pure financing or strategic carve-out. In fact, IC should be central to all corporate carve-out opportunities. IC may be used to create value through several means:

- *Patents and applications.* Such proprietary technology rights can often form the foundation for new products or market-creating improvements.
- *Corporate knowledge base.* The collective experience of a large entity can often apply to an emerging business.
- *Management know-how.* Proprietary business processes can often be the foundation for success or new business opportunities.

Not one to miss an opportunity to participate in the value-creation process, the venture capital community has now begun to recognize the hidden value within the corporate IC vault. New strategies are being developed to fund and capture these assets. In an example of a corporate carve-out, the venture capital partner will work with senior management of an existing large entity to fund the productization of select IC. Typically, this process is intended to bring to market patented technology that was originally developed to support the company's core operation. The new entity is created either as a subsidiary of the parent company or as a separate joint venture.

WHEN SHOULD YOU CONSIDER A CARVE-OUT?

When you are determining whether you should consider a carve-out and what you should carve out, you need to consider some other questions. First, ask what kind and amount of intellectual capital does the company have? For many companies this can be answered by listing all of the known and codified intellectual property and intellectual assets of the firm, collectively IC. The next question is, how does this technology relate to the context of the company? One of the major lessons learned is that the value of a firm's IC depends not only on the kind of

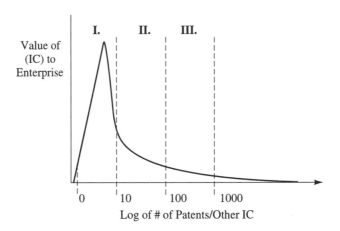

EXHIBIT 13.1   Hypothesized Lognormal Distribution of an IP Portfolio: An Enterprise View

value desired, but also on the company's context—that is, how the company defines value to the organization.

Companies that want to sort through their intellectual property and know-how portfolios to determine alternative ways to commercialize this IC need to first understand how these assets relate to the business of the firm. One way to classify the business use of the portfolio is to look at whether the IC is protecting, enabling, or is utilized in the current business of the firm. Next the same process is repeated, looking at the future business of the firm. And finally, whatever is left over must by definition have no relationship to the current or future business of the firm and is considered *excess*. Having completed that process and then prioritizing the results by the value brought to the enterprise, you will likely see results like the sample portfolio profiled in Exhibit 13.1.

Looking at the IC distribution of a sample portfolio, we see that there are generally three categories into which the value of the IC to the enterprise can fall:

1. *A small number of IC opportunities provide a high value to the company either through commercialization or enforcement.*   Here the IC tends to be more often related to the future of the firm, rather than the current business. In this group, there is IC that is suitable for carve-outs or infringement licensing or standards-based licensing.
2. *Select IC relates to the current business of the firm.*   It is the bread and butter of the company, either by protecting or enabling the current business. In this group there are possible carrot-licensing opportunities often outside the current industry of the firm.
3. *The remaining IC is not related to the current or future business of the firm.*   It is considered excess. These groupings are prime candidates for

a variety of value-extraction mechanisms such as donation, divestiture, or maintenance-fee reductions, all of which can generate a fairly quick return with minimal added investment.

Value-extraction methods and commercialization costs need to appropriately match the expected underlying value. Most value-extraction opportunities outside of productization for a company provide relatively low value (see Exhibit 13.2). Cost avoidance and reduction offer the most opportunities but the smallest returns. One example of cost avoidance is termination of an R & D project. Understanding the commercial potential, the marketplace, and the competitive product space—and having a way to develop quick relative valuations for various projects—can result in substantial cost reduction, avoidance, and savings. Similarly, periodically reviewing the IC assets for those opportunities in the tail of this curve in Exhibit 13.1 and having a methodology for assessing relative value can greatly assist in choosing those assets appropriate for abandonment, discontinuation of maintenance fees, or donation.

At the next level up are opportunities for licensing of IC, and above this there are even fewer opportunities for enforcement of patent rights and donation of the assets for tax reduction. As shown in Exhibit 13.2, the most valuable assets are at the same time the fewest and most costly from which to extract value. These are the assets that might involve some equity components or arrangements. Equity arrangements can be in the form of partnerships, joint ventures, start-ups, spin-outs, or carve-outs (or wholly owned subsidiaries). It is these high-value equity opportunities that we want to focus on for the remainder of this chapter.

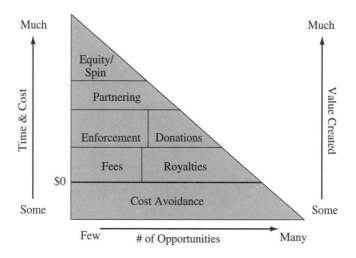

EXHIBIT 13.2   Value Extraction Methods

WHAT IS THE ROLE OF IC IN CREATING VALUE THROUGH A CARVE-OUT?

The latter half of the 1990s were an extraordinary time for technology-driven new business start-ups and new capital and value formation. The market valuation of going concerns and businesses can be very different for an equity-related instrument, in that multiples of revenue or other characteristics, along with comparisons to existing publicly traded businesses, are often used in deriving value. This has resulted in the sort of valuation distribution shown in Exhibit 13.3, which highlights the difference in realizable value as the same technology is moved from an opportunity in R & D, to a license, to an equity possibility, up to a hundred-fold increase! Thus, it can pay handsomely to be able to complete a successful carve-out. In fact, companies that are first to market with products based on advanced technologies command higher margins and gain share. Companies that carve out variants more rapidly and leverage their core technologies across more markets earn higher returns.[2]

A number of elements affect one's ability to move up the value curve in Exhibit 13.3. First and foremost is the state of maturity of the technology and the state of market readiness. Exhibit 13.4 is a graphical representation of the myriad of factors.

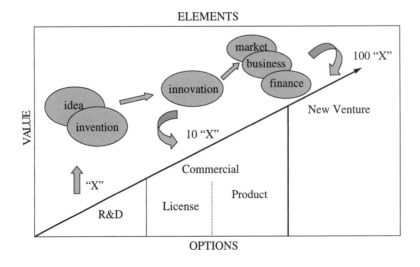

EXHIBIT 13.3 Commercial Context for Value Extraction Methods

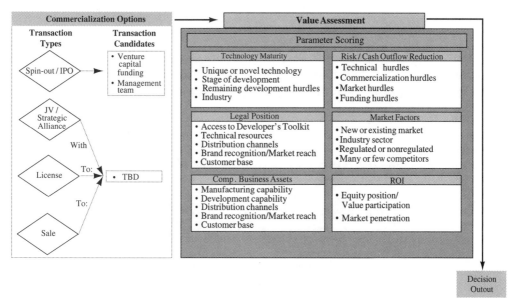

EXHIBIT 13.4   Value Assessment

WHAT CRITERIA SHOULD BE USED
TO JUDGE POTENTIAL OPPORTUNITIES?

The decision to execute a carve-out opportunity is not without trade-offs. The company's ability to manage the operations of the subsidiary will likely be compromised, as new partners will want significant influence on decision making. A short listing of issues that should be considered includes the following:

- The company's ability to devote the resources required to exploit the opportunity under its current operating structure
- The degree to which the underlying IC of the potential carve-out provides competitive advantage to the company's core business
- The ability to recruit and anticipate contribution of new outside management for subsidiary operations

The company has the option of managing its IC in a variety of ways, from maintaining it as proprietary to a complete sale. Each option within this continuum presents its own risk profile. A license agreement from the company to the subsidiary is most often seen as the preferred strategy. Typically, such a license will include those provisions:

- A royalty to the company that may be optioned for further equity interest in the NewCo

- Field-of-use exclusivity, preventing the carve-out from directly aiding the company's core competitors
- Grant-back and grant-forward provisions assuring that both the company and subsidiary benefit from ongoing technology development
- Assignment provisions allowing the NewCo to transfer all IC rights to a third party as part of a sale

Ultimately, the decision to carve out IC depends on the size of the new market opportunity and the present value of profit or sale expectations.

WHAT CRITERIA SHOULD YOU USE TO SELECT POTENTIAL PARTNERS?

In almost all cases, a key motivator for a carve-out is the enhanced ability to partner with third parties to create value. There are generally three classes of partnerships that should be considered: executive management, operations, and financial.

The selection of a senior executive management team for NewCo is the single most critical variable to success. The process of selecting this team should begin with a clean-sheet profiling of the skills necessary to grow and extract value from the business. In this regard, there is no substitute for experience. A management team that has proven its ability to grow and capture value in an entrepreneurial way will benefit the shareholders of NewCo. The selection process is rarely simple and usually involves extensive debate around the decision to use existing company management or to recruit third-party executives.

Company management will likely be far more familiar with the market opportunity and the IC that underlies the business. They should understand the systems used by the company that support the carve-out opportunity. Company management may, however, lack the entrepreneurial, finance, and company sales experience desired. Fast-track executives might view the carve-out as a diversion from their path to the company's executive suite. Participation in common equity incentives due the CEO of NewCo may also create envy by the executives' former peers, making a return to the company difficult.

A third-party executive team has the advantage of being perceived as a neutral party between NewCo joint venture partners. These executives are also more likely to have experience with venture or private equity partners. In any case, it is important that a key member of NewCo's management team has strong relationships with the relevant departments within the company.

The operational management of NewCo must be selected by the CEO of the carve-out. Whether or not the marketing and manufacturing skills exist within the company, the CEO should have the option of recruiting the team he or she thinks will be most effective.

The last key partner represents the growth or acquisition capital necessary to maximize NewCo's value. Selection of such a partner will hinge upon a few variables:

- Willingness/likelihood of the funding partner to assume a minority equity ownership position
- Attitudes toward board of director control
- Industry/carve-out experience
- Valuation opinions
- Views on likely exit structures and timing

Each of these issues will be addressed in further detail.

The Funding Partner (Venture Capital 101)

Given the importance of the venture capitalist to the success of an IC-based corporate carve-out, it is valuable to understand the structure and motivations of a typical venture capital fund when negotiating for funding. The venture capital business model is structured as a limited partnership, with the venture professionals as the general partner and the ultimate capital sources as limited partners.

The *general partner* makes decisions on behalf of the other partners, runs the business on a day-to-day basis, and is personally liable for the partnership's liabilities. In a general partnership, all the partners are GPs, meaning they all have unlimited liability (full liability) for the debts of the partnership. In contrast, a limited partner is an owner in the limited partnership whose liability is restricted to the investment he or she has made in the partnership. The limited partner exerts little or no influence on the way the partnership conducts its business.

The venture capitalist is compensated for his efforts through both a *carried interest* in investments of the partnership and an overriding management fee. The industry standard for the GP's carried interest is 20 percent of net profit. The remaining 80 percent of net profit is allocated according to contributed capital. Management fees are payable quarterly or semiannually to the GP in an annual amount equal to 1.5 percent to 2.5 percent of capital commitments (or more, in the case of a small fund). Following a period of time, typically after the fund's investment period (e.g., 5 years), the management fee declines either by 10 percent per year or to an amount equal to 1 percent to 2 percent of the fund's assets on hand, valued at cost.[3]

An investment into a corporate carve-out may be either common stock or one of several versions of preferred stock. *Common stock* is the basic unit of ownership. It does not carry any special rights outside of those described in the company charter and bylaws. It gives the holder ownership, but that which is subordinated to (1) all government claims; (2) all regulated employee claims; (3) all trade debt; (4) all bank debt; and (5) all forms of preferred stock.

Preferred stock has a liquidation preference over common stock. In the event of sale or liquidation of the company, the preferred stock gets paid ahead of the common stock. Preferred stock may be *redeemable preferred* having no convertibility into equity. Its intrinsic value is therefore its face value plus any dividend rights it carries. In most ways it behaves in a capital structure like deeply subordinated debt. *Convertible preferred* stock can be converted at the shareholder's option into common stock. This forces shareholders to choose whether they will take their returns through the liquidation feature or through the underlying common equity position. Clearly, if the value being offered for the NewCo exceeds the implied total enterprise value at the time of a investment, then the shareholder will convert the preferred stock to common stock in order to realize his portion of the gain in value.

Lastly, *participating convertible preferred stock* is convertible preferred stock with the additional feature that in the event of a sale or liquidation of the company, the holder has a right to receive the face value and the equity participation as if the stock were converted. Like convertible preferred, these instruments carry a mandatory conversion term triggered on a public offering. The net result is an instrument that acts like a redeemable preferred structure while the company is private, and converts to common on a public offering.[4]

Regardless of the equity instrument used, the venture partner will require the subsidiary to meet certain covenants. Covenants are the most basic way venture investors protect their investments. They are contractual agreements between the investor and NewCo and may relate to use of funds, select management decisions, required financial ratios, and so on.

Selection of a Venture Partner

The general partners of a venture fund have a fiduciary duty to their limited partners. Central to this obligation is adherence to the fund's stated investment strategy. General partners will therefore view each investment opportunity in the context of their strategy. This explains why different firms will view the same equity investment in very different ways. In general, the fund's investment strategy will revolve around the stage of investment capital (e.g., seed capital versus early-stage funding versus growth) as well as industry or other sector focus. A short description of the most common investment stages follows:

- *Seed capital.* Seed money refers to financing a potential business that requires substantial research, development, and/or other threshold activities before the entrepreneur can begin revenue-generating activities.

- *Early-stage venture capital.* This refers to financing an entrepreneur who has passed the seed-money stage and is ready to begin (or has recently begun) revenue-generating activities.
- *Growth equity.* This works to assist an existing business enterprise in expansion, such as building a new plant, developing a new product, and so on. The capital requirement might exceed the amount that is available from traditional sources.
- *Consolidation investments.* These are made into industries that are highly fragmented; made up of many small or relatively small competitors and no or few market leaders. Usually, the investor teams up with a high-quality CEO from the industry to form a new entity or platform company that consolidates the industry. The platform is used where the consolidation begins with a reasonably large buyout of an established business, followed by numerous add-on acquisitions.
- *Leveraged Buyouts.* These buyouts occur when a private equity group forms a new company to buy the target, arranges for the new company to borrow a majority of the necessary funds, and contributes a minority of the necessary money as equity capital. Such buyouts come in at least four varieties:

  1. The simplest version of a buyout is the purchase of a *target division* or wholly owned subsidiary from a large corporation, generally where the large corporation has concluded that the division no longer fits the long-term strategy.
  2. The target is privately owned by a family or small group of people.
  3. The target is publicly held.
  4. The private equity partners structure a buyout of any of the previous options as a recapitalization.

- *Turn-around investment.* This is similar to a growth equity investment, but one that is made in a company that is troubled, suffering losses, is over-leveraged, and so on. Since the company is troubled, the investment is generally more risky than that of a traditional growth equity investment.[5]

Unique opportunities exist for minority executives and businesses; a number of new venture funds have been created in the last five years to invest exclusively in a minority business enterprise. Corporate carve-outs that have minority or female senior executives or favorably target a minority community may benefit from such focused venture funds.

Historically, the minority business enterprise and minority executives have been underserved by the private equity market. The IC within the minority sector is unique, has substantial economic value, and is frequently undervalued. Elements of such IC include

- Unique customer and supplier affinity
- Federal and state purchase preferences
- Corporate initiatives relative to carve-outs and joint ventures
- Group buying power

Regardless of investment stage or focus, most financing partners share a common set of concerns and investment criteria. In general, the venture partner wants to minimize the risk associated with the investment and therefore maximize the opportunity for return. There are four risk elements:

1. *Execution risk.* Is the management team capable of growing the business according to plan? Previous experience in the industry with a business of similar scale should serve as a good barometer of management's ability in this regard. The private equity partner whose charter is that of consolidations or leveraged buyouts is most concerned with execution risk. That said, all private equity and venture investments share an element of execution risk.
2. *Business model risk.* Have consumers previously validated their need for the product or service being offered, and have they been willing to pay the pricing anticipated by NewCo? A venture investor will focus on the distinction between *like to have* products and *have to have* products. The latter has a lower business model risk. Unless there is another industry player with a directly competitive offering, business model risk is uniquely high in a corporate carve-out.
3. *Technology risk.* As the term implies, technology risk assesses the chances the underlying IC will not perform. One of the greatest benefits of the corporate carve-out is that the technology is often proven at scale within the originating company. Such reduction of technology risk should lead to a greater likelihood of investment at a more attractive valuation to the company.
4. *Return risk.* Like execution risk, all transactions face a degree of return risk based on numerous third-party elements such as the general economic conditions.

When selecting a funding partner, preparation is critical to success. A strong executive team with a vision for the business that addresses each of the above risk components is mandatory. An understanding of likely capital requirements and anticipated investor returns will facilitate the initial discussions. Even a simple calculation of return on invested capital will force the management team to consider expected growth, margin improvements, and likely exit timing and pricing. The underlying IC of a corporate carve-out might also provide the funding partner with further risk minimization through a security interest and subsequent donation of NewCo's patent rights. (See the chapter appendix describing the authors' Venture Consolidation model.)

As stated earlier, the importance of fit between the proposed corporate carve-out and the investment charter of the funding partner cannot be understated. Both the company and NewCo's management team should take care to verse themselves on the focus of their potential partner. Current Web and other resource tools can help to quickly identify likely partners. The stronger the fit, the easier it will be to secure the first meeting and capture the attention of the venture firm.

As a final thought, the company and the management team must be prepared to hear *no*. It is not unusual for a venture firm to review several thousand investment opportunities annually and select less than a dozen. If you have done the work necessary to select a partner whose charter fits your investment, be certain to assess the basis for rejection. Often such firms are receptive to a revised plan or strategy that accommodates their concerns. Given a fund's diverse experience, the company is well advised to pay careful attention to any objections from a seasoned venture capitalist.

Exiting the Partnership

The goal of any financing partner is to liquefy its investment at a substantial profit when NewCo's value has been maximized through astute management and venture partner supervision. Generally, a venture capitalist will look to exit its investments three to seven years after funding. The three most common exit scenarios are the following:

1. Sales of portfolio company stock to the public—IPO
2. Sale of portfolio company to a large company
3. Sale of the fund's securities back to the portfolio company

In the case of a carve-out, the company may or may not find a repurchase attractive but will certainly want to preserve this option. Depending on investment philosophy, some equity partners may be generally unwilling to sell to NewCo's management team, as they fear management's ability to influence performance prior to sale.

HOW SHOULD A CARVE-OUT BE STRUCTURED?

As discussed previously, an IC-based corporate carve-out has at least three key partners: the company, management (both executive and operational), and the financing partner. All three share a common goal of maximizing the value of the stock of the subsidiary. Each party may also have a separate agenda that must be reconciled and subordinated to the principal of value creation.

In such a partnership, substance follows form. Carefully crafted structuring of the relationship and its incentives will help to assure success of the venture. Key structuring issues will revolve around the likely individual agendas of each partner. A short checklist of such issues follows.

Issues important to the company include:

- *Role as customer.* The market will be eager to purchase NewCo's products and services if they are validated by the company through their use and participation as a customer. Structuring the company as NewCo's first customer is more difficult when dealing with an existing business unit. The company has likely viewed the IC at issue to be a cost center or item of overhead. The cost of such IC was represented by its development and current overhead structure. Once within NewCo, these costs will be burdened by additional overhead and the need for NewCo to capture or earn a profit on delivery of the IC-based product or service. Often, the company may be faced with a substantial cost increase when presented with pricing terms by its subsidiary. The structure and valuation of the company's equity in NewCo must consider this eventuality and compensate the company through a larger relative stake in the common stock of NewCo. The company will still want to protect its interest by limiting any purchase commitments with NewCo to market-based terms of price, quality, and delivery. All parties will want a defined period of commitment and subsequent phase-out option as part of the leading customer relationship.

- *Technology grants.* The IC or technology contributed to the subsidiary might or might not bear a relationship to other activities of the company. The closer the relationship, the more important it will be to address treatment of related technology developments. All parties will want to be certain that developments by either the company or the subsidiary will not impinge upon their core operations. As a result, it is often helpful to carefully define the scope of technology for both entities and ask that each provide a license grant to their sister company for technology or IC that falls outside their core competency. Such grant-backs may be royalty bearing and for specific periods of time.

- *Competition.* It has been the authors' experience that the fear of diminished competitive advantage by the company has been the leading barrier to further carve-out activity. Specifically stated, the company is generally willing to contribute its IC to be developed and marketed outside its industry but is reluctant to let its closest competitors benefit as a customer of NewCo even if the IC is viewed as nonstrategic in the industry at question. This issue is usually resolved in a bipolar manner: Either the company is offered industry exclusivity as part of the transaction or no restrictions are effected. A case-by-case policy of review is to be discouraged, as it can be demotivating to management and open questions of original valuation.

- *Branding and brand management.* Will NewCo benefit from use of a primary or secondary brand of the company? If so, the use and protection of that brand must be carefully managed. A formal royalty-bearing brand license agreement is usually sufficient to address this issue.
- *Infringement and related enforcement.* Given that the NewCo carve-out was founded on core IC of the company, it is likely that at some point NewCo will face the prospect of enforcing its IC rights against competitors or customers of the company. Both present challenges for the burgeoning partnership.

Enforcement of infringement against a customer will place pressure on the company that is adverse to the interests of the subsidiary. A clear shareholder agreement limiting the company's interest to that of a shareholder or defined contract partner can help to manage this situation. It is important that NewCo not be restricted in its growth by such competitive pressures.

An opposite but related challenge results when a potential enforcement action exists against a competitor of the company. The infringer may be well aware of the company's interest in NewCo and look to initiate a parallel infringement action against the company in hopes of putting pressure on the subsidiary to curtail its enforcement efforts. Again, a clear and arm's-length role helps to limit such retaliatory action.

Whether a member of the existing company team or a third-party industry leader recruited to lead the growth of NewCo, management's agenda is far less complicated. Its concerns revolve around current incentive compensation, vesting of equity interests, and the realization of exit value. Following are select comments on these issues:

- *Vesting.* Management will seek to reduce any time period for vesting of shares and will desire acceleration of all vesting rights upon a sale or other change of control. This is a difficult issue for the company and its financing partner, as any likely acquirer or investment banker will mandate that management not immediately leave NewCo on their purchase or an initial public offering (IPO). This concern can be addressed through noncompete agreements, extended vesting schedules post-sale, or on a case-by-case basis depending on the buyer for NewCo.
- *Incentive compensation.* Management will present a plan for the business that will form the basis for creation of NewCo and its financing. Any material success beyond the plan will generally result in incremental cash

or equity consideration to the management team. An understanding of such rewards in advance as part of an agreement with senior management should resolve any potential for later concern.

- *Tag-along rights.* Management will want to benefit from any bargain the financing partner strikes to sell its shares. In common parlance, management will want to tag along with such a sale to realize value from its equity.
- *Autonomy and board participation.* If properly selected, management will be most effective if it can execute the plan of the subsidiary on a reasonably autonomous basis. As a partial guard to such freedom, the CEO likely will demand participation on NewCo's Board of Directors.

As a general statement, the capital or financing partners will want to be sure that all parties are motivated to increase and realize the value of the common stock of NewCo. They are quite willing to be a resource to management and can provide substantial partnership, mergers and acquisitions (M & A), and financing assistance. They are neither interested nor qualified to run the business. That said, if the subsidiary does not mature as planned, the investment partner will want the opportunity to change management and exercise full control over the direction of the subsidiary. Issues likely to be discussed in detail as part of the financing terms for NewCo include:

- *Class of equity.* Private equity or venture capitalists will generally invest in preferred stock. Such preferred equity can come in a variety of forms.
- *Board control.* From the beginning, the financing partner will want significant board participation—usually two of five seats or three of seven. The partner will also want the right to approve the other members, which generally consist of the CEO, a representative of the company contributing the IC, and one or more independent directors knowledgeable of the industry and friendly to the investor.
- *Other leverage (asset or cash flow based).* From inception and certainly as NewCo grows, the financing partner will want to fully leverage its capital and minimize dilution by utilizing bank or other financing for growth or acquisitions. Traditional bank financing may be limited by near liquid assets (such as accounts receivable) or the free cash flow of NewCo and its acquisitions. Continued M & A activity can also be financed in part by seller notes and acceptance of newly issued equity in NewCo in exchange for the stock of any acquired company.
- *The use of earn-outs.* Continued interest and best efforts by management and the parent company can be motivated by earn-out formulas. The equity partner is only too happy to have everyone on the team enjoy the fruits of their equity, but they want to be sure everyone earns their allocated share.

Other issues related to structure that should always be addressed include the company's degree of ownership and related profit recognition. Depending on the percentage of equity held by the company after the financing and retention of management, the company may be required to report the earnings of NewCo as part of its consolidated operations. This might or might not be desired by the company, depending on its own objectives and largely whether the earnings of NewCo are accretive.

Three options must be considered: *no significant influence, significant influence, or control.* These options are based on the percentage equity the company retains in NewCo. If the Company owns less than 20 percent, it is deemed to have no significant influence on NewCo and record its interest as an investment in equity securities. Such interest is recorded using the fair value method reporting unrealized holding gains and losses (e.g., stockholders' equity) at cost. As value goes up or down, the company will report the variation as a change in stockholders' equity.

The company is deemed to have significant influence if its ownership is at least 20 percent but not more than 50 percent. In this case, the company's interest is recorded using the *equity method.* NewCo's stock is recorded at cost and adjusted annually up or down according to earnings. When the company owns such a sufficiently large percentage of common stock, it is able to exert significant influence of the operating and financial policies of the subsidiary. In particular, the company might be able to influence NewCo's dividend policy. Such dividends paid may be affected by the company's cash needs, desire to raise its income, or by tax considerations. The fair value methods recognize income as dividends are received (declared) and are therefore inappropriate when significant influence exists.

The equity method of accounting is used to account for these investments as it (1) acknowledges the existence of a material economic relationship between the company and the subsidiary; (2) is based on the requirements of accrual accounting; and (3) reflects the change in stockholders' equity of the subsidiary.

When the equity method is used, an investment in common stock is recorded initially at its acquisition cost. However, in contrast to the fair value method, income is recorded by the company when it is reported by the subsidiary. The company records income and an increase in the carrying value of the investment account at an amount that is based on its percentage of ownership. Dividends received (or receivable) are recorded as reductions in the carrying value of the investment account whenever they are paid (or declared) by NewCo. Furthermore, since a material relationship is presumed, the effects of all intercompany items of revenue and expense are removed from the Company's accounts to avoid *double counting.* If the acquisition cost is greater than the proportionate book value of the subsidiary, additional depreciation and/or goodwill amortization is recognized. Therefore, it is necessary to make certain adjustments to the investment income:

- Eliminate intercompany transactions in the determination of the company's net income (e.g., sale from the company to the subsidiary).
- Depreciate the proportionate share of any difference between the fair market values and book values of NewCo depreciable assets implied by the acquisition price of the NewCo shares.
- Amortize any purchased goodwill.
- Treat the proportionate share of NewCo extraordinary items as extraordinary items of the company.

If the company owns more than 50 percent, it is deemed to have control. Such an ownership structure requires a consolidation of results.

HOW SHOULD DUE DILIGENCE BE APPLIED TO SELECTING VENTURE INVESTMENTS?

If experienced venture investors really do receive more than 1,000 funding opportunities annually, how do they make a decision? First, of the opportunities received, less than 100 or 10 percent may receive any noncursory review. This is usually based on the fit criteria already discussed. What, then, is the process for selecting the truly compelling investments? How does this process differ if intellectual capital is central to the investment rationale? For the private equity partner, the process is one of due diligence.

A general overview of the *due diligence process* is shown in Exhibit 13.5. The key to effective due diligence is to maintain an efficiency of time and focus. This template is divided into three phases, based on the level of analysis and depth of issues explored. Each of the nine columns represents substantive areas of investigation. For each 1,000 deals received, less than 100 will enter the Phase I: Review stage, 50 may advance to Phase II: Evaluation and Development, and only 15 are likely to be subject to an exhaustive Phase III: Due Diligence.

Although intellectual capital is listed uniquely as one of nine major verticals in Phase I of consideration, a true appreciation of intellectual assets spans at least half of the remaining columns. Indications of such relevance are:

- *Portfolio fit.* The venture firm's own intellectual capital should be assessed to determine the true fit of any investment. Expertise in particular industries or structures will affect advancement beyond the review phase.
- *Management.* The success of any business is strongly influenced by the knowledge, contacts, and experience of its management team. These intellectual assets should be explicitly identified and categorized at an early stage.

Phase I: Review

Portfolio Fit	Intellectual Capital	Management	Business Model	Financial	Technology	Competition	Sales & Marketing	Deal Structure

Phase II: Evaluation and Development

Portfolio Synergy	Existing IC	Executive Skill Set	Mission Statement	Profit %	Product Demo	Market Value	Market Size & Growth	Debt Leverage
	Future IC	Board of Directors	Partnership	Cash Flow	Tech Plan	Differentiate	Customers	Acquisition Strategy
	Competitive IC	Employee Skill Set	Mega-trend	Use of Funds			Outside Influences	Risk Factors
			Futuring	Valuation			Sales Strategy	

Phase III: Due Diligence

Patent Doc	Employee Agreements	Supplier Relations	Debt	External Lab Review	Industry News	Customer Relations	Financial
Trademark Doc	Comp/ Incentive	Agreements	Tax Status & Planning			Distributor Relations	Legal
Trade Secrets	Employee Issues		Audit Review				
IC Threats	Shareholders		Property				

EXHIBIT 13.5   Due Diligence Process

- *Business model.* The advent of process patenting suggests that all investments should be screened to see if their model is either unique or subject to the rights of others.
- *Technology.* The technical plans and products of a business are obviously close to the heart of traditional intellectual property protection. Frequently, a mapping of the five-year technology plan to existing or pending patents shows potential competitive threat or market barriers not previously recognized.

Phase I: Review

The first or Review Phase is designed to provide a quick indication of potential investment value. As Exhibit 13.6 shows, each of the major areas is addressed.

The intellectual capital column represents a need to determine existing or potential assets by type, including utility patents, process patents, brands, domain names, and a formal employee knowledge base. Commentary should simply address whether these items exist, with a quick indication of quality. If not currently present, thought is given to the ability to create such rights and the related potential contribution to value.

Phase I: Review

Portfolio Fit	Intellectual Capital	Management	Business Model	Financial	Technology	Competition	Sales & Marketing	Deal Structure

EXHIBIT 13.6   Phase I: Review

Phase II: Evaluation and Development

Those opportunities that pass the Review Phase enter a more detailed period of Evaluation and Development, or Phase II.

As shown in Exhibit 13.7, this second phase addresses existing, future, and competitive intellectual capital, or IC. Existing IC issues for investigation include the following:

- *A review of key issued patents noting particular claims of interest.* It is important to focus attention on the claims rather than the summary abstract of the patent. Only the claims are going to provide immediate barriers to entry and proprietary market positions for investment purposes. Here a patent attorney or consultant may be helpful.
- *An understanding of the target's process for determining which patents to file and the steps taken in the prior art search.* Such an analysis should provide guidance as to the breadth and depth of the claims reviewed. The determination as to when and what to file may also yield cost-reduction strategies or further areas for proprietary positioning.
- *An assessment of the quality of the patent counsel retained by the target.*
- *A review of the company's inventory of brands and domain names.* The absence of an inventory showing corporate entity ownership and quality procedures for maintenance may be a cause for concern.
- *A comparison between period of product introduction and patent number marking.* Lax practices in this regard may greatly limit perceived competitive barriers.
- *An investigation of cross-licensing activity.* This should note both hidden rights and competitive permissions.

Future IC analysis should focus on a review of pending and potential future patent applications. Often, the presence of a pending application can provide tremendous near-term proprietary positioning. In fact, this right might be more valuable than that provided by the existing claims. Consideration should also be given to the budget for future IC development as shown internally, as well as in the target's funding pro forma statements. A declining future budget may be a means to improve overall profitability but at a cost of not preparing adequately

Phase II: Evaluation and Development

Portfolio Synergy	Existing IC	Executive Skill Set	Mission Statement	Profit %	Product Demo	Market Value	Market Size & Growth	Debt Leverage
	Future IC	Board of Directors	Partnership	Cash Flow	Tech Plan	Differentiate	Customers	Acquisition Strategy
	Competitive IC	Employee Skill Set	Mega-trend	Use of Funds			Outside Influences	Risk Factors
			Mega-trend	Valuation			Sales Strategy	

EXHIBIT 13.7   Phase II: Evaluation and Development

for competitive threats. A rapid rise in budget may indicate an earlier-stage investment than originally believed.

Competitive IC is the most overlooked aspect of the Evaluation Phase. Investors should allocate time to explore competitive patents as well as current processes to gather IC market intelligence.

Phase III: Due Diligence

Only a few opportunities will advance to traditional due diligence. It is at this stage that most investors will retain patent counsel or other advisors when considering IC assets. This portion of the analysis comes after the venture capitalist has made a preliminary intention to make an investment, usually in the form of a term sheet (see Exhibit 13.8).

Patent documentation begins with a complete inventory of existing and pending patents. A notation should be made as to whether the company is practicing the claimed technology and if the key inventor(s) remain with the business. All license agreements providing third-party rights can be similarly categorized. The correspondence between the company and the U.S. Patent and Trademark Office may prove insightful.

Trademark documentation follows a similar effort, with attention to cataloging all marks and domain names checking for the use and availability of domain equivalents (e.g., www.cars4sale.com versus www.carsforsale.com versus www.cars4sale.net). A discussion with the target's trademark counsel may provide great insight into the status of any pending registrations. The investor may make a strong case for valuation discounts for any issues that are not as forecasted.

An analysis of trade secrets documentation usually begins with a copy of any existing trade secrets policies and a review of key employee confidentiality and assignment agreements. Again, valuation discounts might be in order if documentation is not.

Lastly, IC threats should be listed and fully explored with management and counsel because infringement actions may be costly in both dollars and business flexibility.

Phase III: Due Diligence

Patent Doc	Employee Agreements	Supplier Relations	Debt	External Lab Review	Industry News	Customer Relations	Financial
Trademark Doc	Comp/ Incentive	Agreements	Tax Status & Planning			Distributor Relations	Legal
Trade Secrets	Employee Issues		Audit Review				
IC Threats	Share- holders		Property				

EXHIBIT 13.8   Phase III: Due Diligence

CONCLUSION

More and more companies are realizing that their underutilized IC has potentially large value. Seeking to more fully leverage such opportunities, companies are increasingly exploring carve-out opportunities. In this chapter we have addressed a series of questions that companies must answer before they can determine if this is the best value-conversion mechanism available to them. Specifically, how to determine pockets of high-value IC suitable for a carve-out and useful criteria for evaluating such opportunities. Once potential carve-out candidates have been assessed and evaluated, what kind of structure is desirable? What is the criteria for determining the optimal partner? Armed with this information, managers can look forward to more successful carve-outs.

ENDNOTES

[1] Roni Michaely and Wayne Shaw, *The Choice of Going Public: Spin-offs vs. Carveouts.* Financial Management Association, Informal Access Company, September 22, 1995. The specific legal requirements of a carve-out are beyond the scope of this chapter.

[2] T. Nevens, Gregory Summe, and Uttal Bro, "Commercializing Technology: What the Best Companies Do", *Harvard Business Review*, May/June 1990.

[3] Jack S. Levin, *Structuring Venture Capital, Private Equity, and Entrepreneurial Transactions* (Gaithersburg, MD: Aspen Publishers, 2001).

[4] Josh Lerner and Felda Hardyman, "A Note on Private Equity Securities" Boston: Harvard Business School Publishing, 2001.

[5] Levin, 1–9.

APPENDIX: VENTURE CONSOLIDATION

The authors of this chapter have pioneered several proprietary investment techniques based on an understanding of core intellectual capital (IC) in combination with proven consolidation investment strategies. In essence, an opportunity exists to augment a traditional large-scale consolidating investment with a much smaller, parallel venture investment in related technology. When complete, the technology is then levered across the newly aggregated entity to enhance margins through incremental services, price premiums, and/or cost savings. As a result of this innovative approach, an industry that was consolidated at attractive earnings before interest, taxes, depreciation, and amortization (EBITDA) pricing can be enhanced both in terms of profitability and valuation multiples.

Termed a *Venture Consolidation,* such an investment strategy is designed to generate venture capital returns with a leveraged buyout risk profile. The risk profile is managed through both investment weighting as well as aftertax recovery on nonperforming technology investments.

There are three primary criteria for a Venture Consolidation investment:

1. A proven Chief Executive Officer and management team have value creation experience in the industry to be consolidated.
2. A fragmented industry includes a large consolidated entity (sales greater than $100M) that can be built at reasonable acquisition pricing and debt leverage.
3. Proprietary technology is in place and a qualified Chief Technical Officer is capable of a timely deployment of margin-enhancing IC across the consolidated base.

The IC component of each investment must be technically proven and commercially ready. The underlying technology will be patented, patent pending, or ready for filing. If the technology deployment efforts fail, then the investor has limited the downside risk in three ways:

1. Ninety percent or more of all invested dollars were committed to the consolidation of profitable entities with a proven CEO.
2. The consolidated entity may be sold with the technology expense treated as an add-back to EBITDA for pricing purposes, thus not penalizing the company for monies spent.
3. The investor or the company will take ownership of the patents under a security agreement and, after valuation by an independent firm, will donate the patents to a 501(c)3 charitable organization (e.g., a university), using the write-off against the income or gains of the consolidation.

Often, the parties will create a special-purpose IC vehicle (SICV) to hold the patent rights as well as the related technical know-how, source code, and so on. The creation of an SICV allows for enhanced valuation if the business is donated. Elements of the Venture Consolidation strategy are patent pending.

ABOUT THE AUTHORS

James E. Malackowski is an internationally recognized expert in the field of intellectual capital management, valuation, and strategy. He spent 15 years as an entrepreneur focused on professional services, and he has consulted with clients and counsel on business valuation issues as well as all phases of the technology licensing process. He is frequently asked to participate as a member of the board of directors for leading technology corporations. Mr. Malackowski's expertise extends to intangible asset portfolios as well as business segments and complete entities. Mr. Malackowski is a director of ewireless, inc.; Insignis, Inc.; Evince, LLC, InfoCast, Corp. (OTC BB: IFCC.OB); and Solutionary, Inc. He is also president-elect of the Licensing Executives Society; a trustee for the National Inventors Hall of Fame; and a resident advisor for the U.S. Department of Commerce and U.S. Information Agency on matters relating to intellectual capital. In 1988, he cofounded ICC Group, Inc. (now InteCap, Inc.), the nation's largest consulting firm focused on intellectual capital valuation and strategy.

Suzanne Harrison is a founding principal of ICMG Inc., a management consulting firm focused entirely on extracting value from intellectual capital. ICMG is a wholly owned subsidiary of Acorn Technologies, a technology development and commercialization firm. Since 1988, Ms. Harrison has been advising clients on maximizing value from their intellectual assets. Ms. Harrison is a recognized expert in the field of intellectual capital strategy, value extraction, and measurement and reporting. Ms. Harrison is the convenor of the ICM Gathering, a group of leading-edge companies that meet to create, define, and benchmark best practices relating to intellectual capital management. Ms. Harrison is the recipient of the Licensing Executives Society North America Fellowship and has been the committee chairperson of the Intellectual Capital Management Committee for the Licensing Executives Society for the past five years. She holds an undergraduate degree in Economics from the University of California at Davis and an MBA from the University of Chicago. Ms. Harrison has written numerous articles and is a frequent speaker about how companies can extract value from their innovations. She is the co-author of *Edison in the Boardroom,* recently published by John Wiley & Sons.

The authors wish to thank David I. Wakefield, an analyst at VIGIC Services, LLC, for his contribution to this chapter.

14

Licensing and Litigation

By Ronald L. Grudziecki and Arnaud Michel

INTRODUCTION

In many ways, litigation would seem to be the antithesis of licensing. That is, *licensing* is the voluntary granting of rights to another to practice what would otherwise be the sole possession of the licensor to another, while *litigation,* on its face, is an attempt by that same possessor of exclusive rights to maintain those rights exclusive for itself. However, litigation is in many ways an adjunct to licensing, and modern litigation practice and procedure has stimulated licensing. Licensing in its many facets will be dealt with elsewhere. What we will deal with in this chapter is litigation in both the United States and Europe, particularly France, and how it has affected licensing in these jurisdictions.

OBTAINING A PRELIMINARY INJUNCTION

In the United States, one of the most important aspects of litigation, and one that is believed to have had a substantial effect on licensing, is the ability of a patent owner to obtain a preliminary injunction against further manufacture, use, sale, offer for sale, or importation of the infringing product, process, and so on. The *preliminary injunction,* so called because the case is not over yet, may be obtained no later than the time of a determination of infringement and validity (e.g., at the end of a trial on the merits). Although such an injunction is not always granted and it is accompanied by an appropriate monetary bond to compensate for the loss suffered by the putative infringer if the decision is reversed on appeal, it is a significant deterrence to the desire of someone to copy a successful patented product and simply roll the dice on an opportunity to have a judge or jury find the conduct somehow excused. In situations where a person or organization has independently created its product and has a good-faith belief of noninfringement, the risks of an injunction issuing after several years of litigation (and concomitant several years of sales and marketing) have caused some organizations to seek a license.

Also, because of the risks and costs of litigation, there are times when initiation of litigation will cause the named defendant to seriously consider licensing. Sometimes, prelitigation licensing discussions are carried out at a particular level or place within an organization, while litigation is overseen by another group or department, often with a greater appreciation for the risks and costs. Receipt of litigation papers certainly gets the attention of the latter and often brings a new set of eyes to the transaction and results in a more positive view toward licensing. Of course, it sometimes creates the exact opposite reaction. Nonetheless, once understood, it should be viewed as another arrow in the quiver of weapons available to the patent owner.

PRACTICE AND PROCEDURE OF LITIGATION IN THE UNITED STATES

The risks and costs of litigation can best be understood by a brief outline of the practice and procedure. In the United States, patent infringement litigation is conducted in the federal court system. District courts (i.e., the trial courts) are found in each of the states. Most states have more than one district geographically arranged within the state (e.g., Virginia has an Eastern District and a Western District; New York has Eastern, Western, Northern, and Southern Districts, with the Southern District being for Manhattan only).

Suit may be brought within certain of those districts as defined by a statute. In particular, a defendant may be sued in a patent infringement action in any district where it resides or where it has committed acts of infringement and has an established place of business. If the defendant is a corporation, as is often the case, the term *resides* means any state in which it is subject to personal jurisdiction. Whether personal jurisdiction applies in any particular case is a factual question, but it is essentially a question of fairness. That is, has the defendant taken advantage of that location in some way so that it would be fair to subject it to legal process there? If the defendant has offices there, is incorporated there, or has itself sued others in that district, courts may rule that it would be fair to sue them there.

The question of where a particular defendant can be sued is sometimes easy and sometimes complicated, because many corporations can be found in many jurisdictions, and the choice of forum may depend on speed of the court's docket, convenience to the plaintiff, or the like.

Filing the Complaint

Litigation begins with the filing of a paper called a *complaint*. It need only identify the parties, the patent, and what relief is sought, although more of the background as to what is involved is often included. The patent owner (or the person bringing the suit if different from the patent owner) need only have a good-faith belief that infringement is occurring. Prior notice to the named defendants is not necessary, and sometimes it is undesirable. That is, if the patent owner gives notice to a putative infringer of patent infringement (e.g., a *cease and desist* letter) so that the recipient has a reasonable apprehension that it will be sued by the patent owner for patent infringement, then the infringer may be able to bring an action for a *declaratory judgment* that it is not infringing or the patent is invalid. Since many corporations may be found for personal jurisdiction purposes in a number of locations, the declaratory judgment action may be brought in a location inconvenient to the patent owner, thus increasing the owner's costs, or even a location that seems to favor the infringer (e.g., a location where it has a strong local position that may be thought to influence a jury). Although there are also rules about transfer to a different location, the first-filed action often controls jurisdiction, so a declaratory judgment action should usually be avoided if possible. Thus, a warning letter needs to be carefully drafted.

The complaint must be served with a summons upon the defendant to start the action, including the time for the defendant's *answer* (its response to the allegations of the complaint). It is not unusual for a patent owner to file a complaint and informally send it to the named defendant with a request for a meeting to try to settle the matter by licensing. The filing of the complaint shows the seriousness of the situation. Although a complaint can be withdrawn if no answer is filed, generally the filing of the complaint commits the patent owner to going forward with the lawsuit if negotiations are unsuccessful. Usually, the district courts will not dismiss the case for a few months' lack of formal service of the complaint if they are informed of the negotiations. Similarly, service of the complaint can be made and the parties can then talk before an answer is filed. It is desirable to have these discussions before an answer is filed because the answer might contain allegations regarding invalidity and/or unenforceability, which can make negotiations that much more difficult. It is thus best to try to have settlement discussions before either service of the complaint is made or an answer is filed.

Discovery

Assuming no agreement is reached, the litigation commences. In the United States, the portion of the litigation from its beginning until almost before trial on the merits is concerned with what is called *discovery*. Discovery also refers to the information gained during that period. Discovery can be had in various ways. The *Federal Rules of Civil Procedure*, which govern the practices in the federal courts, has a mandatory disclosure rule that requires each side to provide certain information to the other side shortly after the answer has been filed. In addition, the *Rules* provide further vehicles for discovery. The most commonly used forms of discovery are *requests for production of documents* (in which one side asks for all documents that the other side has in defined categories), *interrogatories* (written questions answered in writing), *requests for admissions* (in which one side is asked to admit a fact), and *depositions* (in which an individual personally requested or someone on behalf of a company is designated to answer questions propounded by an attorney for the other side).

Although there are limits on discovery, generally it is fairly broadly construed in the United States and is clearly a bane to companies not accustomed to dealing with the tremendous scope of U.S. discovery. Just the thought of U.S. lawyers poring over a company's business records and its scientists and files is in and of itself a reason to think about the desirability of settlement. U.S. judges are loath to get involved in what they consider minor discovery matters (although they do often get into those details), and they try to get the parties to provide what is more than reasonably necessary so as to avoid disputes. Very often, one of the first issues in a litigation of this type is how to frame a protective order that controls the dissemination of documents and other information. Usually, there is at least one category of "Confidential" or "Business Confidential" in which access is limited to outside lawyers and experts and perhaps a few designated in-house lawyers. Sometimes, there are multiple layers of confidentiality, with at least one level only to be seen by outside lawyers and experts and with no disclosure of this material to the lawyer's client!

Markman Hearing

One of the more important things that can happen in U.S. patent litigation is what is known as a *Markman hearing,* named after a case involving the Markman Company in which the U.S. Supreme Court said that the meaning of the words of a claim were the sole province of the judge, even if a jury was to find the ultimate questions of infringement and validity. In such a hearing, the judge interprets the meaning of a term or terms in a claim of a patent involved in the litigation. The judge's decision is binding and his or her interpretation controls throughout the remainder of the litigation. However, if the parties agree as to the meaning of *all the terms* of *all the claims* in the suit, then no such hearing is necessary. However, if there is a disputed term(s), then the judge can hold a hearing to determine what a word or phrase means in the context of that particular patent. A Markman hearing can be held at any time before decision but is usually held during discovery. The procedures vary from court to court and judge to judge, with some deciding on written presentations and, perhaps, oral arguments by the lawyers, and with others being much more elaborate with live testimony from experts and other witnesses.

Since the meaning of the claim is so important to claim scope and thus to infringement, these types of hearings can be quite important. If a term is given a certain interpretation, there may be no literal infringement; if that term was added to the claim during prosecution to distinguish prior art, then it is likely that there is no infringement to be found under the doctrine of equivalents so that the case may be ended before a trial on the merits.

Motion for Summary Judgment

In such a situation—or any other in which it can be said that there is no material fact in issue—then a party may file a *motion for summary judgment.* This motion presumes that there is only a question of law, not of fact (at least no fact that would make a material difference in the court's ability to decide the case). In that instance, a court can find for the moving party and if, for example, it finds that the claim scope as interpreted by its Markman decision cannot encompass the alleged infringing device (process, article, etc.), then the court can decide as a matter of law that there is no infringement. The case ends at that point as to that patent, pending appeals. If that is the *only* patent in the case, then the case is over, at least at this point (appeals will be discussed later). Summary judgment motions can be made for validity or infringement issues and are an important aspect of the case. Indeed, it is believed that more cases are resolved by summary judgment than from full trials.

Trial. If there is no settlement or disposition by summary judgment motion, then the case will go to trial. In the United States, a case can be tried before a judge or a jury, depending on the demands of the parties. If a jury is used, the jury decides the questions of fact and the ultimate questions of validity and infringement with the guidance of the judge, who gives instructions as to the law before the jury begins deliberating. A jury usually has 12 members, but there can be fewer if the parties agree. Members of the jury are chosen from local citizens in that district. Before the evidence is presented, members of a jury pool are presented and certain questions are asked to elicit possible bias. Usually the judge does the questioning. Jurors are then picked by the parties. Juries are thought to give greater credence to the grant of a patent than a judge might (although there are no scientific bases for that conclusion), so it is generally thought that the patent owner would favor a jury. Another consideration in choosing a judge or jury is the speed in which a decision is desired. A jury verdict is obtained at the end of the trial, whereas the judge's decision may be obtained quite a length of time later. The judge needs to have *findings of fact* and *conclusions of law* for a possible appeal, and therefore, his or her decision often is not known until the final decision is written. This can be months or—unfortunately, on occasion—a year or more after trial. If the patent at issue has a relatively short life after the trial is concluded or if an injunction is the most desired remedy, then trial by a jury may be the most expeditious route.

Burden of Proof

It is the patent owner's responsibility to prove infringement by the defendant's activities and any resulting damages that have accrued. There is a presumption that the patent is valid (by law), so the patent owner does not have to prove validity. Rather, the defendant must prove invalidity and, if raised, *unenforceability* of the patent. These proofs are often presented by experts retained by the parties to explain to the judge or jury what the patent relates to and how the accused device or process does or does not fall within the scope of the claim(s).

Damages in Patent Infringement Litigation

Damages in a patent infringement litigation are a special area. U.S. law says that the patent owner (if it prevails) is entitled to damages in an amount "not less than a reasonable royalty," along with interest and costs. If the patent owner is competing in the marketplace with the infringer for sales of products that fall under the patent, then the patent owner may be entitled to lost profits for those lost sales (if it can show that it would have made those sales but for the infringement), as well as a royalty for remaining sales of the defendant. Obviously there is substantial room for the efforts of licensing specialists and accountants in making these determinations, and such resources are utilized during discovery as well as during the trial.

As mentioned before, one of the most important remedies available to a successful patent owner is an injunction against future infringement. It is usually requested at the end of the trial when a favorable decision is obtained, and it is usually granted, providing that the patent owner posts a *bond,* a security that covers the cost of the damage to the infringer if the decision is reversed on appeal. Decisions on the amount and type of the bond are often hard fought, as are the liability and damage issues. The judge must decide these issues on such terms as the court deems proper.

In exceptional cases—for example, where the defendant's conduct is particularly egregious or if the patent owner is found to have obtained the patent by improper means in dealing with the Patent and Trademark Office—the court might increase the damages by up to three times those found and even award reasonable attorney's fees to the prevailing party.

Appeals

After a trial on the merits, it is possible for the judge to change the decision, particularly if there was a jury, but the chances of such a reversal by the judge are slim. All patent litigants enjoy a right of appeal before the Court of Appeals for the Federal Circuit (CAFC). The CAFC was founded about 20 years ago to hear, among other things, all appeals in patent cases. Previously, appeals went to circuit courts of appeals that were (and still are for other appeals) arranged geographically. The CAFC was created in response to the perceived problem that there was a split in the way the same type of issue was decided among these circuit courts, leading to *forum-shopping* (e.g., trying to get your case into a district court within a "favorable" circuit) and inconsistencies in decisions. The CAFC has more or less ended forum-shopping for favorable decisions and also has more or less ended inconsistencies in decisions. (Some commentators have noted that various three-judge panels at times seem to handle some issues differently from some others.) If an important point of patent law is seen to be at stake, the court can hear the case *en banc,* with all judges participating. In this instance, the decision is the law of the CAFC.

After an unfavorable decision by the CAFC, there is a very, very slim chance that the U.S. Supreme Court will hear a further appeal. The appeal is not as a matter of right, so a *petition for writ of certiorari* must be filed. It is unusual for this court to accept a patent case on appeal. It has typically taken less than one per year over the last several years, and fewer before then.

At the time of denial of such a petition or if none is filed within the prescribed time and assuming the patent owner has been successful, the case returns to the district court for entry of a final judgment and a permanent injunction. Presumably, at that point, the case is over.

Since this procedure takes years (depending a lot on where you started), is obviously expensive, and runs the risks of an injunction and damages of a substantial nature, licensing is an attractive alternative, even if the terms initially seem high. A proper risk analysis may reveal the cost efficiency of a license.

PRACTICE AND PROCEDURE OF LITIGATION IN FRANCE/EUROPE

The previous sections were in regard to the United States. Europe, meanwhile, has also considerably developed its expertise in the intellectual property legal system. The European patent system is built on the Munich Convention when combined with the Brussels Convention (which has now become the Brussels Council Regulation (EC) No. 44/2001 of 22 December 2000 on jurisdiction, commonly referred to as "the Brussels Regulation") relating to the enforcement of judgments within the European Union (EU). It enables judgments rendered by the courts of the different Member states of the European Union to be easily enforceable all over the European Union. Moreover, the recent creation of unitary rights, such as the Community trademark and the Community designs or the proposed Community patent, make Europe even more of a key area in a strategy of development and consequently of protecting one's intellectual property rights.

In this new environment, France holds a particularly interesting position. Its judiciary system for trademarks and patents is composed of professional judges, with only 10 courts all over France having jurisdiction to rule over patent cases. The principles of the Roman law system, applicable before the French courts make legal actions considerably less costly than those in countries of common law without, of course, prejudicing the quality of the judgments rendered.

Litigation as a Weapon

The claimant needs to establish whom to sue. The best targets are the manufacturers, the importers, and the distributors of the infringing products. It may also be possible to sue the customers in certain circumstances. A goal for the claimant should be, when possible, to set a precedent in order to persuade other infringers to stop infringing.

A claimant may also take action against the foreign parent company—even though it has not committed infringing acts in the country—if it can be shown that it was, in some way, involved with the infringement. In such circumstances, the French system does not require that the parent company show it knew or intended that its subsidiary infringed the concerned intellectual property.

For example, under French law, a person is liable for patent infringement if, without the consent of the owner of the patent, the person:

- Makes, offers for sale, puts on the market, or uses a product subject to the patent
- Uses a process that is subject to the patent
- Offers for sale, puts on the market, or uses the product obtained directly by a process that is subject to the patent

French courts also prohibit the import of products that infringe French or European patents designating France in whole or in part, or by equivalence (the counterfeited patent gives a result similar or used same means). Moreover, it is unlawful to supply on the French territory or to offer to supply a person other than a person entitled to practice the patented invention, with the means of implementing the invention.

Patent infringement may be caught either under civil law or under criminal law. In the latter case, any person who has knowingly infringed the rights of the owner of a patent may be liable to imprisonment of up to two years and/or a maximum fine of FF 1,000,000.

With respect to trademarks, any person who reproduces, imitates, uses, affixes, suppresses, or modifies a trademark, or is in possession of counterfeiting products, offers them for sale, or sells them is liable for trademark infringement. As for criminal law, a person who reproduces, imitates, or uses a trademark without the owner's authorization may be subject to imprisonment for a maximum period of two years and/or a maximum fine of FF 1,000,000.

Before proceedings begin, the owner of the IP right must make sure that its title is valid.

The checklist should include these points:

- Is the registration still valid?
- Have the renewal fees been paid on time?
- Has the intellectual property right that is licensed been formally registered?
- Does the owner have an up-to-date copy of the registration?

A nonexclusive licensee whose license has been duly registered may ask for damages to compensate its own injury that results from the commercial losses and the unfair use by the infringer of its promotional investment in the right. However, the licensee may not sue for patent, copyright, and registered designs infringement. In regard to trademarks, unless the license provides otherwise, the licensee may call on the proprietor to sue. If the proprietor gives no answer, the licensee may bring action in its own name if the infringement affects its interests. However, an exclusive licensee may sue in its name for patent and copyright infringement but not for registered designs.

As regards to trademarks, the license agreement may provide that an exclusive licensee may sue in its own name. In the case where the trademark's owner effectively initiates proceedings, the licensee is entitled to join the procedure in order to claim compensation for its own damages. In that case, the licensee's cause of action will be a tort claim for unfair competition.

Methods of Proof in France

There are major differences in the methods of proof between France, on the one hand, where parties may recourse to the seizure procedure, and the countries of common law, on the other hand, where parties use the discovery system.

The common-law system knows a specific phase unused in France, called *pretrial discovery.* The system of discovery and cross-examination as a means of establishing proof is seen by lawyers of the common law as the guarantee of the quality of the system of justice. As has been explained, under this procedure, a party to the trial and third parties have to reveal to the other party to the trial the existence of pertinent and substantial information they know, keep, or control. Such process cannot be avoided because it permits to each party the best knowledge of the case.

The *seizure (saisie-contrefaçon)* system used in France is quite different from the pretrial discovery. It is simple, fast, economic, and still very reliable. It has proven to work so well that the European Union authorities are considering expending it to the rest of the European Union.

In practice, prior to the initiation of a lawsuit, the IP rights holder requests that the presiding judge of the court in the proper jurisdiction issue an order authorizing a seizure of a few samples of the allegedly counterfeiting items or devices. (The jurisdiction is determined by the location of the alleged infringed products.) The request needs to be made by the intellectual property right's owner or its exclusive licensee through its attorney. The presiding judge issues an order for a seizure, either immediately or within a very short period, on the basis mainly of the evidence of the validity of the IP rights invoked.

Usually, the party seeking the seizure is authorized to have a bailiff seize a few (two or three) samples of the counterfeit products in order to establish the infringement. However, the judge may also order a seizure of the entire stock of the allegedly counterfeit products. The bailiff is also permitted to search for and copy any documents (invoices, order forms, or bills of lading) relating to the considered goods. The result of the seizure should put the claimant in a position where it has gathered information on the size of the infringement, the origin thereof, the sales of the infringing products, the costs involved, and the margins performed. This will permit the IP rights holder to assess in good conditions whether initiating a legal action on the merits is relevant. An important guarantee of the French seizure system is that it is managed by the judge, whereas with the discovery phase, it is only directed by the parties.

In order to avoid abusive seizures, French law provides that the claimant must sue the defendant for infringement within the short deadline of 15 days following the seizure; otherwise, the seizure is invalidated.

For trademark infringements, the customs services also play a major part, since they are entitled in France and in the other member states of the EU to seize the goods that seem infringing. For this purpose, the trademark holders lodge a file with the customs each year where the characteristics of their IP rights are described. The watch performed in France by the customs services is gorgeous and costs hardly anything.

Civil versus Criminal Action

Once the evidence of the infringement is collected, the plaintiff has to choose between a civil or criminal action. Most of the time, the civil route is elected, but in cases where the bad faith of the infringer is obvious (such as by professional counterfeiters), a criminal trial may be sought.

Civil Action. Usually, the civil action starts with the service at the request of the claimant of a notice of claims to the defendant(s). Once the notice of claims has been filed with the court, the parties exchange their arguments in writing, as well as their supporting documents under the supervision of a judge. The lawyers of the parties meet regularly with the judge for procedural hearings. When the judge considers that the parties have sufficiently developed their arguments, the judge closes the procedure and schedules the date for the oral pleadings. For patent cases, the procedure lasts about 18 months to 2 years (for trademark cases, about 1 year).

In quite a few cases, the duration of the legal action is too long and the plaintiff is anxious to get a ruling as soon as possible, or at least some immediate provisional measures. The French legal system offers the following possibilities:

- *The plaintiff may serve a notice of claims on the defendant with a short notice date for the oral hearing.* This requires the prior specific authorization of the presiding judge, to whom the urgency of a ruling must be shown. This procedure is difficult to perform. It is sometimes used for trademark matters, but almost never for patent cases.
- *A party may initiate summary proceedings, but only when a lawsuit on the merits has already been filed against the alleged infringer.* To obtain preliminary injunction, the claim for such a preliminary injunction must be instituted shortly after the IP rights owner or the exclusive licensee has known about the infringing facts. The case on the merits must appear serious.

  This procedure is expedited and the president renders an order in a short period of time (about one or two weeks). If in the past the courts were quite reluctant to grant such preliminary injunction, nowadays orders in summary proceedings are much more frequently granted when the statutory conditions are met. The president of the court may require the claimant to post security to cover any damages that may be suffered by the defendant in the event that the infringement action is subsequently judged unfounded.

- *Pan-European injunctions.* Europe has gone even further and lately developed an impressive system of Pan-European injunctions. The patent owner's task in preventing patent infringement is not easy where this extends over several countries. International systems for the registration and grant of patents such as the Patent Cooperation Treaty have been introduced with great success. However, as yet, there is no organized judicial system at a multinational level concerned with acts of patent infringement. Therefore, infringement must be attacked at its source in its country of origin in order to prevent multinational infringement. But it is not always possible, and in many cases the claimant has to commence proceedings in each country where infringing goods are sold.

  One early attempt to correct this difficulty was forged at the Convention on the Grant of European Patents (Munich, 1973). The Munich Convention made it possible to acquire patents in one or more, or even all, of the contracting states of the EPC by means of a single application and a single granting procedure with the European Patent Office (EPO) in Munich. The EPO performs the role of the national patent-granting authorities for all the contracting states in which patent protection is desired. It could be said that the contracting states have *delegated* their patent-granting authority to the EPO.

During the past few years, a number of patent owners have attempted to bring proceedings in one European country in respect of infringing acts committed in a number of other European countries. In Europe, Dutch courts have appeared as particularly willing to accept such applications and have ordered the cessation of infringing acts occurring in several countries, thanks to *cross-border injunctions.* It seems now that judges from other European jurisdiction would be ready to do the same.

A cross-border injunction is granted by a court in one country (e.g., the Netherlands) forbidding infringement in several countries, including the country where the claim was filed (e.g., Netherlands, France, UK, Germany). These cross-border injunctions are based on a continued implementation of the provisions of the Munich Convention and of the Brussels Regulation relative to the judiciary competence and the execution of civil and commercial decisions within the European Union.

- *Immediate enforcement of the judgement despite an appeal.* After the court renders its judgment, an appeal may be filed by any of the parties before the competent court of appeals. The appeal suspends the enforceability of the judgment of the district court, but in most IP cases, the plaintiff asks the district court to rule that its judgment is immediately enforceable, despite an appeal. Here again, French judges are very much concerned by the duration of the procedure. In most cases, if they acknowledge the infringement exists, they grant an immediate injunction to the defendant not to pursue the infringing acts.

  Judgments of the courts of appeals may again be reviewed by the Supreme Court (Cour de Cassation), but only on the basis of violation of law, since the Cour de Cassation does not rule on the facts of the case but only on the manner in which the rule of law was applied to the facts.

In order for the French system to be effective and attractive, the remedies granted to the prevailing party must be appropriate. We have seen that injunctions immediately enforceable are ordered. This is very satisfactory. Even if the French courts are not accustomed to granting millions of damages as the U.S. courts are, the amounts of the damages granted have considerably increased in the past years, and French IP judges are keen to have adequate information to be able to grant the appropriate remedies.

Therefore, the parties and their lawyers should not neglect this part of the case as they often tended to do in the past, thinking that it was a waste of time because the judges were reluctant to grant substantial damages. This is not true any longer. Judgments for damages can be substantial. However, it is still true that the reimbursement by the succumbing party of the legal costs of the prevailing party is not satisfactory, although it may, in some cases, exceed $10,000. But this works both ways: should the IP right holder have made a wrong assessment of rights, it will not cost the plaintiff a lot in reimbursement of the defendant costs. To advertise against infringement and infringers, the court usually orders the publication of the judgment in different newspapers at the defendant's expense.

Criminal Actions.   In criminal proceedings, the plaintiff lodges a claim before the criminal court against the alleged infringer. If the owner has obtained an order of seizure, the claim must be served within 15 days following the seizure. The claim sets forth the date of the first hearing, at which time the case will be examined from a procedural standpoint and the court will fix the amount of the deposit to be paid by the plaintiff. At the second hearing, the case is pleaded on the merits. If the facts are clear and there is no need for an additional investigation, a judgment will be rendered within four to five months from the date of the filing of the claim. Otherwise, a decision may take anywhere from six months to two years.

Criminal proceedings may also be initiated as a result of investigations conducted by the police empowered to do so by letters rogatory issued by the investigating judge. The results of the investigations must be transmitted to the public prosecutor, who remains free to decide whether to bring a criminal indictment. The investigating judge finally decides either to charge the defendant with patent infringement and refer the defendant to the criminal court or discharge the proceedings against the defendant.

The remedies available to the plaintiff in the criminal court are similar to those available in civil proceedings (damages and confiscation of the articles recognized as constituting an infringement). In addition, the defendant is subject to criminal penalties consisting of fines and/or imprisonment, with or without suspension.

Litigation is not only a weapon used against infringers. It can also be used as a shield in order to avoid a trial. Before taking an action against a potential infringer, the claimant should consider the relevance of the potential defenses available to the defendant. There is a surprising range of defenses, including the procedural ones already referred to, consisting of taking advantage of a step missed by the plaintiff if the pretrial check referred to above has not been properly conducted.

The defendant may also take advantage of the exhaustion of the IP right invoked by the plaintiff. Indeed, the European Union law limits the intellectual property owner's rights to restrain the free movement of goods within the

European Economic Area (EEA) where goods are first put on the market of one of the member states, either by the IP right owner or with its consent.

In some cases an IP right holder is prevented from using or licensing out its technology because of the threat of an intellectual property legal action by a third party, based on alleged prior rights. Such a situation is not bearable because it penalizes the good development of the business. The legislature has therefore provided for a specific procedure, for patent rights only, enabling to clear the situation.

Under French patent law, every manufacturer who can prove its industrial production in a European member state may ask a patent right holder to acknowledge that its production does not infringe its patents. In case the patentee contests the noninfringement or does not answer the request during three months, the manufacturer may sue the patentee and ask the court to rule that there is no infringement.

CONCLUSION

In conclusion, there are many reasons to particularly consider Europe and notably France when defending one's intellectual property rights. Moreover, coming to Paris to attend a trial is never a burden. It lasts for just half a day, it helps you to improve your French language, and leaves you plenty of time to taste French wines and cheeses.

ABOUT THE AUTHORS

Ronald L. Grudziecki is a partner in the Alexandria, Virginia office of the IP firm of Burns, Doane, Swecker, & Mathis, L.L.P. He is a past president of LES (United States and Canada) and is currently chairman of the LESIAC (International Affairs Committee of LES). He is also an adjunct professor at the Georgetown University Law Center. His practice concentrates on patent and trademark litigation before the U.S. district courts and the International Trade Commission, licensing, and client counseling.

Arnaud Michel is a member of the Paris Bar and has been a partner of the French law firm Gide Loyrette Nouel for 14 years, where he has co-headed the IP department since 1993. He has expertise both in IP and EU law. He headed the Brussels office of Gide Loyrette Nouel for seven years. In addition to extensive commercial and litigation practice, Michel has advised central European governments on the redrafting of their IP laws in the context of future membership of the EU. Mr. Michel is a member of the LES, chairman of the European Committee of LES International, president of LES-France, and past president of the main French trademark association (APRAM). He is also a member of the AIPPI (French group).

15

Alternative Dispute Resolution: Fighting Smarter, Spending Less

By Tom Arnold

INTRODUCTION

Transaction lawyers generally bring inadequate alternative dispute resolution (ADR) skills and negotiation energy to the negotiating table. There are many dispute resolution processes, none of them near perfect even in their optimum application.[1] They vary in their costs in time, money, quality of process, and likely results. Hence, the dispute-resolution process needs sophisticated and energetic attention at contract negotiation time, as well as at the time when the dispute arises.

Unfortunately, the client and often the transaction lawyer tend to think of the dispute-resolution clause as *boilerplate* (a standardized form) not worth much attention. Transaction lawyers who draft licenses and other contracts only rarely are experienced in even *one* ADR process, never in three or five. Almost uniformly, they are unsophisticated in dispute-resolution system design and evaluation required in the negotiation of a dispute-resolution clause. In the context of friendly negotiation of a contract, transaction lawyers erroneously tend to exhaust their client's and the other party's and counsel's time, interest, and negotiating energy on commercial aspects of the contract with virtually no intellectual energy or interest left to give to the dispute-resolution clause, which often is among the most difficult to design well.

Transaction lawyers tend to plug a dispute resolution clause into the contract almost as an afterthought. It is usually an arbitration clause, which is often *not* the clause of choice for the purposes of balancing time, cost, quality of process, and result. It lacks the dispute-resolution sophistication and negotiating energy that such an important clause deserves—sometimes with poor to near catastrophic results.

Negotiation techniques by which to get a well-considered, well-crafted, well-designed dispute-resolution clause is a topic beyond the allotted scope for the ADR chapter in this book. However, do not let the omission of negotiating techniques be taken as an implication that such techniques are not important. They are very important.

THE LITIGATION PLAYING FIELD

For clients who are at risk of a significant dispute to fully understand the dispute-resolution concept of *fighting smarter, spending less,* they must first understand the playing field upon which we play expensive litigation games. Warren E. Burger, former chief justice of the U.S. Supreme Court, wrote:

> Our litigation system is too costly, too painful, too destructive, too inefficient, for a civilized people.[2]

Would you recommend to your client a system of dispute resolution so schlocky as to beget that quote from its highest officer? Indeed, would you be guilty of malpractice before any jury in the land if you recommended that system to your client without discussing the alternatives?

Do I believe that Chief Justice Burger was correct? Yes, for U.S. practice I believe it in spades, based on a number of example cases:[3]

- Two patent infringement suits were in the court for 27 years.
- One case cost nearly $100 million (total both sides) through trial and appeal.
- One case had been in active trial in court for a year when the judge ordered it transferred to another district, where the trial had to start over again.
- A case involving a suit on a patent, a counterclaim on another patent, and an antitrust counterclaim went to trial at 9:00 A.M., went through trial on all those complex issues, and I was on the airplane with a signed judgment in my pocket at 3:30 P.M. that same afternoon. The merit in that practice was that this judge was keeping current on the overloaded docket that Congress had given him.

Most countries other than the United States, civil law countries, have much lower litigation costs than the United States has begot by its striving overly hard for unobtainable perfection in court dispute resolution. In such countries the differential in cost, time, quality of the process, and result between the various dispute-resolution processes (court and noncourt processes) is not nearly as great as in the United States. But the various countries with proportionally more international markets than the United States seem to have greater need to avoid a presumed bias of the adversary's local courts, and hence, more often suffer a need from that quarter to use an ADR process.

Chief Justice Burger was probably indulging an understatement in the previous quote, particularly but not solely as applied to the United States. That fact should motivate us all to look for where the waste most commonly is, and how to control the waste at those locations.

AVOIDING THE WASTES OF LITIGATION

Party/Counsel Attitude

Waste occurs, *inter alia*, because of the attitude the client representative often brings to the trial counsel at the commencement of a dispute or litigation, and because of the natural and expected response of most winning-warrior-type trial lawyers to a somewhat bellicose or aggressive client. In licensing and other intellectual property (IP) cases, the plaintiff wants a monopoly, wants that other party out of the business segment involved, or wants that party to pay big license fees that debilitate a business perceived by the defendant to be noninfringing and hence outside any royalty obligation. Those plaintiff-sought results are seen as strongly obnoxious by the adverse party and counsel, who see the accused structure as justified by the prior art, and see no credibility in the patentee's arguments for validity or infringement of the patent. So the suit or threat of suit tends to beget harsh adversarial feelings on both sides.

But the fact that the burden of proof of invalidity of a patent, registered "trademark," and registered copyright is on the accused infringer biases the result in such cases. If the accused infringement is close enough to be importantly competitive, the question of whether there is an infringement of a valid scope of the alleged protection is probably a close enough issue for the plaintiff to argue equivalents, or derivation, or some other pro-plaintiff theme. So the attitude tends to be or rapidly becomes aggressive, seeking a harsh remedy.

By mood as much as by words, the client often makes it clear that it wants a successful warrior for a lawyer. When the client and counsel are thinking emotionally about drawing blood, the mood is simply not right for most lawyers to appear to put their tail between their legs and say to their client, "Well, I understand your case. It seems solid. But I think we should seek to mediate the case and settle it now."

It takes a peculiarly strong lawyer to take that position at that time and place; most don't do it often. So the patentee's warrior lawyer with a litigious, sometimes somewhat hot-headed client in hand, often says, "Well, to get what you want, I guess we will have to sue them."

And on the other side, the defendant's lawyer often asks for information about values at risk versus cost of litigation, and so on, but almost invariably ends up saying something like, "Well, I guess we better get to work on our answer and counterclaim."

The client's experience with most ADR procedures is nonexistent to shallow. The lawyer's own experience with more than one alternative process most likely is not very deep—and the lawyer *believes* in the litigation process that has been his or her life's career. Ten years ago, most law schools offered several courses in litigation but not a single course in ADR. So the trial lawyer is going to suggest the familiar path most of the time.

Neither counsel is very likely to take the smart step: pick up the phone, call the adversary counsel on the phone, and say

> Joe, we got a problem on our hands. Let's you and your VP in charge of…, and me and my VP in charge of…, have lunch tomorrow and talk about how we are going to solve our problem. And by the way, do you know a good ADR person you trust? I'd like to invite him/her, somebody you trust, to come to lunch with us and talk to us about mediation, about arbitration, arb-med, med-arb and MEDALOA,[4] about collaborative dispute resolution, and about whether one of those processes is the cheapest and most fair way for us to resolve our dispute.

In about 35 years as a trial lawyer and a dozen years of ADR neutral work in mediation and med-arb, in arbitration and arb-med, in MEDALOA and collaborative dispute resolution and related dispute resolution system design work, I made such a call (or coached some others to call) dozens of times, and that opening move begot a very good timely settlement ratio. Perhaps only three times was such a call made to me or to my client and relayed to me. We got all of them settled within 60 or 100 days or so, for what I think was probably less than $100,000 per side—cases typically budgeted between $1–2 million and often running over budget.

Was that fighting smarter? Was that spending less?

Litigation, you see, is like making love to a gorilla. You are not through until the gorilla is through. And the spirit of competition and combat biases the sides to fight over every picky discovery issue that comes to mind. Once you start a complex commercial or IP litigation, it is very hard to stop it before hundreds of thousands of dollars have been spent.

So much for the unthinking knee-jerk attitudinal reaction of both client and lawyer to litigate, and to be very competitive about the combat aspects of litigation, rather than instantly initiating a settlement exploration process.

Sometimes it is the house IP counsel who committed overly strongly in an area of law not known well or where, as in license and IP law, nearly every legal standard is uncertain in its application. In one case we spent perhaps $2 million in litigation costs, including a minitrial early on, fighting disengenuity from a major "reputable" corporation and firm. That corporation's house counsel had written a stupid, self-serving opinion to the corporation. Apparently in reliance on that opinion, the corporation did a big, stupid, infringing thing, litigation followed, and the house counsel's career path was at grave risk.

The house counsel and his trial counsel fought viciously without regard to right, honesty, or ethics. When the corporation woke up shortly after trial and fired the offending house counsel who had written the stupid opinion and supervised the big litigation expense, the corporation paid $60 million and apologized for the way the litigation had been conducted. This settlement came two months after trial but before the trial decision came down; I think it fair to say that settlement for that same figure was available during the early minitrial settlement effort. In truth, we were entitled to recover attorney fees for the trial, but took the settlement without them.

In any big-value license or IP case, the client representative's or lawyer's career path may be to some degree at risk, as in that case. But at least commonly, the lawyer intensely wants some vindication either way. And either way, the lawyer can weasel essentially unlimited money from the company to fight a cause he or she intensely wants to win. Such counsel blame the high cost on the trial lawyers, as though they had no responsibility for them or their actions, because as they tell it, they hired the very best. And outside of the insurance bar, most lawyers are very poor at cost control.

Lack of Effective Budget Control

Waste occurs because (1) most lawyers are untrained in and are notoriously poor at budget control of litigation and (2) an unwitting conspiracy, often unknown to the client and lawyer who participate in it, begets, effectively, a nearly unlimited budget for a major commercial case. As IBM General Counsel Kastenback testified to the U.S. Senate about a big case against IBM: "The lawyers have an unlimited budget for this case, and every year they exceed it."—a not unfair metaphor for many an IP, license, and other commercial disputes.

Not atypically, the client representative, the vice president in charge of whatever, approaches the trial lawyer in a self-righteous mood, somewhat testy as to the perceived infringer, looking for vindication. The client representative has probably already reported to the corporate president or board that the defendants are dirty thieves of the corporation's very important and valuable invention—or, on the other side, that the patent is completely and undeniably invalid because we've been doing something *nearly* like it since long before the application for the patent was filed and *so we ought not be paying license royalties!*

Trial lawyers have an understandable competitive spirit to win and want to win to bolster their own reputation and for other reasons. They seem always to find a sincerely felt reason to look at all the other side's 12 million quality control cards, or whatever, in search of evidence of non-obviousness of the patented invention. Or in a trademark case, likely the lawyer suggests a perceived "need" for expensive public opinion surveys and suggests, "You know the importance of this evidence; if we don't get it, we just might lose a case that could have been won." The house VP commonly wants to vindicate his or her own business judgment more than he or she wants a tight budget of the corporation's money, and yields to slight but expensive suggestions by counsel. Often the concept of "need" is a gross exaggeration, but one each counsel and VP can tolerate and be sympathetic with—and this begets expenditures of money and time.

And there are other factors motivating the big effort or lack of control on the budget.

I do not here argue that either the trial lawyer or the VP client representative are blatantly dishonest in deciding to spend big sums that may exceed the value of the trademark or settlement of the infringement suit by a design-around. Rather I argue that their focus of attention is primarily upon their career path, the competitive combat, getting along with each other in that competitive endeavor, and winning that competitive endeavor they both want to win, irrespective of merit.

Relatively little attention is focused on the cost-effectiveness of the individual acts in the litigation, measured in context of things like the inherent uncertainty anyway of the predicted outcome in any event, and the perhaps equally good market under an alternative trademark or for a product design that is free of any charge of infringement. Neither side of the lawsuit mounts any meaningful effort at examining and evaluating the dispute-resolution plan and its elements under a cost-effectiveness microscope. The actions of one party elevate the knee-jerk reactions of the other until, distressingly often, there is a veritable flood of motion papers being dispatched weekly, mostly about issues the parties should and would settle amicably, but for the by-then intensity of competitive attitude, often sprinkled with animosity and an absence of an overall dispute resolution manager.

Indeed, both sides, driven by their common desires and interests, unwittingly become co-conspirators devoted to excesses in the fight and their will to win it, with no objective evaluation of their budget decisions in sight.

Absence of Overall Dispute Resolution Manager

Nobody, including the judge, is really proactively in charge of the budget management of the overall dispute-resolution project, with skills and under instruction to make it all cost-effective. With or very soon after a Complaint or Answer, many counsel are biased to serve a broad request for documents, and the genetic instinct of 65 percent of litigators on the other side tends to be to write a motion to quash a major part of it, and the fight mode is off and running. No overall proactive manager intervenes to get the counsel to work it out with each other. The judge, nearly always perceiving his or her docket as the overload it very often is, doesn't usually attempt that efficaciously. The competitive reaction to many a client and lawyer is a strong knee-jerk instinct to try to get the better of the other party, and the trial court does not intervene effectively except in response to motions that are expensive and time consuming. A subpart of this concept is thereby telegraphed.

In a majority of litigation the difference between chaos and a project is a project manager. A project manager can do many managerial things like:

- Schedule an early date for both parties' discovery requests to be exchanged and objections outlined and exchanged
- Call the parties together with their objections and the discovery they concede
- Mediate a pattern of recognized and accepted meritorious discovery plans
- Include trade-outs of issues arguable both ways with appropriate cost allocations worked in
- Seek to address all other discovery issues that by now have come to mind

Sometimes, indeed usually in simple cases, a project manager is able to resolve all of the potential future discovery disputes in this one conference by inducing an attitude of cooperative trade-outs between counsel, and is able to precipitate essential completion of discovery in a few weeks in circumstances where via court motion practice and related delays that same discovery would routinely take six months and often more.

When counsel get along well, the amount of time and money saved may be little to nothing in your case, but by comparison with contentious discovery fights, such savings are often prodigious. It is truly rare for a judge to be an effective hands-on project manager.

Absence of an Instinct to Talk to the Adversary

Counsel are not practiced in, and have no confidence in their skills in, persuading a competitive adversary to be objective and fair in a process of work-outs and compromises.

Mostly, it would never occur to trial lawyers to pick up the phone, set an early meeting to negotiate and trade out their respective requests, find alternative ways to accomplish what the other lawyer really needs without the burdens his or her request entails, and allocate costs of the searches inherent in the several requests. All these points are argued to the court in motions, but not to the other party in a cooperative spirit dedicated to working it out. In the context of the competitive combat, to "work it out" is simply not what litigators often do— they do not see "working it out" as an option.

Is that common pattern the best example of "fighting smarter, spending less"?

Agreed Basic Discovery

By agreement, or under the auspices of a mediator/special master, sort of overall dispute resolution project manager, or a pair of counsel and parties who execute a collaborative dispute-resolution contract, the parties could voluntarily produce four categories of discovery:

1. All documents the party is going to rely upon
2. All documents that are inconsistent with any theme to be presented by the party
3. All documents that support a theme being urged by the adversary
4. As to the most likely appropriate number of witnesses, the names and brief recitation of the role making the named witness relevant to the case

Is that doing it smarter, spending less?

Some documents are privileged, of course, but perhaps 85 percent of arguments over what is privileged can be resolved by a reasonable joint effort in lieu of motion practice. Those who will execute the collaborative dispute participation agreement (as discussed later) are prone to work and resolve the privilege issues.

Is that doing it smarter, spending less? You can bet your bottom dollar it is.

Ethics Standard

It seems only ethical that you not advocate a theme while concealing documents in your own files that contradict that theme, that you not deny or argue against a theme of the other party while concealing documents that support its theme. Many will observe accurately that that is common U.S. practice, but none, I hope, will say that it is ethical to do those things, however common it may be.

Ethics on that point is the law in England. The theory, of course, is not nearly perfect in the practice, but it works pretty well—much better than the U.S. motion practice I've seen on the same subject.

So when I am arbitrator, I take on a measure of proactive initiative and control as project manager of this traditional source of waste: I visit with the parties/counsel and essentially always get their acceptance of an order of the four categories of discovery right out of the starting blocks. And I set up the mediated trade-out session as soon as the parties can determine their basic discovery needs and request responses. As counsel, you usually can precipitate that smarter, less costly approach even in court cases where you appear. Or you can influence all the parties and counsel to execute the four-way participation agreement of collaborative dispute-resolution practice, explained later in this chapter.

But in the U.S. court litigation of commercial, license, and other IP disputes, that much discovery typically costs $100,000 to $400,000, plus 6 to 20 months of time. Why? Because there is no dispute-resolution process project manager, and we litigators tend to litigate almost every arguable issue, sometimes for no more important reason than because it is there to be litigated. Not in all cases to be sure, but in too many cases, the quantity of waste in court discovery process is mind boggling.

Recently I was mediator in a case in which each side had already spent roughly $16 million before doing final trial preparation. Without any doubt, a cooperative discovery effort would have put on the table all the information they relied upon in the mediation at a cost of something like $250,000 or $300,000—certainly not chicken feed, but definitely less than $16 million. Perhaps it is telling that nobody ever suggested that any of the $16 million per side had been wasted.

Vague and Indefinite Legal Standards in IP Law

Vague legal standards dominate all intellectual property law, and some other legal areas as well. The result is unpredictability of result in any tribunal. This is yet another factor that argues in favor of the compromises of ADR.

In fiscal 1997 and 1998, it was reported by Federal Circuit sources that trial court decisions in patent cases were reversed on appeal in some determinative part in nearly 50 percent of the cases. This high number occurs because most intellectual property and complex commercial disputes have multiple determinative issues, and the legal standards for many of them are unavoidably vague and indefinite. Thus, reasonable, unbiased people (like trial judges versus appellate judges or trial lawyers versus any judges) differ in their judgment on one or more issues. More recent figures appear to be lower, though still large. The raw data relied upon by these reporters appears to be soft, but the point I make still seems valid.

These reversals were reversals of a decision by a neutral trial judge after all discovery was closed, after all cross examination, after the entire trial transcript was frozen in stone and briefs on the merits written and considered.

By comparison, do you think lawyer opinions are any more reliable, when they are rendered before discovery is complete, before cross examination of the adversary expert and some others, before the trial transcript is made, before seeing the other side's law briefs, and when the opinion is written by a nonneutral lawyer who received a biased story of the evidence from the client, and whose speculations on the further development of the evidence are always, unavoidably, biased to favor the client's case?

In patent cases where, when the house internal support costs and outside expenses are added together, clients bet something like $1.2 to $2 million per side in litigation costs—bet that much and sometimes much more on the correctness of the counsel's opinion, which inherently is less reliable than the trial court's nearly 50 percent reliability in some modern years.

A better—and cheaper—bet would be to meet me at the local tavern. I'll buy the beer and supply the quarter. For cases with less than $1 million at risk, we will flip the coin only once. For big cases, two out of three. You will get instant results that way, and they would be more reliable, on average, than the opinions of U.S. district courts in some recent years in patent cases. That would be funny if most folks did not find a coin flip to be a process too disrespectful and low-class to apply to issues deemed so serious as these parties' dispute, even when the coin flip is fighting smarter and spending less than what lawyers do at the courthouse.

ARBITRATION

To save words and space I skip over arbitration lightly, not because it is not an important process, but because (1) anything less than a book may tend to mislead about arbitration, (2) you have other sources of sophisticated information on this widely used process, and (3) it is highlighted elsewhere in this chapter where arbitration is compared with other processes, like *baseball* or *last offer* arbitration, which work well either as a standalone process or as the way, when a mediation has not produced a settlement, to beget an assured resolution of a dispute and not leave it dangling. In this hybrid arrangement, the mediation process tends to frame the high and low limits of any fair compromise settlement.

Indeed, by contract, those or other high and low limits can be fixed, can be established as a binding feature of the process being used. High–low limited arbitration is very popular in personal injury insurance cases. One of its features is that the insurance company, being protected from a runaway jury on the amount of damages, can address the case with a fixed low budget because it is fighting against only the difference between the limits, and has no exposure to, shall we say, a $3 million verdict.

In international arbitration the time/money costs might not be materially better via arbitration than via the litigation practice of some civil law countries, but the bias and quality of dispute resolution may be. So you must investigate the bias, quality, cost, and time realities for your case and court versus arbitration practice in any appropriate countries.

"Baseball," or "last offer," arbitration is popular in sports salary disputes and some other dispute niches as well, as a hybrid part of MEDALOA. I discuss this proposition both as a standalone and particularly as part of the MEDALOA hybrid, shortly.

MEDIATION

Mediation often will give you a much better considered and just result than the courts afford on the average IP or big-market commercial case after considering costs in time and money.

Mediation is, of course, a good and useful process in most cases, but as the size of the case goes up to the numbers common in big-market commercial and IP cases, the bias of saving the litigation money slips downward, dragging with it the settlement percentage.

Further, some insurance companies are increasingly *not* using the mediation session truly to mediate a compromise; rather, they tend to evaluate the case, give authority to their agent to settle for their evaluation figure, offer that number in very short order, and declare an impasse if the figure is not accepted. They choose to take their chances on litigation rather than give the mediation reevaluation and trading a chance to work. It does take time and cost money, particularly when the opposing counsel is not competent, prepared, or psychologically facile at decision making, which is not uncommon.

Similarly, some of the best plaintiff's lawyers evaluate their case, invite defense counsel to look at all their documents—the whole case—and comment on the plaintiff's case and explain why plaintiff's case is not sound. The plaintiff's lawyer says:

> If you can't show me now why my case is not sound, I want X (a big number) dollars; if you can justify a responsible odds number for my losing point A or point B in my case, I'll multiply by that odds number and take that much less: if you are not willing to work candidly with me in that framework, let's all go home and get ready for trial.

Both these approaches are begot by high levels of confidence and impatience with mediation's efficacy borne of a lot of wasted time in past mediations with adverse counsel who are poorly prepared, poor at advocacy, and/or afraid to make a decision. As a result, mediation is losing ground as a dispute-resolving tool.

Like other ADR processes, mediation performed by Homo sapiens is imperfect, and increasingly it seems the process does not resolve the majority of disputes, as some of us were taught would happen when mediation was novel. Among cases sent to mediation and mediated, a rate of 55 to 75 percent settled in or shortly after mediation may be a better guess now than the 75 to 90 percent settlement rate we used to hear about, although big settlement rates still fill some niches.

But when reasonably well practiced by parties and counsel, mediation often is so very much better than traditional U.S. litigation as to make it almost criminal for litigants to give mediation's potential merit no consideration for any given case.

One large class of disputes almost uniformly resolved substantively much more justly by mediation than litigation is the contract dispute over an issue not really thought through during the negotiation, such that an issue arises as to construction of contract language. Perhaps the language was not chosen with the problem in mind or intent to decide the issue at hand, with the result that the contract is not economically viable for one party or the other to perform as written. But 95 percent of litigators don't recognize that class of cases when they see one, as a class uniquely well-served by the mediation or collaborative dispute-resolution processes better than by litigation.

Mediation remains recommendable, but it may be that as a standalone or hybrid preliminary to litigation it is not the sole process of choice.

MEDALOA

The second phase after a mediation where settlement was not obtained can be a court trial or any one of several binding arbitration varieties grouped as *med-arb*, mediation followed by some form of arbitration.

MEDALOA, Mediation And Last Offer Arbitration, a hybrid so named about 1992 by Bob Coulson, then president of the American Arbitration Association (AAA), is one of them, and among knowledgeable people is high on the list of preferred dispute-resolution processes.[5]

In last offer arbitration mode, parties can use the mediator as the follow-on arbitrator in standard arbitration. After the mediation, the mediator has good knowledge of the case and saves a lot of time and money by being able to use that knowledge investment. A possibility arising from this is that the parties will fear a mediator turned arbitrator with mediation-process knowledge the party has not heard or rebutted (most of us run much too afraid of that basically correct concern) and might comfortably name a new neutral for the arbitration. The choice doesn't have to be made until the mediation is concluded, and the subject framed for the process is thereby better understood.

Or the mediator who is not selected to be the follow-on arbitrator can serve as a sort of special master or project manager in charge of administering the trial preparation to be cost effective—and in a big, complex case can save a bunch above and beyond his or her fee and get a better reasoned result. All of these alternatives as to use or nonuse of the mediator in the arbitration process are within the MEDALOA group of processes. There is little experience I know about with the mediator as special master of the get-ready-for-trial.

In the MEDALOA, last offer arbitration format, each party—having been through the mediation process and given a candid rereview to all the risks, costs in time and money, and what is fair and/or likely in terms of relief—makes a final or last offer in written form. The amount and style of preparation and presentation in the evidentiary hearing is varied, depending on what is deemed appropriate in light of whether the neutral party is new and fresh to the subject matter or is highly informed about it during the prior mediation.

The arbitrator(s) (maybe you want three), in due course after the evidentiary hearing and arguments, choose the last offer they think is most nearly fair, just, and consistent with the applicable law, in their neutral judgment. The arbitrators' hands are tied to adoption of one of the submitted offers as the final award; they may not run off on a frolic of their own.

This approach, in combination with the mediation set of prior offers, effects a sort of set of high–low influence on their authority. Indeed the parties may contract that neither party shall, in the arbitration last offer, back away from their most-adverse-party-favorable offer in the preliminary mediation—one way to provide true limits, which I think are advantageous. Since the parties have already defined the width of the compromise spectrum by their prior offers in the mediation process, this most favorable offer to the other party is likely to be so close together that the arbitrator is not really deciding a big lot of value in most cases.

The widespread use of last offer arbitration of sports salaries, particularly baseball salaries (from which the process derives a nickname baseball arbitration), has made a good track record for the process there and in other types of cases as well, but when complex terms of an injunction need to be worked out, that step is a sometimes frustrating problem. Even so, experienced neutrals find MEDALOA to be a truly recommendable process.

A number of interesting psychological motivations come up in different cases to beget tweaks in the process. For example, in *daylight baseball,* the arbitrator reads the two final or last offers before deciding the case (frequently more than two last offers: I was mediator in one 13-party case where the process worked magnificently and inexpensively).

By contrast, in *night baseball,* the arbitrator writes out and commonly reveals the award before receiving or reading the last offers, and thereafter selects the party-offer closest to the arbitrator's own as the final binding award. Perhaps a party wants to offer to take very little or to pay very much because it doesn't trust the credibility of its own key or expert witness, and if the arbitrator sees the oddball last offer he or she will be biased by that implied admission. Such a party doesn't want that, and it is avoided if the arbitrator has already locked in a judgment founded on the evidence and arguments, without the evaluation-by-counsel aspects of an offer being yet known.

As you see, there are many aspects to arbitration practice whether used as a follow-on to mediations or as a standalone process.

ARB-MED

Arb-med, or *mediation against the box*, involves a full-scale discovery and arbitration and award that is written out but not delivered to the parties. The award is put in the box—perhaps a cigar box on the table. The parties and counsel heard and saw all the final evidence and heard the errors and corrections on cross or redirect examination; they can no longer speculate about what the evidence not yet discovered *will* show or how the adversary's expert is going to crumble under the cross examination, because all that is history, frozen in stone and unchangeable. All participants are evaluating the same question of what the final evidence *did* credibly show. There will be no surprises in later discovered evidence. The parties remain in complete control—nothing is yet turned over to an outsider like an arbitrator to decide. This is a context for a mediation sharply different from pretrial mediations.

But in *mediation against the box*, the arbitrator turns into a mediator. The mediator is not contaminated by any evidence heard in private that one party has not heard or rebutted. Responses to the evidence have been heard.

In complex, big-value cases handled in this arb-med context, the parties almost invariably agree to a settlement. Indeed, in every case I have knowledge of (only four cases, pretty complex and of moderate to large value), this process produced a settlement that assured on average, in terms of balance of equities, greater future business practicalities and creative solutions than any form of adjudicative black-and-white decision. That's pretty good value to obtain in a case with large values at risk. Note that the parties do not have to decide to use the mediation phase of this process until after the close of the evidence and the summation argument in the arbitration phase.

Why not mediate after both parties have heard the same identical evidence—all of it, including the responses? Normally, they can avoid errors or impractical entrapments that are likely in the decisions of judges and arbitrators. Mediation against the box is clearly fighting smarter than most court trials.

If the settlement occurs, what do you do with the *award*? There are some giggles and smiles while parties and counsel talk about it, but in the few of these cases that I have performed, it was thought better to destroy it so nobody knows how much value was left on the table. The mediation settlement becomes the arbitration award enforceable under the New York Convention in about 127 foreign countries.

COLLABORATIVE DISPUTE RESOLUTION

Consider last my favorite newly developed and studied collaborative dispute resolution, keyed and characterized by

1. An early-stage contract (*participation agreement*) among and between all counsel and all client persons who have a responsibility for or a significant interest in the dispute[6] or its resolution.

2. One contract among all the adversaries providing explicitly that all such signatories agree to collaborate in resolving the dispute using only the highest standards of which they are capable, with ethical and respectful behavior, integrity, respect, and cooperation, including *inter alia* and initial reciprocal, voluntary discovery of

   - All potentially relevant, discoverable documents that the possessing party may rely upon at trial
   - All potentially relevant, discoverable documents in one party's control that rebut or are inconsistent with that one party's advocacy themes
   - All potentially relevant, discoverable documents in one party's control that are consistent with and support the advocacy themes of the other party
   - The names of the most relevant potential witnesses, together with a brief statement of the role the witness played that makes him/her relevant

3. The collaborative participation agreement provides *inter alia*, that if the process fails to produce a settlement, the initial counsel resign from the case and don't talk to their clients anymore, and new counsel are employed. This is multifunctional as an incentive to counsel to keep the collaboration going and limit adversarial use of confidential information learned by counsel during the collaborative work.

4. The counsel become the planners and schedulers not only of the cooperative discovery process but also of a series of conferences among both counsel and the parties, where counsel talk through the process and evidence, what has been learned and/or will be learned, where to go from here, and how to get there. At the first such conference, the lawyers' draft participation agreement is read out loud and discussed clause by clause to assure everybody's full understanding and informed consent and joinder in the contract.

Though not yet widely used in commercial disputes, the hundreds of divorce cases handled since 1991 in accord with now tried-and-proven procedures has demonstrated this *collab* process's great value. It is such a pity that the commercial trial bar is not yet using it much.

As aforesaid, no dispute-resolution process is perfect or trouble free; you will find things to criticize and get angry about if that is your style. But among lawyers and clients who will execute such a contract (that screens out perhaps 90 percent of the chronically unethical schlocks, among others), the substantial or vast majority will behave (or can be induced by citing the contractual commitments to behave) close enough to the spirit of the contractual commitment so as to make surprisingly high the batting average of the process producing a highly cost-effective pursuit of good, responsible, cost-effective results. There are ADR horror stories, but they are less frequent than litigation horror stories, and ADR stories estimate out to be only about one-third as horrible. Any breach of this participation agreement is an original new cause of action.

All I can promise you is that collab, MEDALOA, and arb-med beat the socks off of the average that you can get in a big-value IP or other commercial case at the typical courthouse, in terms of the quality of result and the cost in time and money of getting there.

Those who have never performed a collaborative dispute resolution or studied the process may be well advised to employ a neutral coach who has studied or experienced the process, to *ride shotgun* with the parties and counsel in the process. This person functions as a proactive mediator coaching the ethical practices of the process. Lawyers who have gone through this process twice likely do not need a coach.

Let me fictionalize, to protect confidences, a real-life experience that exemplifies the kind of performance commonly generated in the process. Joe and Mary's marriage is sliding downhill. Joe blows up with every little disagreement or impatience with Mary. Mary is increasingly unforgiving of his late arrivals home in the evening, often after too many drinks. They agree to get a divorce. They and their lawyers execute a version of the collaborative participation agreement discussed with them by their lawyers, where all of them commit to conduct themselves with the highest standards of candor, equity, respect, and ethics of which they are capable. Monday afternoon, Joe blows up again as he departs the house on a business trip. He can't recall the reason when he gets where he is going. Mary can't take it anymore. She takes the kids, the new Mercedes, and all the stuff she can load into it, and moves to a secret apartment where Joe can't find her. Both of them complain bitterly to their lawyers about the other's behavior and want loose from the collaborative participation agreement. Their lawyers have been through this before and know how to handle it.

First they touch base with each other. Then Mary's lawyer takes her to lunch, where he asks few questions about what happened and why, points out that she has to get along with Joe to conduct the ongoing co-parenting of the children, as they had agreed to do, and asks whether this unilateral appropriation of the children, the new Mercedes, and community property was an example of her highest standard of cooperation, ethics, integrity, and respect. Says her lawyer, "We've got to manage some kind of an apology."

Pretty soon she is sorry to have messed up, asks him to arrange to get on with the divorce, and says she will behave. But she swears, "No, absolutely not. I will not apologize to that hot-head. Since the first baby, every time I've tried to apologize or ask for forgiveness, that has been the trigger for another blow-up I don't deserve."

Joe's attorney talks to Joe, telling him, "Look, I need her goodwill and cooperation if I am to get you equal time with your children instead of only every other weekend, and you stab my efforts in the back by a silly, emotional blow-up! That habitual blow-up behavior of yours won't play well before a jury if you have to go back to the courthouse for this. Gee, can you see, we *need* your wife's goodwill and cooperation—a lot of it."

Pretty soon, Joe wants forgiveness, is persuaded he should and will initiate the apology, and will take her guff when he does it. If he keeps his temper, he can make her accept it.

The lawyers move gradually as the process unfolds into a pair of co-mediators handling the discovery issues, child support, and so on—or they may carve out a single tough issue, such as rights as to the children, for litigation by other counsel, while they collaboratively handle all the other issues, such as property disputes and the sale of house and furniture. And so the whole project is saved by the collaborating attorneys, who find that their collaboration is in both their clients' best interests.

If it works so well in the midst of divorce animosities, why not in license disputes when the partnership of the licensor and licensee blows up? It seems only logical that using collaborative dispute resolution beats the socks off of the process, costs, and results of litigation, and can certainly be termed as fighting smarter, spending less.

CONCLUSION

Remember,

> "Our [U.S. court] litigation system is too costly, too painful, too destructive, too inefficient for a civilized people."—Warren Burger

> and

> "A dispute is a problem to be solved together, not a combat to be won."
> —Anonymous

ENDNOTES

[1] See, for example, Tom Arnold, "A Vocabulary of ADR Procedures," *Les Nouvelles,* Vol. XXXVI, 407, no. 1 (March 1991), p. 4; revised and republished, *American Arbitration Association Dispute Resolution Journal,* 1996; and again revised and republished in course book of 1999, American Lawyer Media, Inc. and Price Waterhouse Coopers seminar titled *Dispute Resolution Summit, Bypassing Traditional Litigation: Fighting Smarter, Spending Less.*

[2] Chief Warren Burger, Speech to the American Bar Association (February 28, 1984), reported at 52 *United States Law Week* 2471.

[3] Tom Arnold, "Why ADR?", *Patent Litigation 2000*, New York: Practising Law Institute, 2000 (619 PLI/Pat 1031).

[4] *MED*iation *And Last Offer* Arbitration, where the mediator may or may not serve also as the follow-on arbitrator at the parties' choice, but the format of the arbitration step is "baseball" or "last offer arbitration." MEDALOA gives a quality result without debilitating the process nearly as much as most folks fear may occur, by its letting the mediator serve as the follow-on arbitrator.

[5] My papers on MEDALOA and a score of other ADR topics have been published in the ALI-ABA course books for each of its annual ADR seminars in 1995 through 2000.

[6] See Tom Arnold, "Collaborative Dispute Resolution, an Idea Whose Time Has Come," *Corporate Counsel Review* 19, 407 (The Journal of the Corporate Counsel Section of the State Bar of Texas)(Nov. 2000), which explains the process, how to use it, and what results to expect.

ABOUT THE AUTHOR

Tom Arnold is a co-founder of Howrey, Simon, Arnold, & White, comprising nearly 500 lawyers in many cities in the United States and abroad. He is a fellow of the Chartered Institute of Arbitrators (London), the Advisory Board, the Institute for Transnational Arbitration, and the Large Complex Case Panel of the American Arbitration Association. He is a fellow of the American College of Civil Trial Mediators and a member of the American Institute of Collaborative Professionals. Mr. Arnold is the former president of each of the following: AA White Dispute Resolution Institute, AIPLA, LES, Houston Bar Association, Houston Executives Association, IP Section of the American Bar Association, and the National Council of IP Law Associations. He is on the Commission for Codification, Texas Business and Commerce Code. He is also an adjunct professor at the Universities of Texas and of Houston teaching IP and Alternative Dispute Resolution law. Mr. Arnold is the co-author of several books, including *Patent Alternative Dispute Resolution* (West Group, 1991), *Licensing Law Handbook* (West Group, 1990), *Invention Protection for Practicing Engineers* (New York: John Wiley & Sons, Inc., 1971), *Patent Law Handbook* (West Group, 1990), and more than 100 speeches and papers on ADR, litigation, and commercial and intellectual property law and practice.

Part Five

Licensing in the Global Community

16

Ignore Europe at Your Peril!

By Prof. Dr. Peter Chrocziel, Nigel Jones, and Thierry Sueur

INTRODUCTION

To a large extent, licensing and technology transfer is global. Many of the issues licensors and licensees have to grapple with are not influenced by local or regional considerations, and agreements in this area are often expressed to have worldwide effect. But there are many exceptions to this generalization. Although a negotiator with experience of, say, U.S. practice, will be able to negotiate many of the commercial and legal points arising in the context of a global deal, the negotiator risks failing to achieve the best possible deal (or in some cases, any worthwhile deal at all) if he or she is not aware of local or regional nuances. This chapter covers some of these issues from a European perspective.

It begins with an overview of some salient points about Europe itself. It then addresses two particular areas that those involved in licensing in Europe need to understand, especially as the law and practice is changing fast: competition and patents.

WHAT IS THE EUROPEAN UNION, AND HOW DOES IT WORK?

The European Union (EU) is currently made up of 15 member states. The total population of Europe is about 375 million. This includes countries of varying sizes and populations, from Germany, with a population of about 83 million, to Luxembourg, with a population of less than half a million.

Despite the fact that all the member states are members of a single union, there remain many cultural and political differences that enable each member state to enjoy a certain amount of individuality. Each member state also has its own legal and political systems, with its own parliament and judiciary. This enables national autonomy. There has, however, been much progress in the harmonization of the laws and systems of the member states via the key EU bodies, namely, the European Parliament, the European Court of Justice, and the European Commission (EC). Each member state also has an obligation to implement EU law.

Each country within the European Union has its own language and culture. Despite economic and political convergence between the member states, these cultural differences remain. This can make the process of harmonization more difficult, but it is important for nationals of each member state to be able to emphasize their individual identity to some extent. And although a single currency is about to be implemented in the majority of the member states, some have yet to agree to adopting it at all.

There are also key differences between the laws of the member states. The UK has a common law system whereby the law develops incrementally with case law, whereas both Germany and France have codified systems.

In trademark law, it is possible to register a Community trademark (CTM). This enables a party to register a mark throughout the European Union, avoiding the need and expense of registering the mark separately in each member state. However, this is largely irrelevant when considering patents and technology.

In relation to patents, it is not yet possible to apply for a single patent that affords Communitywide protection, although there are ongoing attempts to deal with this issue. The second part of this chapter discusses this topic. Copyright also remains, at least to some extent, national in nature, although again there has been much harmonization.

EUROPEAN COMMISSION COMPETITION LAW

This section reviews the provision of the Treaty of Rome that is most relevant to technology transfer, namely Article 81.[1] It explains the way in which block exemption regulations work; considers the regulation most relevant to technology licensing (namely, the Technology Transfer Regulation),[2] and briefly summarizes the changes that have been proposed in this area—changes that, if implemented, will have a major effect on licensing in Europe.

Article 81(1)

Article 81(1) of the EC Treaty prohibits agreements that may affect trade between member states and that have as their object or effect the prevention, restriction, or distortion of competition with the common market.

Article 81 does not apply to minor agreements, but few commercially significant agreements will benefit from this.[3] Agency agreements and agreements between a parent and its subsidiary are also not covered.

An agreement that infringes Article 81(1) is automatically void and unenforceable. The parties to an agreement prohibited by Article 81(1) may also, depending on their conduct, be exposed to heavy financial penalties and can be sued by third parties who suffer loss as a result of the anticompetitive agreement.

Article 81(3)

Under Article 81(3) of the EC Treaty, agreements may be exempted if they contribute to technical or economic progress and give consumers a fair share of the resulting benefit, so long as the restrictions imposed are necessary to achieve the benefits of the agreement and do not give rise to the possibility of eliminating competition in a substantial part of the market in the products in question.

An individual exemption may be obtained only by making a formal application to the Commission. This is the area in which the proposed reforms will have their most significant impact in relation to licensing. (This is discussed in more detail later.) If granted, the exemption takes effect from the date of the application. So if you consider that your agreement might affect competition but the relevant restrictions are reasonable, you must notify the Commission of the agreement and ask for an exemption.

Notifying the Commission will generally protect the parties against fines even if the restrictions are not exempted. The parties may nevertheless be fined for conduct prior to making an application. Notification must be submitted by completing a form prescribed by the Commission.[4] The notification must contain the following:

* Names and addresses of the parties to the agreement
* A summary of the nature, content, and objectives pursued by the agreement being notified
* The definition of the relevant market that, in the applicant's opinion, should form the basis of the Commission's analysis of the notification
* Description of the activities of each party to the agreement in the relevant market and neighboring market
* The position of competitors and customers in the relevant market
* Any other relevant information identified on the form[5]

The parties to an agreement being notified should also indicate the reasons for the application for the exemption; in other words, how the agreement fulfills the conditions of Article 81(3).

The individual exemption procedure presents considerable difficulties for parties to technology transfer agreements. Particularly for exclusive agreements, parties need to be certain about their rights. It may be that the licensee or licensor or both are only interested in an exclusive license and that a nonexclusive license is not an acceptable commercial alternative. If they need to be certain that exclusivity will be enforced by the courts, they must notify them about the agreement and hope for an early decision by the Commission. Often it will be unreasonable to wait. And if parties are entering into many agreements, this process may be very expensive and time consuming. (Again, all this may change if proposed reforms are introduced.)

Block Exemptions: General

The European Commission recognizes that efficient technology transfer is important for the development of the EU's economy. To reduce the number of cases in which an individual notification is necessary, the EC has enacted various regulations granting *block exemption* from the effects of Article 81(1) for certain categories of agreements. These include patent and know-how licensing agreements, which are covered by the Technology Transfer Regulation.

If the guidelines in the block exemptions are followed, the parties can be reasonably sure that their agreement will be exempted from the effects of Article 81(1) and that the relevant restrictions will therefore be valid and enforceable.

Most block exemptions follow a standard format: Article 1 lists restrictions that are permitted notwithstanding the provisions of Article 81(1); Article 2 lists further clauses (*white* clauses) that will not affect the position; and Article 3 lists certain restrictions that will deprive an agreement of the benefits of the block exemption (*black* clauses).

Technology Transfer Block Exemption Regulation No. 240/96. For technology licensing agreements, the most relevant block exemption regulation is the Technology Transfer Block Exemption Regulation (no. 240/96). It covers patents that include utility models; semiconductor chip topographies; supplementary protection certificates (SPCs) for pharmaceuticals or for any other products for which such certificates are available (which, since 1996, includes agrochemicals); plant breeders' certificates; and applications for any of these rights[6] and know-how. This is defined as technical information that is *secret, substantial,* and *suitably identified.* Commercial or marketing information is excluded.

The regulation does not cover all technology licensing agreements. Licenses for other intellectual property rights such as trademarks, copyrights (including computer software), and designs are covered only if these are part of an agreement that is mainly a patent and/or know-how license, and where the additional rights contribute to achieving the objects of the licensed technology and the provisions concerning them are only ancillary to the main provisions. It does not apply in certain joint venture situations; nor does it apply to agreements between members of patent or technology pools that contain territorial restrictions on the parties' activities.

Generally, however, the regulation provides a reasonable set of rules for technology licensing in the European Union. This enables parties to conclude agreements that they can reasonably expect to be enforceable and clean from a competition view point.

Types of licenses and obligations exempted (Article 1).

- *Sole licenses.* The licensor agrees not to grant any further license but reserves the right to compete with the licensee.
- *Exclusive licenses.* The licensor also agrees not to use the technology.
- *Territorial licenses.* The licensees are assigned specific territories in the EU and are forbidden to compete with one another in their respective territories.
- *Marking requirements.* The licensee is obliged to use the licensor's trademark or get-up.
- *Production limited to own requirements.* The licensee is obliged to limit production of the licensed products to what it needs for making its own products and to sell the licensed products only as integral or replacement parts for its own products.

Exclusive or *sole licenses* and *territorial restrictions* on competition between licensees (with one exception) are exempted while the relevant patents are in force, or where know-how is involved, for *10 years* from the date when a licensed product is first marketed in the European Union by a licensee, whichever is longer. The exception is competition between licensees in response to unsolicited orders. Here the exemption is for a maximum of *5 years* from the relevant date, whether patents or know-how are involved. It does not follow that longer periods are prohibited. They are simply not automatically exempted and will require an individual notification.

It is important to note that the regulation specifically allows the licensor to reserve its patent rights to restrain a licensee from operating outside its licensed territory (Article 2.1(14)). So while the maximum period for contractually banning a licensee from meeting unsolicited orders from other territories is 5 years, the licensor may reserve its patent rights to combat such activity by an action for infringement.

Additional Typical License Provisions That Do Not Affect Exemption: White Clauses (Article 2).

The regulation lists additional obligations (often called *white clauses*) that will generally not restrict competition and that may therefore safely be included in a license agreement without prejudicing the automatic exemption. This white list is summarized below:

- Bans on assignments or sublicenses
- Post-termination use bans while patents subsist or know-how remains secret
- Obligation on licensee to license improvements back to licensor, provided:

- • Licensor agrees to grant licensee exclusive or nonexclusive license of his own improvements
  - • If licensee's improvements are severable from licensor's technology, the license back to the licensor is nonexclusive
- • Obligations on licensee to observe minimum quality (including technical) specifications, and tie-in obligations (i.e., obligations on licensee to procure goods or services from the licensor or the licensor's designee, provided that the products or services concerned are necessary for a "technically proper exploitation" of the licensed technology or for maintaining quality control)
- • Obligations to report and assist in combating infringements
- • Obligations to pay royalties after patents expire or know-how becomes public (unless this is the fault of the licensor), provided this is to facilitate payment or is freely agreed between the parties
- • Field of use and product market restrictions
- • Minimum royalty and minimum production requirements
- • Most favored licensee clauses
- • Obligation to mark licensed product with licensor's name or patent details
- • Obligation not to use licensed technology to construct facilities for third parties
- • License limited to right to supply a particular customer, or license given to a customer to make or have made licensed products, to meet a second sourcing requirement
- • Reservation of patent rights against a licensee's activities in unlicensed territories (discussed above)
- • Right to terminate agreement if licensee challenges validity of a licensed patent, or secrecy or substantiality of licensed know-how, or claims that a licensed patent is not necessary
- • Best endeavors obligation
- • Right to make exclusive agreement nonexclusive and stop licensing improvements if licensee enters into competition with licensor in respect of R & D, production, use, or distribution of competing products.

This is an extensive and useful list, and it includes many provisions that have or may have been the source of uncertainty in the past. It is worth noting that national rules may be stricter than the European competition rules.

Provisions That Preclude an Exemption: Black Clauses (Article 3). The Commission views certain provisions with sufficient suspicion to deny an exemption to any agreement that includes one. These are listed in Article 3 and are often called *black clauses.*

It is important to remember that these clauses are not necessarily anticompetitive and that, even if they are, they will not necessarily never be exempted by the Commission. They are simply clauses that the Commission does not believe it can include in a block exemption, and for which it will continue to require an individual notification.

The list in the new regulation is shorter than the lists in the old patent and know-how block exemptions. The black clauses now include the following:

- Price restrictions
- Noncompete clauses (without prejudice to the right to terminate exclusivity and rights to improvements discussed above)
- Obligations without objectively justified reason, to refuse to supply users or resellers who will market in other EU territories, or to make it difficult for users or resellers to obtain the products from other resellers (in short, to frustrate parallel imports)
- Customer restrictions between parties who were already competing manufacturers before the grant of the license
- Limitations on manufacture or sale (without prejudice to "own use" limitations discussed earlier)
- Obligation on licensee to assign improvements to licensor
- Clauses that seek to extend periods of exclusivity or restrictions on competition between licensees in different territories beyond the maximum exempted periods.

Gray Clauses and the Opposition Procedure of Article 4. If an agreement contains a provision (often called a *gray clause*) that infringes Article 81(1) and that is not specifically exempted, the entire agreement is void, notwithstanding that other clauses might be in full compliance with the block exemption. This all-or-nothing approach has been criticized as too restrictive. Although calls for it to be changed were not taken into account when this regulation was being finalized, the Commission now seems to have accepted that it does need to be amended.

Any significant clause that is not in the black list or the white list must therefore be considered carefully for possible anticompetitive effects. Its inclusion in a license agreement may prevent the parties from benefiting from a block exemption under the regulation. If this gray clause does infringe Article 81(1), the agreement is not exempted, and the enforceability of important provisions like exclusivity will be at risk.

For such situations, the regulation offers a quick notification or opposition procedure in Article 4. If an agreement containing a gray clause is notified to the Commission and the Commission does not oppose an exemption within four months, the agreement will benefit from the block exemption.

Furthermore, the Commission may relieve the parties of the obligation to make a full, formal submission such as would normally be required for a notification. Instead, it will now generally be content to receive the text of the agreement, and an estimate "based on directly available data" of the market structure of the subject matter of the license in question and of the licensee's market share.

Two specific examples are cited in the regulation of clauses that might benefit from use of the opposition procedure. Both are clauses that were blacklisted under the previous patent and know-how regulations:

1. A tie-in obligation, which is not necessary for a technically satisfactory exploitation of the licensed technology
2. A no-challenge clause (as to validity of a patent, or secrecy or substantiality of know-how)

It is illuminating that the Commission considered that such provisions, previously regarded with extreme suspicion, might well be worthy of exemption under the opposition procedure.

Withdrawal of Exemption

The Commission has the power at any time to withdraw an exemption under the regulation where it finds that the exempted agreement nevertheless has effects that are incompatible with Article 81(1). Some examples of situations in which it might exercise this power are given in Article 7:

- Where the licensee refuses without objective justification to meet unsolicited orders
- Where parallel imports are impeded
- Where the parties were competing manufacturers when the license was concluded, and minimum quantity or best endeavors obligations on the licensee are preventing the use of competing technologies
- Where the effect of the agreement is to prevent the licensed products from being exposed to effective competition in the licensed territory by "identical goods or services, or by goods or services considered by users as interchangeable or substitutable in view of their characteristics, price and intended use." It is specifically stated that this may in particular occur where the licensee's market share exceeds 40 percent (discussed later).

Proposed Reform

As has been explained, the traditional way of seeking confirmation that one's agreement does not fall foul of EU competition law is to notify the

European Commission of the agreement and ask for the exemption. The advent of block exemption regulations eliminated the need for notification in many circumstances, but users of the system remained concerned about the administrative burden imposed by this form-based system. With the implementation of the *vertical restraints block exemption* in June 2000 came a broader, effects-based or economics-oriented regime (at least for agreements that qualified under that regulation), in which the parties have to consider the economic impact of their agreement and decide for themselves whether it is anticompetitive under EU law. A far more radical reform has also been proposed, and so far has received strong support from a broad range of interest groups, in the Commission's "White Paper on Modernisation of the Rules Implementing Articles 85 and 86 [as they then were] of the EC Treaty" (1999 OJ C 132/1). This white paper aims to reduce the administrative burden on the Commission arising out of the notification system, giving the Commission time to focus on new markets and new competition issues.

For many years, it had been thought that national authorities would be given the power to grant exemptions. In fact, the proposal is to do away with the notification regime altogether and make Article 81(3) directly applicable.

Agreements satisfying the conditions laid down in Article 81(3) would not require any official act conferring exemption: they would simply be exempt as a matter of law. If and when a question of compliance arose before an authority or court, its decision on the agreement would merely be declaratory, not constitutive—that is, the decision would recognize that an agreement is, and always has been, exempt, or would declare that it infringes. Therefore, national authorities and courts will be given an enhanced role. Whether they have the resources to deal with it remains to be seen.

Interestingly, the white paper refers to the continuing use of the block exemption system for agreements that fall within its scope, and applies the new *exception legale* rule only to those that fall outside their scope. In other words, block exemptions would exist in parallel, by way of reinforcement.

Much will have to be done by way of flanking legislation to clarify the principles by which industry and its advisers will be called upon to make the difficult judgment as to whether an agreement is exempt.[7] Presumably member states will also be expected to do away with their national notification procedures.

Reform of this kind now seems inevitable: not least because of the need to reduce the burden on the Commission of dealing with its ever-longer backlog of notifications. And recent indications suggest that it will come very soon—with a real possibility of the framework legislation being adopted by the European Union legislature by the middle of 2002.

REFORM TO PATENT LAW: THE LONG AND PAINFUL WAY TO A COMMUNITY PATENT

Although there are many European success stories, taken overall, companies based in Europe have failed to match the performance of innovative companies based in the United States. This innovation deficit can be attributed to many factors; some are internal within the companies themselves, but many are external:

- European society is less supportive of risk-taking, entrepreneurship, and the adoption of new technologies—key requirements for successful innovation.
- Europe's markets for products and services do not offer the appropriate balance of opportunities, pressures, and incentives for innovation.
- Europe allocates too few resources to the creation and diffusion of knowledge, particularly research and development.
- European education systems are less successful than those in many other countries in equipping its citizens with key skills in areas such as mathematics, science, technology, ICT (information and communication technologies), and management.
- Europe's burden of taxation is too high, particularly on innovators, entrepreneurs, managers, employees, and their companies.
- Europe's regulatory and fiscal frameworks inhibit the development of modern, high-performance workplaces.[8]

One of the key issues is that starting from a creation of knowledge that is already minor compared to that of the United States or Japan, in terms of percentage of GDP (U.S.—2.8%; Japan—3%; EU—1.8% in 1998/1999), the European Union is, in addition, not the best in exploiting innovation through licensing, either.

There are, of course, many reasons for this, but apart from traditional obstacles to collaboration and commercialization, such as taxes and also the legal environment, the European Union does not have the proper tools for licensing because the European Union has no Community patent.

Today, Europe has national patents, and Europe also has the European patent. It may be necessary to describe here the situation in more detail.

European Patent System

Europe at large and the European Union understood very soon after World War II that the construction of Europe should and would have consequences in the field of intellectual property.

With respect to patents, the first step was the creation of the European Patent System in 1975, which created a unique law and a centralized organization in the form of the European Patent Office (EPO) granting European patents.

The EPO now has 20 members—the 15 members of the EU plus Monaco, Liechtenstein, Switzerland, Cyprus, and Turkey—and about 10 other states will join in the second part of 2002 or after.

Of course, the EU patent is a useful tool because it enables the applicant to obtain a patent through a unique grant procedure. Things become more complicated thereafter as, after being granted, the national aspect comes on board again. The European patent has in each designated state the same effect that a national patent would, and is submitted to national laws and courts, for interpretation and licensing.

About at the same time that they were creating a European Patent, the EU members had agreed on a Community Patent Convention, complemented a few years later, in 1989, by a further convention creating a common appeals court specializing in the field of patents.

None of these conventions came into force for various reasons, one of them being that some states had ratification problems, but it is generally agreed that the main reason was that the potential users—that is to say the industry, big enterprise, and small and middle-size enterprises (SMEs), and inventors made clear that they would not use the proposed Community patent established by these conventions, the system being too complicated and too expensive.

After many years and due to the insistence of the industry, the European Commission proposed, after various consultations, a draft regulation by mid-2000.

In addition, the 15 heads of state of the European Union, during the European Council of Lisbon (March 2000) asked the Council and the Commission to take the necessary steps to ensure that a Community patent is available by the end of 2001, "so that Community-wide patent protection in the Union is as simple and inexpensive to obtain and as comprehensive in its scope as the protection granted by key competitors." This commitment was reaffirmed in the conclusions of the Stockholm and Gothenburg Summits in 2002.

After such strong demand from the users and an equivalent strong political will at the highest level, we have to examine where we stand today with respect to the regulation.

The Possible Future of Community Patents

Focusing on the hot topics only—that is to say the issues that seem to create difficulties in achieving the goals just described—we can mention four hurdles:

1. The language regime
2. The judicial/litigation system
3. Decentralization
4. Membership of the EU in the EPO

The Language Regime. The commission's draft regulation proposes maintaining the three languages of the European Patent Office (i.e., English, French, and German). Where litigation ensues, the patentee would be required to provide the alleged infringer with a full translation of the patent in the alleged infringer's own language, unless the patentee could establish that the alleged infringer understood the patent in the language in which it was granted.

Seen from the user's side, the language issue is directly connected to cost. The main argument of the users is that as the European Union is, from an economic point of view, similar to the United States, and as a patent is essentially an economic tool, there is no reason why a Community patent should be more expensive than a U.S. patent. Today, a European patent costs about three times as much as a U.S. patent.

The EU figures show that 40 percent of the cost of an average EU patent is due purely to translation, and this share would be greater if a full translation had to be provided in the 11 languages of the European Union (and more in the future).

From the member states' side, various reactions have to be mentioned. Certain states, more particularly from the south of Europe, would like to have Italian and Spanish added. Spain and Italy also propose as an alternative solution the "English-only" solution, which is likely not to be supported by France.

Judiciary System. First of all, it should be noted that the European Court of Justice (CJCE) is only competent to interpret the EU treaties but has no competency with respect to litigation between private parties. The Commission proposes the creation of specialized intellectual property chambers within the tribunal of first instance of the European Court of Justice.

The industry has underlined the importance of having qualified and specialized judges who possess appropriate technical expertise, and of establishing uniform substantive law (covering *inter alia,* evidence, procedure and damages). If necessary, a limited number of decentralized chambers could be considered, located in regions or countries where infringement litigation occurs frequently. Wandering chambers would be another acceptable alternative.

It should be mentioned that in order to have the right to create such courts, the European Union will have to change the Amsterdam treaty. This possibility has been provided in the Nice treaty of December 2000, which had yet to be ratified by Ireland as of this writing.

Decentralization. This recent question was not touched on at all in the original draft of the EU Commission, which of course intended to rely on the EPO to examine and grant Community patents.

The issue is that some states are asking for compensation for the possible loss of skill of their national patent office. For the purpose of, and in order to maintain a competent office for their own SMEs, they wish to be entitled to make prior art searches or even examinations of Community patents.

This has created a controversy in the industry, which considers, first of all, that this would be in total contradiction with the centralization principal that led to the creation of the EPO 25 years ago. In addition, the industry states that if searches or examinations are handled in various national patent offices, the Community patent, then granted, will have a very different quality, depending on which office has searched or examined the application. It is feared that this would result in a kind of forum shopping, whereby the applicants would shop around, trying to have their applications handled by a less difficult office. The EPO, apart from its excellent quality, is by definition and conception a neutral organization.

Membership of the European Union in the EPO. The European Union wants to become a member of the EPO to make sure that the law and procedures that will lead to the granting of Community patents take into full consideration the *acquis communautaire.* Of course this will require the consent of non–EU members such as Switzerland and others, but this also implies solving other issues like money distribution and votes. With respect to money, the EPO makes a substantial profit, which is shared between the members.

How will things be organized when the EU becomes a member of the EPO? With respect to votes, will the EU vote as an additional state, which some non–EU members might consider as not being fair, and will it oblige all the EU member states to vote just like the EU representative votes? These are diplomatic and not IP questions, but solutions will have to be found fast.

Lastly, the adhesion of the European Union to the EPO will have to take place prior to the end of June 2002—that is to say, prior to having new states from central and eastern Europe joining the EPO.

Impact on Licensing by the Community Patent

We now discover that in a territory like the European Union, it may be more complicated to create a Community patent than a single currency, because IP touches on issues of justice and language that many countries consider a matter of sovereignty.

Will the politicians of the third millennium in Europe be as creative and European oriented as were those who created the EPO in 1975 for the sake of competitiveness in the industry and welfare of the people through innovation? We will have the answer in the very near future, and it is hoped that the answer will be positive, in the interest, among others, of licensing.

Today, even companies of significant size, which have internal intellectual property departments and use a network of national EU law/patent firms, experience difficulties when they want to license European patents in the European Union, because in each country the scope of the patent will probably be different as the claims will be interpreted according to each country's national laws and court decisions, and in the different countries of Europe some courts have a broad interpretation, whereas others have a narrow interpretation, and others again a variable interpretation.

The situation is rendered even more complicated by the fact that a translation into the local language has to be filed at the national patent office in most countries, and that in certain countries, the interpretation will be based on these translated claims and specification provided it is identical or narrower than the originally granted patent. The differences are so important that during the last revision of the Munich Convention, the member states were unable to agree on a common definition of the equivalence.

This variety of treatment also applies, to a lesser extent, to the regulations of licensing, which may differ from one state to another. It is obviously easier to license in a unique territory, such as the United States, when you have one patent, interpreted in the same way. Nevertheless, the European Union is supposed to be one unique market.

One additional difficulty, more of an administrative nature but a real one anyway, is the payment of an annual fee, as the fees that have to be paid to the designated national offices vary to a great extent from one country to another, and this in many circumstances forces applicants to abandon a European patent in a specific country in order to save money. Ultimately, they regret this later on when opportunities arise to license the patent in this country.

Now, is all this true for smaller enterprises? It has been suggested many times that the Community patent was in the interest of big industry but that SMEs would have no or limited interest.

As a matter of fact, the Community patent might be of greater interest to small and middle-size enterprise, and this is due to licensing.

If it becomes possible to obtain, through a unique patent application, a protection covering 15 countries and a unique market, which would in fact be the biggest market of the world, SMEs would then discover the possibility of simultaneously reaching two goals:

1. *Protect a specific territory where the SME wants to use the patent as a monopoly in order to prevent others from using or implementing the same technology.* That is to say, the SME would keep a competitive advantage. Outside of what could be called their own territory or territories, the SME will very quickly understand that it has potential rights in the other EU countries where protection exists but where the technology is not used.

2. *The SME will then have the option to license or to establish alliances in the countries where the Community patent extends its protection and where the SME has no industrial or commercial activity.* This will allow the SME to extract more value from its intellectual property rights.

Today, with a European patent, this possibility is limited because at the time when SMEs file a European Patent application or even later when the patent is granted, and when the time comes for the validation in the countries originally designated, statistics show that in most or at least in many circumstances, the SMEs are not seeking protection outside the territory where they operate because this is too expensive and there is no direct and automatic payback.

The situation will be completely different when the Community patent exists because, first of all, at the time of the application, the 15 countries will be automatically designated. If, at the time when the patent is granted, there is no additional cost directly connected to designation of a country and more particularly if no translation is required, then, with no or little additional cost, the protection will then be obtained for the whole EU territory.

At this time, SMEs would be in a situation similar to the situation that exists in the United States. For example, a company located in Florida and operating in this specific state or in the surrounding states would see no problem and, in fact, many advantages to licensing its patent to a company acting in the same field but located and operating in the state of Washington, in California, or in Maine. This means that the creation of the Community patent could ultimately favorably affect licensing.

Of course, in this respect, licensing should be understood in a very broad sense and include any form of cooperation such as alliances, joint ventures, or partnerships, which should be based on the existence of a Community patent, as will any alternative solutions that each and any SME will be able to choose in order to get additional value from its intellectual property portfolio.

It should be noted that in addition to having unique protection for a unique market, the judicial aspect will have some impact. Thus, in case of conflict, instead of risking contradictory decisions within the various countries of the EU, the Community patent will give the SMEs the option to litigate in one place only, the decision rendered by the judges applying throughout the whole EU territory.

In this respect, it could be mentioned that there are still hesitations in the European Union concerning alternative dispute or SMEs, to obtain fast decisions and avoid the publicity of court actions. It is hoped that, as was recently contemplated in an intergovernmental conference in which all the member countries of the European patent convention participated, arbitration will become a more and more possible option for parties—as long as, of course, they agree to use such arbitration.

One of the major interests of patents for governments is the dissemination of information and the increasing use of new technology. From a company perspective, in addition to the traditional creation of a competitive advantage, the trend is to focus on the extraction of value from patent rights. From a law firm's/consultant's point of view, the goal is to enable clients to understand what kind of return they may have on their R & D and patent expenses. In all these cases, licensing, in a broad sense, may be the answer.

Licensing does not have the place it should have in Europe, and it is likely that the existence of an affordable Community patent of good and uniform value, granted by one central office, with a unique judiciary system, will have a decisive and major effect on its development. It will happen as it is needed, and it is in the interest of the economy, but when? Several recent cases discussed in the remainder of this chapter provide insights on these questions.

LICENSING AS RIGHT—NOT DUTY

It is one of the trivialities of intellectual property law that whatever intellectual property right a company may own, this very intellectual property right will create a monopoly. Only the owner of such right will have the enjoyment of the subject matter, may it be an invention, a trademark, or a copyright. Aside from historical developments questioning the rationale of creating intellectual property rights as such, it is common understanding that intellectual property rights add to the greater good of both the economy and society in fostering technical and creative, if not to say artistic, developments. Especially the copyright has been looked at over the centuries as being an integral part of rights that should be available to a human being (as well as a corporate entity) when certain creative objects are brought into being.

It is also one of the basic principles of the business of licensing that it is up to the IP right owner to decide whether it wants to enter into a license arrangement for the exploitation of its patents, trademarks, or copyrights. Aside from any compulsory licensing set forth in national law, it is an understanding of all the practitioners involved in licensing around the world that licensing is a voluntary act in which an IP owner opens itself to an interested party to make available part or all of its protected monopoly position for the benefit of its contract partner. It is therefore no surprise that the Block Exemption Regulation on Technology Transfer Agreements (No. 240/96 of January 3, 1996) in its Whereas-Clauses (Whereas-Clause No. 5) talks about licensing agreements as "agreements whereby one undertaking . . . *permits* another undertaking to exploit . . ." (italics added). It is the permission by the IP right owner that is needed to make a licensing deal work.

As discussed earlier, antitrust law is concerned with the content, that is the conditions of such licensing, to avoid a situation whereby an IP right owner enjoying such a monopoly would misuse this position and overstep the acceptable boundaries.

CORRECTION BY EUROPEAN LAW

To look at licensing agreements as purely voluntary understandings between two or more companies is a very traditional approach and a tradition that is present in all of the European member states.

When it came to making available the listing of television programs in the United Kingdom and Ireland, the local courts of the member states had no doubts that using a monopoly granted by an intellectual property right in not making available the use of this right would make perfect business sense. The same happened when the German courts had to decide whether not making available a copyrighted structure of collecting pharmaceutical data that identifies drug sales in Germany was acceptable. In finding copyright protection for this system to collect and identify the data, the courts came, without any further ado, to the conclusion that such a copyright should be enjoyed by its owner without any disturbance.

Such a traditional, if not to say local, approach to licensing might be too short-sighted and the conclusion might be reached too easily, when it comes to evaluating the same behavior under the European antitrust standards (i.e., Article 82 of the HEC Treaty).

A refusal to license may be deemed to be an abuse of a market-dominating practice when judged under the applicable standards of European antitrust law. It would be today almost a case of imprudent business due diligence—for an advisor, a case of negligence—in not going the next step and considering whether such a national solution reached by application of European law might come to a different result. This may require the IP right holder to open up its legally granted monopoly position to anyone who claims to need access to the technology.

H CASE LAW

The Commission has been struggling for years with the concept of abuse of intellectual property rights and the question when such rights may not be exercised or when the position has to be opened to competitors. A quite impressive line of cases has dealt with the principle and the details of such a behavior:

- In *Tetrapack,*[9] the Commission found that a dominant company has responsibility not to reach out for a new technology in an in-licensing situation where it already enjoyed an absolute market domination for its existing technology. Any new entrant into the market will not be able to ever compete with this dominant company if even any new developments are monopolized—may the license be as legal as it ever can be.

- In *Volvo v. Veng*[10] the European Court of Justice found that the mere refusal to grant a license to a registered design as such will not amount to an abuse. Only certain ways of exercising the monopoly position represented in the registered design may lead to such a result.

- In *Magill*[11] the Commission as well as the European Court of Justice for the first time found that a refusal to license could be and was such an abuse, as the companies who wanted to publish a weekly TV guide could not do so because of the exercise of its rights and the refusal to license by the copyright owner. In preventing the introduction of a new product to the market, which new product could only be produced in making use of the copyrighted information, an abuse of a dominant position had occurred.

- In *Ladbroke,*[12] a couple of years later, the Commission rejected the idea that the refusal to make available television pictures of horse races from France in Belgian betting shops amounted to such an abuse of a dominant position. The refusal to grant the license did not foreclose the aspiring licensee to enter the market, as it already had a large share of that market. There was no restriction of competition to be found in the refusal to license.

- In *Bronner*[13] the Commission as well as the European Court of Justice seemed to show the world that it backed the understanding of the courts of the member states and the businesses around Europe that a refusal to open up a protected, genuinely built system cannot be an abuse as such, excluding any other abusive activities. The refusal to also distribute newspapers of a competitor through their own proprietary distribution system was found not to block access to this market, as the competitor could always build up its own distribution network. Again, the exercise of whatever intellectual property rights were available did not as such constitute an abuse of a dominant position. The court held that it would still be necessary to plead the existence of an abuse, to show not only that the refusal of the service comprising home delivery was likely to eliminate competition on the daily newspaper market, but also that the service in itself was indispensable to carry out the business that was desired.

IMS HEALTH CASE: THE COMMISSION'S FINDINGS

It was therefore safe for the German courts to decide that the refusal to license the system for identifying drug sales in Germany by IMS Health, Inc., after access was desired by National Data Corporation (NDC), was the right thing to do. The Commission, however, again took a more European approach to this problem.

In 2000, NDC, a competitor of IMS, complained to the EU Commission that IMS had refused to license to NDC its "1860 brick structure" for reporting German sales data to the pharmaceutical industry. The structure segments Germany into 1,860 sales zones, or bricks, and allows the reporting of sales to be broken down into useful geographical areas, each covering a small group of pharmacies. IMS created the structure, largely based on the official German postal code, in cooperation with the pharmaceutical industry in the 1970s. The structure has since become the recognized standard in industry. NDC's complaint followed a series of decisions by German courts that NDC had infringed IMS's copyright by using the structure. The competitors then asked IMS for a license to use the structure, which IMS refused.

The Commission found that IMS's 1860 brick structure was the industry standard and that the refusal to license it prevented competitors from entering or staying in the pharmaceutical sales data market. IMS had therefore abused its dominant position within the market; in breach of article 82 of the EC Treaty. Having surveyed the pharmaceutical market, the Commission found that the sector was economically dependent on the 1860 brick structure, and it would not be viable for a competitor to use an alternative method.

The Commission therefore granted interim measures, pending its final decision. It ordered IMS to license the use of the structure to its current competitors on nondiscriminatory, commercially reasonable terms. The order requires IMS to agree with each licensee on the royalties payable under the license; in the absence of agreement, royalties will be determined by independent experts using transparent and objective criteria. The Commission said the interim measures were justified because IMS's abuse of its dominant position was likely to cause serious and irreparable damage to NDC. The Commission therefore had to act before making its final decision.

The European Court of First Instance doubted whether this decision (ordering in a rare movement preliminary measures to enforce the evaluation of the European Commission) would prevail and temporarily suspended in an evenly unusual decision the Commission's forcing a licensing arrangement on IMS. In suspending the order of the Commission, the court found that the Commission was wrong to follow the *Magill* decision, as the facts of the two cases seemed to be substantially different. But, even more important, the court opined that the Commission exceeded its powers in ordering a license, an active step, rather than making an order preserving the status quo.

LICENSING IN EUROPE—A DEMAND OF LICENSEE?

The IMS decision raises important issues for any IP right owner, which by the IP right might enjoy not only a legal monopoly but whose rights could be reviewed as an industry standard.

In developing the essential facilities doctrine and granting equal access to essential facilities for all market operators, a refusal of a license under such circumstances will be the risk of the IP rights owner in any given market. A company that is excluded from entering or remaining in a market by lack of access to another company's IP right might consider whether to approach the Commission, irrespective of what this company might have heard on a national level within Europe, as to enforceability of IP rights.

On the other hand, IP owners should consider an appropriate licensing structure to avoid a complaint being made against them. If the right structure is chosen, licensing of technology need not lead to a loss of the position as a market leader.

ENDNOTES

[1] Articles 28 and 30 of the Treaty are also very important but will not be dealt with here. The paper also briefly refers to Article 82, and the relationship between the competition rules and the exhaustion of rights principle, but does not deal with these issues in detail.

[2] Regulation 240/96. (Note: This Regulation and all of the existing and draft legislation referred to in this paper are accessible via the European Commission's Web site (http://europa.eu.int/index-en.htm)).

[3] Minor agreements are defined by the Commission as those in which the market shares of participating undertakings do not exceed in any of the relevant markets where the agreement is made between undertakings operating at the same level of production or marketing ("horizontal agreements"), a threshold of 5%; or where the agreement is made between undertakings operating at different economic levels ("vertical agreements"), a threshold of 10%; or, in the case of a mixed horizontal/vertical agreement, a threshold of 5%. See Commission Notice on Agreements of Minor Importance, OJ C 372, 9 December 1997.

[4] Referred to as "Form A/B."

[5] See Commission Regulation No 3385/94 of 21 December 1994.

[6] Article 8(1).

[7] If they get it wrong, the consequences could be huge: a national court could declare the agreement null and void; and there will be no immunity against fines from the Commission.

[8] The Union of Industrial Employers' Confederations of Europe (UNICE), "Stimulated Creativity and Innovation in Europe," Benchmarking report 2000. UNICE is composed of 35 central industry and employers' federations from 27 European countries, and is the official voice of European Business and Industry vis-à-vis the EU institutions.

[9] OJ 1988 L 272/27.

[10] 1988 ECR 6211.

[11] 1995 ECR 743.

[12] 1997 ECR 812.

[13] 1998 ECR 7791.

ABOUT THE AUTHORS

Prof. Dr. Peter Chrocziel is a partner of Freshfields Bruckhaus-Deringer, a leading international law firm comprising some 2,300 lawyers, resident in the firm's Frankfurt office. He is joint leader of the global IP/IT Practice Group, comprising 170 lawyers in 19 locations worldwide. His clients include major international companies engaged primarily in modern technologies such as information technology, software, and telecommunication. His practice covers all aspects of intellectual property work, including trademark, patent and copyright, antitrust, licensing, and litigation.

Peter Chrocziel was admitted to the German Bar in 1983 and to the New York Supreme Court. He is a professor at the University of Erlangen-Nürnberg, Bavaria, where he teaches trademark, patent, and competition law. He is author of a number of books and articles on intellectual property issues. Presently, he serves as vice president of the Licensing Executives Society International. He holds a Doctor of Laws degree (Dr. iur.) from the University of Munich and an M.C.J. degree from the New York University School of Law. He was a research fellow of the Max-Planck-Institute in Munich, and interned as visiting expert with the European Commission (DG IV).

Peter Chrocziel is included in the Commercial Lawyer's List of Europe's Top 50 lawyers, described as one of Germany's best IT lawyers, having an "exceptional presence," and was also included in the Chambers Global 100 Lawyers. Recommended repeatedly both for intellectual property and information technology by practice area guides, he is labeled as "one of the leaders in the field."

Nigel Jones is a partner in the intellectual property group of Linklaters & Alliance, and chairman of the firm's health care group. He is currently based in the firm's Cologne office. He has a degree in biochemistry and is a qualified English solicitor. His experience and expertise include dealing with licensing, distribution, and other forms of technology transfer agreements, including in relation to competition law; United Kingdom and multijurisdictional patent litigation; IP and regulatory issues in the context of mergers, acquisitions and other commercial transactions; and providing IP advice in relation to the flotation of biotech and other health care bodies. He is a fellow of the Chartered Institute of Arbitrators in the United Kingdom, and, within LES, immediate past chair of LESI's European Committee, and of LES Britain and Ireland's EU Laws Committee.

ABOUT THE AUTHORS (continued)

Thierry Sueur, currently vice president, intellectual property and vice president, European and international affairs, of Air Liquide, graduated as a chemical engineer from CEIPI (Strasbourg Law University) before becoming a European patent attorney. After nine years in private practice, he joined Thomson Multimédia as vice president, intellectual property, in 1984 until 1992. From 1988 to 1992, he was director of the board of RCA licensing and was president and CEO of the GIE Mac Packet (licensing of high-definition TV patents). In addition to his current responsibility at Air Liquide since 1992, Mr. Sueur was president of LES France from 1993 to 1996 and co-chair of the LESI Chemical Committee. From 1996 to 1998, he was treasurer of LES International. Since 1997, he has been chairman of the Intellectual Property Committee of the MEDEF (French Industry) and since 1999, he has been vice chairman of the Patent Working Group of UNICE (Union of Industrial and Employers' Confederation of Europe). Mr. Sueur is currently president of LES International.

17

Challenges of Licensing to and from China and Hong Kong

By Larry W. Evans with a contribution from Chi Shaojie

INTRODUCTION

The purpose of this article is to review in some detail the issues that should be considered by parties involved in licensing intellectual property to and from China and Hong Kong. It should be noted at the outset that there has been only limited licensing from China and that Hong Kong has a totally different legal system and, to some extent, a different negotiation culture from that of China. It is my understanding that Hong Kong's legal system is very similar to the English common-law system and, thus, those who are experienced in U.S. and European licensing will find licensing to and from Hong Kong to be consistent with this experience.

Accordingly, this chapter will concentrate on licensing to China. The different stages encountered in negotiating a license and the particular licensing clauses that should be considered will be discussed. Additionally, the article will address the special considerations one should keep in mind in negotiating with the Chinese and specific negotiation tactics that will be encountered and that have been effective in actual negotiations. Finally, the article examines China's legal framework with respect to technology transfers with some discussion of draft regulations known as Uniform PRC Regulations on Technology Import and Export, which were submitted on September 1, 1999, to China's State Council for ratification and publication.

BACKGROUND

Nearly 30 years ago, even before Dr. Henry Kissinger traveled to China via Pakistan to make arrangements for President Richard Nixon's historic visit to China in late 1972, Standard Oil Company (SOHIO) was approached by one of its Japanese acrylonitrile licensees. The licensee was interested in sublicensing SOHIO's world-famous acrylonitrile technology to China as a critical part of a synthetic fiber complex to be built in the vicinity of Shanghai. At the time, the United States and China had been pursuing more than a decade of chilly nonrelations following the Korean War. After considerable internal discussions, SOHIO decided to apply for an export license from the U.S. Department of

Commerce. Because an export license had not been granted for China since the Korean War, the Commerce Department balked at granting the license. However, when the export license request was brought to the White House, President Nixon personally approved it because he had decided to open the door to China.

In early 1973, negotiations began between SOHIO's Japanese licensee and China National Technical Import Corporation (CNTIC) for a license to construct and operate a plant based on SOHIO's technology. SOHIO was invited at the final stages of the proceedings to negotiate several important provisions of the agreement, including term of secrecy, improvements exchange, capacity, and the currency in which the license fee would be paid. These negotiations were successful, and the Chinese were willing to agree to secrecy and nonuse terms (except as expressly licensed), which limited their continued access to the technology for plants not licensed under the agreement.

Since these initial negotiations, there have been seven additional negotiations to license the technology in its current form to other plants in China. What is important to note from these negotiations is that the Chinese remember their old friends and reward success and positive relationships.

WHY LICENSE IN CHINA?

China offers the most potential growth for business transactions in the world. It is a large country of nearly 8 million square miles, and within China's borders all of the world's 140 industrially useful minerals are found. China has a population of 1.2 billion friendly, educable, and industrious people and has recorded double-digit GNP growth for each of the past 10 years. Moreover, China's private enterprises are growing even faster. Inflation (while somewhat high at present) has largely been controlled. China has essentially an endless supply of coal and, until the early 1990s, it exported oil. Since 1993, China was forced to import oil because of the slow progress in developing its northwest oil fields.

Although China has a socialist, centrally planned economy and its politics are not democratic, China truly has opened its doors to the outside world. Currently, there are three major economic trends in China:

1. The increasing privatization of the economy as part of an overall shift from state planning to market mechanisms
2. The increasing integration of the Chinese economy into the world economy (which includes membership in the WTO)
3. The opening of the Chinese market to consumer-led boom

Chinese policy has always been formulated in simple slogans. When SOHIO's licensee began negotiating with the Chinese in 1973, the ruling slogan was

"Adherence to Leninist/Mao Tse-Tung Thought," which meant that the medium of production and all trade were to be decided by the Communist Party in Beijing as part of the state planning and/or political process. While the Chinese economy was devastated by the Great Leap Forward and the Great Proletariat Cultural Revolution, China's economic revolution began in 1979 with the Party Congress, which adopted Deng Xiao Ping's open-door policy under the slogan of the Four Modernizations. This policy led to the first foreign rush to China in the 1980s, when executives of most U.S. corporations visited China and announced plans to penetrate the market of 1 billion consumers. The chairman of Nike referred to China as a market of 2 billion feet.

Since the mid-1990s, the slogan is "Socialism with Chinese Characteristics." A Beijing economist has described this policy as follows: "We have finally decided to take the capitalist road; we just can't put up the road signs." But even without road signs, some of the characteristics of this new socialism are surprisingly like capitalism. For example, non–state-owned town and village enterprises have rapidly emerged as a growing industrial force in China. In fact, these non–state-owned enterprises account for nearly half of the country's industrial output and more than half of the total industrial employment in China.

Under China's new socialism, the government encourages foreign investments and the importation of foreign technology and does not require foreign manufacturing firms to commit to a specified percentage of exports. As a result, by the end of the century (only 12 years following the advent of the open-door policy), China had approved more than 100,000 foreign investment contracts with a total value in excess of $100 billion. In the early 1990s, China began approving foreign investments in the service industries, and began granting licenses to accounting firms, law firms, insurance companies, and banks so that they could establish operations with China. Foreign exchange adjustment centers (swap centers) were established at about the same time to permit joint ventures that have difficulty obtaining foreign exchange to swap Chinese currency for foreign exchange.

Furthermore, the new socialism has encouraged the privatization of efficient state-sector companies. However, inefficient state-sector companies are still being subsidized by the government because nearly half of the total industrial work force is still employed by these enterprises and there are few employment alternatives. Finally, another feature of socialism with Chinese characteristics has been the rapid growth of stock markets in China.

CONSIDERATION OF CHINA'S POLITICS

If "socialism with Chinese characteristics" is appearing increasingly like capitalism in disguise, "politics with Chinese characteristics" do not even remotely resemble Western democracy. One of the curious aftereffects of the

Tiananmen Square incident, which caused most American companies to back away from China, was that investments from Taiwan (which had been negligible before June of 1989) and Korea increased dramatically. The reason for this significant increase was probably the perception of political stability in China; that is, the Chinese and Koreans consider stability through dictatorial control by the Communist Party as a positive, not a negative.

The Chinese desire for order over chaos indicates that the Chinese, whether the old guard or the younger emerging technocrats, do not plan to liberalize the political structure in China any time soon. Of late, China has begun to select its leadership based on personal merit (i.e., education, experience, and capability), rather than whether they participated in the Long March that took place more than 50 years ago.

PRACTICAL ASPECTS OF LICENSING IN CHINA

In attempting to license technology to China, the licensor is faced with many challenges. China is a long way from the United States (more than 12 time zones), and communicating with the United States is inconvenient, even though telephone and fax service is quite acceptable in China. In addition, China's laws are complicated, and the negotiating style in China is similar to Chairman Mao's concept of guerilla warfare, discussed later.

First, the licensor must develop the project at its own office. Because many negotiations have failed when only one negotiator was sent to China, a team should be put together to complete the licensing transaction. The team must involve the very best people in the company and include a responsible management person as the leader. This person must have credibility within the corporation and must be able to establish credibility with the Chinese. The leader must also be able to make snap decisions in China even in areas that have not been discussed with company management. Furthermore, the leader of the team should have a good general understanding of the technology.

Although the Chinese will supply interpreters for the negotiations, the team should also include an individual with Chinese language skills who understands the technology and the business. This individual should not be identified only as an interpreter, but rather as a member of the negotiating team. This individual should form personal relationships with members of the China team and act as an informal communication link between the two leaders. Furthermore, the team should also include a technical specialist who has a complete understanding of the technology. The Chinese will know about the technology, and it would prove embarrassing if the licensing team did not have a true expert.

The team that is sent to China must be completely prepared for the negotiations. The negotiating team must know (1) all costs involved in implementing the license; (2) its competition; and (3) the company's strengths and weaknesses. The negotiating team should also be prepared to spend an extended period of time in China in order to maintain continuity in the negotiations; the Chinese will extend the effort, and the licensing team should as well.

If a company might be involved in many projects in China, a Beijing office is highly desirable. Additionally, the licensor should not hesitate to use consultants because the presence of any experienced "China hand" on the negotiating team is invaluable.

Before beginning licensing negotiations in China, it is important to ask several questions:

- Who are the negotiators on the Chinese side?
- What are their names, positions, and companies or organizations?
- What is the reporting relationship?
- Are they part of the provincial government or the central government?
- Is the project government-approved?
- Is the project part of the central government's five-year plan, or that of the provincial government?
- Is foreign exchange available, or will you be asked to accept counter-trade?
- Does the project have to be an export-oriented project, or can it be based on domestic sales?
- Who are the customers, and will the project have any competitors in China?
- What will be the size of the plant?
- Are raw materials and other facilities available?

Obtaining the answers to these preliminary questions will make the rest of the negotiations proceed much more smoothly. The Chinese do not want to be surprised, and neither should the negotiation team.

Generally, there are five phases in a typical negotiation in China. First are the introductory seminars. The Chinese want to learn about the technology and form an opinion about the individuals on the negotiating team and their company. Second, the fundamental structure of the project is discussed, and usually a letter of intent is signed. The third phase consists of formal contract negotiations. In this phase, the Chinese usually begin with technical negotiations, including these factors:

- A technical appendix that describes in detail the products or technology licensed
- A description of the technology transfer process

- The terms of the license
- A description of technical documentation with specific delivery dates
- Training programs, if any, that typically limit the number to be trained and specify technical competence and language capabilities
- Any technical assistance programs that are offered during the contract
- Warranties of ownership of the technology
- Personnel issues, such as visas, medical care, housing, training cost, travel, and other related issues

The fourth phase deals with commercial terms, including all necessary legal and commercial provisions. Usually in this stage the licensor is presented a form agreement. It is not only unnecessary but also dangerous for the licensor to agree to the form agreement. The licensor should not depart from its policies regarding the technology. If the technology has been licensed elsewhere (which is almost always the case), it is unfair to the licensor and its other licensees to agree to China's form agreement instead of the licensor's standard agreement. Chinese organizations will understand the licensor's position and adapt to the licensor's agreement so long as it generally complies with the Chinese laws, which are covered later in this chapter.

The final stage of the negotiations concerns price. Price negotiation is the most difficult stage of the entire process. Generally, the Chinese will not make any counterproposal on price until all other issues are resolved. Serious price negotiations are intentionally delayed until the end of the negotiations.

Since the Chinese negotiators simultaneously conduct price negotiations with the licensor's company and its competition, the initial license fee should be priced high enough to allow for significant discounts at critical points, but the fee should not be unrealistic. That is, it is essential that the opening price be defendable (i.e., a discounted cash-flow analysis should show that the licensee will make money even if the licensee pays a license fee at the initial asking price). The negotiating team should have an understanding of its final offer before beginning negotiations. This offer should be at least as high as other licenses in other countries. While license fees should be based on benefit rather than cost, implementing a license in China is more time consuming and costly than licensing in many parts of the world.

During the final stage, the payment schedule should be negotiated first. The time value of money (and the interest) should be included in the bottom price. That is, the price should be expressed as dollars at the time the agreement is executed. When the State Planning Commission (SPC) was responsible for approving all license agreements, it was important early on to determine, if possible, the "budget price" that had been approved by the SPC because this price could only be exceeded by 20 percent without going back for additional approval. Therefore, if the license has to be approved by the SPC, the Chinese should be given an idea of the license fee at a very early stage, ideally before they go to the central government for approval.

With respect to contract guarantee provisions, the licensing guidelines, suggested by China's Ministry of Foreign Economic Relations and Trade (MOFERT), normally require that the technical information supplied by the licensor will be "without mistake and will enable the licensee to manufacture a qualified product simply by using the document."[1] This guarantee should not be made because the licensor ordinarily is not able to control the construction of the plant or the raw materials used in the plant. Rather, the licensor should indicate in the agreement that the technical documents are similar to the documentation used by the licensor in the United States where the licensor produces a product meeting all the specifications in the license agreement. The licensor, however, should not use this requirement as an excuse to minimize control in other aspects of the agreement.

The area of contract guarantees raises other concerns. Many of the Chinese officials whose positions are "on the line" will do their utmost to ensure that every aspect of the license transaction is guaranteed by the licensor. That is, they do not want to accept any responsibility for the success or failure of the plant. If the licensor oversells its technology, it will have a very difficult time fulfilling the guarantees in excess of its typical guarantees in other license agreements. Therefore, the licensor's sales pitch should be realistic, and the guarantee levels in the agreement should be well within the likely performance of the technology on matters of capacity, output, product quality, and so on.

One technique that may be used to satisfy the guarantees is to provide for credit when guarantees are exceeded in certain areas. This credit can then be used against the failure to achieve guarantees in other areas. For example, with respect to the quality of a petrochemical product, 10 to 15 items are usually specified. If the licensor exceeds the guarantee level in 10 of the items but does not reach the guarantee level in the other 5, credits for exceeding the guarantees could more than balance out the liabilities for not achieving guarantee levels in the remaining areas.

One other matter that deserves particular attention with respect to the guarantees is the plant acceptance test or product acceptance test. Depending on the kind of technology being licensed, only one acceptance test should be performed. This test should occur reasonably close to the actual start-up of the plant. For example, with respect to petrochemical plants, it can be specified that a 48-hour test be performed in which the raw materials consumed, capacity, and product quality all meet the necessary guarantees. If this test is performed too soon after the introduction of feeds into the plant, there is a possibility that the licensee may operate the plant in a manner that will affect the guarantee test run. Therefore, it is important to negotiate guarantees that are realistic and incorporate safety factors, since the plant in its earliest operating stages may not operate at its optimum level. During this start-up period, the licensor and licensee should try to develop a good working relationship so that each has trust and confidence in the other. Furthermore, the licensor must assure the licensee's personnel who visit the licensor's facility that, if the plant is operated well, its performance will continue to improve over the life of the license.

In regard to technical assistance (i.e., assistance by foreign engineers and operators in China and training of Chinese engineers and operators in the United States), the Chinese will usually ask for more assistance than the licensor believes is necessary. Thus, the licensor should limit the amount of time that must be spent by personnel in China and the amount of time (expressed in "person days") that the Chinese trainees will spend at the licensor's facilities. The agreement should also specify which party will be paying for this assistance, along with the other costs such as travel and living expenses. Likewise, the agreement should specify the living accommodations and transportation for the foreign engineers while they are in China.

During these negotiations, the Chinese will certainly require specific delivery dates for technical documentation, equipment (if equipment is to be supplied by the licensor), and other items connected with the license. Usually, the Chinese will insist on penalties for the failure to meet the delivery dates. If delivery dates and penalties are specified, the Chinese will have no choice but to enforce the provisions. Therefore, the license should be drafted so that the penalties apply only to the items to be delivered and not to the overall agreement.

In addition, the licensor should make sure that the contract protects it against delays by the Chinese. For example, if a petrochemical plant is not started up for three or four years after delivery of the catalyst, the agreement must provide for retesting the catalyst prior to the start-up of the plant in order to make sure that it is still in acceptable form. Therefore, the licensing team should advise their company to expect and plan for delays on the Chinese side.

With respect to payment provisions, if the license fee is a lump sum rather than a running royalty (as is most usually the case in China), the agreement should specify that the entire lump sum is an irrevocable payment and is not tied to the start-up of the plant. Although this provision may be very difficult to negotiate, it is a desirable goal because the start-up of the plant may be delayed interminably through no fault of the licensor. As a result, the licensor will be denied the time value of the license fee.

Depending on the status of the licensee within the Chinese system, the licensor may try to insist on a letter of credit issued by a U.S. bank with payment made against the tender of noncontrovertible documentation. Alternatively, the licensor may require a letter of credit issued by the Bank of China. There are no hard and fast rules for whether the licensor should insist on a letter of credit, but the licensor should take this matter into consideration before executing a license with the Chinese.

Although the Chinese may agree to running royalties, the choice of a lump sum versus a running royalty is a complex one. Most Chinese negotiators prefer a lump-sum payment because it can be included in the project financing, which may be available from a foreign government bank such as the Japan Ex-Im Bank or the World Bank; and they do not want to have their production and sales records audited, which would be necessary if the agreement specified a running royalty. Likewise, the licensor might prefer a lump-sum payment for the following reasons:

- The money is usually guaranteed.
- Hard currency is available immediately.
- Tax consequences (i.e., running royalties) will almost certainly be regarded as ordinary income.

On the other hand, there are disadvantages to lump-sum agreements. First, they tend to provide unlimited capacity to the licensee unless there are specific provisions in the agreement that provide for additional payments if the licensed capacity is exceeded. Furthermore, the technology transfer regulations (discussed shortly) limit the term during which running royalties can be collected. These regulations set the term at 10 years; however, the Chinese will usually negotiate for a much shorter term.

When license payments are being negotiated, the Chinese will often suggest the possibility of paying for the technology with something other than cash. Usually, Chinese negotiators begin with discussions of payments based on a cash price. However, late in the negotiations, the Chinese will require that the compensation be based on countertrade. Licensors should remember that countertrade is most often handled by third parties who demand a commission. Therefore, the commission must be considered in determining whether the countertrade payment exceeds the bottom-line price.

Other areas that deserve consideration are *force majeure* and arbitration (or dispute resolution). In 1973, it was very difficult to negotiate a *force majeure* because this term literally means "act of God," and China was, by definition, an atheistic country. Today, all Chinese negotiators will probably agree to a *force majeure* clause. The essential elements to cover in this clause are acts of God, natural disasters, imposition of government controls over import and/or export, riots, war, power interruptions, strikes, and all other clauses beyond the reasonable control of the licensor.

With respect to arbitration, China's Foreign Economic Contract Law provides that disputes can be submitted to Chinese or other arbitration bodies. In practice, the

Chinese have agreed to arbitration in Sweden under the rules of the Arbitration Institute of the Stockholm Chamber of Commerce. Because of China's general preference for Stockholm, a large percentage of arbitration in Sweden is based on disputes with respect to China. Although this is probably an acceptable arbitration forum, it seems likely that Swedish arbitrators will tend to favor the Chinese in order to continue to be named as arbitrators in the future. Therefore, licensors should insist on arbitration before other international arbitration bodies or even the American Arbitration Association (AAA). Furthermore, with respect to American licensors, arbitration in China may be preferable to arbitration in Sweden because the U.S. government has influence on the government of China that can be used to support fairness in the arbitration process. Consequently, the arbitration clause must carefully provide for all of the various aspects of arbitration, such as the number of arbitrators, appointing authority, place of arbitration, language of arbitration, governing law, and the qualifications of the arbitrator(s). The arbitration clause should also provide a basis under which the arbitrators will operate.

Even though recent changes have brought Chinese law largely in line with the industrialized world, the confidentiality provisions in the agreement should be drafted carefully. Until recently, trade secret protection in China was only contractual (i.e., there was no trade secret law, and trade secrets were not regarded as protectible property). Today, China's Tech Transfer Regulations provide for confidentiality terms of no longer than 10 years "without special approval of the examination and approval authority." As a practical matter, the status of the licensee and the advanced nature of the licensor's technology will often permit a term longer than 10 years. However, the licensor should be prepared for a very difficult negotiation of this point.

Another area that must be considered is whether the licensee will be permitted to export the product. Although this is a difficult point to negotiate (i.e., the Chinese are reluctant to forgo the right to export), it must be kept in mind at least as a bargaining chip.

An additional point is that a U.S. export license is required from the Commerce Department in order to disclose the technology to the licensee. The Chinese side will often require evidence of this export license as a precondition to the agreement's effectiveness.[2]

SPECIAL CONSIDERATIONS IN NEGOTIATING WITH THE CHINESE

In the 31 short years since China has opened its doors to the West, tremendous strides have been made. The Chinese have progressed from being cautious and relatively inefficient negotiators to respected business partners. Their negotiation style is characterized as having similarities with Chairman Mao's 16-character poetic description of guerrilla warfare:

Enemy advances,
we retreat.
Enemy halts,
we harass.
Enemy tires,
we strike.
Enemy retreats,
we pursue.

Negotiation with the Chinese today retains some of these characteristics, but great strides have been made toward more efficient negotiation. However, many negotiators still leave the table feeling pessimistic about their future partners. China's negotiating style can be described as a blend of the Byzantine and the Evangelical.

Chinese negotiators often frustrate Western businesspeople not accustomed to Chinese tactics. In negotiating with the Chinese, foreign businesspeople must realize that successful business dealings in China depend on personal relationships, known in China as *guanxi.* China's Confucian traditions have established a society that is ruled by man rather than by a strict legal system. Chinese are taught that the law is a tool used by the ruling class to suppress opposing classes and to control the people. As a result, the Chinese are still less trustful of laws than of personal contact.

Chinese negotiators believe it is important to achieve a sincere commitment to work together rather than an airtight legal package. They also believe that business dealings will inevitably involve some troubles that might be impossible to predict and very difficult to solve. As a result, the Chinese try to devise solutions only for problems that are anticipated and to rely on personal relationships to solve all of the other problems. Moreover, any foreign company that licenses technology in China automatically establishes the company as a friend. In China, a friend has a responsibility to assist the Chinese partner in times of difficulty.

To the Chinese, nothing is ever cast in stone. A signed contract merely marks the end of the initial stage of negotiations, which will be followed by more discussions and thus, more compromises and concessions. In fact, the Chinese often push relentlessly for further concessions after an agreement has been concluded. This uniquely Chinese view means that negotiations are an endless process and that a signed contract does not indicate that the deal has been completed. Foreigners are often caught unprepared by frequent Chinese requests to continue negotiations that have supposedly been concluded. This does not imply that the Chinese will not keep their word. On the contrary, the

Chinese can be expected to uphold the bargain and will not try to cancel or refuse to honor the contract without a good reason. However, a foreigner can be assured that the Chinese will continually bring up small matters. By continuing the negotiations in this way, the Chinese are testing whether their foreign counterparts are truly committed to the *relationship* as opposed to the *contract.*

After becoming familiar with the Chinese culture, one often discovers that there is a close link between the negotiating tactics of the Chinese and their traditional values. Indeed, Chinese negotiating tactics can only be understood after realizing the various strategies that have historically been used by Chinese negotiators to lead the other side into doing business the Chinese way.

The Chinese style of negotiating involves at least three distinct stages: a sounding-out stage, a substantive stage in which hard bargaining begins, and a final stage that theoretically concludes with the signing of the contract. During the first stage, the Chinese assess the trustworthiness of the foreign partner. The Chinese will focus on general principles and common goals before moving on to possibly contentious issues. (This could be culturally based because the Chinese try to avoid or postpone confrontation). Foreigners should not consider this stage as only a formality. Rather, it is a time in which fundamental issues are discussed. The Chinese will always remind their foreign partners about these fundamental principles during the hard bargaining phase, and it is helpful if the foreigners also remember the fundamental principles that tend to favor their side during the difficult stages of the negotiations.

During this initial stage of negotiation, the foreign partner should obtain as much information as possible about the Chinese partner and its place within the Chinese hierarchy. The foreigner should also be aware of the possibility of internal conflicts among the parent organizations to whom the Chinese report. It is also important that both corporate and personal relationships be established.

Throughout the course of the negotiations, foreigners should expect that bargaining will extend beyond the negotiating room. Social activities are used not only to cultivate business relationships but also to deliver messages (i.e., use of banquets with higher-ranking officials on the Chinese side to deliver both positive and negative messages). An example of a positive message is praise for the Chinese negotiators, while an example of a negative message is asking the potential licensee to do the impossible by violating a strong company policy.

There is no clear ending of the first negotiation stage and beginning of the second, more substantive stage. Usually, the licensor has no choice but to allow the Chinese to control the pace of the negotiation. When the Chinese negotiator begins to discuss very specific issues, the second stage has begun. During the second stage, there will probably be numerous disputes over the language of the contract clauses. However, there may be an agreement on issues that seemed unsolvable earlier. Although foreigners are more accustomed to solving issues one by one as they arise, the Chinese prefer to make concessions at the end of a negotiation.

Foreigners should be aware of typical Chinese negotiating tactics before attempting a negotiation in China. The following Chinese negotiating strategies are often used:

- *The Chinese will control the location and schedule of the negotiations.* This is done not just to minimize expenses, but also to keep the upper hand. Chinese negotiators sometimes simply try to wait the foreign party out in order to test whether their position is firm.

- *The Chinese will utilize weaknesses observed in the other side's position.* This strategy can also extend to the personality of the foreign negotiator. For example, if the negotiator is susceptible to flattery, the Chinese may lavish the negotiator with praise.

- *The Chinese are known for using shame tactics, such as reminding the Japanese of their country's atrocities in China during the 1930s and 1940s.* Furthermore, if a foreigner makes an unfriendly remark or violates any of the fundamental principles established during the initial negotiation stage, the Chinese will seek to embarrass the foreigner into carrying out the negotiations their way.

- *The Chinese will pit competitors against each other.* It is a favorite Chinese tactic to set competitors against one another in order to start a bidding war. Although the competitors mentioned by the Chinese may be imaginary, they are often real. Therefore, foreign negotiators must understand the competition and its advantages and disadvantages.

- *The Chinese will often feign anger.* Even though public expressions of anger are considered bad manners in China, it is not uncommon for Chinese negotiators to suddenly fly into a rage, pack up their papers, and leave the room. These incidents are usually staged to gain concessions. For example, the writer has experienced the good cop–bad cop routine after such an incident during negotiations in the past.

- *The Chinese are known for rehashing old issues.* This strategy is used to gain additional concessions and may occur at any time—even after the negotiations are officially over. Therefore, foreign negotiators should keep good notes and sign a protocol reviewing the areas of agreement after each negotiation stage.

- *The Chinese will often try to control expectations.* After several months or years of negotiation, the Chinese will often express a strong sense of urgency in order to gain concessions. They will also attempt to renegotiate previously negotiated issues by taking advantage of the foreigner's desire to end the negotiation quickly and return home (e.g., for a holiday).

In light of these tactics, negotiations with the Chinese will be much more effective if these guidelines are followed:

- *Choose the right leader.*   Make sure the leader has status and credibility.
- *Maintain a consistent team.*   Continuity is key to a successful negotiation. The Chinese will exploit discontinuity by misrepresenting previous understandings. Therefore, a member of the foreign team should have the ability to ensure that both sides understand the issues being agreed upon. This individual can further act as a cultural bridge in order to overcome misunderstandings and to promote harmony in the negotiating process.
- *Identify the real decision makers.*   Foreign negotiators should determine who is actually making the decision on the Chinese side. The real authority may often take a low profile during the negotiating process.
- *Stay calm.*   Foreign negotiators should refrain from making gestures of frustration or using abusive language. These are signs of defeat and weakness to the Chinese. Confucian traditions run deep in China. Social or business interactions should be conducted in such a way that nobody ends up backed into a corner and thereby forced to "lose face." Foreign negotiators should practice *restrained steadfastness.*
- *Use litigation only as a last resort.*   Although litigation is often used as the first resort in some countries, a foreign licensor should use litigation in China only if it has no other choice or concern about ending the relationship. The Chinese believe that the settlement of a dispute in the courts or through arbitration is a failure of the relationship.
- *Leave the door open.*   If there is a break in negotiations, both sides should proceed carefully in order to smooth the process. Foreign negotiators should avoid casting blame on Chinese counterparts or describing the negotiations as a failure. Furthermore, foreign negotiators should try to keep bad news from becoming public knowledge unless a deliberate leakage of information is calculated to take advantage of public pressure and help save the negotiations.

Many of the foregoing tactics and observations are applicable generally to all negotiations and not just those with the Chinese. Foreign negotiators should remember that the Chinese begin learning their negotiating style from the time they are able to communicate and thus are generally more adept at negotiation than foreigners. Professor Lucian Pye, a noted China scholar from Harvard University, advises that foreign negotiators in China should be patient, accept prolonged periods of no movement as normal, avoid exaggerated expectations, discount Chinese rhetoric about future prospects, resist the temptation to blame themselves for difficulties, and try to understand Chinese cultural traits.

However, Professor Pye cautions that "foreigners should never believe they can practice Chinese tactics better than the Chinese." As Sun Tzu, China's most admired military strategist, said: "Know yourself, know your enemies; 100 battles, 100 victories."[3]

CHINA'S LEGAL FRAMEWORK

Although China essentially had no legal system as of late 1979, it has created and enacted many laws. Among the new laws adopted in the 1980s are Contract Law, Foreign Contract Law, Joint Venture Law and Implementing Regulations, Joint Venture Tax Law and Implementing Regulations, Regulations Regarding the Registration of Joint Ventures, Foreign Exchange Control Regulations, Regulations Governing Permanent Representative Offices in the PRC, Regulations on Doing Business in the Special Economic Zones, Bankruptcy Law, Import/Export Regulations, Patent Law, Trademark Law, Regulations Governing Arbitration, Insurance Regulations, Advertising Regulations, and two sets of regulations on the Administration of Technology Import Contracts. In the 1990s, Chinese patent law was amended to protect chemical and pharmaceutical compounds, as well as other subject matter. In addition, China enacted a Trade Secrets Law that provides that trade secrets are protectible property.

With respect to technology transfer, three basic laws apply: (1) the Regulations for the Control of Technology Import Contracts, promulgated on May 24, 1985; (2) the Foreign Economic Contract Law, adopted on March 21, 1985; and (3) the Procedures for Examination and Approval of Technology Import Contracts, issued on September 18, 1985. These Transfer Regulations apply to the transfer of patents and technology, technical services, and technology contracts involving joint ventures. Although each of the laws emphasizes different aspects of the technology transfer process, they overlap in certain areas.

In order to enjoy favored treatment under these Transfer Regulations, the technology being licensed must be described as *advanced technology*. The definition of this term was clarified by the Rules for Examining Export and Advanced Enterprises with Foreign Investment, which were issued on January 27, 1987. To qualify as advanced under these rules, the technology should (1) lead to the development of new products; (2) expand exports; (3) substitute imports; or (4) provide products that are in short supply on the domestic market. Therefore, the licensor should convince the Chinese party that the technology is advanced and suitable for the practical Chinese situation.

Furthermore, these Transfer Regulations contain a list of prohibited or restrictive clauses. For example, the licensor cannot require the licensee to accept tie-in conditions that are unrelated to the technology to be imported, including the purchase of unnecessary technology, technical services, raw materials, equipment, or products. The licensor also cannot (1) restrict the licensee from acquiring, from another source, similar competing technology; (2) unreasonably restrict the licensee's sales channels or export markets; or (3) require remuneration for unusable or invalid patents. The regulations further state that "the supplier may not compel the recipient to accept an unreasonable requirement of a restrictive nature."

Although many of the foregoing restrictions are similar to the provisions in Western antitrust laws, some prohibited restrictions may cause difficulty. For example, if the licensor is required to guarantee the performance of the technology, the licensor may be quite reluctant to allow the licensee to purchase materials, parts, and equipment from third parties that might not meet the technical requirements to implement the technology. In the case of a catalytic chemical process, the licensee should be required to purchase (at least for the initial operation) a catalyst from an approved source. If a prohibited restriction is present in the contract, the contract is subject to special approval.

The Transfer Regulations specify the procedures to obtain approval. These procedures deal with the following four aspects of the approval process:

1. The identities of the examination approval authorities
2. The application process
3. The factors considered in examining and approving a contract
4. The effect of approval or disapproval

The regulation, Detailed Rules for Implementing Technology Transfer Contracts by the Ministry of Foreign Economic Relations and Trade (MOFERT), published on January 20, 1988, also provides details for obtaining approval of technology transfer contracts. The Detailed Rules for Implementing Technology Transfer Contracts give MOFERT the primary authority over all technology import contracts, and only MOFERT has the right to print and number the Technology Import Contract Approval Certificates. Depending on the size of the contract, MOFERT might authorize other responsible ministries or administrations to examine and approve the contract. These approval procedures provide that the application must be submitted within 30 days after execution, and the examining authority shall decide whether to approve the contract within 60 days after receiving the application. If no decision has been made after 60 days, the contract will be deemed automatically effective. In addition, these procedures provide that the licensor must defend any infringement lawsuits and must indemnify the license against any costs or damages from such infringement.

The Transfer Regulations also require the licensor to guarantee that the technology is capable of achieving the objectives stipulated in the contract. The statutory liability is provided as a penalty for licensors whose technology fails to achieve the stipulated objectives. As a result, the licensor should be careful in making any guarantee that it is the lawful owner of the technology and that the technology provided is complete (without error), effective, and able to obtain the objectives provided in the contract. Therefore, the technology transfer contract must be carefully drafted to ensure that the scope of the guarantee is limited and clearly defined in order to avoid statutory liability.

With respect to confidentiality, considerable discretion is left to the contracting parties. The Transfer Regulations require the Chinese licensees to keep confidential any part of the technology that is secret and has not been made public in accordance with the terms agreed upon by the parties. Therefore, the licensor may include the scope and period of confidentiality with the licensee in the contract. Although the regulations ordinarily limit the term of secrecy to 10 years, this term can be extended with special approval.

China's Foreign Economic Contract Law is the Chinese version of Western contract law. There are provisions on contract formation, contract breach, the scope of contractual relations between foreign businesses, and Chinese enterprises. It generally creates a positive environment in which the Chinese and foreign parties can negotiate contracts freely. However, a Chinese entity is not allowed to enter into a contract with a foreign party without permission from the Chinese government. This reflects the obvious conflict between free market practice and the state-owned socialist economy.

The Foreign Economic Contract Law also acknowledges that if Chinese law does not have provisions on particular points, the generally accepted international principles apply. It further provides that international or bilateral treaties with China prevail over Chinese domestic law. Clearly, with this law, the Chinese are trying to fulfill their international agreement and treaty obligations.

With respect to dispute settlements, the Chinese prefer negotiation and consider lawsuits abhorrent. However, if negotiation fails, they will agree to arbitration. The Foreign Economic Contract Law provides an institutional infrastructure to facilitate dispute resolution. Article 37 of the Law specifies that "disputes arising over a contract should be settled, if possible, through consultation or mediation by a third party" and "in case the parties concerned are not willing to, or fail to, go through consultation or mediation, they may submit to China's arbitration agency or other arbitration agencies in accordance with the arbitration agreement reached afterward." Article 8 of the Agreement on Trade Relations between the United States and the People's Republic of China states that the Arbitration Rules of the United Nations Commission on International Trade Law (UNCITRAL) may be used. Although the Chinese contend that both Chinese enterprises and foreign contracting parties have equal rights under Chinese law, foreign technology owners should insist on international arbitration and rules, especially in the case of the term arrangements that carry the possibility of a change in the initial parties. In any event, arbitration in Sweden under the rules of the Stockholm Chamber of Commerce is not recommended. Instead, the International Chamber of Commerce (ICC) or the American Arbitration Association should be used.

Although Chinese laws are very detailed and complex, their overall effect is similar to that found in many other countries. American-style license agreements will usually be acceptable to the Chinese provided that the specific restrictions in the Technology Transfer Regulations satisfy a Chinese *rule of reason* analysis. Further, if a licensor desires a longer term than 10 years, the licensor should provide the basis for this longer term and enlist the licensee in a joint effort to convince the approval authorities that the basis is sound.[4]

CHINA'S DRAFT REGULATIONS

As already indicated, China is now formulating Uniform PRC Regulations on Technology Import and Export. A draft regulation was submitted on September 1, 1999, to China's State Council for ratification and publication by the Council. China does not have an antitrust law; the draft regulations are not intended only to prevent monopoly or promote competition. The Ministry of Foreign Trade and Economic Cooperation (MOFTEC) is the ministry responsible for drafting the new regulations, and it apparently intends to retain its role as the supervisor/monitor of the business of international licensing. To do this, it must convince the State Council of the necessity to control, to some extent, the conduct of licensing-in and licensing-out by Chinese entities. As a result, the regulations have retained the old policies on administration of technology transfer, approval, and recording of international technology transfer contracts, capacity to contract, and so on. Despite these vestiges of China's central planning system, the draft regulations appear to represent a step forward with respect to licensing to and from China.

Capacity to Contract

Under the central planning regime, only so-called foreign-trade corporations were permitted to enter into international contracts involving purchase or sale. Deng Xiaoping's open-door policy enlarged the scope of organizations permitted to enter into such contracts; however, limitations remain. MOFTEC administers the international licensing business and decides whether particular organizations can enter into contracts with foreign parties. It is therefore necessary to determine whether a Chinese party is authorized by MOFTEC to sign a license agreement prior to spending time and money in negotiations. It should be noted that, while the validity of a contract signed by a party lacking MOFTEC authorization can be challenged, its validity is decided by a judicial or arbitration body after due consideration of relevant facts. The fact, however, remains that draft regulations do not change this central planning characteristic of China's foreign contract administration. It is expected that this practice will be discontinued in order for China to achieve WTO membership.

Approval and Recordation

As just indicated, international license agreements must be approved by MOFTEC under the current regulations. In 1995, MOFTEC initiated a policy of simply recording normal license agreements (i.e., eliminating the examination and approval steps). After being recorded by MOFTEC, a certificate is issued, and the Chinese licensee may proceed with all formalities for foreign exchange remittance, tax payment, and so on. The draft regulations divide technology into three groups: (1) technology that is prohibited to be imported or exported; (2) technology that is limited with respect to its licensing (in or out); and (3) technology that may be freely licensed. MOFTEC, in consultation with the Ministry of Science and Technology, is expected to publish lists for the first and second groups from time to time. Contracts for technology in the second group must be approved within 15 days (compared to 60 days under the existing regulations), and those in the third group must be recorded within 5 days. The validity of such contracts depends on approval or recordation (i.e., if the procedure is not followed, the contracts may be declared to be unenforceable).

Terms and Conditions

Following is a comparison of how certain terms are treated in the existing regulations versus the draft regulations.

Term of License.   Under the current regulations, the term of a license is generally no longer than 10 years. Special approval is required in order to have a longer term approved. The draft regulations require an explanation by the licensee. It is expected that the authorities will normally respect the parties' agreement.

Confidentiality.   Under the current regulations the confidentiality term shall not exceed 10 years unless special approval is received. The draft regulations provide no such mandatory limit. Also, an undertaking by the licensor with respect to the licensee's confidential information is required.

Improvements.   The current regulations require equality with respect to licensees' and licensors' improvements. The draft regulations are more liberal but still stipulate that the principle of "who makes, who owns" is to be followed.

Use of Licensed Technology after Termination.   Under the current regulation, licensors cannot prohibit licensees from continuing to use the licensed technology after expiration or termination of the license. The draft law is expected to leave this matter to the parties' agreement.

Restrictive Practices.   The current law contains the following nine prohibitions in license agreements:

1. Tie-in clauses
2. Restrictions on a licensee's purchase of raw materials, parts, or components from others
3. Restriction on license improvements
4. Restriction on licensee's sourcing similar technology from others
5. Unequal exchange of improvements
6. Restrictions on quantity, quality, or price of licensed products
7. Restrictions on licensee's distribution or export of licensed products
8. Prohibition on continued use of licensed subject matter after expiration or termination of the license
9. Payment of royalties on unused or expired patents

In the draft regulations, the number of prohibited clauses is reduced to the following six:

1. Tie-in clauses
2. Restrictions on license improvements
3. Restrictions on licensee's sourcing of other technology
4. Payment on unused or expired patents
5. *Unreasonable* restrictions on licensees' purchase of raw materials, parts, or components
6. *Unreasonable* restrictions or export of licensed products

Guarantees/Warranties.   China's fear-of-failure, risk-averse mentality is exhibited in the need for licensors to guarantee performance, legitimacy (ownership of technology by licensor), and noninfringement. Technical annexes detailing specifications of the licensed technology are negotiated and attached to license agreements. Licensors also must guarantee that they are the legitimate owners of the technology and that they will indemnify the licensee against infringement claims by third parties. It is expected that the new regulations will somewhat relax these requirements, but because Chinese licensees are so risk-averse, licensors should anticipate that they will be required to agree to these guarantees and warranties, especially patent indemnification.

It can be said that the draft regulations will certainly represent a step forward as compared to the existing laws. However, there remains a vestige of China's central planning regime. It is believed that, in order for China to realize entry into the World Trade Organization (WTO), it must further improve its regulations on foreign contracts, especially in the areas of capacity to deal with foreign companies and the extent of state intervention and control of foreign contracts. A free market–based modern law on technology transfer will most likely be adopted when (and if) China enters the WTO.

CONCLUSION

Although considerable effort is required to establish a relationship with the Chinese and to negotiate a viable licensing agreement, the time and effort are not wasted. The Chinese will remember and reward good relationships and successful licensing arrangements. The concept of *mutual benefit,* which is so often expressed by the Chinese, is not an idle one. Licensors should always look at a licensing situation with the Chinese from both sides. If a negotiator asks for a concession, the negotiator should ask how he or she would react if a similar concession were requested by the other side. Confucius must have said something about putting oneself in the other person's shoes, but if he didn't, he should have.

ENDNOTES

[1] The MOFERT "licensing guidelines" are unofficial but are followed by Chinese negotiators.

[2] For additional treatment of this topic, see Wang Zhengfa, "Issues Affecting Licensing Technology," *Les Nouvelles* (March 1989), 1; and Chi Shaojie, "PRC View of Technology Transfer," *Les Nouvelles* (September 1986), 124.

[3] For more information about China's unique negotiating style, see Min Chen, "Tricks of the China Trade," *China Business Review* (March–April 1993), 12–16.

[4] For further information concerning China's legal framework regarding licensing, see Ellen R. Eliasoph and Jerome A. Cohen, "China's New Technology Import Regs," *Les Nouvelles* (March 1985), 16; and Meimei Fu and Frank D. Shearin, "Technology Transfer in the PRC," *Les Nouvelles* (March 1988), 32.

ABOUT THE AUTHORS

Larry W. Evans is a consultant in licensing and intellectual property with an office in South Barrington, Illinois. Following his nearly 25 years in intellectual property management and international licensing at BP America and its predecessor, Standard Oil of Ohio (as Chief Patent Counsel and VP of Licensing), Mr. Evans now provides counsel and related services with respect to international licensing and negotiation to companies around the world. Additionally, he serves as an expert witness in litigation involving patent infringement, licensing, contract interpretation, trade secrets, damages, and related matters. He is a past-president of the Licensing Executives Society International and of the Licensing Executives Society US & Canada. In May 2000, Mr. Evans received the Gold Medal of the Licensing Executives Society International, the Society's highest award. Mr. Evans received a bachelor of science degree in chemical engineering from Purdue University and a juris doctorate from the George Washington University School of Law.

Chi Shaojie, attorney at law and patent agent, is a senior advisor of the CCPIT Patent & Trademark Law Office. He is also an arbitrator at the WIPO Arbitration Centre, the China International Economic and Trade Arbitration Commission, and the Beijing Arbitration Commission. He is an international delegate of the Licensing Executives Society International (LESI) and vice chairman of Trademark and Character Licensing Committee of LES International, as well as secretary-general of LES China. Mr. Chi is experienced in litigation and arbitration representation, arbitrating, and licensing. His major fields of legal practice are IP infringement and licensing, Sino-foreign joint venture disputes, and international trade. He has won 90 percent in litigation and arbitration representations. He has arbitrated approximately 70 international and domestic disputes as presiding arbitrator, for 40 percent handlings. He has been invited by the PRC Ministry of Foreign Trade and Economic Cooperation to be a special advisor in Sino-Japanese & Sino-German model licensing contract negotiations. He has also published about 170 articles in Chinese and foreign magazines and newspapers, lectured to many training courses at home and abroad, and is a frequent speaker at international conferences and seminars.

18

Is There a Future for Japan?

By Dennis Unkovic

Japan is a country in permanent and irreversible economic decline.

Adecade ago, the mere suggestion that Japan would soon find itself in a state of economic decline would have been deemed outrageous. Today, however, this statement reflects reality. At the beginning of the twenty-first century, Japan is mired in the most serious and long-running economic slump in its history.

After 60 trips to Japan since the early 1980s, I have come to admire the Japanese people and their country, but the Japan of today is not the same as it was 20 years ago. This chapter will examine the current state of the Japanese economy and its future prospects. My purpose is not to criticize, but rather, to objectively analyze where Japan is today and describe what steps it must take if it expects to reverse its current depressed state. This seriously affects the prospects for future technology transfer and licensing in Japan and elsewhere throughout Asia.

About 10 years ago, at the request of a Japanese publisher, I wrote a book titled *Revisioning Japan: Inside the American Mind*. My publisher gave it a different title, *America in a Great State of Irritation*.[1] The book attempted to explain to Japanese readers why many Americans at the time perceived Japan as such a threat. *Japan bashing* was the label the Japanese invented to refer to those foreigners who were viewed as unduly critical of Japan. My book came out at the same time many observers feared that the Japanese would fulfill Professor Ezra F. Vogel's prediction in his book, *Japan As Number One: Lessons For America*, and dominate the world economy.[2] All that changed rather abruptly during the early 1990s when the "bubble" burst.

In the Japanese language, there are two words—*tatemae* and *honee*—that convey the uniquely Japanese way of communicating. *Tatemae* refers to a statement by someone that is essentially politically correct and nonconfrontational. For example, when you ask someone in Japan what they think about a debatable issue, you normally hear *tatemae*; in other words, the polite, uncontroversial response. The Japanese use *tatemae* because they are not eager to offend. *Honee,* on the other hand, means saying exactly what you think with little or no regard for how it will be received by the listener. For example, if you are getting ready for a party and your spouse says, "You can't wear that outfit!" that is *honee*. This chapter is about the concept of *honee,* and what you can really expect to encounter in Japan.

OVERVIEW OF JAPAN

Most people have heard or read about Japan, but few have ever actually visited there. Japan is quite dissimilar to how it is portrayed in the popular press. Japan's economy, despite its current depressed state, still represents 8 percent of the global economy. When you combine the economic potential of Japan and the United States, they represent more than 30 percent of world productive output and power. Together they far outstrip the European Community, which collectively represents less than 24 percent. That is why Japan's long-term success or failure as an economy and technological innovator will clearly have a far-reaching impact on the rest of the world's economy.

For decades following World War II, Japan emerged as the second most important center for technological innovation (after the United States). Licensing played an important role. Japan at first spent much time learning from U.S. companies about the importance of technological innovation and research. Beginning in the 1970s through the end of the 1980s, Japanese corporations emerged as not just licensees of foreign technologies but also licensors of many of its technologies (such as ceramics and machine-tool fabrication) around the world. This development quickly made Japan both powerful and rich. As a result, Japanese corporations were seen as not just successful in their own right but, in some cases, a serious threat to their U.S. and European competitors. The idea of a powerful corporate Japan was unsettling.

THE BUBBLE PERIOD

Japan really began to take off in the mid-1980s. Through a combination of both good luck and cheap money, the Japanese economy grew at an unprecedented rate. One fundamental reason behind the growth was that a large percentage of the savings of individual Japanese was directly deposited in local savings banks and other financial institutions. These institutions willingly lent those funds to borrowers at extremely low rates. Although this also occurred prior to 1980, it escalated in the 1980s. Japanese financial institutions thus provided unprecedented sums to Japanese corporations, which then massively invested throughout the country and around the world. The stories of Mitsubishi Estate purchasing Rockefeller Center in New York and other Japanese business groups buying up golf courses such as Pebble Beach for astronomical amounts are now legend. During its *Bubble Period* (1985 through early 1990), Japan and its corporations appeared able to do no wrong. As Japanese companies grew and became immensely powerful, many outside observers witnessed a growth in what was perceived as arrogance. The same Japanese business executives who prior to the

1980s would respectfully listen and learn from others were now asserting to the world that the Japanese way was the only way. This set off a round of Japan bashing both in America and Europe.

If you look at the statistics, Japan actually began to emerge as a true power-house much earlier. As early as the time of the Vietnam War, Japan was already a fierce competitor in a number of areas. Landmarks of this are the Japanese automobile export boom of the late 1970s and the emergence of its RAM chips during the 1980s. The key point is that the emerging Japanese industrial sector intentionally kept a low profile, and it was only in the 1980s when those outside of Japan began to recognize it.

Money was lent to Japanese corporations and individuals, who then reinvested the borrowed funds into real estate and the swiftly emerging Japanese equities market. It was like a Ponzi scheme. The speculative excess came tumbling down at the beginning of the 1990s, shocking Japan and frightening others, who foresaw what it would mean.

FOUR MAJOR CHALLENGES FACING JAPAN

After experiencing more than 10 years of recession, there is no hope that Japan can correct its current state of economic malaise without adopting significant changes. It faces four major challenges, each of which needs to be addressed:

1. The banking system must be fixed.
2. Japan's political system must have new leadership.
3. Government must release the economy from central planning.
4. Corporations must restructure to promote excellence.

Challenge One: The Japanese Banking System

The Japanese banking system spun completely out of control during the 1980s. Basically, Japanese banks found themselves flush with cheap capital and massive reserves and thus made unwise loans within Japan and around the world. At a time when international competitor banks were looking to charge 1 percent to 2 percent margin rates on commercial loans to good customers, Japanese banks were essentially giving away loan commitments for as little as 25 basis points to almost anyone who showed up asking for money. This meant that many corporations and wealthy individuals could borrow massive amounts with very little interest or justification. Since the Japanese people have traditionally prized real estate over any other form of wealth, much of the loaned money went into speculative real-estate ventures. Other loans went to individuals and corporations betting on a rapidly rising Japanese stock market.

At one point, Japan's Nikkei stock index rose to around 40,000. Financial institutions were lending money to individuals to buy stock. When the stock appreciated, it would be used by the same borrowers as collateral for new stock purchases. When the bubble burst, the Nikkei dropped 60 percent to 70 percent to its current levels, and has remained in that range for more than 10 years. After the crash, corporate and individual borrowers found it impossible to repay the loans. Even Japanese brokerage houses were betting their own money and their clients' money on speculative investments. The crash fundamentally changed the Japanese psyche.

When all of this came crumbling down in the early 1990s, Japanese banks were faced with the unenviable prospect of holding enormous numbers of non-performing loans on which neither principal nor interest had been paid for more than six months. Japan's Ministry of Finance has estimated that the face value of nonperforming loans left over from the Bubble Period still held by Japanese banks are in the range of $400 billion to $500 billion. In fact, some well-known financial experts outside of Japan have estimated that the actual size of these nonproductive loans is as much as $750 billion to $1 trillion. In any case, the Japanese banking system is still struggling under this enormous burden. However, the political establishment in Japan has been unwilling to take the controversial step of closing insolvent banks or underwriting the debts with tax-payer funds. In fact, Japanese policy in the past has helped exacerbate the problem. For years Japan's Ministry of Finance has pursued a policy of trying to prevent the yen from rising against the U.S. dollar by not cashing in dollars for yen. This practice contributed to the bubble and, in my view, continues to undermine the economic relationship.

To put the size of the Japanese banking crisis into perspective, America's savings and loan crisis during the 1980s was a $200 billion problem. To solve that problem, taxes were raised by the U.S. Congress and assets of insolvent U.S.-based institutions were sold. Even then, it took more than four years to straighten out the financial mess. Since the Japanese economy is approximately one-half the size of the U.S. economy, and if you accept the conservative estimates that Japan's bad loans are in the range of $400 billion to $500 billion, then the problem facing the Japanese banking system today is five to seven times as large as the U.S. savings and loan crisis. If the actual amount of the nonproductive loans is closer to $1 trillion, as some believe, then the size of the problem facing Japan is truly staggering. Although the Japanese government has taken some tentative steps to deal with the problem, there are still large holes in the asset bases of Japanese banks that make the situation highly fragile. Simply put, the Japanese economy can never significantly improve without this problem being solved, and at this point the prospects are dim.

Challenge Two: Japan's Moribund Political System

Japan is not a democracy in the traditional sense. One political party, the Liberal Democratic Party, has controlled the Japanese political system for all but a handful of years since the 1950s. The LDP, as it is known, has had a stranglehold over the political process in Japan. Without effective challenges to the LDP's leadership by other parties for most of the last 50 years, things have changed very little.

Traditional LDP constituencies, whether agrarian or industrial-based, have a long history of giving financial support to the LDP. As a result, there has been very little change, as Japan has been governed by a long line of LDP prime ministers. I believe that if Japan is to significantly restructure itself, it must begin in the political arena. At this point, though, that appears highly unlikely. There is a precedent for Japan to think about. In the mid-nineteenth century, England faced similar problems in its political system, which eventually led to "one-man, one-vote" reforms in 1866. Those reforms are normally opposed by entrenched political interest groups, so firm political leadership is essential.

As this book is going to press, Japan has a new prime minister, Junichiro Koizumi. Koizumi has declared himself a true reformer and has benefited from high public approval ratings in his first months in office. He is trying to reduce the power of the traditional factions within the LDP, which in the past have undercut the ability of his party to make changes. His campaign slogan was *"Change the LDP! Change Japan!"* As a kind of maverick, Koizumi will try to deregulate Japan's economy and initiate needed reforms. It is too early to predict whether he will ultimately succeed, but if he does not, Japan will decline even further.

Challenge Three: The Japanese Economy and Central Planning

Following the devastation of World War II, Japan lacked the financial resources it needed to rebuild its economy and industries across the board. As a result, beginning in the 1950s the Japanese government played a controlling role in deciding where and how the country's economy would grow. This was primarily done through the judicious allocation of financial resources (loans) to certain industries that Japanese bureaucrats in the Ministry of International Trade and Industry (MITI)[3] judged as important to its economy and as a way of generating much-needed hard foreign currencies from exports. Beginning with basic metals and steel through automobiles to electronics and computer hardware, Japan's economy grew steadily throughout the 1980s. Other Japanese industries, such as chemicals, financial services, insurance, and retailing, were protected from foreign competition through informal tariff barriers permitted by the government.

One of my father's favorite expressions was, "Nothing lasts forever; all you can expect is a good run." This can apply to the Japanese model. Although government-dominated central planning worked well for almost 30 years, there was no guarantee it would work forever—and it didn't. The problem with central economic planning is that government bureaucrats, rather than the marketplace, decide where resources will ultimately be allocated. When the Japanese economy came to a grinding halt at the beginning of the 1990s, the government nevertheless still insisted on exercising control. Although there have been some efforts to deregulate the financial industry, Japan still has numerous domestic industries that directly benefit from subsidies and indirect trade barriers that discourage foreign competition.

One thing the Japanese government did in response to the recession was to issue hundreds of billions (U.S. dollar equivalent) in government-backed bonds to build bridges, highways, and other infrastructure projects to restart the economy. Public-funded construction was seen as a panacea for Japan's economic ills. This massive building incentive plan simply did not work. There were multiple reasons for this. Some were low-priority agricultural projects and were only authorized as a form of reward to party loyalists. Others were fantastically expensive because of the high cost of real-estate acquisition. In the end, Japan is suffering under an enormous debt, and its economy remains very weak.

Challenge Four: Corporate Japan

If you looked at the obvious success of Japan's corporations during the 1980s, many public and private observers believed that the Japanese corporate model would dominate the world economy for generations. However, most Japanese corporations, while once strong, have failed to adapt to the new world economy. The hierarchical management structure in most Japanese companies has changed very little over the last 15 years. It was the opposite in the United States. American companies, which were badly hurt by Japanese competition during the 1980s, forced themselves to restructure as a matter of survival. Almost across the board, U.S. corporations instituted programs to limit unnecessary levels of corporate management, downsize wherever possible, and find new markets both domestically and internationally.

Japanese multinational corporations were far less adept at remaking themselves in the 1990s. Although some were highly successful (such as Toyota Motor Corporation and Sony), most have refused to make the difficult decisions necessary to adapt. Restructuring goes beyond downsizing the number of workers. The kind of incentive-based compensation and authority that is now in most American corporations is absent in Japan. Unfortunately, in most Japanese corporations how old you are is still more important than your level of competence and experience. This acts as a direct disincentive to many bright young Japanese workers who would like to rise through the corporate ranks. Realizing that they might be 45 years old before they have any real authority or influence, younger Japanese increasingly elect to pursue other paths. Ten years ago it was difficult for a European or American company doing business in Japan to recruit top Japanese talent, but that is no longer true. Many ambitious Japanese workers are more interested in working for American or European models where promotion and advancement in one's career is dependent more on personal ability than longevity.

Another factor is the *keiretsu* system, which has dominated Japan for decades. Essentially, the term *keiretsu* refers to industrial groups that are composed of an interlocking corporate directorate of manufacturing, trading, and financial resources. There are about two dozen major *keiretsu* groups today that collectively control more than half of Japan's economy. Without a doubt, over the last 20 years the system has begun to break down, so it is no longer true that member companies within one *keiretsu* find it impossible to deal with companies outside their group. Nevertheless, the *keiretsu* system still exists and remains a barrier to effective restructuring for corporate Japan.

The basic problem is that while a limited number of major Japanese corporations have successfully restructured and become more effective competitors, the rest tend to be relatively backward. They are protected within the Japanese economy and are becoming increasingly noncompetitive multinationals. Over time, this weakens the long-term viability of all of Japan.

THE IMPACT ON LICENSING IN JAPAN

Since it appears unlikely that Japan's economy, at least in the short run, will make a rapid or meaningful rebound from its current levels, it is important to look at what this means for those interested in technology and licensing with the Japanese and throughout Asia. I see five basic trends:

1. A short-term licensing upswing
2. Lack of entrepreneurs
3. Increased venture capital
4. Less reliance on Japanese multinational corporations
5. Avoidance of Japanese markets

Trend One: A Short-Term Upswing in Licensing

Licensing and technological innovation are like the tides; they periodically rise and fall. Beginning in the mid-1980s, Japan emerged as a significant licensor of its own home-grown technologies in a broad variety of fields. At that point it appeared that

Japan would continue to grow in importance as a licensor and would require less technologies from outside its borders. The 1990s significantly altered the equation. Very few companies in Japan during the last decade grew at all or had healthy balance sheets. As a result, research and development suffered.

For the first time, companies in Japan are being faced with the prospect of emerging international competition within Japan's borders. I have recently observed a kind of desperation among Japanese companies that have finally woken up to the fact that they need to change but are not quite sure how to do it. One potential quick fix is for a company to acquire a technology by way of a license and incorporate it into its activities. I have seen a growing interest among Japanese companies seeking to license any type of technology. U.S. or European companies with technologies that they feel would be interesting to a potential Japanese licensee would be well advised to explore the prospects for licensing opportunities in Japan. Whether this trend will continue beyond the next two years is unclear.

Since the domestic Japanese economy is not growing, its long-term prospects for licensing are poor unless the licensed technologies are incorporated as part of a product or service sold in international markets. Since most sophisticated licensors have their own international networks, the depressed Japanese economy suggests that over time the licensing prospects within Japan should decline rather than rise. This may come as a shocking observation to those who have historically viewed Japan as a formidable economic competitor, but it is a reflection of reality.

Trend Two: The Missing Japanese Entrepreneurial Class

Within a year or two after the bubble burst, bureaucrats in MITI (now METI) and other parts of the Japanese government began to recognize that the economy needed corporations different from the traditional vertically integrated Japanese model. It is a fact of life that you cannot always license the technologies you most want or need. Japanese central government and prefectural officials decided to pursue an active strategy to incentivize and foster the growth of entrepreneurship in Japan. As a result, from the mountains of Hokkaido in the north to Kyushu and Okinawa in the south, government-funded and sponsored high-technology incubators popped up like cherry blossoms in the spring. Usually housed in gleaming new buildings, some incubators focused their recruiting efforts on particular industrial fields or sectors (such as robotics or software), while others catered toward more general populations of technology entrepreneurs. I have personally visited a half dozen of these facilities throughout Japan. Unfortunately, few of these incubators have met with success. The Japanese made the mistake of focusing on building impressive physical facilities as opposed to developing the human systems that help to nurture new companies.

Such systems are at the heart of successful incubation programs in the United States and elsewhere.

After a decade of big spending and little success on incubator projects, most of the major research and development that does take place in Japan emerges from the larger traditional corporations. Although Japanese multinationals have had some success at R & D, the type of growth generated by licensing and innovation in America has in large part come from small and emerging companies. This poses a structural problem to Japan in the long run that will be difficult to reverse. There are insufficient new technologies being developed in Japan at this time. This limits the prospects for maintaining Japan's status as an important licensor of emerging technologies. If this trend continues, it will have serious consequences.

Trend Three: Venture Capital in Japan

Much has been written in the Japanese press about the exciting venture capital industry supposedly developing in Japan. Frankly, most of these published reports are more form than substance. Japan has not yet been successful in developing an indigenous venture capital class capable of identifying and funding new and emerging technologies. Those venture capital activities that have met with some success have primarily been the result of foreign money coming into Japan seeking opportunities.

Without question, the Japanese economy will be forced to open itself to outside influences more in the future. I am working now with a number of companies seeking opportunities to invest and/or acquire existing Japanese companies. The continued deflation in Japan makes investments from abroad into selected industries much more attractive now than at any time during the last three decades. This trend toward acquisition in certain industries, including financial services and insurance, suggests that over the long run this will be a top priority for foreigners, while licensing into Japan will hold a lower priority. Licensing may later occur between an acquired entity in Japan and its parent, but the major focus appears to be in that direction rather than licensing.

Trend Four: The Japanese Multinational Corporation as a Partner

There was a time when it was difficult to successfully conduct business in Japan without first having forged some kind of partnership or license arrangement with a leading Japanese multinational corporation (MNC). The past dominance of Japanese MNCs within their market mandated such a relationship. In addition, Japanese companies were traditionally so strong throughout Asia that U.S. companies thought they needed a Japanese partner if they wanted to be successful.

The fact is that most Japanese corporations are less powerful and influential in the twenty-first century than they were just a few years ago. There are obviously exceptions. Toyota, for example, during fiscal year 2000, had a consolidated pre-tax profit that grew 22 percent over the previous year to 972.2 billion yen. Toyota is benefiting from both a demand for its new car models and, more importantly in my view, its continual rationalization measures. Despite its success, Toyota has still undertaken significant cost cutting under its current president, Fujio Cho, in order to heighten competitiveness. Toyota's efforts have paid off. According to published reports, Cho's streamlining efforts at Toyota have added almost 200 billion yen to its overall profit on a consolidated basis. Obviously, the effects of cost cutting have genuinely helped Toyota, but it is truly unfortunate that other Japanese companies have not followed this lead. As a result, I see many Japanese multinationals becoming increasingly noncompetitive on an international basis. This makes them less desirable as either licensing partners or business partners.

Ironically, it was the shock of Japanese competition during the 1980s that forced U.S. companies to restructure and improve the way they do business. However, the same pressures placed on Japanese companies during the 1990s have not resulted in the same reaction. Unless this trend changes, it bodes poorly for the future prospects of the competitiveness of Japan's corporations and its economy.

Trend Five: The Bypassing Phenomenon

When I first started to do business in Asia more than 25 years ago, there was one clear preference: Any company looking to target the Asian market would go to Japan first. Japan was the center and the heart of Asia. Once established there, foreign companies could look to Korea, China, or Southeast Asia as they continued to expand. This occurred even though the Japanese made it difficult to invest and do business in Japan through informal trade barriers. During the Bubble Period, Japanese companies openly rebuffed efforts by European and American companies to do business in Japan.

In my view, the most serious trend influencing Japan's future is the concept of *bypassing*. Simply put, when foreign companies seek to do business in Asia, they no longer go to Japan first. China appears to have overtaken Japan as the most favored destination for businesses seeking Asian markets. While Japan remains a leading financial center in Asia, its influence both economically and politically appears on the decline.

The truth is that the Japanese made it so difficult to do business there over such a long period that foreign companies are simply heading elsewhere. The People's Republic of China recognized this years ago and has artfully played itself off against Japan both formally and informally. Japan ought to be terrified of the bypassing phenomenon. Opening up its markets to more foreign business and competition is not simply a question of economic growth; it is a key to survival. The bypassing phenomenon, if it continues, guarantees that leading technologies emerging in both the United States and Europe are more likely to go to China or other parts of Asia instead of Japan.

KOREAN COUNTERPART

The Japanese experience is not unique. During the 1950s, one country in Asia that found itself in even more desperate straits than Japan was South Korea. Following the end of the inconclusive Korean War, South Korea appeared to have no future. Burdened with a devastated national infrastructure, few natural resources, and a large agrarian sector, few thought Korea would ever be anything but a third-world backwater. Then, the people of South Korea surprised everyone, including perhaps themselves.

In just two generations, South Korea posted a remarkably sustained record of economic growth. To put it into perspective, the average per capita income for a Korean was U.S. $75 in 1953, and in 2000 grew to U.S. $9,628. Korea achieved this enviable period of growth by adapting an economic model similar to the one used in Japan. The theory was to combine a high level of individual savings that were loaned to private companies with heavy direct and indirect subsidization of key selected Korean industries by the central government. The form originally chosen by the Koreans was the family-owned holding companies called *chaebols*. Later, the *chaebols* evolved into more public entities.

Beginning with shipbuilding and followed by steel, automobiles, and electronics, targeted industries in South Korea emerged as world-class competitors and strong exporters. Early on, Koreans understood the need to aggressively seek out foreign licensed technologies (even some of the computer chip technologies now in widespread use in South Korea were licensed out of Japan). By nature, the Koreans are aggressive entrepreneurs. They entered into the nuclear power industry with licensed technologies from Westinghouse Electric and other industries as the lead contractors for major projects, such as constructing the twin Petronis Towers in Kuala Lumpur (currently the world's tallest buildings).

The Asian financial crisis of 1997 that first emerged in Thailand derailed South Korea's growth. In 1998, Asia's economic downturn hit Korea particularly hard and forced it to borrow more than $60 billion in funds from the International Monetary Fund (IMF) in order to remain solvent. Since then, South Korea has made significant strides in turning around a weak economy, despite ongoing weaknesses through Asia.

What I find most remarkable about the Koreans is their fierce individual drive and flexibility. Despite being surrounded by China, Mongolia, and Manchuria, Korea for centuries[4] has been able to maintain peace through excellent diplomacy and negotiations with its much more powerful neighbors.

South Korea has done much to embrace technology on a nationwide basis—some would argue even more than Japan. South Korea currently has the highest Internet supply rate in the world. It is also the only country to have installed a high-speed communications net in all elementary, middle, and high schools. This reflects the fact that Koreans appear willing to share their knowledge and information with others.

There is another development worth nothing. The Korean *chaebols* have had serious economic problems recently; some, such as Daewoo, even faced the prospect of bankruptcy. This has made the need for restructuring a higher priority, and they appear to have begun real efforts at restructuring in order to reverse the trend. Just look at how rapidly Samsung has achieved a dominant position in the worldwide cellular telephone market. Although it is by no means clear what will happen in South Korea in the future, the innate flexibility of Koreans suggests that South Korea is more likely to undertake serious steps toward the necessary restructuring of its key industries and economy before Japan.

CONCLUSION

Japan is and will remain a country with enormous economic resources and potential. Unfortunately, since its bubble burst more than a decade ago, Japan has seen itself decline, but has done little to reverse the trend. This has affected Japan's economy and its political and economic influence throughout Asia. As both a licensor and a licensee of technologies, Japanese corporations must take aggressive steps to reverse this current trend; otherwise, Japan in the twenty-first century will indeed find itself in permanent and irreversible economic decline.

ENDNOTES

[1] This book was published in Japanese by Diamond, Inc. (Tokyo, 1990). It is out of print now, but copies may be found in libraries in Japan (and possibly other countries). The book was not translated into any other language for publication.

[2] Ezra F. Vogel, *Japan As Number One: Lessons for America* (Bridgewater, NJ: Replica Books, 2001).

[3] MITI is now known as the Ministry of Economy, Trade and Industry (METI).

[4] Except for 35 years of Japanese rule (1910 through 1945).

ABOUT THE AUTHOR

Dennis Unkovic is a partner with Meyer, Unkovic & Scott, LLP in Pittsburgh, Pennsylvania. His practice primarily focuses on international business deals including acquisitions, divestitures, strategic alliances, and joint ventures. Prior to joining Meyer, Unkovic & Scott, he served in Washington, D.C., as the legislative director for Hugh D. Scott, former U.S. Senate minority leader. He simultaneously served as assistant counsel to the Senate Judiciary Subcommittee on Patents, Trademarks and Copyrights. Mr. Unkovic is frequently invited to speak to government, business, trade association, and academic leaders on issues such as international negotiations, mergers and acquisitions, strategic alliances, technology transfer, intellectual property, venture capital, and countertrade. He has authored four books and more than 100 articles for domestic and international publications. He received his B.A. with distinction from the University of Virginia and his J.D. from the University of Pittsburgh School of Law.

19

Licensing in Russia:
Opportunities and Pitfalls

'ia Karpova

INTRODUCTION

1omy is marked by globalization, and the transfer of science,
1d intellectual property have emerged as key ingredients in this
1y. At the same time, intellectual property transfer and man-
emerged as an independent discipline. A viable patent system,
based on commonly held principles, underpins and facilitates this growing
business of technology transfer and establishes prerequisites for participating
in the economic benefits accruing thereto. As Russia's economy shifts toward
capitalism, many international businesses exhibit increased interest in partnerships with Russian firms. To be a good partner, Russia must improve its
system of legal protection for intellectual property as well as transferring
technology. The purpose of this chapter is to describe the changing landscape
of Russia's intellectual property system. We begin with a brief discussion of
the historic context.

INTELLECTUAL PROPERTY YESTERDAY

The Former Soviet Union (FSU) possessed vast scientific and engineering
potential. The Soviet Union and the United States shared second place in the
number of registered inventions annually in the world; Japan registered
the largest number of inventions. Before 1991, the number of Soviet inventions exceeded 1.5 million.[1] Each year about 80,000 inventions were registered in the FSU, 64 percent of which were invented in Russia. Russia also
gave more than 80 percent of other industrial property subject matters.
Therefore, the available data can be interpreted as representative of Russia. An
analysis of the data available for the years 1985–1991 yields similar results
(see Exhibit 19.1). Clearly this constitutes a powerful basis for technology
transfer activity that could yield economic benefits for Russia today.

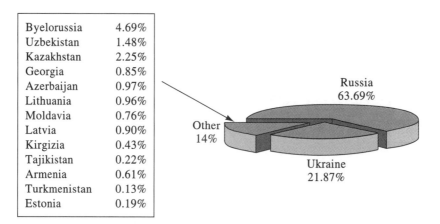

Byelorussia	4.69%
Uzbekistan	1.48%
Kazakhstan	2.25%
Georgia	0.85%
Azerbaijan	0.97%
Lithuania	0.96%
Moldavia	0.76%
Latvia	0.90%
Kirgizia	0.43%
Tajikistan	0.22%
Armenia	0.61%
Turkmenistan	0.13%
Estonia	0.19%

EXHIBIT 19.1   Registered Inventions in Former Soviet Republics (in Years 1990–1991)

Intellectual Property Organization

Russia adopted a patent law in 1812; the law was annulled in 1919. The legislation enacted thereafter remained intact until 1991, when the Soviet Union was dissolved. From 1919 to 1991 only foreigners could obtain exclusive rights to an invention. The state owned most inventions registered and receiving an Inventor's Certificate. An *Inventor's Certificate* recognizes the individual inventor's authorship but provides the state with the right to practice the invention. Inventors might receive a modest remuneration from their employer.

In addition, anyone could use the invention without the inventor's permission. Likewise, the Inventor's Certificate could not be sold or licensed. This situation for intellectual property protection and the rights to implement the technology was the result of the FSU policy that new technical solutions did not belong to anyone in particular. This view causes great difficulty for those wishing to transfer technology to or from Russia today, as enterprises believe they can use (and profit from) other persons' inventions without permission or payment. The situation has been exacerbated by the speed with which the state and its business infrastructure were privatized. The structure of the state changed rapidly, and without an opportunity for the citizens to learn the principles and practices of capitalism.

Inventions.   The largest number of domestic inventions registered during 1985 to 1991 are in the following fields[2] (the sections are given according to the International Patent Classification (IPC)):

- Machine building, mechanical processing of materials (Section B)
- Chemistry (Section C)
- Energetics (Section H)

- Aerospace research (Section G)
- Arms (Section F)

Foreign inventors sought protection for their inventions in

- Chemistry (Section C)
- Technology processes (Section B)
- Consumer goods (Section A)
- Arms (Section F)

In 1991, 52 countries availed themselves of patent protection in the FSU; leading industrial country firms owned 79.8 percent of the foreign patents; Eastern European firms owned 19.8 percent of the patents; and developing country firms owned 0.6 percent of the patents. In 1991, of the industrialized countries Germany held the most patents (1,643), the United States held just over 1,080, Japan held 803 patents, and France held 782.[3] The numbers of patents owned by foreign firms drops off rapidly thereafter.

Industrial Designs.   Design patent filings followed a similar pattern, though foreign firms did not hold more than 1 percent of FSU registrations. At the end of 1991, firms from 28 countries protected 281 industrial designs.[4]

Trademarks.   The pattern for trademark protection is entirely different. A sharp increase in trademark registration occurred between 1989 and 1991—particularly by foreign firms. About 60 percent of all trademarks belonged to foreign firms from the 64 countries of the world. In 1991 alone, nearly 8,000 trademarks of foreign firms were registered. Most of them originated from Germany (1,796), France (1,357), the United States (917), and Italy (885). By the end of 1991 in the FSU the total number of valid trademarks (including domestic) neared 100,000.[5]

Commercializing Intellectual Property

Before 1991, there was no basis for domestic licensing. The state controlled all aspects of patenting and licensing abroad and bore all the costs related to it.

The Chamber of Commerce of the USSR was responsible for foreign patenting of Soviet inventions. And international license trade was carried out by the state organization *Licensintorg*. The beginning of the USSR participation in international license trade may be referred to 1962.

Exports.   The FSU began active exporting technologies in 1976 and had entered into about 5,000 licenses by 1992. Between 1976 and 1990 (see Exhibit 19.2) licenses were sold to 69 countries of the world, with the greatest

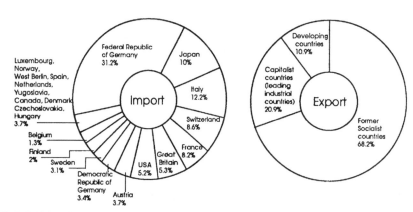

EXHIBIT 19.2   Geographic Structure of Soviet Licensing Export and Import, 1976–1990

percentage of agreements written with former socialist countries (Bulgaria, Czechoslovakia, German Democratic Republic, and Hungary). About 21 percent of licenses were sold to firms in 23 capitalist countries (e.g., Finland, Japan, Germany, Italy, the United States).[6] The number of licenses with capitalist and developing countries was growing. The distribution across industries is shown in Exhibit 19.3. The largest license suppliers to the world market were metallurgy, gas industry, power engineering, instrument-making, heavy machinery contruction, oil-extraction, geological prospecting, and medicine.

Imports.   Licenses with the Democratic Republic of Germany, Czechoslovakia, Hungary, and Yugoslavia make up about 6 percent of imported technology.

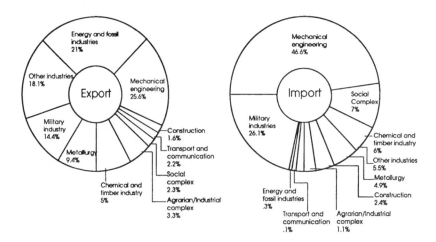

EXHIBIT 19.3   Industrial Structure of the Soviet Licensing Export and Import, 1976–1990

Ninety-four percent of imported technology results from licenses with 20 countries, with Germany, Italy, Japan, Switzerland, and France collectively representing 70 percent of the licenses. With respect to industry distribution, Exhibit 19.3 illustrates that almost 47 percent of licenses focused on machine building, with other sectors significantly smaller. These factors represent the past. Today all of this has changed.

INTELLECTUAL PROPERTY TODAY

The dissolution of the USSR and the changing economic order resulted in the following:

- Russia is an independent state—one of several participating in a Commonwealth.
- A free-market economy is emerging.
- New kinds of property (including private property) have appeared.
- About 150 political parties replace the single party.
- The legislative foundation of the nation is changing.
- Foreign firms can invest in Russia.

On July 4, 1991, the Law on Foreign Investments in the RSFSR provided that foreign firms/organizations could invest in Russia. The foreign investments were defined as "all types of material and intellectual values invested by foreign investors in objects of business and other kinds of activities for the purpose of gaining profit (income)" (Article 2). Article 31 of the law states that the current legislation protects foreign investments based on intellectual property. Improving the Russian system to protect and commercialize intellectual property comprises an important component of building a new economy and improving the nation's relationship with other nations.

The Russian Agency for Patents and Trademarks (Rospatent)

The Russian Agency for Patents and Trademarks (Rospatent) was established in 1992. The organization—a federal, executive body—is authorized to grant, register, and maintain the rights to inventions, utility models, industrial designs, trademarks, service marks, appellation of origin, computer programs, databases, and masks (i.e., topographies of integrated circuits). Rospatent combined the functions of the State Patent Office and the agency providing protection for software-related technology. The organization holds the power to implement policies to protect industrial property rights, computer programs, databases, and topographies of integrated circuits to strengthen intellectual property legislative and statutory foundations, to improve the climate for commercialization, and to implement international policies related to commercialization. In addition, in April 1999 the organization was empowered to improve legislation, international cooperation, and interaction with public organizations in the field of copyrights and related rights.[7]

Rospatent is broken down into several bodies:

- *A Central Office.* This office formulates intellectual property policies in cooperation with other government bodies, manages financial aspects of the intellectual property system, registers licenses, certifies and registers patent attorneys, and responds to questions about the intellectual property system.
- *The Federal Institute of Industrial Property.* This body accepts and examines applications, registers titles, publishes data, provides industrial property protection, and solves specific legal and methodological problems.
- *The Board of Appeals.* This board examines objections to the examiner's decisions and the award of registration; if dissatisfied with the Board of Appeals decision, an applicant can appeal to the PRO Patent Court.
- *The Higher Patent Chamber.* This body examines appeals, applicant statements and requests, ownership, and rights of third parties.

The State Anti-Monopoly Committee monitors businesses' compliance with the new legislation. The committee's activities are founded on the Law on Competition and Limitation of Monopoly Activities on the Markets. Article 10 of this law bans the sale of goods produced in violation of someone's intellectual property rights and prohibits misleading buyers about the source and manufacturer of goods.

New Intellectual Property Legislation

Between 1992 and 1993 the government passed a series of new laws related to intellectual property designed to protect property of individuals (i.e., private property). Patents and certificates of equal jurisdiction can be awarded to individuals, who can then commercialize them in a private-enterprise fashion. For those interested in technology transfer to or from Russia, the most important of these laws are described in the following sections.

Patent Law of Russian Federation No. 3517-1 (September 23, 1992). This legislation describes the structure of legal protection for industrial property. In particular, it permits postponement of invention examination. It also regulates the relations that occur with the development, legal protection, and use of the inventions, utility models (UM), and industrial design (ID).

To qualify as patentable, an invention must be

- New (i.e., not known from the prior art, which includes any information that is generally available in the world before the priority date of invention)
- Not obvious (i.e., does not follow obviously, for an expert, from the prior art)
- Applicable in industry, agriculture, public health, and in other fields of activity

The patent subject matter may be a device, a method, a substance, a strain of microorganism, cultures of plant/animal cells, or an improvement of any one of these. Scientific theories, mathematical methods, and methods for organization and management provide examples of nonpatentable items. Invention is protected by a patent, which provides protection for 20 years.

Utility models and designs are defined in the law. A *utility model* is a structural embodiment of a means of production or consumer goods. The *industrial design* refers to the outer appearance of an object or its artistic/structural embodiment. Utility model can be protected by a certificate for five years, while industrial design is protected by a patent for 10 years.

A national, who created an invention, is recognized as an inventor. The inventor's rights are inalienable personal rights that are protected permanently. The patentee holds exclusive rights to use an invention, and the rights may be retained by the inventor or assigned to any of the following:

- A national or legal entity specified by the inventor
- The inventor's heir
- The inventor's employer, when there is an applicable employment agreement

A patent application must be filed with the Russian Patent Office. National and stateless persons living outside Russia, as well as foreign legal entities, must file using the services of a Russian patent attorney who is registered by the Russian State Patent Office (RPO) or Rospatent. Nationals and foreign organizations have equal rights in the patent system.

Priority in the patent system is established by the filing date. Alternatively, priority can be established using a filing date in a country belonging to the Paris Convention if the Russian application is filed within 12 months from the foreign filing date (the time is six months for an ID patent). Provisional applications are effective for three years from the date of publication. To obtain full patent protection, the application must move to examination within the three years (see Exhibit 19.4 for the Organization of Legal Protection of Industrial Property in Russia).

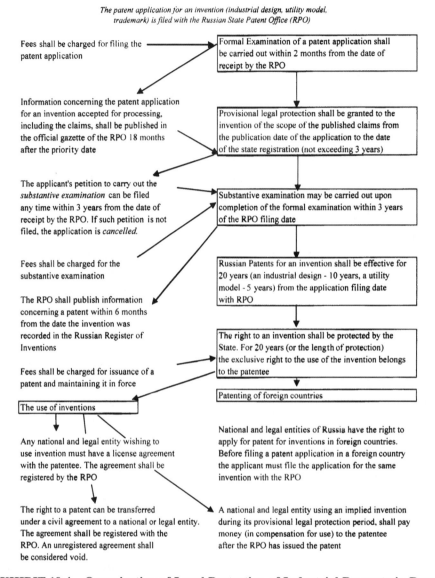

The patent application for an invention (industrial design, utility model, trademark) is filed with the Russian State Patent Office (RPO)

Fees shall be charged for filing the patent application

Formal Examination of a patent application shall be carried out within 2 months from the date of receipt by the RPO

Information concerning the patent application for an invention accepted for processing, including the claims, shall be published in the official gazette of the RPO 18 months after the priority date

Provisional legal protection shall be granted to the invention of the scope of the published claims from the publication date of the application to the date of the state registration (not exceeding 3 years)

The applicant's petition to carry out the *substantive examination* can be filed any time within 3 years from the date of receipt by the RPO. If such petition is not filed, the application is *cancelled*.

Substantive examination may be carried out upon completion of the formal examination within 3 years of the RPO filing date

Fees shall be charged for the substantive examination

Russian Patents for an invention shall be effective for 20 years (an industrial design - 10 years, a utility model - 5 years) from the application filing date with RPO

The RPO shall publish information concerning a patent within 6 months from the date the invention was recorded in the Russian Register of Inventions

The right to an invention shall be protected by the State. For 20 years (or the length of protection) the exclusive right to the use of the invention belongs to the patentee

Fees shall be charged for issuance of a patent and maintaining it in force

Patenting of foreign countries

The use of inventions

Any national and legal entity wishing to use invention must have a license agreement with the patentee. The agreement shall be registered by the RPO

National and legal entities of Russia have the right to apply for patent for inventions in foreign countries. Before filing a patent application in a foreign country the applicant must file the application for the same invention with the RPO

The right to a patent can be transferred under a civil agreement to a national or legal entity. The agreement shall be registered with the RPO. An unregistered agreement shall be considered void.

A national and legal entity using an implied invention during its provisional legal protection period, shall pay money (in compensation for use) to the patentee after the RPO has issued the patent

EXHIBIT 19.4   Organization of Legal Protection of Industrial Property in Russia

The Law of the Russian Federation on Trademarks, Service Marks and Appelations of Origin No. 3520-1 (September 23, 1992).   Under this law, a trademark or service mark is awarded to distinguish manufactured goods and services of one organization from those of another. A private owner or juridicial person can apply for a mark; when awarded, the applicant receives a certificate. Certification is effective for 10 years and may be renewed every 10 years. A certificate of appellation or origin is granted only once and lasts forever.

Rules on Recognition of Trademark as Well-Known Mark in the Russian Federation (effective in 2000). These rules were promulgated to harmonize Russian practices with the Joint Recommendations Concerning Protection of Well-Known Marks adopted by the General Assembly of the Paris Union on Protection of Industrial Property and the General Assembly of the World Intellectual Property Organization in September 1999. The rules characterize a well-known mark as (1) used intensively, (2) maintaining a strong reputation (notoriety) among relevant groups within the populace of the Russian Federation, or (3) maintaining its reputation as a mark for a specific manufacturer's goods. The rules also name the documents—and describe their content—that can be attached to an application for a mark.

Civil Code of the Russian Federation, Part 1 No. 51-FL (November 30, 1994) and Part 2 No. 15FL (November 26, 1996). This document provides for implementing the law protecting the trade names. Article 51 states that the legal protection for trade names begins after registration of a legal entity by the Ministry of Justice.

Law of Russian Federation on Legal Protection of Computer Programs and Data Protection No. 3523-1 (September 23, 1992). This law provides the basis for regulating the development, legal protection, and use of computer programs and databases:

- *Computer program* means the objective form of presenting a totality of data and commands that are intended for the operation of computers and other computer devices for the purpose of obtaining a certain result. It is understood that the use of a computer program also includes the preparatory materials.
- *Database* means the objective form of presenting and organizing a totality of data (e.g., articles, calculations) systematized in such a way that this data may be found and processed by a computer.

Computer programs and databases are protected by copyright. Protection extends to all kinds of computer programs (including those for operational systems and software complexes) expressed in any language and in any form (including initial text and object code). Database protection covers databases that result from the creative work to select and organize data whether or not the data they include, or on which they are based, are protectable. To announce database rights, from the first issuance of a computer program or database the owner must use the copyright symbol, name of the owner, and year of first issuance. When the materials in a database cannot be copyrighted, the rights vest in the creator of the database.

Law of the Russian Federation on Legal Protection of Topographies of Integrated Microcircuits No. 3526-1 (September 23, 1992).   The law defines topography of integrated microcircuits as "a three-dimensional disposition as fixed on a material carrier, of a totality of the elements of an integrated micro-circuit and the interconnections therebetween." The law protects only original topographies, for 10 years, and ownership resides with the creator. The owner receives exclusive rights to use (by manufacturing and distributing integrated microcircuits) the topography and prevent others from using them without per-mission. (Article 8 of the law contains some exceptions.) All topography may be marked with the uppercase letter T ("T," [T], T*, or T), the date when exclu-sive rights began, and identity of the owner.

Law of the Russian Federation on Copyrights and Allied Rights No. 5351-1 (July 9, 1993).   This law regulates copyright issues related with the develop-ment, legal protection, and use of research works, literature and art, phonograms of performances, and programs (allied rights). There is no method for official registration; copyright occurs when the work is complete and protects the work during the author's life plus 50 years.

Law of Russian Federation on Legal Protection of Achievements in Selection No. 5605-1 (August 6, 1993).   The law regulates development, protection, and use of new plant varieties and animal breeds (i.e., Achievements in Selection). The rights are protected by patent for a period of 30 years.

The laws summarized here provide the basis of intellectual property law in Russia (see Exhibit 19.5).

International Intellectual Property Conventions

Russia holds a membership in several international intellectual property con-ventions. The Paris Convention allows applicants to file a patent application in their native country; thereafter they have one year to decide if they wish to file a patent application in another country. Applicants can use this time to assess the commercial potential of the property that is protected.

If an applicant wishes to file a PCT application, Russia runs a receiving office for inventors. Applicants also can file a European application, even though Russia is not a member of the European Patent Convention. Another option for applicants is the Eurasian patent. Most former Soviet republics belong to this convention, nonmember nationals may apply for this patent, and an application may be filed in the Eurasian Patent Office in Moscow. A Eurasian patent remains whole (i.e., does not divide into national patents), and the maintenance fee sums the national maintenance fees.[8]

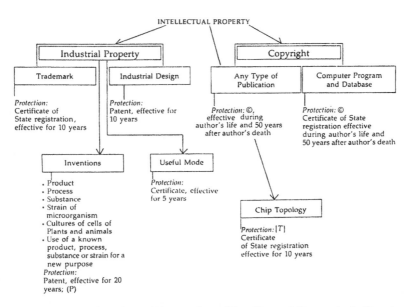

EXHIBIT 19.5   Legal Protection of Intellectual Property in Russia

TRENDS IN RUSSIAN INTELLECTUAL PROPERTY PROTECTION

Russia's intellectual property laws have been in force for more than nine years now. Several trends appear in the areas of the various types of protection. Inventive activity decreased after the 1992 implementation of the new patent law. The number of Russian invention applications dropped sharply from 200,000 in 1989 to 28,000 in 1993. There are at least two reasons for this:

1. Unstable economic conditions within Russia, including a sharp decline in production
2. Changing legal status of patents, including the assignment of exclusive ownership to the patent holder who is interested in protecting the invention

Changing conditions required a concomitant shift in the requirements for selecting patentable inventions. The most noteworthy change required applicants to pay a fee for thorough examination of inventions and ongoing maintenance of patents (previously Inventor's Certificates were issued at no cost to the inventor).[9] The number of patent applications decreased until 1998, after which inventive activity in Russia rose again (see Exhibit 19.6).[10] A small decrease in absolute numbers of foreign applications occurred, while the share of foreign applications vis-à-vis the total number of applicants increased from 1.2 percent in 1989 to 20 percent in 1999.

EXHIBIT 19.6	Applications to Rospatent						
	1993	1994	1995	1996	1997	1998	1999
No. Russian Applicants	28,478	19,482	17,551	18,014	15,106	21,362	19,900
No. Foreign Applicants	3,738	3,599	4,651	5,197	4,886	4,908	4,759
TOTAL NO. APPLICANTS	32,216	23,081	22,202	23,211	19,992	21,362	24,659

Beginning in 1985, applications from the developed nations increased substantially. Today, the United States ranks first in foreign patent filings (28 percent of the foreign total). Japanese and German filings increased to 14.3 percent and 19 percent, respectively; Great Britain and France follow. At present, the number of foreign filings from developed countries has reached more than 10,000.

Although foreign filings have increased, the policy of foreign firms regarding protecting their inventions in Russia remains the same. Firms in the industrialized nations continue to seek patent protection in other industrialized nations before Russia. Among the CIS nations, the Ukraine files the largest number of patent applications, achieving a rank of number four in filings (immediately after France).

The creation of a market for buying and selling intellectual property depends on growth in protected inventions (i.e., a growing number of valid patents and certificates). The number of protected inventions is increasing steadily in Russia. By 2000 there were 191,129 valid patents in Russia, of which 38,143 were filed from 85 nations (see Exhibit 19.7).[11]

The majority of inventions registered annually belong to a juridical entity. The number of patents awarded to juridical entities from Russia typically is twice the number awarded to individuals. Among foreign applicants for patents the ratio is about six times that in Russia. For example, in 1999, 14,138 of 19,508 patents were awarded to juridical entities—10,378 of these patents were given to Russian representatives and 3,760 to foreign firms. Further analysis of patents awarded demonstrates that industrialized countries maintain their policies toward Russia. Their filings fall into the same categories mentioned earlier: chemistry and metallurgy (C), technological processes (B), armaments (F), and necessities of life (A). Russian applicants have absolutely changed their priorities. Previously, the smallest number of national applications were made in the necessities of life (A); today this is the most active category. Russian enterprises are moving to gain markets providing the *necessities of life* rather than armaments and explosives as previously.

EXHIBIT 19.7 Valid Protection in Russia						
	1994	1995	1996	1997	1998	1999
Patents: Inventions	60,321	76,186	109,467	155,247	173,081	191,129
Industrial Designs	——	4,700	5,560	6,400	7,234	8,651
Certificates: Utility Models	186	2,971	3,361	5,700	8,185	11,591
Trade and Service Marks	81,675	92,915	102,241	109,993	107,561	117,920
Registrations: Computer Programs	534	1,018	1,601	2,322	3,071	4,087
Databases	43	84	133	224	302	463
Microchip Topologies	8	16	20	23	31	43

Utility Models

Legal protection for utility models exists now in Russia, as demonstrated by the increase in Russian applications for utility model protection (up from 14 in 1992 to 3,444 in 1999), as well as in the number of registrations for certificates. Foreign applicants show little interest in this protection within Russia. Between 1993 and 1999, foreign firms submitted only 202 applications, and these came mainly from the Ukraine and Byelorussia. Further analysis of registered utility models proves that Russians file the most applications in the category different technological processes (B), then necessities of life (A), mechanics, light, weapons, ammunitions (F), and finally physics (G). Foreign applicants are ranked as follows: different technological processes (B), textiles, paper (D), necessities of life (A), and mechanics, light weapons, ammunition (F). By January 1, 2000, 11,591 valid certificates for utility models were in force.

Industrial Design

Under free-market conditions, industrial design constitutes a significant component of industrial intellectual property protection. At present, foreign firms attend to industrial design as a means to ensure the sale of products. This type of protection does not constitute a component of economic value in Russia. The number of domestic applications to register industrial designs confirms this fact (see Exhibit 19.8).[12]

The volume of foreign applications to register industrial designs increases steadily. However, the total number filed in Russia does not compare with

EXHIBIT 19.8 Dynamics of Applications for Industrial Design Patenting

	1994	1995	1996	1997	1998	1999
Total Applications	1,423	1,370	1,266	1,302	1,509	1,585
Russian participants	1,225	1,165	994	929	1,076	1,274
Foreign participants	198	205	272	373	433	311

applications in developed countries. Thus, in 1999 France submitted 44 industrial design registration applications, the United States submitted 36, Germany submitted 30, Great Britain submitted 10, and the Netherlands submitted 31. Japan, the most active nation in protecting its industrial designs, submitted only 17 applications to Russia in 1999. Foreign firms tend to protect consumer goods, sporting goods, and light industry items, while paying little attention to mechanical engineering items. The level of unsophisticated technology in Russia and market conditions explains this tendency.

Trade and Service Marks

Trademark and service mark protection constitute a strong segment of intellectual property protection in Russia. In Russia, like the rest of the world, marks are acquired through registration. An analysis of mark registration is contained in Exhibit 19.9.[13]

A total of 117, 920 marks were effective in Russia on January 1, 2000. The number of marks registered increases steadily. Domestic applications increased to 63 percent of all mark applications in 1999. The number of registered and used foreign marks previously held at 60 percent. Now the new economic structure in Russia caused many Russian companies to recognize the value imparted by trademarks. In 1999, Russian firms accounted for more than 50 percent of the total new registrations.

Foreign firms remain concerned about protecting their goods in Russian markets. Applications are received from 64 countries, including Germany, France, the United States, Switzerland, the Netherlands, Great Britain, and Spain. Czechoslovakia and Poland lead registrations from FSU countries, and Byelorussia and Ukraine lead the CIS nations.

The number of service mark applications increased dramatically; between 1994 and 1999, about 23 percent of mark registration applications were for service marks and came from Russian firms. The increasing market for services within Russia accounts for this increase. Foreign applications represent less than 10 percent of the new applications.

EXHIBIT 19.9	Changes in Submission of Applications for Registration of Trademarks (TM) and Service Marks (SM)						
Years	1993	1994	1995	1996	1997	1998	1999
In total number of applications for registration TM and SM in Russia:	25,920	23,875	21,403	24,127	28,157	28,581	28,995
• Russian applicants	18,028	14,419	11,829	13,513	15,998	15,583	18,254
• Foreign applicants	7,892	9,456	9,574	10,614	12,159	12,993	10,741
Total number of new registrations:	11,246	12,805	12,647	20,313	17,401	17,701	19,507
• Russian applicants	3,996	5,780	10,256	10,108	8,249	7,791	9,181
• Foreign applicants	7,250	7,025	2,391	10,205	9,152	9,910	10,326
By the end of the year of registration	74,676	81,675	92,915	102,241	109,993	107,561	117,920

Appellation of Origin

This is a new form of legal protection in Russia and, as such, Russian firms typically do not take full advantage of registration. Even though they have been protected by law since 1992, only 129 Russian applications have been submitted to Rospatent, with 104 certificates granted. Most registrations protect signs associated with traditional goods (e.g., gzhel, Khokhloma, Fedoskino, Vologodskoye maslo, mineral waters). Foreign firms did not apply in this area.

Computer Programs, Databases, and Topology of Integrated Circuits

Official registration of these items began in 1993. Exhibit 19.10 contains data demonstrating that legal protection is developing in Russia.[14] Between 1997 and 1999, the number of appeals for official registration of computer programs increased dramatically. Both domestic and foreign firms (IBM, Microsoft, and Unigraphics are particularly active) have applied for protection demonstrating that foreign firms wish to protect their positions in the Russian software market.

EXHIBIT 19.10   Registration of Computer Programs, Databases, and Topology of Circuits

	1994	1995	1996	1997	1998	1999	TOTAL
Computer Programs	534	484	583	721	749	1,016	4,087
Databases	43	41	49	91	78	161	463
Integrated Circuits Topology	8	8	4	3	8	12	43

RUSSIAN LICENSING SYSTEM

Legal protection for intellectual property assumes an intent to commercialize the subject matter. At the same time, today's economic relationships assume constantly increasing volume of intellectual property transfer—especially technology. Typically, firms accomplish this transfer through licenses. For most countries, licensing occurs both domestically and on an international level (i.e., firms exchange technologies within a country and use licensing as part of their international trade practices).

Technology Transfer Regulation

All scientific and technical achievements in the former Soviet Union belonged to the state. Therefore, in the USSR there was no basis for domestic licensing; licensing existed only as a tool for foreign economic relationships. Now Russia does not have the special laws that governs technology transfer.

These legislative acts and regulations adopted between 1991 and 1999 laid a foundation for a domestic legal infrastructure permitting licensing:

- The Civil Code of the RF
- Patent Law of the RF
- On Legal Protection of Computer Programs and Databases
- On Legal Protection of Integrated Micro-Circuits Topologies
- On Legal Protection of Achievements in Selection
- On Copyrights and Allied Rights
- On Export Control
- On Competition and Limitation of Monopoly Activities on the Markets

Domestic System of Technology Transfer.   Today in Russia there are a variety of ways to exchange technology: (1) a patent assignment contract, (2) a license agreement granting the right to use protectable industrial property, (3) a contract

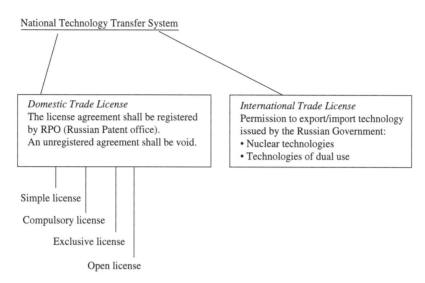

National Technology Transfer System

Domestic Trade License
The license agreement shall be registered
by RPO (Russian Patent office).
An unregistered agreement shall be void.

International Trade License
Permission to export/import technology
issued by the Russian Government:
• Nuclear technologies
• Technologies of dual use

Simple license

Compulsory license

Exclusive license

Open license

EXHIBIT 19.11   The National Technology Transfer System

granting know-how, and (4) a commercial concession contract providing the user with exclusive rights, including a trade name or a business name. The patent assignment contract is designated in Article 10(6) of the Patent Law of the Russian Federation. In this case, rights are transferred to a national or legal entity using a civil agreement that is registered in the Rospatent (see Exhibit 19.11).[15]

Article 13 of the Russian Patent law defines four types of licenses:

1. *Simple license.*   A licensor provides a licensee with the right to use the invention but retains all rights arising from a patent, including the right to grant a license to a third party.
2. *Compulsory license.*   If an invention or industrial design fails to work or perform sufficiently within four years from the date of publication of a patent (or three years from an industrial design), a person willing and able to commercialize the invention may sue for a compulsory, simple license. Terms for the invention's use, amounts, time limits, and payments are set by the Patent Court of Russia. Payment must compare with the market value of the license. A license will be granted if it is not possible to conclude a license agreement with the patentee and if the patentee cannot justify failure to commercialize or insufficiently perform.
3. *Exclusive license.*   An exclusive right can be assigned to a licensee for use of an invention within a specific scope. The licensor can retain the right to use the invention in part.
4. *Open license.*   A patentee may offer to give any person the rights to the invention by applying to the Russian Patent Office. In this case, the maintenance fee is reduced by 50 percent, beginning at the date of application.

License agreement registrations are governed by Regulations on Consideration and Registration of the Contract for the Assignment of a Patent and Granting the Rights to Exploit the Invention, Utility Model, Industrial Design. Registration ensures the legality of contracts assigning and exploiting intellectual property rights. The process is designed to prevent assignment of intellectual property rights to an unauthorized person, inclusion of clauses contradicting current legislation, and revocation of rights under the contract. Documents required to register a contract are enumerated in paragraph 2 of the regulations. The protecting document (i.e., patent for invention, utility model, industrial design) and access to State Registers Databases allows examiners to confirm the licensor's ownership and the patent's validity on the date of registration. Contract amendments and additions must also be registered (paragraph 6) if they relate to identification of contracting parties, the object of the contract, the scope of rights transferred, the territory where valid, the contract term, and premature contract expiration.[16]

Licensing Trademarks and Trade Names. The Law on Trademarks, Service Marks and Appellations of Origin, Article 26, states that any national and legal entity wishing to use a trademark must conclude a license with the owner. Russian legislation only protects signs registered by the Patent Office as trademarks. In Russia, the signs used to mark goods that are not registered are not protected as trademarks. Therefore, they cannot be licensed. Note that this discussion does not include well-known trademarks that are protected without registration.

The RU Law on Trademarks, Service Marks and Appellation of Origin, Article 2, states that a trademark owner can be a legal entity or individual engaged in entrepreneurial activity. A legal entity may be a commercial or noncommercial organization; daughter companies and affiliates are not regarded as legal entities. A legal entity must be registered by the Ministry of Justice. Russian legislation permits a citizen to engage in entrepreneurial activity without establishing legal entity if registered as an individual entrepreneur. An individual engaged in entrepreneurial activity may own a trademark.[17]

Legal protection of *trade names* is regulated differently. As a member of the Paris Convention for the Protection of Industrial Property, Russia provides legal protection for trade names without mandatory filing or special registration. This international obligation is included in Russian legislation. Thus, a trade name can be licensed if the owner is registered as a legal entity. When the owner of the rights is not a Russian company, a trade name can be licensed in Russia if it can be protected in the owner's nation. There are legal requirements for trade name owners. Only a *commercial organization* can own a trade name. *Commercial organization* means an organization with the objective of making a profit from its activities.

Successful trademark and trade name licensing depends greatly on correctly determining the legal status of the licensor. Not respecting registration requirements and ownership regulations will result in annulment of a license.

License contracts must be registered according to the Rules for Registration of Trademark Assignment Contracts and License Contracts for the Grant of Rights to Exploit a Trademark, which is departmental normative.[18]

In Russia, the franchising agreement is replaced by commercial concession and widely used, especially Article 1027 ("Commercial Concession") of the RU Civil Code:

> Under a franchising arrangement, one party to the agreement (i.e., franchiser) shall be obliged, in exchange for consideration, to allow another party to the agreement (i.e., franchisee) for a certain period of time or without indication of time limits, to use in the franchisee's commercial activity, the system of exclusive rights belonging to the franchiser, including the right to a trade name and/or business name of the franchiser, right to undisclosed information as well as the other objects of exclusive rights provided for in the agreement—a trademark, service, mark, etc.

Licensing Computer Programs, Databases, and Topographies of Integrated Circuits. In accordance with Article 13 of the RU Law on Legal Protection of Computer Programs and Databases, those who hold economic rights in a computer program or database may, with the term of copyright protection, register an application. An application for registration of the topographies of integrated circuits should be filed within a two-year period from the date of first use. Contracts assigning all property rights and contracts for licensing property rights for computer programs, databases, and topographies are registered with Rospatent.[19] This registration is governed by the Rules on Registration of Contracts for the Complete Assignment of Rights and Contracts for the Transfer of Rights for Computer Programs, Databases, and Topographies:

> In particular, the contract (or copying) of any intellectual property, the application to register a contract, and proof of fee payment are filed within the Patent Office to register the license contract. All documents must be written in Russian or accompanied by a certified Russian translation. The application will be considered within two months of filing.

Information related to granted licenses is recorded in the Official Register of the Russian Federation and is published in the Patent Office Official Gazette.

Know-How Transfer

There is no law that combines rules related to know-how in Russia. At the same time, including know-how in a license is a popular method for transferring technology. And know-how is transferred in the majority of license agreements and commercial concession contracts. According to Article 139 titled "Commercial Secrets of Civil Code of the Russian Federation":

> The various valuable commercial knowledge connected with manufacturng, management, financial activities, etc. are recognized as know-how. Know-how may include technical knowledge such as scientific reports design drawings, methods of carrying out experiments, methods of calculations, principles of prescription-writing, test documents. Economic and confidential management information may be protected as know-how or commercial secrets. For example, client and suppliers contact information, financial records, business plans, analytical information, work processes.

One must note the RU government Resolution of December 5, 1991, No. 35, On the List of Data which Cannot be Regarded as Commercial Secrets:

> [The term] "know-how" requires special care to take into account peculiarities of the RF legal system. In some countries know-how is defined to include all commercially valuable information as well as information that is not kept secret. However, in the Russian Federation this term has a more narrow construction and is equivalent to the notion of a trade secret. To avoid possible misunderstandings, parties to an international licensing agreement should strictly define the term "licensed information."[20]

Otherwise any agreement can be held invalid. A contract assigning know-how rights need not be registered. Trends in registering license transactions provide evidence that Russia can convert intellectual property into goods.

Licensing Inventions

Formation of an intellectual property market began with invention licensing (see Exhibit 19.12). Between 1992 and 1999, 9,643 license agreements were registered in Russia including:

Patent concession agreements	3,512
Exclusive licenses	860
Nonexclusive licenses	5,271

Most signed agreements are for nonexclusive licenses (57.6 percent); patent-concession agreements represent 33.8 percent; exclusive licenses constitute the remainder of signed agreements. Changes in the numbers of nonexclusive licenses (down from 72 percent in 1994 to 40 percent in 1999) are accompanied by an increase in the share of patent concessions (see Exhibit 19.13).[21] Exclusive licenses constitute only 8.6 percent of the total number of agreements.

The Russian situation differs greatly from world practice. Around the globe keen competition exists and licensees, aiming to protect markets, desire

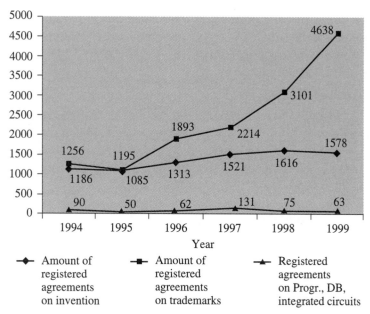

EXHIBIT 19.12   Technology Transfer Regulation in Russia

exclusive licenses. In Russia, a large market capacity, the complexity of guaranteeing exclusive rights, and the low cost of nonexclusive licenses explain the predominance of the latter. Sometimes, a license agreement can stipulate use of the licensed object in only one industry (e.g., aircraft manufacturing). Furthermore, in Russia agreements have limited validity within Russia and CIS countries, and distant foreign countries do not participate in the licensing process. License agreements that are valid across the territory of Russia contribute to 78 percent of the total number of license agreements:

- In CIS countries   10%
- In specific regions, districts, or cities   5.7%
- Within some firms   6.3%

EXHIBIT 19.13	Registration of Agreements							
	1992	1993	1994	1995	1996	1997	1998	1999
Patent Concession	98	97	214	292	422	757	851	781
Exclusive License	98	80	101	101	82	115	115	168
Nonexclusive License	433	579	820	702	809	649	650	629
TOTAL	629	756	1,135	1,095	1,313	1,521	1,616	1,578

Licensing Utility Models and Industrial Designs. The number of utility model (UM) and industrial design (ID) agreements is growing. Since 1996 the number of ID agreements increased from 60 to 161 in 1999; UM agreements increased from 37 in 1996 to 159 in 1999. This increase proves that the demand for small inventions is increasing.

During this period, considerable changes occurred in the activity of the participants of all license bargains. Until 1995, individuals were the most active licensors (57 percent), with state-owned firms holding 26 percent of the licenses. Non–state-owned firms' licenses have increased from 17 percent in 1995 to 58 percent in 1999.

Until 1995, most licensees were state-owned firms (62 percent), nonstate structures at 22 percent, and individuals at 16 percent. In 1998, the number of agreements in which state structures (e.g., firms, research institutes, design bureaus, and higher education institutions) were identified as a licensee decreased to 7 percent. Simultaneously, the share of individual licensees decreased to 12 percent, but the share of licensees that were privately owned organizations increased sharply, to 81 percent.

The increase in agreements with foreign firms constitutes an important trend in Russia. In 1996 the share of agreements in which a foreign firm participated in a license was less than 4 percent while in 1999 it was 12 percent. Examining the distribution of agreements across industries also indicates considerable change. Between 1992 and 1995, most agreements were concluded in the field of medicine (22 percent). Other industries in which agreements were concluded include the following:

Light and food processing	14.5%
Chemicals/petrochemicals	15.0%
Engineering, machine-tool building, and tool manufacturing	11.3%
House construction/building materials	11.2%
Power engineering/electrical engineering	8.3%
Electronics engineering and computer facilities	5.7%
Metallurgy	3.6%
Other	8.4%

By 1999, the number of agreements in the field of oil and gas increased 2.4 times, engineering increased 2.0 times, and medicine decreased by 50 percent. Agreements in the fields of house construction, light and food processing, power engineering, and electrical engineering decreased and then stabilized. The share of agreements in the fields of chemicals/petrochemicals, electronics/computers, and instrument making is stable.

Licensing Trademarks and Service Marks.   Today, trademarks constitute a very important type of intellectual property. More than 80 percent of all items produced and exported by firms in industrialized nations are trademarked. In global markets there is more competition among trademarks than goods, and the transfer of marks continues to increase steadily. Russia is developing this process (see Exhibit 19.12). An analysis of the data contained in Exhibit 19.14 reveals steady growth in the number of license and concession agreements for marks.[22] In 1999 the number of agreements grew to 4,638 from 450 in 1993, demonstrating that the Russian market for marks is developing more quickly than it is for inventions.

On January 1, 2000, 14,677 agreements had been registered. Of these, 8,813 agreements were concession trademarks and 5,864 were licensed trademarks. Note that trademark concessions were reduced from 85 percent to 56 percent. At the same time, the ratio of national and foreign subjects of agreements shifted. At the inception of trademark agreement registration in Russia about 75 percent of the agreements included the participation of foreign firms. Their share was reduced to 20 percent in 1999. These changes are attributed to the progress of privatization in Russia. There appear to be a great number of new firms with different ownership to which the old firms sell their trademarks. Further, firms close, merge, detach their affiliates, and so forth.

The situation with license bargains differs substantially from those of concession agreements. As the total number of license registrations increases, the share of licenses with foreign participation remains stable at about 25 percent of the total. Practically all foreign corporations license their trademarks to their own representatives in Russia. Foreign firms, especially multinational corporations, create affiliate and representatives offices as part of their marketing strategy. This strategy reduced risks for the firms.

U.S. corporations hold more than 13 percent of Russian mark registrations, then come firms from Germany, Canada, the Netherlands, Great Britain, and Finland. About 75 percent of the license bargains in Russia are made between Russian firms and organizations. An analysis of the license bargains shows that the largest number of agreements, about 20 percent, relate to food processing (manufacturing drinks and cigarettes). Approximately 17 percent relate to

EXHIBIT 19.14	Registration of Trademark Agreements						
	1993	1994	1995	1996	1997	1998	1999
License Agreements	47	600	111	691	929	1,456	2,030
Concession Agreements	403	656	1,014	1,202	1,285	1,645	2,608
TOTAL	450	1,256	1,125	1,893	2,214	3,101	4,638

petroleum production, about 11 percent to electrical industry and manufacture of instruments, 8 percent for light industry, about 7 percent to services including finance, about 5 percent to chemicals and pharmaceuticals, and about 5 percent to publishing. The increase in volume of license bargains appears to be a consequence of new forms of business (e.g., franchising, merchandising) in which transferring trademark rights is part of the overall agreement. In Russia, the term *franchise* is replaced by *commercial concession.* Commercial concession agreements came into existence in 1997, when Part 2 of the Russian Federation Civil Code was adopted. Today the largest share of the Russian franchise markets belongs to foreign firms like McDonald's, Coca-Cola, Pizza Hut, Baskin-Robbins, Beeline, and PepsiCo. There is no legislative base that regulates trademark licensing in merchandising.

Licensing Computer Programs, Databases, and Topology of Integrated Circuits

Markets for computer programs, databases, and integrated circuit topologies emerged in 1993. Exhibit 19.15 includes data for these items.[23]

Since 1997, 471 agreements were registered. Agreements transferring rights constitute the majority of agreements in this category. Note that their share of the total number of agreements decreased from 80 percent in 1994 to 57 percent in 1999. The analysis provided here does not include agreements for transfer of such items as "know-how," research results, development results, engineering, and so on. Russia does not have a legislative base for registering of the "know-how" agreements. That is why the development of the license market is slowing.

Particulars of International Technology Transfer

Until 1992, the state held a monopoly on foreign trade. Under the Russian Federation Presidential Decree dated November 15, 1991 (On Liberalization of Foreign Economic Activities in the RSFSR Territory), entrepreneurial firms and individuals are given the right to engage in export–import commercial operations. These operations include the purchase and sale of licenses. Russian Federation Law No. 2551-1, On Conversion in the War Industry,

EXHIBIT 19.15 Concession and Rights Transfer							
	1994	1995	1996	1997	1998	1999	TOTAL
Concession Agreements	17	9	8	39	32	15	120
Rights Transfer Agreements	73	41	54	92	43	48	351
TOTAL	90	50	62	131	75	63	471

dated March 20, 1992, permitted firms in the military industrial complex to transfer technology and know-how, as well as scientific and technical achievements. Private firms and individuals obtained the right to license internationally with foreign partners without registering the resulting agreements. Note that this does not apply for technology needed to create military equipment.[24]

Today, the Russian Federation law No. 157-FL On the State Regulation of Foreign Trade Activities, dated October 13, 1995, regulates economic activity. It establishes the legislative authority for foreign trade regulations, defines the roles of organizations, and defines the rights as well as obligations/responsibilities for government agencies. The transfer of technology with military uses, special uses, and dual uses, as well as sensitive technology, is strictly regulated under the law. Currently, Russia has a paradoxical situation. The national technology transfer system regulates licensing only within Russia, while making no provision for regulating the sale of licenses overseas.

A commission for export control was established on April 11, 1992, under Presidential Decree No. 11, On Measures to Establish the Export Control System in Russia. This decree identifies goods that cannot be exported without authorization of the Department for Export Control inside the Russian Ministry of Economy. These goods are identified as strategically important to the nation. The decree is supported by a Russian Federation Government Ordinance (No. 1132) dated September 29, 1998, On Legal Protection of Achievements of Research, Development, and Technological Works having Military, Special, and Dual Purpose. This document calls for a Federal Agency for the Legal Protection of such technology and the intellectual property protecting it. This agency registers, controls, and maintains records of technology that falls into these categories.[25]

At this time it is not possible to appraise the scope or number of international intellectual property transactions. There are, however, indirect means to assess the transfer of Russian technology to foreign firms. Over the past few years, licensing activity has shifted into science-capacious industries (e.g., instrument manufacturing, biology, radio-electronics). Also, new problems have emerged in licensing. These relate to employee inventions, export controls, legal protection of intellectual property created in the Russian Federation, contractual relationships, and invalidity of agreements. Typically, parties to agreements do not pay attention to Russian requirements emerging from administrative proceedings and court proceedings. In this case, the licenses themselves may be invalid. If this is the case, economic losses may occur for both parties.

Problems also can emerge when Russian firms execute export–import agreements that introduce scientific and technical products into non-Russian markets. Problems can result from Russian licensing professionals' poor skills. Under the USSR structure, the *Licenzingtorg* governed a state system for licensing that maintained the skills of licensing professionals. Besides, during the Soviet period most licenses were sold to former socialist countries (about 66 percent). Only about 24 percent of all licenses were concluded with foreign countries.[26] Today, Russian firms seek technology buyers/sellers from all countries. Often the Russian firms do not have the financial and business contacts to effect the license.

Another problem results from Russian firms trying to license the latest knowledge of purely scientific character and early-stage technology without providing needed expertise (e.g., manufacturing technology, trade secrets) for the licensee to succeed. Often the developers focus on the development rather than providing the infrastructure needed to produce a product with the invention. Many of these technologies cannot be implemented in industry because of their early stage of development. This may be the most significant problem for Russian licensors. Finally, many Russian firms simply do not protect their technology so that it can be transferred.

When Russian firms license-in foreign technology, they often do not account for obtaining legal protection, maintaining quality assurance, and securing the possibility to use this technology when the license expires. This constitutes an area of naivete that education and experience can overcome—but for the moment, the problem exists.

Price is another problematic issue when importing licenses. Unfortunately, not all Russian entrepreneurs and managers realize that royalties constitute only part of the payment. Besides the royalty, payment quite often includes the cost of production, which is necessary for technology development. The cost of equipment may be 2 to 3 times higher than royalty for license.

The most promising fields for licensing Russian technology include

- Vacuum and plasma technologies
- Informatics
- Optical instruments and spectrometers
- Laser technology, advanced optical means for information transmission
- Production technologies for special materials (e.g., synthetic diamonds, nanoparticles, crystals)
- Biotechnology equipment (e.g., environmental protection technology)

Tax Issues Affecting Licensing

The Tax Code of the Russian Federation, Part 1, No. 147-FL (July 31, 1998) and Part 2, No. 118-FL (August 5, 2000) regulate tax issues related to licensing in Russia. Article 148 of this code states that payments for export licenses and patents (when the license contract and patent assignment are attached) are exempt from value-added tax (VAT).

CREATING A FAVORABLE ENVIRONMENT FOR LICENSING

The legal bases for regulating technology transfer processes in Russia are not yet complete. The government focuses on creating a positive climate for licensing between Russia and other nations.

Common Problems

Despite the progress made to date, new and increased technology transfer activity has revealed four sets of macro and micro problems within the legal system:

1. The legislation remains vague with respect to

   - Ownership rights when the intellectual property covers the results of federally funded research and/or development
   - How to transfer know-how and trade secrets that support product implementation
   - How to govern unfair competition and restrict monopolistic licensing activity

2. The participants of the licensing process both foreign and Russian

   - Often have different meanings for the same definition
   - Do not take into account the specifics of legislative base of respective countries

3. Many foreign partners

   - Do not take into account that most Russian scientific research organizations are state enterprises and financed by the state
   - Suggest to Russian customers out-of-date achievements, while there are modern technologies provided at fair prices

4. Russian participants face the problem of information vacuum on foreign up-to-date technologies. At the same time, there is a lack of information on Russian progressive technologies abroad.

Despite these problems, the Russian system of intellectual property protection and technology transfer continues to improve steadily.

Opportunities

Several areas concerning intellectual property and technology transfer offer opportunities.

Information and Organizations. LES Russia operates to assist partners in searching for and finding desirable technology within Russia and the CIS. For more information, see the organization's Web site: www.LES-Russia.org. Potential partners will find a system of science and technology parks, business incubators, and innovation-technology centers in Russia. These organizations contain science and technology that may be licensed.

Many international centers can be found in Russia, including the Russian-German space technology center, the International Science and Technology Center (partners: European Union, United States, Japan, Norway, Republic of Korea), and others.

Intellectual Property Rights Enforcement.   Effective protection of intellectual property rights takes on increasing importance in today's Russia. According to the data published in *Patents and Licenses* magazine, about 100 assignments and licenses are registered each month in Russia. Intellectual property documents find a place in businesses every day.

There are many ways to fight intellectual property infringement. The Patent Office and other agencies oversee administrative controls. The State Anti-Monopoly Committee implements the Law on Competitions and Limitation of Monopoly Activities on the Market. Article 10 focuses on unfair competition and bans the sale of goods that violate intellectual property rights. Trademark owners often avail themselves of this legal remedy to stop the use of a mark. The Coca-Cola case in Russia illustrates this protection. Coca-Cola lodged a complaint with the Anti-Monopoly Committee and forced the local producer to cease using a similar trademark. A case may be brought in Moscow, regardless of the infringer's location.[27]

A mark owner can also bring a civil action in the case of infringement. Suits are brought at the infringer's location, creating some disincentive for the plaintiff. Both domestic and international law govern civil actions.

Finally, a criminal action can be brought in the case of intellectual property infringement. The RU Criminal Code (1996) includes protection for intellectual property owners in two ways. First, the existing code distinguishes between crimes committed in the sphere of patent protection and the author's rights (including neighboring rights). For example, in a case where an author's and neighboring rights are infringed, criminal responsibility relates to illegal exploitation of the intellectual property. Second, the RU Criminal Code provides additional protection for computer software; Chapter 28 identifies the operations considered criminal offenses. Articles 272–274 constitute the basis for prosecuting infringers in the field of computer information.[28]

Technology Transfer.   An analysis of court and arbitrage practice shows that the RU Civil Code and RU Patent Law govern contractual relationships related to transferring patent rights for commercialization. The relationship between

EXHIBIT 19.16 Court and Arbitage Dispute Settlement Practices	
TYPES OF DISPUTES	**GROUNDS FOR ACTION**
Contract conclusion	Not registered with Rospatent Legality of registration agency requirements Coercion of patent holders to contract registration
Contract amendments; premature expiration	Contract not executed (payment, technical warranties, patent/legal guarantees)
Invalid contract	Provisions not fulfilled Not registered with Rospatent Patent/legal guarantees not fulfilled

licensor and licensee are governed by the license contract registered with the Patent Office (Article 13, Patent Law of the Russian Federation). Rospatent has no authority to oversee execution of obligations contained in the agreement. And disputes related to assignment of rights are not governed by the current legislation. Article 31 of the Patent Law provides for the courts to settle disputes arising from licenses. Exhibit 19.16 contains an analysis of court and arbitrage practices in settling intellectual property disputes.[29]

In contract disputes, there are two primary reasons for voiding a contract: (1) the lack of registration with Rospatent, and (2) the coercion of one party to register with Rospatent. Article 165, Paragraph 3, of the RU Civil Code states that if one party is avoiding registration, a court has the power to invalidate the agreement.

In disputes related to contract amendments and premature expiration of validity, two issues emerge: Clauses are often badly written—especially the technical guarantees—and the licensor sometimes engages in unfair trade practice. In the second case, the licensor imposes burdensome clauses to establish a barrier to exploitation. Currently, other than compulsory licensing (Article 10 of the RU Patent Law), only Article 2, Paragraph 2, of the RU Law on Competition and Restriction of Monopoly Activity on Commodities Markets provides protection against monopoly abuse. This article states that protection is provided when contracts governing the exploitation exist that restrict competition. The RU Civil Code, Chapter 54, governs unfair trade practice under commercial concession contracts (i.e., franchise agreements).

Infringement of patent and legal agreements (including patent validity) classically revolve around issues related to guaranties of validity and the existence of third-party claims. These have increased according to courts and arbitrage practitioners that determine the validity or invalidity of agreements.

Participants in agreements need to pay special attention to the details and formalities of licenses and patent assignments in order to conform to existing law.

Furthermore, the requirements of the Rules on Examination and Registration of the Contract on Assignment of Rights of Use Inventions, Utility Models, Industrial Design, Trademarks and Trade Names need attention.

State Intellectual Property Policy

Today, the effective use of Russian science and technology through private exploitation (including technology transfer) is seen as a basis for economic growth. The national government has adopted several documents to support this process, which are as follows:

- The Interdepartmental Commission on Intellectual Property Protection has been established to coordinate the activity of state bodies involved in the development and exploitation of intellectual property—both domestically and internationally.
- Russia took an active part in establishing the Eurasian Patent Convention (August 12, 1995), which creates a unified patent space on the territory of 11 CIS member states. The participation of Russia in this convention promotes the development of its national IP system.
- The Russian Federation Government Ordinance adopted the "Conception of Innovation Policy for 1998–2000," which focuses on intellectual property enforcement for innovations.
- For government-funded technology, Russian Federation Presidential Decree No. 863 (dated July 22, 1998) identifies the need to balance rights and legal interests of parties (including the state) to agreements as a major problem. The objective is to actively support economic development through innovation and new product development/commercialization.[30]
- The opportunity to cooperate with investors participating in financing new technology development depends on their being able to use the results of R & D resulting from state-funded projects. The Russian Federation Governmental Ordinances 982 (dated September 2, 1999) and No. 1132 (dated September 29, 1998) state that the results of all scientific and technology activities funded by the state belong to the Russian Federation. Such technology, not related to government needs, may be licensed. These licenses are nonexclusive and, accordingly, licensees are not protected from competition of others.
- A separate system is being developed for state control and export regulation of Russian technology having a civil purpose, including those funded by the state.
- To realize intellectual property rights, it is necessary to improve the system for assessing exclusive rights. The federal Law on Evaluation

Activities in the Russian Federation, No. 135 FL (dated June 29, 1998) provides standards for evaluation, development, and drafting. This effort will be completed by state bodies and approved by the Russian Federation government. Today, intellectual property and intangible assets are valued in accordance with international standards.

These items demonstrate that Russia has undertaken a new approach to implementing an economic system in which intellectual property holds a proper position. Corporate policy includes intellectual property as part of the overall business development strategy, taking into account the concerns of both the firm and the nation.

In conclusion, legislative improvements and new mechanisms for protecting and licensing intellectual property are very important to the growth of Russia's scientific and technological potential. These are also important for developing international technology exchange and expanding international trade and business.

ENDNOTES

[1] Natalia Karpova, "Insights into IP Licensing in Russia," *les Nouvelles* (December 1996).

[2] Statistics of the USSR State Committee of Inventions "GOSCOMIZO-BRETENY," 1985–1991rr.

[3] Id.

[4] Id.

[5] Id.

[6] Id.

[7] ROSPATENT Annual Reports, 1992–1999.

[8] V. Medvedev, "Protection of intellectual property in Russia and the use thereof in international technology transfer," International workshop, International Aviation & Space Salon, Zhukovsky, Russia, 1999.

[9] Natalia Karpova, "Legal protection and licensing of intellectual property in Russia," International workshop, International Aviation & Space Salon, Zhukovsky, Russia, 1999.

[10] ROSPATENT Annual Reports, 1992–1999.

[11] Id.

[12] Id.

[13] Id.

[14] Id.

[15] Natalia Karpova, "Legal protection and licensing of intellectual property in Russia," International workshop, International Aviation & Space Salon, Zhukovsky, Russia, 1999.

[16] V. Evdokimova, "Law enforcement practice in the field of IPR related to technology transfer in Russia," Regional seminar of technology, transfer based of licensing, Moscow, 2000.

[17] V. Orlova, "Licensing of trademarks and trade names in Russia," Regional seminar of technology, transfer based of licensing, Moscow, 2000.

[18] Id.

[19] M. Fomichev, "Peculiarities of registration of computer programs, databases and topographies of integrated circuits," Summary of Reports of the Scientific and Practical Conference, Rospatent, Moscow, 1999.

[20] N. Zolotykh, "Licensing in foreign operations in the transfer of technologies," Regional seminar of technology, transfer based of licensing, Moscow, 2000.

[21] ROSPATENT Annual Reports, 1992–1999.

[22] Id.

[23] Id.

[24] N. Orlova, "Features of legal regulation of the technology transfer," Regional seminar of technology, transfer based of licensing, Moscow, 2000.

[25] A. Korchagin, "Formulating and implementing the state policy in the field of legal protection and use of intellectual property rights," Summary of Main Reports of the Scientific and Practical Conference, Rospatent, Moscow, 2000.

[26] Natalia Karpova, "Legal protection and licensing of intellectual property in Russia," International workshop, International Aviation & Space Salon, Zhukovsky, Russia, 1999.

[27] V. Medvedev, "Protection of intellectual property in Russia and the use thereof in international technology transfer," International workshop, International Aviation & Space Salon, Zhukovsky, Russia, 1999.

[28] N. Finkel, "Ways of improvement of intellectual property rights protection," Summary of Reports of the Scientific and Practical Conference, Rospatent, Moscow, 1999.

[29] V. Evdokimova, "Law enforcement practice in the field of IPR related to technology transfer in Russia," Regional seminar of technology, transfer based of licensing, Moscow, 2000.

[30] A. Korchagin, "Formulating and implementing the state policy in the field of legal protection and use of intellectual property rights," Summary of Main Reports of the Scientific and Practical Conference, Rospatent, Moscow, 2000.

ABOUT THE AUTHOR

Dr. Natalia Karpova is director of the International Business Division (Graduate School of International Business) of the Academy of National Economy at the Russian government, the leading training and research center for top-level managers in the Russian Federation. The academy is currently engaged in retraining and upgrading the qualifications of managers in the state industrial enterprises, associations, and newly developing sectors of the economy. As a Professor, Dr. Karpova specialized in business strategy, international license trade and investment, legal protection of intellectual property, IP management, and IP and IA valuation. She has taught at the Moscow State Academy of Foreign Trade, the Russian Institute of Intellectual Property, the Russian Academy of Management, and Harvard Business School. Dr. Karpova delivered lectures at the University of Washington, Central Washington University, Microsoft Corporation (USA), the University of British Columbia (Canada), the Royal Academy (Sweden), and Company Nortan & Rose (England). Dr. Karpova worked at Tetrex International Company, Unigraphics Solution, Hewlett Packard, and Sterling (Switzerland). She has published 104 scientific works, including 14 monographs. Dr. Karpova is associated with the Russian Chamber of Commerce and Industry, the Scientists Board of the Russian State Patent Office, and the American Business Congress. She is a member of the Russian Patent Lawyers Association, and she is president of the Licensing Executives Society Russia (LES Russia).

20

Australia: Licensing Opportunities in the Medical and Biotechnology Areas

By Rodney DeBoos

INTRODUCTION

Research undertaken in Australia is well regarded internationally. For example, after adjusting for the relative size of our science system, Australia leads the world in terms of the impact of its research in medical and biological science, and also in the fields of atomic, molecular and chemical physics, astronomy and astrophysics. Across a range of other fields Australia's share of the production of knowledge, as measured by its output of scientific publications, significantly exceeds its share of world trade.[1]

At the start of the new millennium, Australia is a far different place than that described by Ava Gardner during the making of *On the Beach*, a film about the demise of the planet following a nuclear catastrophe. On a chilly morning at a beachside suburb of Melbourne, Australia, she described Australia as the perfect place to make a film about the end of the world. While Australia might still be geographically isolated, the advent of modern communications and travel means that it is accessible and its influence in the global technological village is significant.

In terms of innovation, Australia has been responsible for more than its fair share of developments that have had a major impact on the populations of the world, particularly in the medical and biotechnology fields. As successive Australian governments have come to realize the importance of science, engineering, and technology to Australia's future, more and more effort has been put into investment in the ways and means of encouraging and developing the innovation process and the commercialization of outcomes.

Although medical health and biotechnology are not the only technological areas where Australian research ranks as a world leader, they are the fastest-growing technology sectors and the principal focus of this chapter.

THE IMPORTANCE OF THE MEDICAL AND BIOTECHNOLOGY REVOLUTIONS

The importance of the biotechnology or life-science revolution is becoming readily apparent to countries and companies around the world. The completion of the mapping of the human genome and the successful cloning of animals are but two of the recent technological successes that are set to presage whole new industries. An important fact about life sciences is that, as an industry, it is likely to replace many existing technologies. Harvard University's Jonathan West said recently that life sciences could replace existing industries representing approximately 7 percent of the gross national product of Australia.

In addition to the other advantages that Australia has, it is one of a few countries in the world with extreme botanical diversity. The life-science revolution has opened the door to bioprospecting in Australia, and this is one area in which Australia can play a central role. The race is now on to ensure that Australia is at the center of this revolution. Crucial to success in this endeavor are the intellectual property regime and the research infrastructure that now exist in Australia.

THE INTELLECTUAL PROPERTY REGIME

Australia is a signatory to the major intellectual property conventions and has a sophisticated and robust set of laws dealing with intellectual property. These laws cover patents, plant breeder's rights, designs, circuit layouts, trademarks, copyright, and geographical indications. Over the past decade these laws have been under intense review, with the result that new legislation for patents, plant breeder's rights, trademarks, and copyright was introduced in 1990, 1994, 1995, and 2001, respectively.

Significant changes are also proposed to be made to the Designs Act and to the Copyright Act in the immediate future. The following summary of the patents regime represents the law as of June 30, 2001. This is the most relevant regime to the biotechnology and medical sectors.

The Patents Act of 1990 governs applications for and the maintenance of patents in Australia. The subject matter that qualifies for patent protection is a product or process within the field of the useful (as opposed to fine) arts, one that is economically valuable, is new, and involves an inventive or, in the case of an innovation patent, an innovative step. Essentially, patent protection has applicable to all areas of technological development, involving products, processes, or compositions. The applicability of patent protection has now extended beyond traditional areas of technology to such things as computer programs, business methods, bacteria, gene sequences, and microorganisms. However, patents are not available for human beings or the biological process for their generation.

Patents are obtained by application to IP Australia with prescribed documentation describing and defining the alleged invention. There are two types of patent available in Australia—standard patents and innovation patents.

Standard patents follow the traditional British model. The system is a *first-to-file* system, and standard patents are examined before grant. The Australia legislation provides for pregrant opposition, and the validity of a patent can also be called into question postgrant. This inevitably occurs in the context of infringement proceedings.

Innovation patents were introduced in early 2001 and supersede the previous petty patent system, which was considered to have failed in its purpose. Innovation patents require a lower standard of inventive advance than standard patents but have a shorter term; a maximum of 8 years rather than the maximum 20-year term available to a standard patent. Innovation patents are particularly suitable for inventions with a short commercial life or inventions that do not meet the criteria for a standard patent.

As long as it does not claim human beings, plants and animals, or biological processes for the generation of these, an innovation patent application will proceed to grant after a formalities check (i.e., without examination). Examination only occurs if directed by the Commissioner of Patents or if requested by the patent owner or a third party. If the patent meets the requirements of examination, it will be certified.

Innovation patent owners can only enforce their rights if the patent has been certified. That is, an innovation patent cannot be enforced until after examination.

Unlike the requirements for standard patents (and petty patents), the application need only disclose an *innovative* step, rather than an *inventive* step. An innovative step has two parts:

1. There must be a difference between the invention and what is currently known about that technology.
2. The difference must make a substantial contribution to the working of the invention.

The innovation patent system is new, and it remains to be seen how it will be used by inventors. Although an innovation patent will be granted without examination, the *right* is essentially worthless until it has been examined and certified. Prospective licensees under patents will need to clarify whether the patent under which they are to be licensed is a standard patent or an innovation patent.

At the time of this writing, the Patents Act is slated for further amendment. The proposed amendments cover a number of areas but, importantly, include the prior art base and the introduction of a grace period. These amendments are controversial and, if proceeded with, will significantly alter the patent regime in Australia.

THE RESEARCH INFRASTRUCTURE

The research infrastructure in Australia involves both Australian and State Government organizations, universities, and private industry. The largest research agency in Australia is the Commonwealth Scientific and Industrial Research Organization (CSIRO). CSIRO employs more than 7,000 staff and receives the majority of its funding from the federal government. CSIRO engages in research across a broad range of areas including the biotechnology area.

One of the recent successes of CSIRO researchers and one that resulted in the researchers winning the 2001 Prime Minister's Prize for Science was the discovery of the *Flowering Switch Gene*. This gene determines when plants stop their vegetative growth phase and start flowering. The discovery is the subject of patent applications by CSIRO and has the potential to boost the productivity of the world's crops by billions of dollars a year.

Plants respond to environmental signals (such as length of daylight or periods of low temperatures) in a process called *vernalization*. The Flowering Switch Gene is switched on and off by vernalization. By isolating the gene, the researchers are well on the path to manipulating the gene to produce crops that, for instance, flower at the right time for the climate in which they are grown or preventing other plants from flowering for long periods. The manipulation of the growth and flowering stages of plants could result in a dramatic increase in world production of various crops.

The funding for health and medical research in Australia is administered by the National Health & Medical Research Council (NH & MRC). The NH & MRC provides grants to organizations for health and medical research with an increasing emphasis on biotechnology research.

As part of its biotechnology initiatives, the Federal Government has established Biotechnology Australia,[2] with the responsibility for developing a national strategy for biotechnology. Biotechnology Australia is a multi-department government agency that coordinates nonregulatory biotechnology issues for the Australian government. One objective is to provide balanced and factual information on biotechnology to the Australian community in order that the development of the industry is not hampered by ill-informed comment. The National Biotechnology Strategy includes a biotechnology innovation fund designed to support the early stages of commercialization of biotechnology.

The organization is also attempting to ensure better access to genetic resources and gene collections and, in this respect, is working with the newly created Office of Gene Technology Regulator, which regulates the production and use of genetically modified products and organisms.

The federal government provides a series of grants and concessional loans through various structures. Importantly, the federal government allows a 150 percent research and development tax concession to Australian-based companies that undertake innovative or risky research and development activities in Australia. Although not an effective inducement to start-up companies that are in a loss situation, the concession has been an important factor in stimulating the provision of funding for research activities.

Perhaps the most adventurous initiative of the federal government in recent times was the establishment of the Cooperative Research Centres Program. It is believed that the program is unique on a global basis. The program was established in 1990 with the objective of strengthening collaborative research links between industry, research organizations, educational institutions, and relevant government agencies. The traditional pattern is for a formal long-term agreement to be put in place between research providers and research users in the public and private sectors. The federal government contributes approximately one-third of the funds, while the other participants contribute the remainder. The involvement of the users of research means that a Cooperative Research Centre (CRC) undertakes research in a highly focused way. The bringing together of researchers and research users also results in a quicker uptake of outcomes of the research because the users and the researchers have been involved directly in the development of the technology from the outset. The commercialization of the results is undertaken either by the participants or third parties under license. The CSIRO is a major participant in a number of these programs. CRCs cover many research areas; however, a number are active in the biotechnical and medical science areas:

- CRC for Tissue Growth and Repair[3]
- CRC for Cellular Growth Factors[4]
- CRC for Eye Research and Technology[5]
- CRC for Cochlear Implant and Hearing Aid Innovation[6]
- CRC for Vaccine Technology[7]
- CRC for Diagnostics[8]
- CRC for Aboriginal and Tropical Health[9]
- CRC for Discovery of Genes for Common Human Diseases[10]
- CRC for Asthma Ltd[11]

Currently there are 72 CRCs in Australia.

There are a number of success stories involving CRCs. Examples of these follow.

- *The CRC for Cellular Growth Factor and its commercial partner, AMRAD Corporation Ltd[12] (AMRAD) successfully completed Phase I Clinical Trials of emfilermin, a formulation of human leukemia inhibitory factor (LIF) in 1999.* As a result of basic research showing that LIF is capable of enhancing the survival of nerves following injury, one of the participants, AMRAD, embarked on a program of developing LIF as a treatment for neuromuscular diseases. A Phase II trial testing the efficacy of emfilermin in alleviating chemotherapy-induced peripheral neuropathy commenced in September 1999. In November 2000, AMRAD announced the grant of IND status from the U.S. Food & Drug Administration to extend the Phase II trial into the United States. These studies are due for completion by the end of 2001. AMRAD also has entered into a partnering agreement with Serono in relation to emfilermin for human infertility. The partnering by AMRAD at an early stage is intended to expedite worldwide commercialization. Similar arrangements have been made by AMRAD with Aventis and Edwards Lifesciences in relation to VEGF-B cardiovascular projects, although this particular project is being undertaken outside the CRC Program.

- *The CRC for Cochlear Implant and Hearing Aid Innovation deals with a more visible piece of Australian technology.* In 1978, Rod Saunders, who had received a head injury that resulted in him becoming profoundly deaf, became the first recipient of the *bionic ear.* This was the prototype for the cochlear implant that has now been implanted in more than 30,000 people throughout the world, including over 15,000 children. The cochlear implant was the result of centuries of pioneering work that started with Voltar, the scientist who discovered the electrolitic cell. Voltar experimented on himself by inserting into his ear metal rods connected to a battery. While the result was not necessarily pleasant, it did spawn other efforts over the centuries to stimulate the auditory system electrically. This work culminated in Professor Graeme Clark producing an implant package and a speech processor that are now widely used throughout the world. The CRC for Cochlear Implant and Hearing Aid Innovation[13] now develops implants with expanded capacity for information transmission, improved control of auditory nerve stimulation, and enhanced cosmetic appeal.

- *GroPep Limited[14] was established by CSIRO and the University of Adelaide to commercialize intellectual property relating to a novel insulin-like growth factor.* The CRC for Tissue Growth and Repair[15] was established in 1991 by CSIRO, Adelaide University, the Dairy Research and Development Corporation, and the Child Health Research Institute. In 1997, GroPep and Flinders University were added. GroPep was listed on the Australian Stock Exchange and is also now the exclusive commercial agent for the Center. The company has established an effective business with a cash flow from product sales. It develops novel factors that increase cell growth and manufactures and commercializes these globally. The company has 14 active patent families that underpin its existing and future products. The patents fall into two broad groups:

those that cover insulin-like growth factors and those that cover growth factor mixtures or individual factors isolated from dairy products.

Many other CRCs have proven that the model of bringing researchers and users together works and serves Australia well.

The State Governments are also taking a keen interest in biotechnology; particularly the states of Victoria and Queensland. Victoria, for instance, accounts for more that 40 percent of Australia's NH & MRC funding and is the home to key research and education organizations, hospitals, and industry through precincts including the Parkville strip, the Werribee animal and food precinct, the Alfred Hospital Medical Research and Education precinct, and the Monash Health Research precinct. The Premier of Victoria has indicated the government's intention of having the state recognized internationally as one of the world's top five biotechnology locations by the year 2010, alongside Boston, Silicon Valley, Cambridge, and Martensried.

As part of this initiative, the state has created an ambassador for biotechnology and appointed Professor Adrienne Clarke as the first incumbent. Professor Clarke is a renowned researcher, particularly in the plant area. During her term as ambassador, Professor Clarke aims to attract further biotechnology investment to the state, including more research facilities for multinationals similar to the GlaxoSmithKline Research and Development Center, which already exists in a suburb of Melbourne.

Melbourne already boasts an impressive group of medical institutes and hospitals in the precinct called *the Parkville strip*. These include the Howard Florey Institute,[16] the Murdoch Childrens Research Institute,[17] the Ludwig Institute,[18] and the Walter and Eliza Hall Institute.[19] These Institutes exist alongside the Royal Melbourne, Royal Children's, and Royal Women's Hospitals, CSIRO, and the University of Melbourne.

As an example of the reputation of the companies and institutes comprising the Parkville strip, the Walter and Eliza Hall Institute of Medical Research was recently offered a grant by New York's Leukemia and Lymphoma Society to investigate the role of cell death in the development of blood cell tumors. The grant is for a five-year project that will consolidate existing research efforts of the Institute and the oncology unit at the adjacent Royal Melbourne Hospital.

Recently, the state of Victoria announced a decision to proceed with the construction of a privately funded synchrotron. A synchrotron is an electron accelerator that acts as an extremely powerful microscope. It can be used to investigate the structure of molecules and is widely used in the biomedical area. For instance, the ability to study the atomic structure of human proteins allows researchers to design drugs to combat disease. Relenza, the world's first drug to fight influenza, was developed by Biota Limited,[20] an Australian biotechnology company, partly by using a synchrotron in the United States. A five-year timeline has been set for completion of construction.

At the same time, the state of Queensland has announced that it will lead the establishment of a Center of Excellence for the development and commercialization of nano-applications. *Nanotechnology* is concerned with the isolation of individual atoms and molecules and their use as building blocks to construct devices and materials with properties that cannot be created with other technologies. There is a wide range of applications for nanotechnology, from medicines to computer hardware and peripherals. The Queensland government expects the Center of Excellence to attract funding from universities, CSIRO, and private-sector companies.

The various universities in the different states and territories of Australia also contribute significantly to R & D in biotechnology and other areas. In many cases, the technology developed in a university is commercialized by spin-off or other local or multinational companies.

For instance, technology originally developed at the University of Adelaide, South Australia, is now being developed by BresaGen Ltd.[21] BresaGen was originally incorporated by an Adelaide University researcher and is now a listed company. It has developed a cost-effective process for the production of recombinant proteins.

BresaGen is also a world leader in the production of genetically modified pigs whose organs are suitable for transplant into humans. Again this technology came out of Adelaide University. The xenotransplantation program is conducted in collaboration with St Vincent's Hospital, Melbourne, Victoria. The company is also developing novel biotherapeutics for myeloid leukemia, breast cancer, and allergic and organ disease.

Another good example of promising university technology is the platform technology termed Co-X-Gene, discovered by CSIRO and ANU and being developed by Virax Holdings Limited.[22] Co-X-Gene technology allows the simultaneous expression of antigen and cytokine so as to optimally modulate the immune response. The required genes are delivered to target cells by a harmless, nonreplicating recombinant viral vector (avipox). The technology has applications in a wide variety of areas, including infectious diseases, cancer, and autoimmune diseases. At the present time, Virax is focusing on the treatment of HIV-infected individuals, a Phase I/IIa trial having commenced in May 2001.

Virax technology is also being utilized in the development of a prophylactic vaccine for HIV/AIDS. The promise of this approach was emphasized by the fact that the U.S. National Institute of Health (NIH) awarded an Australian consortium, of which Virax is a member, $27 million to fasttrack the development and testing of this *prime and boost* vaccine. The prime vaccine will be DNA based, while the boost vaccine will be based on fowlpox virus.

AIDS sufferers have more to look forward to in that, in July 2001, researchers at Monash University in Melbourne announced that they may have found the missing link in the search for an AIDS cure. Their discovery focuses on the stimulation of the thymus gland, which is a key organ in the immune system. The thymus produces, programs, and distributes T-cells. The Monash researchers are now carrying out clinical trials with AIDS and chronic cancer patients and those needing a bone-marrow transplant following chemotherapy for leukemia with a drug called GnRH Analogue.

Monash University has also successfully transferred the work of its researchers in the in vitro fertilization (IVF) field to the marketplace. In the 1960s, IVF pioneer Professor Carl Wood teamed up with Professor Alan Trounson, who had been conducting IVF research in relation to animals. The combination of these two talented people resulted in the technology being utilized in humans, with the result that thousands of infertile couples around the world have been able to become parents. The technology was successfully transferred to the United States and is currently being commercially exploited by IntegraMed Inc. IntegraMed is listed on the Nasdaq exchange. Professor Trounson is also now involved in stem-cell research, being one of the world's leading stem-cell scientists. He is able to continue his research in Australia, as stem-cell research is supported there.[23]

AUSTRALIA'S PERFORMANCE IN THE MEDICAL AND BIOTECHNOLOGY INDUSTRIES

The Australian biotechnology and pharmaceutical industries are the best performing of Australian industries in technological terms. While small on a global scale, they continue to grow. The examples just given are but a few of the successful innovations made by Australian companies. However, there are many developments that go unnoticed, notwithstanding their potential value in the marketplace.

In terms of patenting growth, patents for Australian inventions in the biotechnology area have increased by 240 percent between the two five-year periods of 1989 to 1993 and 1994 to 1998. This compares to a rate of growth of 118 percent for all U.S. patents.[24] The same study found that Australian patented technology is relatively leading edge and that, in the biotechnology area, Australia is a technology-driven country.[25] However, while biotechnology is an area of excellence and emphasis for Australia, the study found that it was a small part of the overall U.S. patent system, amounting to only 2 percent.

When it comes to citations of scientific papers in patents, the linkage is strongest in the areas of biotechnology and pharmaceutical patenting. In Australian patents there is heavy citation of Australian scientific research; however, this citing of Australian scientific research does not find itself replicated in U.S. patents for inventions made outside Australia. In these patents, there is a low ratio of citation of Australian science, which indicates that Australian science is not as visible to the rest of the world as it might be.[26]

The fact that Australian science in the biotechnology area tends to be at the leading edge but is not cited in the United States in the same ratio as it is cited in Australia suggests that there is an opportunity in Australia for commercializers, both overseas and in Australia, to capitalize on technology that is currently overlooked. The Australian biotechnology industry is dominated by small to medium companies, and its relative geographical isolation has meant that alliances with larger multinational companies are a major means of access to international markets for these companies. For instance, Proteome Systems[27] is an Australian company that has developed a suite of novel technologies to make the world's first integrated, high-throughput platform for proteome analysis. Proteome Systems has formed alliances with Shimadzu Corporation, Sigma Aldrich, and Millipore for the marketing of instruments and consumables developed by it.

Numerous multinational corporations have subsidiaries in Australia that both market the parent's products and sponsor continuing research in the biotechnology and pharmaceutical areas. Thus, it is not unusual for scientific developments made in Australia to be commercialized outside Australia. The *Australian Biotechnology Report 2001* said that Australian biotechnology companies had more than 150 potential products in clinical or field trials during 2001.[28]

One of the reasons the biotechnology industry has been able to develop so quickly and at the forefront of various technologies is that Australia is a low-cost location for biotechnology investment. As of December 2000, Australia was found in a benchmarking study to be the lowest-cost country when all of the facts considered by the study were aggregated and modeled for the establishment and running of a 30-person biotechnology business.[29]

The *Australian Biotechnology Report 2001* sets out the strengths of the Australian biotechnology industry. These strengths have been adapted from the benchmarking study and are as follows:

- When measured relative to the available national labor force and resources, Australia has a globally competitive industry—although still small in size compared with the U.S. and EU nations.
- There is a clear business cost advantage in running R & D facilities compared with other nations.
- The supply of graduates and excellent training/skills provide a quality and readily available labor pool.
- Australia has a strong international reputation for quality of science and source of intellectual capital.
- An excellent, cheap communications infrastructure is in place—both internationally and nationally.

- High expenditure, relative to GDP, compares well with competitor nations of public sector R & D in fundamental areas driving biotechnology.
- Improving links between public-sector R & D providers and industry, for example the links between CSIRO/CRCs and industry, is a world-class model.
- Australia consistently rates high on a comparative basis with other nations on the quality of life and cost of living indexes—meaning very attractive conditions for expatriates.
- A new focus for support of the Australian bio industry through the establishment of a dedicated national agency, Biotechnology Australia, drives new national bioinnovation initiatives.
- Australian state governments have all raised levels of support for bioindustries with significant funding and infrastructure support.
- Commonwealth, state, and territory governments have identified biotechnology as a national priority for investment attraction efforts.

Importantly, in the weaknesses highlighted by the *Australian Biotechnology Report 2001*, was the "great lack of awareness by international analysts of the capability of the Australian biotechnology industry." All in all, it would appear that the Australian medical health and biotechnology industries present commercialization opportunities of global proportions.

FINDING THE OPPORTUNITIES

The unearthing of relevant technologies is often a hit-and-miss affair. However, the use of the Internet as a searching tool does provide an excellent starting point.

In Australia, the Department of Industry, Science, and Resources has established a search tool that it calls *Research Finder*. Research Finder is an Internet search tool that allows for the discovery of Australia's researchers, research activities, and emerging technologies using a high-quality keyword search capability. Research Finder currently covers 190 government-funded research and research-support organizations, institutions, departments, and agencies. It can be located online at http://panoptic.act.cmis.csiro.au/research-finder/.

CONCLUSION

Australians have always had to struggle against the disadvantages that a small population base and distance have bestowed on it. On many occasions, these drawbacks have lead to innovation, as necessity is often the mother of invention. They have also meant that Australian companies are receptive to dealing with foreign licensees.

Moreover, the successful exploitation of Australia's vast natural resources has provided a sound educational infrastructure from which good science has been produced. The time is now right for Australia to capitalize on its knowledge resources, and this presents licensing opportunities for both Australian and off-shore enterprises. The combination of a relatively low cost base, a supportive government, and good science decrees that these opportunities will continue well into the twenty-first century.

ENDNOTES

[1] Dr. Robin Batterham, "The Chance to Change: Discussion Paper" (Canberra: Department of Industry, Science, and Resources, August 1990).

[2] Biotechnology Australia

[3] CRC for Tissue Growth and Repair
    E-mail: leanna.read@crc-tgr.edu.au
    Web site: http://www.crc-tgr.edu.au

[4] CRC for Cellular Growth Factors
    E-mail: crccgf@wehi.edu.au
    Web site: http://www.ludwig.edu.au/crc-cgf

[5] CRC for Eye Research and Technology
    E-mail: b.holden@cclru.usw.edu.au
    Web site: http://www.crcert.org

[6] CRC for Cochlear Implant and Hearing Aid Innovation
    E-mail: cowanr@mail.medoto.unimelb.edu.au
    Web site: http://www.medoto.unimelb.edu.au/crc

[7] CRC for Vaccine Technology
    E-mail: annek@qimr.edu.au
    Web site: http://www.crc-vt.qimr.edu.au

[8] CRC for Diagnostics
    E-mail: Peter.Hudson@hsn.csiro.au
    Web site: http://www.crc.sci.qut.edu.au/cdt.html

[9] CRC for Aboriginal and Tropical Health
    E-mail: tonyb@menzies.edu.au
    Web site: http://www.ath.crc.org.au/

[10] CRC for Discovery of Genes for Common Human Diseases
    E-mail: genecrc@cerylid.com.au
    Web site: http://www.genecrc.org

[11] CRC for Asthma Ltd
E-mail: philipb@mail.med.usyd.edu.au

[12] AMRAD Corporation Ltd
E-mail: amrad@amrad.com.au
Web site: http://www.amrad.com.au

[13] CRC for Cochlear Implant and Hearing Aid Innovation
E-mail: cowanr@mail.medoto.unimelb.edu.au
Web site: http://www.medoto.unimelb.edu.au/crc

[14] GroPep Limited
E-mail: geoff.francis@gropep.com.au
Web site: http://www2.gropep.com.au

[15] CRC for Tissue Growth and Repair
E-mail: leanna.read@crc-tgr.edu.au
Web site: http://www.crc-tgr.edu.au

[16] Howard Florey Institute
E-mail: info@hfi.unimelb.edu.au
Web site: http://hfi.unimelb.edu.au

[17] Murdoch Childrens Research Institute
E-mail: murdoch@cryptic.rch.unimelb.com.au
Web site: http://murdoch.rch.unimelb.edu.au

[18] Ludwig Institute
Web site: http://www.ludwig.edu.au

[19] Walter and Eliza Hall Institute
E-mail: information@wehi.edu.au
Web site: http://www.wehi.edu.au

[20] Biota Limited
Web site: http://www.biota.com.au

[21] BresaGen Ltd
E-mail: adelaide@bresagen.com
Web site: http://www.bresagen.com.au

[22] Virax Holdings Limited
E-mail: virax@virax.com.au
Web site: http://www.virax.com.au

[23] Between the time of writing and the time of publishing, the Australian government surprisingly forecast a ban on embryo stem cell research. The announcement has led to a lively debate with several state and governments and many institutions opposing the move. At the time of publication a final decision had not been reached and, in the meantime, stem cell research continues.

[24] F. Narin et al., "Inventing Our Future—The Link Between Australia Patenting and Basic Science." (Canberra: AusInfo, 2000).

[25] Id., p. 39.

[26] Id., p.17.

[27] Proteome Systems
      Web site: http://www.proteomesystems.com

[28] *Australia Biotechnology Report 2001* (Canberra: AusInfo).

[29] "Benchmarking Study of R & D Costs in Selected Segments of Australian Biotechnology" (Ernst & Young, Hay Group, and Strategic Industry Research Foundation, January 2001).

ABOUT THE AUTHOR

Rodney DeBoos is a partner in the Melbourne law firm of Davies Collison Cave Solicitors (formerly Davies Ryan DeBoos), which is associated with Davies Collison Cave, patent and trademark attorneys. His major area of practice is commercial law and, in particular, the exploitation of intellectual property rights. Rodney has held the positions of secretary and president in both the Australia/New Zealand chapter and the international body of the Licensing Executives Society. He also lectures at Melbourne University on the subject of the licensing of patents and technical information in the Graduate Diploma of Intellectual Property course and is the author of the chapter on patent licensing for *The Laws of Australia* (Melbourne: Law Book Co., 1993).

21

Challenges to Arab Industries in Acquiring and Selling Appropriate Technologies

By Talal Abu-Ghazaleh

INTRODUCTION

The Arab world is made up of 22 countries with different economic and political systems and their own unique histories. But they are united by shared language and religion and correspondent similarities in social and cultural traits. Another feature that they have in common is that they are all developing countries. They are distinguished not by the desire to stay ahead, nor to keep up, but to catch up. The means of doing so is to acquire the necessary technological base and capacity to produce more complex value-added products and services that can raise the standard of living of the countries' people. Only 40 years ago, there was virtually no Arab industry of which to speak. In the past decades, oil wealth has funded a remarkable transformation of the Arab Gulf region that has affected not only the Gulf but the entire region. Other Arab countries such as Jordan, Egypt, Lebanon, and Palestine have served as labor pools for the Gulf oil economies, fueling economic development in those countries as well. Despite the great degree of change and development, the Arab countries have nonetheless remained locked into the *developing countries* classification, and economic indicators for the region indicate that the Arab developing countries have not kept pace with their peer nations in South America and Asia. In fact, the Arab countries are, in terms of economic and human development indexes, among the most marginalized regions of the world. Gulf economies still remain heavily dependent on oil-financed consumer imports, although some nations, such as Saudi Arabia, have worked hard to develop local industry to supply consumer goods. Such factories for the most part remain unable to compete internationally and depend on government intervention through tariffs and nontariff intervention to maintain their viability. In other Arab countries, massive state investment has produced large industries but with mixed results. The Arab countries are far from the basket-case situation that one finds in some least developed countries, but this is nonetheless a region that has not lived up to its potential. There are numerous reasons for this—some historical, some economic, some political—but clearly the inability to acquire the right technologies, to develop these, and to become not only a consumer but also a producer of technology is a significant part of the reason why the Arab countries are still lacking in attainment of their economic and social objectives.

REASONS FOR ARAB DIFFICULTIES IN
TECHNOLOGY TRANSFER

There are many reasons why Arab countries have had difficulties in acquiring appropriate technologies. Intellectual property laws have been weak or lacking. Courts and legal systems often suffer from ineffective administration and/or the appearance or existence of bias. Police and other enforcement agencies have suffered weaknesses in funding, training, motivation, and overall success in enforcement operations in IPR issues, related to licensing and technology issues, although corrective measures have been introduced in many countries in recent years. Investment laws often place serious restrictions on entry of foreign firms, which is often the means through which companies are likely to transfer the most cutting-edge technologies. Even if such transfer tends to be of a proprietary intra-company nature, its technological and financial impact is significant, and it does become generalized, while supporting human capacity development. This leads us to the first and foremost challenge to Arab countries in acquiring and selling appropriate technologies, and that is the issue of *human capacity*.

Arab investors often have limited experience in international systems of technology exchange; they have little familiarity with licensing issues. Furthermore, the necessary professional support they require to make decisions and operate is not available, either. In the West, businesses rely heavily on specialized support from attorneys regarding the complex issues involved in domestic and international transactions, both in regard to technology transfer and intellectual property rights (IPRs). In the Arab world, few attorneys are familiar with these issues, and those that are face a challenge in explaining such concepts to business and government sectors that have only recently become familiar with elementary intellectual property concepts. There is very little understanding by Arab businesspeople and attorneys, even those specialized in intellectual property, of the complexities and subtleties of licensing arrangements. Although there is a general understanding of the basics of patents and trademarks, the mechanisms for licensing and assigning such rights are not well known.

In the last few years, several Arab countries have acceded to the World Trade Organization (WTO) and thus have had to comply with WTO rules on intellectual property as laid down in the Tripps agreement. The process of updating national laws for WTO members, or of accession for those who have not yet joined, has greatly expanded discussion and general familiarity of IPRs in the

Arab world. However, the situation in many of the Arab countries was very poor in the area of IPRs until very recently. Patent protection as such was not enforced in Kuwait among others; Lebanon had virtually no protection of copyrights; pirating of software and other products was rampant across the region (and still remains a significant issue); and in general intellectual property rights were considered mostly a foreign concept conceived for foreign benefit. But new legislation and new enforcement efforts have changed the situation drastically in most Arab countries.

CURRENT CLIMATE IN THE ARAB REGION

We now face a climate in which intellectual property is becoming a widely known and discussed concept in the Arab region. Thanks to basic minimum standards established by the Tripps agreement, the legal environment is becoming somewhat harmonized. Arab attorneys are becoming increasingly familiar with the basics of patents, trademarks, and copyrights. There are an increasing number of Arab attorneys with specialized knowledge of IPRs. But because this is a recent development, the knowledge base is shallow. In fact, even among IPR attorneys very few are familiar with the full range of standard licensing issues found in international business. This is not altogether their fault, as Arab countries do not generally have special legislation regarding licensing. To the extent that there may be particular licensing laws, they normally regard registration of the license agreement or mandatory licensing provisions for patents. So, there is little basis in local laws or legal tradition to provide the necessary knowledge and skills that would enable the Arab lawyers to be aware of all the concepts involved in a routine license agreement.

Because intellectual property laws have only recently been passed, updated, or begun to be strictly enforced, the result is that licensing is somewhat of a new issue for the Arab world. Naturally this is not to say that various types of licensing agreements have not been made over the course of the years, but the participants have not necessarily seen them as IPR licensing agreements, but more often as simple agency agreements or commercial transactions. And because there are not really specialized laws on licensing, it generally falls under the area of standard contract or civil law in most countries. The business possibilities afforded to an international licensor are sometimes as good or better than those under their own nation's law, but sometimes are not fully understood due to miscommunication or misunderstanding.

For example, sometimes foreign lawyers may come to believe that they are unable to enact a licensing agreement that fully protects them or satisfies their goals, when in fact they can. In some cases, foreign business owners or attorneys have mistakenly believed they could not legally protect their interest because of an absence of certain legislation familiar to them, when in fact, they could do so by drafting comprehensive contracts, enforceable under contract law.

Another problem that occurs is that foreign partners may have certain expectations or understandings from their own experience and sometimes from their own attorneys, but they might neglect formalities or other details in laws in the licensee's country that might result in forfeiture of some or all of their rights. This happens when a foreign company relies too heavily on its home country attorneys and fails to consider the different legal situation in the licensee's country.

Licensing is very poorly understood in the Arab world. Even many specialized Arab intellectual property attorneys may not be fully informed when confronted with a foreign licensor's questions regarding licensing stipulations that might or might not be permitted under local law. In many cases, there is no clear legal precedent or parallel for answering such questions, and one weakness of Arab attorneys is that they are less likely to acknowledge when they do not know something. As often as not, an Arab attorney will try to answer a question, though coming from a different legal tradition there might only be the *appearance* of mutual understanding, rather than the reality.

It is not uncommon for a foreign firm to enter into a licensing agreement only to discover later that its licensee is not complying with the terms of the agreement, and that there is little it can do to solve the problem. Another common problem is that Arab businesspeople may sign an agreement that they do not fully understand, nor which did their attorneys, and then find themselves legally liable for significant costs that they had not anticipated and that may result in losses. There are many unhappy stories from both sides. The end result is that we must focus on two key lessons, both of which involve a joint appreciation for the value of mutual communication.

1. When a foreign firm seeks to enter into a licensing agreement with an Arab firm, the standard advice around the world still applies. Seek local counsel, and be flexible.
2. It is important to realize that licensing is not a well-understood practice. Intellectual property laws and practice have only recently been established, and questions regarding licensing must be posed to prospective partners with the expectation that they may not necessarily be familiar with the concepts.

HISTORICAL REVIEW

Arab businesspeople have a long history as merchants at a global crossroads. They are clever and wily. It is not difficult for them to understand these concepts that may be new to them. The problem arises through miscommunication, when both sides have misunderstandings. Both foreign firms and local partners have suffered disappointment and loss from lack of mutual understanding. The foreign companies usually lose on the basis of bureaucratic rules or processes that they never understood or considered. The local firms usually lose from not understanding the lengthy contracts that they are presented with from international partners.

In the West, and particularly in common-law countries, the contract has evolved to an amazing extent, with a large body of law to support its interpretation. Arab businesses and lawyers are generally not as familiar with this and tend to see the law as much more cut and dried and simple than Westerners do. The custom drafting and negotiating of complex contracts jointly by corporate business and legal teams is not familiar to most Arab attorneys. They generally expect more of the legal implications to be resolved by statutory principle.

In general, then, the most serious impediments in the Arab world to acquiring appropriate technologies are

- Lack of Arab personnel familiar with licensing and technology transfer
- Perception that intellectual property laws are weak (despite major improvements)
- Past mistakes by international companies in their approach to business in the region, which continue to affect foreign perceptions
- Insufficiently developed science and technology infrastructure

Of all these issues, the most significant is in relation to the lack of familiarity with international systems of technology documentation and transfer. In order to acquire a technology, you must first know of it and find it, or the opposite—which is to find it and then know it. In other words, you must find something you want or look until you find something you want.

The Arab world has a poorly developed science and technology infrastructure and so, although business and government leaders always aspire to acquire the most impressive cutting-edge technologies, there is just as much to be gained from many older technologies. With the Internet, these technologies can be identified and located with greater ease than ever before. So, a principal way in which to facilitate technology acquisition in the Arab world is to train its business leaders and scientists to utilize the massive global resources regarding technical information, such as patent databases, technical exchanges, and so on.

Arab business leaders are beginning to work on these important issues. The Licensing Executives Society—Arab Countries (LES-AC) was formed only two years ago, but is already making a major contribution to awareness of these issues in Arab countries. By developing our professional people, we develop our countries. The technologies are acquired and developed by people, so it is people on whom we must first concentrate. Whenever you speak to an Arab businessperson, you will find a tremendous interest in what technologies and products are available around the world, but too often finding an answer to this question has been hit or miss for the Arab participant. Now with information technologies like the Internet, and professional development associations like LES-AC, the situation is changing.

MOVING FORWARD

For foreign entities interested in licensing technology to the Arab region, it is advisable to utilize LES-AC as a focal point in the search for licensees or for professionals such as business agents or attorneys. This is mutually beneficial because it provides the foreign entity with access to the Arab world's small body of licensing professionals and it supports the work of LES-AC and the process of interesting other Arab professionals in developing the Arab licensing field. Ultimately the best interest of both licensors and licensees is to negotiate a win–win agreement based on full and mutual understanding of the terms and implications thereof. In order to make this possible on a wide scale, a great deal more needs to be done, particularly in human capacity building, for which professional associations are an appropriate resource. As this human groundwork is built, the science and technology infrastructure will be subsequently developed, increasingly allowing a higher level of technology acquisition.

Although the focus here is on the human aspect, it is important to refer once more to the legal background of the situation. In the past, insufficient intellectual property laws and serious restrictions on foreign investment prevented businesses in the Arab region from transferring technologies. Although some restrictions remain, the situation is markedly improved from the past, with even 100 percent foreign ownership allowed in some countries. Meanwhile, as noted already, the intellectual property laws have improved remarkably from the influence of the WTO and the Tripps agreement. Thus, the Arab countries are in a situation where many of the factors necessary for progress have been aligned, and there seems to be no reason not to expect significant progress in the next few years. The efforts of organizations building human capacity in professional fields, information technology, the Internet, science, and education in general will be crucial to the long-term successful development of the Arab science and technology infrastructure.

AUTHOR'S NOTE

Like so many millions of others around the world, I was shocked, dismayed, and horrified by the terrible tragedies of September 11 in New York and Virginia. We all share with you in grieving for the great loss and great blow, which is not just to the United States but to the civilized world and civil society in general. We pray that the blessings and comforting presence of almighty God will be with all those who lost friends and loved ones, and that justice will be given to all those who perpetrated and instigated this horrible crime.

Catastrophes bring out the best and the worst in people. In a way, they are a fire that tempers the human character. Some people give way to looting and wanton crime as social order disintegrates, while others willingly risk and sometimes sacrifice their lives to help and save others. New Yorkers, Washingtonians, and Americans have distinguished themselves with their calm courage and stoicism, their giving spirit, and their patient, moderated response in channeling their anger and retribution. They have also shown their generosity of spirit, their kindness, and their understanding. I know so many Arab Americans who, though feeling strained, have expressed gratitude and appreciation for all the support their American friends have given them, at a time when they feel somewhat apprehensive.

As for me, I am not American, I am an Arab, but I was very touched by the letters I have received from Americans I know, some of whom I met only days before the September 11 tragedy, urging us to strengthen our cooperation and dialog, as businesses, nongovernmental organizations, and as people in a global community. These people see that the way to ultimately marginalize and then extinguish the terrorists and their supporters is to enhance international dialog, cooperation, and partnership, and to empathize our common human bond and our common brotherhood under one shared universal God.

On behalf of LES—Arab countries, I offer my sincere condolences to all Americans, my goodwill and my hope for the future.

ABOUT THE AUTHOR

Talal Abu-Ghazaleh is the chairman and founder of Talal Abu-Ghazaleh & Co. International (TAGI), the largest and foremost Arab group of professional service firms in the field of accountancy, consultancy, intellectual property, and digital knowledge, with 34 offices in the world. He currently serves as the president of the Arab Society of Certified Accountants (ASCA), the Arab Knowledge Management Society (AKMS), the Arab Society for Intellectual Property (ASIP), Licensing Executives Society— Arab Countries (LES-AC), and the Arab Internet & Domain Names Association (AIDNA).

Among his numerous international contributions, he chaired a vast number of United Nations and international committees, including the Telecommunications and Information Technologies Committee of the International Chamber of Commerce (ICC), and was the first chairman of the Arab Internet Names Consortium (AINC). He also serves as an observer member of the United Nations Commission on International Trade Law (UNCITRAL), and most recently has been chosen to chair both the Lebanese IP Committee (ICC) and the Jordanian IP Committee (ICC).

He is also a founding member of the United Nation's Information Communication Technologies (ICT) Taskforce, the World Intellectual Property Organization (WIPO), and the Industry Advisory Commission (IAC) in Geneva. He is also a member of the International Chamber of Commerce (ICC) Working Committee on Intellectual Property, Paris; Advisory Board on Dispute Settlement in International Trade, Investment and Intellectual Property of the United Nations Conference on Trade and Development (UNCTAD); Electronic Commerce Committee of the Licensing Executive Society International (LESI), New York; Business Constituency of the Domain Name Supporting Organization (DNSO) of the International Corporation for Assigned Names and Numbers (ICANN); and the Intellectual Property Constituency of the DNSO.

22

The South African Experience in Economic Development

By Alan Lewis and Don MacRobert

INTRODUCTION

Six years ago, South Africa welcomed its first-ever democratically elected government, and more particularly, the institution of President Mandela as head of state. This was a momentous occasion, and there was much cause for happiness.

Now that the political goals have been satisfied, it is believed that the real work starts: the economic development of South Africa, which in due course could translate into the rest of Africa. Technology can play a major role in the comeback of nation building during the period of reconstruction and development.

This reconstruction is important because there is much catching up to do. Millions of people have been disadvantaged through the previous laws and practices. They need to be brought into the mainstream, and there is much to be done regarding the provision of services such as education, housing, and health, as well as the creation of jobs.

LICENSING: GOOD OPPORTUNITIES FOR DEVELOPMENT

In South Africa, licensing is now seen as one of the strongest tools for reconstruction and development. It must be one of the major avenues to be followed in addressing some of the main requirements of housing, health, and education, as well as the provision of jobs.

It is widely recognized that through a process of licensing, the licensee stands to gain considerably from the licensor's know-how techniques, knowledge, and experience. Thus, for an emerging entrepreneur in a developing country (which South Africa must now be regarded as), licensing can provide an excellent tool for the transfer of knowledge, as well as bringing an entrepreneur licensee up to steam fairly quickly.

Under the previous government, laws prohibited black people from owning property, from holding certain jobs, and from having their own construction or industrial businesses. The black person was destined to be a worker, as opposed to being an entrepreneur, industrialist, or businessperson. South Africa was faced with economic sanctions because of these laws and regulations. Many U.S. and other foreign companies withdrew from South Africa. They sold their companies at fire-sale prices. This led to economic recession and considerable loss of jobs. There was high unemployment.

CHANGES BROUGHT ABOUT BY DEMOCRACY

With the new democratic society, one is noticing considerable changes. Apart from the happiness with the political changes, one is seeing the arrival or return of many foreign investors. Companies that disinvested but that have returned include IBM and Coca-Cola. Newly arriving companies (having previously decided not to come because of apartheid) include Nike, McDonald's, and many others.

A very novel and interesting development has been the stipulation by some aid donors to link their funds to licensing and similar ventures. Because of the changed political situation, many foreign governments have promised aid packages to South Africa. As an illustration, South Africa has jumped to the number three position for USAID funding (after Israel and Egypt). Part of the aid packages are specific in that they encourage licensing and, with it, the transfer of technology. Thus USAID has set up a special arm that promotes and establishes joint ventures for licensing operations. It has encouraged licensing seminars and has brokered many new licensing contracts that relate to education, manufacture of clothing, and housing.

The Japanese government announced a package of more than $1 billion in aid. Much of it was tied to linkages with Japanese firms, including banking and insurance companies. Again, there is a strong licensing component. Much relates to the training that is imparted from a licensor to a licensee. The Danish government package is another case in point. A large portion of aid is focused on linking Danish businesses with emerging South African entrepreneurs and businesses.

BENIGN BANKS

Part of the development of a good licensing operation also relates to assistance given by banks. A leading bank has set up a special division to handle loans to small businesses. However, this division has stated that it would prefer to grant loans to borrowers who are about to become licensees of licensing transactions.

Most small businesses fail within the first two years of starting up. The bank has found the opposite to be true with licensing and franchising operations.

Most small business licensees are not only still in business after two years, but are also highly successful. This clearly flows from the information, know-how, systems, back-up, and technology given by a licensor in a licensing operation.

Then again, the central bank of the country (the Reserve Bank) recently announced certain changes in the fields of currency and foreign exchange. First, the previously structured two-tier financial system (the commercial Rand and the financial Rand) has been abolished. Second, the Reserve Bank believes that future changes will make the South African investment scene far more attractive to a foreign investor and licensor.

The laws affecting licensing in South Africa are user friendly. The Patent Act grants ample opportunities for monopoly rights to be conferred upon a patentee for a period of 20 years. This easily enables the patentee to grant licenses to licensees. Similarly, the Trademarks Act, which to a certain extent follows the British trademark system, makes provision for registration of trademarks. More specifically, it makes it possible (but not mandatory) to record licensees as registered users.

Again, licensing can involve know-how and intellectual property not covered by patents, trademarks, or designs. This often forms the subject of technology transfers that occur in the newly emerging licensing arrangements aimed at the new businesses in South Africa. Part of the development of a good licensing operation also relates to assistance given by banks.

SUCCESSFUL LICENSING CASE STUDIES

USAID, the developmental agency for the U.S. government, sponsored a licensing seminar about five years ago. This promoted the concept of licensing and the benefits to be obtained by the emerging licensees. It was pleasing to note that at least 10 new license agreements have been concluded between U.S. licensors and South African licensees. Apart from the considerable growth and expansion in well-known licensing operations (such as Kentucky Fried Chicken), these new licensing arrangements provide interesting statistics.

In the case of Coverall Inc., of San Diego, California, they have granted a franchise operation to a South African company (which has taken the licensee's name of Coverall, and is known as Coverall (Pty) Ltd.). The master license was granted not only for South Africa, but for the entire region of southern Africa (covering 10 countries, in all). The master licensee then had the opportunity and right to grant sublicenses to licensees in geographical areas. Of particular interest is the fact that the U.S. government's USAID then provided a loan guarantee scheme to enable licensees from previously disadvantaged communities to obtain loans through commercial banks. The guarantee covers 50 percent of the facility offered by the financial institution.

The Danish Licensing Programme, sponsored by DANIDA (the Danish Government Developmental Agency) in conjunction with the Danish Chamber of Commerce, goes even further. In the case of Padborg A.B., the licensor of Denmark, a license has been granted in connection with the trademark Just Trucks for trucking, haulage, and warehousing services to the licensee known as Just Trucks (Pty) Ltd., which was intended to provide start-up or seed capital. Furthermore, the Danish government DANIDA provided a guarantee to the commercial bank that offered a loan to the licensee.

POSSIBLE VARIATION OF TRADITIONAL LICENSE CLAUSES

It is possible that one may have to vary traditional or normal licensing arrangements and conditions when in South Africa. Many of the emerging licensees may not be in a position to pay an upfront license fee. Some may have to seek funding from friendly banks, as has been described. They might also require special or additional training (which will be most welcome). Moreover, they might have to pay more for certain support services offered by the licensor.

All circumstances indicate that the licensing negotiations need to be worked through very carefully. There can be no hard-and-fast rules based on experience elsewhere. New ground is being covered. One such avenue is the *royalty rate.* This may have to start off at a low level, but as the licensee's turnover increases, it could go to a level that is higher than the normal royalty rate to catch up on the previously depressed royalty rate, as well as other expenses that may have been incurred upfront.

A further interesting development is the desire on the part of some companies to act as mentors or counselors to the emerging entrepreneur. The Swiss business group (IEF), a foundation consisting of major Swiss companies, has volunteered to assist emerging businesses with start-up business plans, management, and an ongoing supply of services and goods (to ensure that these are delivered at the right time, price, and quality). They bring with them an effective license because, in many cases, they are acting as a back-up or support for the emerging licensee operations.

Their focus is also interesting because they are concentrating on tenders awarded by the government for goods and services required by government departments. The Government Tender Board has indicated the desire to ensure that some of the tenders are awarded to previously disadvantaged people. And yet, there has been no proper matching of this desire with tenders being awarded to the emerging entrepreneur. This is where the Swiss IEF group is starting to play an active role in assisting the emerging entrepreneur to complete tender documentation correctly and deliver goods and services at the right time and price as indicated earlier.

BENEFITS OF LICENSING

One of the joys of licensing has seen the emergence of certain black licensors. A case in point is that of Leseding Dressmaking School, just outside Pretoria. Leseding trains pupils and students in the discipline of making clothing. However, where students show a willingness coupled with an ability to learn, they are given extra training so that they may become licensees. Leseding now has 20 licensees operating around South Africa, including countries such as Lesotho and Namibia.

This leads us to realize that elsewhere in Africa there must be great opportunities for development through the tool of licensing. Generally, there will be certain areas in which licensing operations could be successful. These could be in the fields of agriculture, water supply, and certain other sectors such as clothing, light engineering, and food retail.

An essential benefit of a license agreement will be the ongoing transfer of skills to the licensees. This introduction of know-how and technology in the licensing arena certainly helps to uplift and increase the skill of the recipient licensee. One can readily see opportunities that will present themselves through economic development and empowerment. In the field of mining engineering, one is already noting that Africa, blessed as it is in many parts with minerals, is experiencing an ongoing exchange of know-how and technology in connection with the mining and processing of such minerals. The technology would usually be licensed in South Africa or other mining countries. This leads to the creation of the mining industries in the country, coupled with the creation of jobs; and thereby to the economic upliftment of the people within those countries.

Furthermore, through tourism (also a big attraction in many African countries), one is noting the arrival of the international hotel groups (who bring their skills), tour operators, transport companies, and general tourist services. These are often the subject of licensing arrangements, and lead to the transfer of skills and the creation of jobs.

Finally, with the advent of telecommunications and the information technology era, there would be great opportunities for licensing opportunities in Africa as a whole. More especially, the introduction of telecommunications into Africa will lead to an upskilling of its people, coupled with the creation of economic and job opportunities. Orion Telecommunications Inc. of New York is one example. It was the first privately owned company to launch a satellite in the universe. This was a costly affair, but it was serviced by renting out user time to the big soaps and cosmetics companies as they launched their marketing and service programs into the former communist Eastern Europe. Their salespeople were on the ground selling products, but because of the poor telecommunications, they could not relay sale and other information back to their head offices in the United States. They could only do so once they had linked up via the Orion satellite. It proved to be a successful venture for both the soap companies and the satellite owners.

GOVERNMENT INVOLVEMENT

During the apartheid era, the nationalist government introduced stringent *exchange control regulations* in an attempt to prevent capital flight. Unfortunately, South Africa still has exchange control, although the African National Congress (ANC) controls the government and has significantly reduced the scope thereof. The ANC vows its intention to remove all restrictions. In terms of these regulations, authority has to be obtained for license fees to be remitted out of the country. If a licensor is happy for royalties and other payments to remain in the country, then the parties have total freedom to negotiate the terms of the license. Although license fees may only be remitted out of the country with approval, dividends are freely transmittable, and many licensors have opted to set up local corporations as a conduit for their remuneration, depending on tax and other considerations.

The South African government and various nongovernmental organizations (NGOs), such as the Industrial Development Corporation, have a number of programs to assist entrepreneurs in setting up and developing businesses. The Department of Trade and Industry (DTI) is particularly active in this regard. The primary role of the DTI is to facilitate access to sustainable economic activity and employment for all South Africans. The key objectives of its incentive schemes are

- Attracting higher levels of domestic and foreign investment
- Increasing market access for foreign investment
- Achieving a fair, efficient, and competitive marketplace for domestic and foreign businesses and consumers

The DTI hopes to achieve the following results:

- Promoting the development of small, medium, and micro enterprises (SMMEs)
- Increasing opportunity for black economic empowerment
- Reducing inequality and poverty
- Strengthening the international competitiveness of South African business
- Developing the South African Development Community (SADC) region

SMALL AND MEDIUM ENTERPRISE DEVELOPMENT PROGRAM

One of the incentive schemes administered by the DTI is the Small and Medium Enterprise Development Programme (SMEDP). The objective of this scheme is to create wealth, generate employment, develop entrepreneurship, promote empowerment, utilize local raw material, ensure sustainability of projects receiving incentives in the long run, and reduce investment loss by small and medium investors.

The scheme is available countrywide to local and foreign firms investing not more than R100 million (approximately U.S. $12.5 million) in land, buildings, and plant and equipment in new projects or expansion of existing projects. Legal entities, as well as sole proprietors and partnerships (excluding trusts), are eligible for assistance. Suitable activities include manufacturing, high-value agricultural projects and agro-processing, aquaculture, biotechnology, tourism, information and communication technology, recycling, and business services.

In terms of the program, an investment grant for two years on approved qualifying assets is provided, on a sliding scale, depending on the value of the project. A grant of 10 percent a year is provided for the first R5 million, decreasing to 1 percent for the final R25 million. An additional investment is available in the third year if the human resource remuneration component of manufacturing cost is at least 30 percent. These incentives are tax exempt. These schemes are particularly suited for joint ventures and license arrangements between foreign parties and local entrepreneurs.

CONCLUSION

All in all, there are considerable opportunities for licensing ventures and operations in the emerging economies in Africa. Licensors stand to gain considerable advantages through discovering new markets. Furthermore, there are advantages to be gained by the emerging licensees through the acquisition of know-how, technology, and other skills.

ABOUT THE AUTHORS

Alan Lewis has a BSc in Physics and Mathematics, a BSc in Electrical Engineering (cum laude), and a BProc law degree. Currently, he is a South African patent attorney. He joined Adams & Adams in 1972 and has been a partner since 1977.

Lewis was president of LES South Africa in 1994–1995. He is treasurer of LES South Africa and vice chair of the Investment Committee of LES International. He has presented a number of papers at conferences, seminars, and courses in South Africa and overseas on a variety of IP and licensing issues.

Don MacRobert is a director of Edward Nathan & Friedland (Pty) Ltd, corporate law advisors, of Johannesburg, South Africa. He is the former president of LES South Africa, as well as the former president of the Chamber of Commerce in Pretoria. He serves on the International Chamber of Commerce (Paris) and has been a director of public companies quoted on the Stock Exchange in South Africa. MacRobert has published several articles in international journals, covering various aspects of intellectual property.

23

Prospects for Increased Licensing in Latin America

By Fernando Noetinger and Gabriel F. Leonardos

INTRODUCTION

Latin America has been viewed as an area of the world where there are still great opportunities for business. It has a tradition and a culture that make it attractive to all those who have had the chance to visit, and above all, there is a total integration of its population, regardless of ethnic origin and religion.

In Latin America, licensing is an increasing activity even though it is still dependent on the factors that slow economic development in this part of the globe. Latin American countries have attempted to achieve economic integration for decades, and although this goal has still not been achieved, the fast pace of economic change cannot be underestimated.

In fact, if a few strong factors unite, there could well be a movement toward the rapid building of an economic union that would allow each country to concentrate on the industrial or service areas in which it has a competitive edge, and in which entrepreneurs would be eager to receive up-to-date technology through licensing. Economic union would receive a great push forward from the U.S.-sponsored Free Trade Area of the Americas (FTAA), which is still being discussed. Many expect that the agreement will be signed and put into force until 2005. The FTAA is discussed in greater detail later in this chapter.

It must be said from the onset that part or all we say in relation to Latin American countries in general might not be applicable to one or more countries, and certainly Mexico is one of those countries that must be treated separately. Mexico, due to its special relationship with the United States that resulted in the North American Free Trade Agreement (NAFTA), has a much more open economy than other Latin American countries. In particular, Mexico has no controls or restrictions at all regarding the acquisition of foreign technology, and there is broad freedom of negotiation for the parties in the legal environment with regard to licensing agreements.

HISTORY OF LICENSING IN LATIN AMERICA

For many decades and until the end of the 1980s, most Latin American countries had policies that tried to control the inflow of technology. The idea behind those policies was not that the acquisition of foreign technology was harmful, but rather that such acquisition should be controlled in order to guarantee that local engineers and technicians were being trained, in order to break the dependence from foreign sources of technology. Another important objective for many Latin American governments was to minimize the flow of hard currency to foreign countries.

Many governments exercised a material control on licensing agreements, and such control was effective because government approval of the agreement was usually a condition for the licensee to be allowed to make payments abroad in hard currency. The shortage of hard currency still is a common feature in Latin America, and it is not uncommon to see news concerning the difficulties some countries face in order to pay the debts incurred in foreign currency (usually U.S. dollars, which is the paramount currency throughout Latin America).

The main type of restrictions that used to be (and to some extent still are) practiced in Latin American countries in connection with licensing agreements could be summarized as follows:

- Licensees should not be impaired in their rights of freely using the technology after the agreement has expired (unless, of course, a licensee had committed a breach of contract).
- Confidentiality covenants are forbidden or restricted to only a few years after termination of the agreement.
- Licensees should present evidence that local engineers and technicians are being trained in the know-how being acquired.
- The hiring of foreign engineers and technicians should be limited to a minimum because preference should be given to local professionals whenever possible.
- There are limitations on amounts of payments and terms during which payments could be made (usually a maximum of 5 years), as well as ceilings on the tax-deductibility of the expenses incurred by the licensee with the agreement.
- High taxes are levied on the remittances of payments abroad, such as withholding income tax and taxes on the purchase of foreign currency, and also special taxes are levied only on the payment of royalties.

Many of these measures were consistent with the economic policy of substitution of imports, according to which developing countries should locally produce all goods and services they needed in order to avoid balance of payment problems.

Latin American countries have had a history of controlling currency flow, as well. Commonly all transactions in Latin American countries are conducted in the national currencies of the various countries. Such currencies (like the Brazilian real, or the Chilean peso) are not accepted outside the territories of the countries that issue them. As a result thereof, all foreign exchange transactions are controlled by the Central Banks, and the banks that engage in foreign trade, purchasing and selling foreign currencies, can only do it within the tight rules prescribed by the Central Banks, and subject to close scrutiny. Thus, whenever a local company needs to make royalty payments abroad, this company must purchase foreign currency in an exchange transaction controlled and authorized by the respective Central Bank.

In Argentina, the 1991 Convertibility Law established a parity of the Argentine peso vis-à-vis the U.S. dollar, something that has provided the pillar of price stability but severely constrained monetary policy. Apart from the fact that the Argentine peso did not float in relation to the U.S. dollar, remittance of payments to foreign or local residents was free and not subject to any prior approval by the authorities. In late 2001, following years of economic difficulties, Argentina was rocked by riots and looting. President de la Rua imposed a state of siege but was forced to step down, and at this writing many expect that Argentina will have to abandon its policy of tying the peso to the dollar as one step in getting its finances in order.

Historically, the balance of payments of developing countries always carries a deficit, because the lack of internal savings requires that such countries borrow money from foreign lenders. (Argentina is shackled with a ponderous $132 billion in debt.) For developing countries, the possible surplus in the commercial balance (i.e., the result of the sale and purchase of tangible goods) is usually offset by other financial commitments already incurred by these countries, including payments of royalties (in a minor part) and interests of loans (in a major part). This shows that there are important reasons for the Central Banks to control the remittance of payments abroad.

EFFECTS OF GLOBALIZATION

With the globalization trend of the 1990s, old selective controls such as a list of types of payments that could be made from a developing country to a foreign resident were substituted by less-intrusive methods, and today basically all kinds of payments can be made to a foreign resident, as long as the withholding income tax levied by the developing country's fiscal authorities is paid, and evidence is shown that the origin of the money in the developing country is legal. Latin American Central Banks commonly deny approval of the remittances abroad if the money was earned from illegal activities, as well as they do with the inflow of money, which is under close scrutiny in compliance with the laws that control money laundering.

As the import of foreign technology often follows the general economic policies concerning the opening of an economy to trade with the rest of the world, in the 1990s most Latin American countries also abolished their controls on the acquisition of foreign technology, not the least because there is a widespread recognition that such controls proved to be ineffective and did not contribute to enable any country to be self-reliant with regard to the development of technology that would be applied into new products and services.

The changes were not caused simply by the increase in world trade and the exhaustion of the economic model of substitution of imports. As we shall see, tax changes during the 1980s in the developed countries also fostered changes in the rules of developing countries governing the remittance of royalties between related companies. This major change was triggered by a modification made in the mid-1980s in the U.S. tax laws (namely, the modification in Section 482 of the Internal Revenue Code through US Law 99-514, of October 22, 1986), according to which the U.S. parent companies of multinational groups with subsidiaries in foreign countries should always recognize an income of royalties from their subsidiaries as a consideration for the use such subsidiaries make of the intellectual property rights of the parent company. Several other developed countries followed the U.S. lead and adopted similar rules.

There was a recognition in the United States and in many developed countries that one of their primary comparative advantages resided in their intellectual capital, when they compared themselves to the so-called emerging countries (such as South Korea and many Southeast Asia countries, or Latin American countries such as Mexico, Brazil, and Argentina). Emerging countries could produce high-quality goods at lower prices, but still lacked advanced R & D facilities. As a consequence of such recognition, the developed countries began to push for stronger protection of their intellectual property rights all over the world, a trend that would produce many fruits, and eventually result in the Tripps agreement of 1994.

In such context, protection of intellectual property in developing countries would be only a half victory for developed countries if the flow of royalties from developing countries were still forbidden or severely restricted. The liberalization of remittance controls in developing countries that followed in the 1990s was much needed by developed countries, and this liberalization is still far from completed.

LICENSING OF FOREIGN TECHNOLOGY

In fact, one can say that "old habits die hard," and nowadays one can notice striking differences among various Latin American countries in connection with their attitudes toward the licensing of foreign technology.

Some countries still treat differently the agreements executed between related companies and those with third parties. In Argentina, transfer of proprietary information is not subject to government control, regardless as to who are the parties to a contract. Until 1993, those agreements between related parties (parent-subsidiary, or subsidiary-subsidiary) were subject to approval. Since 1993, all agreements are treated in the same way: They only need to be registered for information purposes, but this is not mandatory. Lack of registration does not render the contract illegal or invalid. The only consequences for not registering it is that the licensee will not be able to deduct as an expense on the balance sheet the amounts paid to the licensor, and the withholding tax rate applied to payments made to the licensor will be higher. Lack of registration will prevent the licensor from benefiting from the provisions of the treaty to avoid double taxation (being taxed in both the licensor's country and in Argentina).

The Argentine Patent Law was amended in 1995, and although some concern has arisen as to whether it complied with Tripps, the objections that some countries have raised have in practice disappeared. The U.S. Supreme Court has rendered decisions making clear that Tripps is fully in force in Argentina and that all internal laws (such as the Patent Law) must comply with its provisions, since otherwise it will be considered to be unconstitutional. As of October 2000, full protection for pharmaceuticals is available.

In the trademark field, Argentina has had a long tradition in the area of granting strong protection to trademarks. Piracy of foreign marks has been strongly condemned by courts, which have also applied Article 50 of Tripps granting full injunctions in case of infringements. Parties to a license agreement are free to agree to the terms of the contract, with the only limit imposed by the antitrust law. In this respect, not only the duration of the agreement but also the royalties have no ceiling.

In Brazil, since the 1960s the remittance of royalties for trademark or patent licensing from the Brazilian subsidiary to the parent company was completely forbidden; such rules were extensively applied by the Brazilian Patent and Trademark Office (BPTO) to preclude remittances for transfer of know-how as well. At the end of 1991, however, under pressure of multinational companies (MNCs) with subsidiaries in Brazil, a new statute was enacted by the Brazilian Congress that was designed to liberalize this rule. Although the language put into the law is not straightforward, the official interpretation has been that payment and remittances of royalties between subsidiaries or controlled companies and the parent company should be henceforth admitted, as long as the agreements are executed and registered as of January 1, 1992.

Brazil has still not abolished a strict control over all know-how licenses, but patent and trademark licenses are treated in a more liberal manner, and copyright licenses enjoy absolute freedom. This apparently incoherent set of rules is a result of the strong force of pressure groups dedicated to copyrights (software owners; movie and record industries), as compared to the lack of organization (and of political power) of companies that are actively engaged in know-how licensing.

The number of patent applications in Brazil is rapidly increasing since the enactment of the 1996 Patent and Trademark Law. A considerable part of this is due to the possibility opened by the new law of issuance of patents for both products and processes concerning chemicals, food, and pharmaceuticals.

TRADEMARK LAW

In the field of trademarks, the scenario is similar. The new law made it easier to obtain valid registration for, and rights in, a wider range of marks and, therefore, to increase the confidence of enterprises that their distinctive signs cannot be easily copied. Such simplified procedures make the system more attractive to licensing.

The intellectual property laws of most Latin American countries are fairly modern and fully in compliance with the Tripps agreement. However, the major issue in the region is still enforcement, because the border controls are too soft (and the customs authorities are underpaid, ill-equipped, and poorly trained), and also because the courts are overburdened with too many lawsuits for too few judges.

In many Latin American countries, the number of judges in comparison with the population is simply too small, if compared to highly developed countries like the United States or Germany. Thus, it is understandable that inadequate enforcement of intellectual property (IP) rights is merely a consequence of the general economic situation of Latin American countries and by no means could be explained—as some people do, in an oversimplification of the matter—to a lack of regard of IP rights.

In most Latin American countries there is full democracy, and one can notice that the stronger the democratic rule is, the better the courts of law will work, not the least because judges are also subject to the investigations made by a free press (the press has sometimes been called a *fourth power*, so large is its influence). In most Latin American countries one can certainly say that the courts of law are fair, and also that cases are tried without prejudices against foreign plaintiffs.

In Andean Pact countries (Bolivia, Colombia, Ecuador, Peru, and Venezuela), the liberalization of the trade regime, initiated in 1989, was complemented by the improved transparency resulting from Venezuela's accession to GATT in 1990. Import prohibitions and licensing have generally been reduced to the extent necessary for security or health reasons or in keeping with international commitments; current exceptions include certain important consumer goods. Agriculture remains relatively protected, as this is also the rule in the United States, Canada, and Europe. There have been advances in intellectual property protection and in competition policy.

In fact, we could not review the treatment conferred to licensing without remarking on the more than striking similarity between Brazil, Argentina, and the Andean group laws. This indicates a clear pattern of cooperation and collaboration between Latin American countries on a scale hitherto unknown. That such cooperation should exist within the Andean group countries is in itself remarkable enough. That it should include countries more industrialized such as Argentina or Brazil, not within the Andean community group, is an indication of the scope of the movement to regulate foreign capital and foreign licensing contracts in all Latin America on a uniform basis.

Finally, apart from the enormous task of implementing the new laws in an effective and meaningful way, there remains to be completed the reconciling of the new policies with the older legislation still in effect. The new emphasis on the substance and value of the individual transfer of technology is hardly consistent with the arbitrary differences in treatment of royalties and technical assistance fees that remain in some countries.

TRADE RELATIONS

In recent years, trade relations have become increasingly focused on the negotiation of preferential agreements. Apart from the already traditional Andean Pact, the 1990s saw the birth of Mercosur, uniting Argentina, Brazil, Paraguay, and Uruguay, and NAFTA, which brought Mexico into a trading union with the United States and Canada.

Apart from the regulatory environment, another breakthrough in licensing in Latin American countries during the 1990s was triggered by the privatization of state-owned companies. Large companies, leaders in their respective countries and with a strong worldwide presence, have been privatized. Subsequently, as they received much-needed funds to invest in their activities, practically all of them received fresh technology, either from the new owners or from other sources.

Privatization not only brought a more efficient way of managing these companies, but also removed a burden to the economy, as privatized businesses began to generate profits and consequently became important taxpayers. Since these state-run companies had generated artificial employment, when privatized, a realistic approach showed that they employed many more people than needed. Layoffs were a consequence of this process, and what was a disguised unemployment suddenly became a reality, which generated unjustified criticism.

This pattern was clear in Argentina, Brazil, Chile, and in many other countries. Privatization reached all areas of activities in which previously there were large state-owned monopolistic companies, such as energy (oil, gas, electricity), mining, chemical industries, telecommunications, banking, and railways.

Moreover, where there was no privatization (e.g., the Brazilian oil company Petrobras was not privatized, due to political concerns), the monopoly was revoked and such companies now compete on an equal basis with new entrants in the market. This breadth of competition also demands that all companies quickly incorporate modern technology in their businesses.

The days of protectionism and trade barriers are coming to an end. The future of the United States and Latin America lies in free trade and competitive economies. To this end, the Free Trade Area of the Americas (FTAA) is methodically taking shape.

There has been much speculation about the Presidential Trade Promotion Authority—formerly referred to as *fast track*—that President George W. Bush sought from the U.S. Congress. Under such authority the U.S. government may sign an international treaty and submit it to the U.S. Senate for either approval or rejection in its entirety, but the Senate may not modify it. It is clear that the harsh negotiation conditions imposed to the U.S. government by the Congress act that approved the trade promotion authority shall create additional difficulties for a final agreement to be reached.

THE NORTH AMERICAN FREE TRADE AGREEMENT

The North American Free Trade Agreement (NAFTA) provides a good model on how equitable and balanced these kinds of agreements can be. Trade among the United States, Mexico, and Canada has doubled during NAFTA's first five years. As an example, Mexico has become a world-class exporter. Before NAFTA, Mexico was the twenty-sixth largest exporting nation in the world; today it is the eighth. If this trend continues, Mexico will soon be one of the top five. Anyone who does not believe that free and fair trade can open the door to prosperity should listen to Mexico's testimony.

In Brazil, the FTAA has been interpreted by some as a threat to Mercosur. It is not. Mercosur is an important player in the world trading system today, and it will be tomorrow. Mercosur also serves as a key pillar of political stability in Latin America, a role that the United States applauds.

Now it is not time to line up on either the side of Mercosur or FTAA, because these trade areas should not be viewed as if they were on opposite sides. Latin American countries have made great strides in fiscal and democratic reform and in building a competitive economy. We are confident this will continue. We should all prepare to compete with other trading blocs around the world, with other economies that are modernizing rapidly.

However, one major competitive advantage of countries like Brazil and Argentina lies in the agricultural sector. Brazil and Argentina are both large exporters of grains, fruits, meat, and hens, and protectionist measures of Europe, the United States, and Japan strongly harm the exporting capability of these emerging countries. It seems clear today that without serious concessions of the United States in terms of opening its internal market for Latin American agricultural products, the FTAA will not go forward.

The cornerstone of the Bush administration policy in the Americas is the FTAA, which will prepare our hemisphere for the new economy, opening the doors of free trade to an integrated market of 800 million people, with more than $10 trillion in GDP.

Latin American countries have already begun their homework, ensuring that local companies can compete under the fairest possible conditions in a continentwide open market. Should the restructuring process launched in the 1990s not be completed, the overall economic conditions of Latin American countries might well undermine the survival of many domestic enterprises, while discouraging foreign investments. It must be made quite clear that in a free trade area, capital will always tend to flow toward countries with stable, deregulated economies that work in an efficient manner.

The FTAA does not mean turning Latin America into a huge depository for the better-developed economies of the continent, particularly the United States and Canada. Latin American countries are eager to be partners of developed countries, as long as they are received into such partnership in positions that reflect the potential of the region.

For instance, Brazil and Argentina are significant partners of the United States: these Mercosur leaders account for two of the ten highest trade (in tangible goods) surpluses posted by the U.S. economy in 2000. Brazil's trade deficit with the United States reached U.S.$1.5 billion in 2000, while Argentina's deficit reached U.S.$1.6 billion. Overall, the United States exported more than U.S.$21 billion to the four Mercosur countries in 2000, outstripping its sales to countries such as France or China over the same period.

The high levels of complexity found in Latin American economies require much care during the FTAA negotiations, in order to prevent any backsliding in the regional growth and development process, while ensuring that integration does not turn into a one-way street benefiting only developed countries.

Discussions with local business leaders will surely endow Latin American negotiators with the necessary feedback, helping them make the right decisions. This is the proposal of the Foreign Trade and Integration of the Americas Committee. It would also be extremely valuable for negotiators in all countries involved to assess the consolidation process within the European Union (EU), which is one of the most successful regional integration movements in history. It could well offer many valuable lessons on the problems and impacts of eliminating national borders across an entire continent.

The manner in which market integration is implemented will basically define whether the FTAA succeeds as a long-term project supported by society or proves to be a trade offense launched by North America against its neighbors' markets. Criticism on the way the United States asserts itself in the international arena are widespread inside the United States, as well, and there is a lesson to be learned with each critic. On July 18, 2001, economist Paul Krugman published the following comments about the Argentinean financial crisis in his prestigious column in *The New York Times:*

> And then, of course, there's Argentina. What's shocking about the political and economic crisis there is not so much its severity—though it is amazing to see the punishment now being inflicted on a country that just three years ago was the toast of Wall Street—as how gratuitous it is. We're talking about a government whose debt really isn't very large compared with the size of its national economy, and whose fairly modest budget deficit is entirely the product of an economic slump, forced into drastic spending cuts that will further worsen that slump. It wouldn't be tolerated here—but the bankers in New York tell the Argentines that they have no alternative. And Washington—not the Bush administration, which has been eerily silent as Argentina melts down, but the conservative think tanks that helped the country bind itself in a monetary straitjacket—agrees.
>
> Does it have to be this way? Is Keynesianism good only for the U.S. and selected other Western countries, but out of bounds for everyone else? Maybe. But I suspect that the core of the problem is that small countries, and even big countries like Japan that have lost their self-confidence, are too easily bullied by men in suits who give them advice dictated by a hard-line ideology they would never try to impose back home.
>
> My advice would be to stop listening to those men in suits, and do as we do, not as we say.

U.S. FTAA negotiators, of course, are much more sensitive to the needs and demands of other countries than international bankers. But the message from several Latin American presidents in the last Summit of the Americas was clear: If the concerns about the opening of the U.S. market and the social development of Latin America are not adequately addressed in the FTAA agreement, the negotiations might end up in a deadlock.

The mistrust among many governments and leaders in Latin America is quite justified. Recent events give reason to worry. The Canadian ban on Brazilian beef exports, claiming a possible risk of mad cow disease (completely nonexistent in Brazil, as attested by the United States and Europe) was a childish vindication against the success of the Brazilian aircraft manufacturer Embraer, which often wins clients over its competitor, the Canadian company Bombardier, owned by friends of Quebec's prime minister. This ban has already been revoked after a serious diplomatic crisis that jeopardized Canadian subsidiaries in Brazil. Another problem are surtaxes imposed on Brazilian steel and orange juice imports by the U.S. government after intense lobbying of local industries. These measures show how developed nations can play rough when defending their own interests, even when they are simply protecting inefficient and subsidized sectors. This type of stance is not a good omen and could well constitute a serious stumbling block to the ongoing progress of the integration process linking up the Americas.

Latin American countries are not ready to accept a hemispheric trade deal at any cost, Brazilian President Fernando Henrique Cardoso recently said, but he also said: "A Free Trade Area of the Americas is welcome if its creation is a step toward providing access to more dynamic markets; otherwise, it would be irrelevant—or worse, undesirable." Cardoso's intent on strengthening the trading bloc of Mercosur countries was seen as one of the main reasons the United States was unable to achieve its target date of 2003 for the proposed deal. Instead, the United States had to settle on a target date of 2005.

Several Latin American leaders emphasized social problems in the second Summit of the Americas, including Venezuela's Hugo Chavez, another leader who has yet to embrace free trade for the Americas: "We have advanced very little—almost not at all—in the social objectives." During the same summit, Colombia's Andres Pastrana joined his neighbor Chavez in making social problems a priority for Latin America: "When hunger, misery, and unemployment strike, it is very difficult to believe in structural (solutions) and it is very easy to fall for irresponsible populism." In the same meeting, Mexico's Vicente Fox argued that NAFTA has succeeded in Mexico, bringing an "unprecedented level of trade and of job creation." And he assured his colleagues, including doubting leaders like Cardoso and Chavez, that "this is what awaits you with a continental free trade agreement."

The preamble to Decision 24 of the Andean Pact declares that the transfer of foreign technology represents a necessary element in the development of the member countries and should receive guarantees of stability to the extent that it provides a positive contribution. In that principle is expressed the two-fold challenge presented by the new legislation: on the one hand, the challenge to Latin America to establish and maintain institutions that recognize the value of such technology; on the other, the challenge to the possessors of the world's technology to demonstrate the contribution that technology can make to developing countries. It must be confessed that the tasks are both so novel that their accomplishment will surely have to be a cooperative effort.

CONCLUSION

To conclude that the elimination of trade barriers and the implementation of modern and effective IP protection and enforcement is somewhat a disadvantage for emerging economies is indicative of a naíve and short-sighted attitude. It is our opinion (and probably the opinion of others who have their career in international licensing) that the most likely result of the protectionist trade and IP regimes that existed in Latin American countries until the end of the 1980s, had they continued, is that emerging countries like Argentina and Brazil would not even still be called *emerging*—they could possibly have *submerged!*

Such countries would only have the opportunity to license-in low-tech, infrastructure technology; thus not improving their economies through licensing. The opening of a country to foreign trade is always coupled with the acquisition of foreign technology, and we are confident that FTAA talks will continue and develop, and eventually an agreement will be reached (if not in the currently set date of 2005). With more free trade, licensing will increase even more in Latin America.

ABOUT THE AUTHORS

Gabriel F. Leonardos, LL.M, is an attorney-at-law in Brazil. He is a partner of Momsen, Leonardos & Cia., an intellectual property law firm with offices in Rio de Janeiro and São Paulo. Mr. Leonardos is the author of a book and several articles about intellectual property matters, including licensing and taxation of intellectual property. He is a professor of intellectual property in post-graduation courses in the Catholic University of Rio de Janeiro–PUC and in the State University of Rio de Janeiro–UERJ. He is also a former guest researcher of the Max-Planck Institute, Munich (1988–1989); post-graduate in German law by the Ludwig-Maximilian University, Munich (1989); and LL.M. by the University of São Paulo (1996). Mr. Leonardos was the president of LES Brazil in 2000–2001 and vice president (1996–2001) of the Brazilian Association of Patent & Trademark Attorneys–ABAPI. He is a member of the International Federation of Industrial Property Attorneys–FICPI.

Fernando Noetinger is an attorney at law, graduated from the Buenos Aires University Law Faculty in 1968. Since 1969 he has been practicing law in the fields of intellectual property, licensing, and commercial law. He is a founding partner of the firm Noetinger & Armando, established in Buenos Aires, Argentina in 1994. Mr. Noetinger is currently a professor of IP in graduate courses at Austral University and Palermo University, both in Buenos Aires, and Siglo XXI University in the city of Cordoba, Argentina. He has conferenced in events organized by WIPO, LES, AIPPI, ASIPI, IBA, and other international organizations. He held the position of president of the Licensing Executive Society International in 1990/1991. He is currently president of the Argentina Association of Industrial Property Agents and of the Argentine Chapter of LES.

Further Reading List

BASIC WORKS

Barker, Joel Arthur. *Future Edge*. New York: William Morrow, 1992.

de Bono, Edward. *Six Thinking Hats*. New York: Penguin Books, 1985.

Drucker, Peter F. *The Effective Executive*. New York: Harper & Row, 1967.

Drucker, Peter F. *Management in Turbulent Times*. New York, Harper & Row, 1980.

Drucker, Peter F. *Management: Tasks-Responsibilities-Practices*. New York: Harper & Row, 1974.

Drucker, Peter F. *The New Realities*. New York: Harper & Row, 1989.

Drucker, Peter F. *Technology Management & Society*. New York: Harper & Row, 1970.

Endres, Al. *Improving R&D Performance: The Juran Way*. New York: John Wiley & Sons, 1997.

Epstein, Michael A. *Epstein on Intellectual Property*. Gaithersburg, MD: Aspen Law and Business, 2001.

Goldscheider, Robert. *Technology Management: Law/Tactics/Forms*. Cleveland, OH: West Group, 1988—revised annually.

Kuhn, Thomas S. *The Structure of Scientific Revolutions,* 2d ed. Chicago: University of Chicago Press, 1970.

Schumacher, E. F. *Small Is Beautiful*. New York: Harper & Row, 1983.

Toffler, Alvin. *Future Shock*. New York: Bantam Paperback, 1971.

Toffler, Alvin. *Power Shift*. New York: Bantam Paperback, 1990.

Toffler, Alvin. *The Third Wave*. New York: Bantam Paperback, 1991.

Walton, Mary. *The Demming Management Method*. Berkeley, CA: The Berkeley Publishing Group, 1986.

CREATIVITY

Levy, Steven. *Hackers*. New York: Dell Books, 1984.

Petroski, Henry. *The Evolution of Useful Things*. New York: Vintage Books, 1992.

von Oech, Roger. *A Kick in the Seat of the Pants*. New York: Harper Perennial, 1986.

von Oech, Roger. *A Whack in the Side of the Head: How You Can Become More Creative*. New York: Warner Books, 1990.

THE FUTURE

Carlson, Richard, and Bruce Goldman. *Fast Forward: A Revised Edition of 2020 Vision—Where Technology, Demographics, and History Will Take America and the World in the Next 30 Years*. New York: Harper Business, 1994.

Davis, Stan, and Bill Davidson. *2020 Vision: Transform Your Business Today to Succeed in Tomorrow's Economy*. New York: Simon & Schuster, 1991.

FM-2030. *Are You a Transhuman?* New York: Warner Books, 1989.

Kennedy, Paul. *Preparing for the Twenty-First Century*. New York: Random House, 1993.

McRae, Hamish. *The World in 2020: Power, Culture and Prosperity*. Boston: Harvard Business School Press, 1994.

Minkin, Barry Howard. *Future in Sight: 100 of the Most Important Trends, Implications and Predictions for the New Millennium*. New York: MacMillan, 1995.

Reich, Robert. *The Future of Success*. New York: Alfred A. Knopf, 2001.

Reich, Robert B. *The Next American Frontier*. New York: Times Books, 1983.

Zey, Michael. *Seizing the Future: How the Coming Revolution in Science, Technology and Industry Will Expand the Frontiers of Human Potential and Reshape the Planet*. New York: Simon & Schuster, 1994.

CORPORATE CULTURES AND STRATEGIES

Allen, Gene, and Rick Jarman. *Collaborative R&D: Manufacturing's New Tool.* New York: John Wiley & Sons, 1999.

Battersby, Gregory, and Charles Grimes. *Licensing Royalty Rates.* Gaithersburg, MD: Aspen Law and Business, 2001.

Berman, Bruce. *From Ideas to Assets: Investing Wisely in Intellectual Property.* New York: John Wiley & Sons, 2001.

Champy, James. *Re-Engineering Management.* New York: Harper Business, 1995.

Davis, Julie L., and Suzanne S. Harrison. *Edison in the Boardroom: How Leading Companies Realize Value from Their Intellectual Assets.* New York: John Wiley & Sons, 2001.

Hamel, Gary, and C. K. Prahalad. *Competing for the Future.* Boston: Harvard Business School Press, 1994.

Hammer, Michael, and James Champy. *Re-Engineering the Corporation.* New York: Harper Business, 1993.

Kelley, Tom. *The Art of Innovation.* New York: Random House, 2001.

Knight, H. Jackson. *Patent Strategy: For Researchers and Research Managers,* 2d ed. New York: John Wiley & Sons, 2001.

Lechter, Michael A. *Protecting Your #1 Asset.* New York: Warner Books, 2001.

Lewis, Michael. *The New New Thing.* New York: W. W. Norton & Company, 2000.

Miele, Anthony L. *Patent Strategy: The Manager's Guide to Profiting from Patent Portfolios.* New York: John Wiley & Sons, 2001.

Parr, Russell L., and Patrick H. Sullivan. *Technology Licensing: Corporate Strategies for Maximizing Value.* New York: John Wiley & Sons, 1996.

Peters, Thomas J., and Robert H. Waterman, Jr. *In Search of Excellence.* New York: Warner Books, 1984.

Razgaitis, Richard. *Early-Stage Technologies: Valuation and Pricing.* New York: John Wiley & Sons, 1999.

Smith, Gordon V., and Russell L. Parr. *Intellectual Property: Licensing and Joint Venture Profit Strategies,* 2d ed. New York: John Wiley & Sons, 1998, and 2001 cumulative supplements.

Sullivan, Patrick H. *Profiting from Intellectual Capital: Extracting Value from Innovation.* New York: John Wiley & Sons, 2001.

Sullivan, Patrick H. *Value-Driven Intellectual Capital: How to Convert Intangible Corporate Assets Into Market Value.* New York: John Wiley & Sons, 2000.

Tellis, Gerard J., and Peter N. Golder. *Will and Vision: How Latecomers Grow to Dominate Markets.* New York: McGraw-Hill, 2002.

Voletto, Kevin G., and David Kline. *Rembrandts in the Attic.* New York: Harvard Business School Press, 1994.

LEGAL COMMENTARIES

Abrams, Howard B. *The Law of Copyright* (2 volumes). Cleveland, OH: West Group, 1991—revised annually.

Arnold, Tom, with Michael G. Fletcher and Robert J. McAughan, Jr. *Patent Alternative Dispute Resolution Handbook.* Cleveland, OH: West Group, 1991—published periodically.

Battersby, Geoffrey J., and Charles W. Grimes. *The Law of Merchandise and Character Licensing.* Cleveland, OH: West Group, 1985—revised annually.

Battersby, Gregory and Charles Grimes, eds. *Drafting Internet Agreements.* Gaithersburg, MD: Aspen Law and Business, 2001.

Cooper, Iver P. *Biotechnology and the Law.* Cleveland, OH: West Group, 1982—revised annually.

Dorr, Robert, and Christopher Munch. *Protecting Trade Secrets, Patents, Copyrights and Trademarks.* Gaithersburg, MD: Aspen Law and Business, 2001.

Dorr, Robert, and Christopher Munch, eds. *Trade Dress Law.* Gaithersburg, MD: Aspen Law and Business, 2001.

Epstein, Michael A., and Frank L. Politano, eds. *Drafting License Agreements.* Gaithersburg, MD: Aspen Law and Business, 2001.

Goldscheider, Robert. *Eckstrom's Licensing in Foreign and Domestic Operations: The Forms and Substance of Licensing* (5 volumes). Cleveland, OH: West Group, 1978—revised three times annually.

Hawes, James E. *Patent Application Practice.* Cleveland, OH: West Group, 1993—revised annually.

Hovey, Craig. *The Patent Process: A Guide to Intellectual Property for the Information Age.* New York: John Wiley & Sons, 2002.

Jager, Melvin F. *Trade Secrets Law* (3 volumes). Cleveland, OH: West Group, 1985—revised twice annually.

Lennon, Michael J. *Drafting Technology Patent License Agreements.* Gaithersburg, MD: Aspen Law and Business, 2001.

McCarthy, J. Thomas. *McCarthy on Trademarks and Unfair Competition,* 3d ed. (8 volumes). Cleveland, OH: West Group, 1992—revised at least twice annually.

Melville, L. W. *Forms and Agreements on Intellectual Property and International Licensing* (3 volumes). Cleveland, OH: West Group, 1979—revised twice annually.

Quinto, David W. *The Law of Internet Disputes.* Gaithersburg, MD: Aspen Law and Business, 2001.

Rosenstock, Jerome. *The Law of Chemical and Pharmaceutical Invention.* Gaithersburg, MD: Aspen Law and Business, 2001.

Simensky, Melvin, Lanning Bryer, and Neil J. Wilkof. *Intellectual Property in the Global Marketplace,* Volume 1: "Valuation, Protection, Exploitation and Electronic Commerce," 2d ed. New York: John Wiley & Sons, 1999.

Simensky, Melvin, Lanning Bryer, and Neil J. Wilkof. *Intellectual Property in the Global Marketplace,* Volume 2: "Country-by-Country Profiles," 2d ed. New York: John Wiley & Sons, 1999.

Smith, Gordon V. *Trademark Valuation.* New York: John Wiley & Sons, 1996.

Smith, Gordon V., and Russell L. Parr. *Valuation of Intellectual Property and Intangible Assets,* 3d ed. New York: John Wiley & Sons, 2000, with 2001 supplement.

Stobbs, Gregory. *Business Method Patents.* Gaithersburg, MD: Aspen Law and Business, 2001.

Toedt, D. C., III. *The Law and Business of Computer Software.* Cleveland, OH: West Group, 1989—revised annually.

West, Thomas L., and Jeffrey D. Jones, eds. *Handbook of Business Valuation,* 2d ed. New York: John Wiley & Sons, 1999.

INTERNATIONAL COMPARISONS

Halberstam, David. *The Reckoning.* New York: William Morrow and Company, 1986.

Hanellin, Elisabeth, ed. *Patents Throughout the World.* Cleveland, OH: West Group, 1989–90—revised three times annually.

le Goc, Michel. *Development Techniques for International Technology Transfer.* Westport, CT: Greenwood Publishing Group, Inc., 2001.

Lowe, Janet. *Jack Welch Speaks: Wisdom from the World's Greatest Business Leader.* New York: John Wiley & Sons, 1998.

Porter, Michael E. *Competitive Advantages: Creating and Sustaining Superior Performance.* New York: MacMillan, 1985.

Thurow, Lester. *Head to Head: The Coming Economic Battle Among Japan, Europe and America.* New York: William Morrow and Company, 1992.

van Wolferen, Karel. *The Enigma of Japanese Power.* New York: Alfred A. Knopf, 1990.

Index